Gene Steinberg

D0515061

SAMS
Teach Yourself

the iMac™

in 24 Hours

FOURTH EDITION

SAMS

201 West 103rd St., Indianapolis, Indiana, 46290 USA

Sams Teach Yourself the iMac™ in 24 Hours, Fourth Edition

Copyright © 2002 by Gene Steinberg

International Standard Book Number: 0-672-32420-2

Library of Congress Catalog Card Number: 2002102903

Printed in the United States of America

First Printing: June 2002

05 . 04   03   02   4   3   2   1

Trademarks

Warning and Disclaimer

ACQUISITIONS EDITOR
Betsy Brown

DEVELOPMENT EDITOR
Marta Justak

MANAGING EDITOR
Charlotte Clapp

PROJECT EDITOR
Andy Beaster

PRODUCTION EDITOR
Chip Gardner

INDEXER
Chris Barrick

TECHNICAL EDITOR
Robyn Ness

TEAM COORDINATOR
Amy Patton

INTERIOR DESIGNER
Gary Adair

COVER DESIGNER
Aren Howell

PAGE LAYOUT
Ayanna Lacey

Contents at a Glance

Contents

Part IV Discovering the Internet 207

Hour 12 The Internet: Learning the Ropes 209

Hour 13 The Wonderful World of Email 225

About the Author

Gene Steinberg first used a Mac in 1984 and never looked back. He is a fact and science fiction writer and computer software and systems consultant. His more than two dozen computer-related books include Que's *AOL 4.0 Quick Reference, Sams Teach Yourself AOL in 10 Minutes,* and *How To Use Your Mac*. Gene's commentaries and product reviews appear on CNET and ZDNet, *MacAddict* magazine, and his "Mac Reality Check" column for the Gannett News Service and USATODAY.com. In his spare time, Gene and his son, Grayson, are developing a new science fiction adventure series, *Attack of the Rockoids*.

Dedication

For Wally, who showed me that miracles are indeed possible!

Acknowledgments

I sometimes wonder how it all came together. This book was an incredible challenge. With two operating systems and loads of new hardware to cover (including the original and the flat-panel iMac), there wasn't enough time to do a book of this size and scope all alone. So I'm grateful to the many people who contributed information, tips, tricks, and, most of all, advice in the preparation of this book.

I want to give thanks to my friend and agent, Sharon Jarvis, for her sage advice, and Apple's corporate communications team, including Bill Evans, Keri Walker, and Nathalie Welch.

And extra kudos go to Apple's Jonathan Ive and his industrial design team for giving us the iMac.

I must give special praise to the team at Sams for putting up with my many eccentricities and for allowing me a great deal of latitude in outlining and writing this book. They include Betsy Brown, Marta Justak, Chip Gardner, and Andy Beaster. I'd also like to express my appreciation to the dedicated, fearless technical editor, Robyn Ness, for poring through every written word and every illustration to verify that they were absolutely correct to the last, minute detail.

And last, I wish to offer a heartfelt, loving thank you to my wonderful, beautiful wife Barbara and my extraordinary son Grayson for putting up with the long hours I spent chained to my computer so that my work could be done on schedule.

Tell Us What You Think!

As the reader of this book, *you* are our most important critic and commentator. We value your opinion and want to know what we're doing right, what we could do better, what areas you'd like to see us publish in, and any other words of wisdom you're willing to pass our way.

You can email or write me directly to let me know what you did or didn't like about this book—as well as what we can do to make our books stronger.

Please note that I cannot help you with technical problems related to the topic of this book, and that due to the high volume of mail I receive, I might not be able to reply to every message.

When you write, please be sure to include this book's title and author as well as your name and phone or fax number. I will carefully review your comments and share them with the author and editors who worked on the book.

Fax: 317-581-4770

Email: consumer@samspublishing.com

Mail: Mark Taber
        Associate Publisher
        Sams Publishing
        201 West 103rd Street
        Indianapolis, IN 46290 USA

For more information about this book or others from Sams Publishing, visit our Web site at www.samspublishing.com. Type the ISBN (excluding hyphens) or the title of the book in the Search box to find the book you're looking for.

Introduction

Would you believe that a personal computer can become a legend? Well, consider the 1987 movie *Star Trek IV: The Voyage Home*, where it was clear that one product had been elevated to that status. In the movie, the crew of the Enterprise goes back through time to visit San Francisco of the 1980s. In one memorable scene, the ship's salty engineer, Scotty, walks over to a 20th century computer, picks up the mouse, and says, "computer," expecting it to respond to his verbal commands.

The computer was an Apple Macintosh.

Long gone are the days when that low-powered, uniquely designed computer captured anyone's imagination, but rising from the ashes of lost market share and low profits are worthy successors, such as the iMac. You can also see the iMac featured prominently in TV shows, movies, and, of course, on the cover of *Time*.

Whether you have one of the spiffy flat-panel iMacs or the original tear-shaped design, you have a personal computer that is designed for folks like you and me. You want a computing "appliance" that will get the work done fast, with as little fuss and bother as possible. Well, at least with as little fuss as you can expect from such a highly complex device.

About a third of the folks buying Apple's consumer computers are new to personal computing. Others have switched from that *other* platform (Windows) to the Mac. In either case, I'm sure you'll want to get up and running as quickly as possible, and safely navigate around whatever hurdles might stand in your way.

When I bought my first Mac back in the 1980s, Apple included several big instruction books with their new products—but big computer manuals are history.

New Apple computers these days usually just come with a quick setup card and a brief troubleshooting book. If you want to know more, you've got to check the Help menu on the computer itself.

Or, even better, read this book.

If you're an experienced Mac user—or this is your first Mac—you'll find that *Sams Teach Yourself the iMac in 24 Hours* is the best book you can buy. I've written the lessons just for you, and I've tried to avoid "geek" talk as much as possible. And where I have to be a little technical, I'll try my best to explain everything to you as clearly as possible.

This Book Is Not Just for iMac Users

This book covers the subjects any Mac user would want to know. So whether you have an iMac, an iBook, or a regular PowerMac, or PowerBook, you'll find lots of information in this book that will help you master your new computer.

For this fourth edition, I've added coverage of the latest and greatest from Apple, Mac OS X and the flat-panel iMac, which takes the original concept in a whole new direction.

Mac OS X, as you probably know, is an industrial-strength operating system that is based on the same core (Unix) as the systems that power a majority of the server computers that run the Internet. Yet despite its heritage, Mac OS X isn't hard to use. It's designed, like the older or "Classic" Mac system, to be friendly and accessible.

Because all new computers from Apple come with two operating systems, this book covers both systems, too. You'll learn the differences and you'll be surprised at the amazing similarities, and how knowing how to do something in one system makes it easy to master the other.

How to Use This Book

This book is divided into 24 segments that each take roughly an hour to complete. You can work through the lessons in the space of a day (if you don't plan to eat or sleep), or you can take your time and work through the hour lessons.

The lessons begin with unpacking your new iMac and setting it up in your work area. From there, you'll learn about the great features of the old and new Mac OS operating systems and discover all the terrific software that came with your new computer. In addition, you'll learn lots of tips and tricks that will help you do things it took years for the experts to discover.

At the end of each hour, you'll be able to accomplish a new set of tasks. The lessons contain clear explanations of the program features and how they work. In addition, each hour provides you with the opportunity for hands-on training, simply by following the steps described.

Conventions Used in This Book

Sams Teach Yourself the iMac in 24 Hours uses a number of conventions that are consistent throughout this book:

- Each hour begins with an overview of what you will learn and the highlights of every hour.

- Step-by-step instructions are preceded by a To Do icon.

- Every hour ends with a summary and a series of commonly asked questions and answers; hopefully, you'll find the answers to your questions among them.

In addition, these elements appear throughout the book:

Notes provide you with comments and asides about the topic at hand.

Tips offer shortcuts and hints on getting the task done.

Cautions explain roadblocks you might encounter when you work with your iMac and tell you how to avoid them.

NEW TERM   *New terms* are introduced with this special designation.

The Thrill of Discovery Is Just Beginning...

Your new iMac, regardless of model, has the power that was formerly reserved for the largest mainframe computers. And it all fits in a cute little polycarbonate plastic case. Truly amazing.

A book such as this can only be a starting point. After you've spent these 24 hours discovering the great features of your iMac and the Macintosh operating system, you'll be ready to go on and surf the Internet, write that great American novel, or just sit back and have fun with a colorful computer game.

I hope you will be able to share the excitement and thrill of discovery that I felt when I bought my first Mac. And if you have any questions or comments, feel free to email me or just pay a visit to one of my two Web sites when you have a chance.

Gene Steinberg
Scottsdale, AZ
email: gene@macnightowl.com
http://www.macnightowl.com
http://www.rockoids.com

PART I
Opening the Box

Hour

Hour **1**

Setting Up Your iMac

Whether you have a fancy new iMac or a vintage model, it's a marvel of technology. Inside its cute plastic box lies the incredible power of Apple's G3 or G4 microprocessors, supercharged chips no larger than a postage stamp. These miniature technological wonders have the capability to process millions upon millions of computer instructions every second; in fact, the G4 processes billions of instructions, which puts it in the supercomputer class. In addition, your new computer comes with a sharp, bright color screen; a graphics accelerator; a fast CD drive, even one that can create DVDs; a built-in modem; and lots and lots of great software.

NEW TERM A *microprocessor* is a little electronic component that crunches numbers and gives your computer its incredible computing power.

NEW TERM A *Graphics accelerator* is a chip that makes the images on your computer's screen show up very, very fast.

NEW TERM   A *modem* is a clever device that turns the ones and zeros generated by your iMac and other computers into analog signals that can be sent back and forth over telephone lines.

In the first hour, or part, of this book, I'll show you how to install and set up your iMac. Whether it's a brand new model with that gorgeous flat-panel display, striking, dome-like base, and stainless steel neck, or one you bought via the closeout route (or from another user), you learn

- How to set up your new iMac
- How to get it running
- How to use Apple's Mac OS Setup Assistant
- How to master your mouse skills
- How to master all those strange symbols on the keyboard, if you're new to any of the Mac Operating Systems

Although many of you have worked on other Macs or the computers from that *other* platform (Windows), I realize that some of you are first-time computer buyers. So I'm going to cover a few basics in this first hour, such as how to figure out what plugs in to where and how to use the mouse. If you've already worked on a Mac and have installed new computers, you'll be able to advance to Hour 2, "Exploring the iMac Desktop," in much less time.

Unpacking the iMac

Before you unpack your new iMac, find a convenient table or desk for it. It's not too large to fit on a small desk, but many of you will purchase a special table for it. In addition, you might want to buy a mouse pad, although it's not necessary on recent models because they use an optical mouse that can work just fine on any smooth surface. If you have an older iMac with the hockey-puck shaped mouse, you can still use a smooth surface, but the porous character of the mouse pad will offer more precise mouse movement. And because a mouse pad only costs a few bucks (sometimes they're even given away as a premium), it's worth having.

As with any new purchase, before you attempt to use your new computer give it a once over for visible signs of damage. If something looks broken (or the shipping box is badly damaged), contact your dealer for help. It's a good idea not to try to attempt to use a computer that might be damaged until it has been checked or (if need be) repaired. What's more, most dealers will exchange a computer that's DOA (dead on arrival).

1

Regardless of where you place it, you'll want to think about the following setup for maximum comfort:

- Make sure your shoulders are in a relaxed position when you set up the keyboard. Apple suggests putting your upper arm and forearm at a right angle, wrist and hand making roughly a straight line. Then again, at my age, I doubt that I'm going to change the positions I've learned over the decades.

- The mouse is best placed at the same height as the keyboard. If you buy a computer table with one of those slide-out trays for a keyboard, make sure it's wide enough to hold the mouse, too.

- Don't forget a comfortable chair that provides good support and a reasonable amount of adjustments so that you can easily tailor it to your needs, and the needs of others who might be using your Mac.

- Setting up your iMac for comfort depends on the model. The flat-panel version has a display that moves freely on a pivot. Grab the corners, which Apple calls a "halo," and you can position it in the way that works best for you. The experts recommend you adjust the angle of the display so that it's slightly below eye level. The vintage iMac's adjustment is limited. To raise it slightly, lift the case, pull out the foot beneath it, and you'll gain some precious inches, but that's all.

The View from the Front of Your iMac

Let's take a closer look at your new iMac and see what features are available. First the front view of the new or flat-panel iMac (see Figure 1.1):

The vintage or Classic iMac, however, has a few controls on the front that are pictured in Figure 1.2.

FIGURE **1.1**
*Where do you plug
things in? On the
base at the rear.*

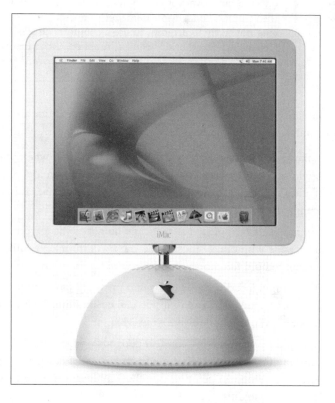

A Look at the Face of the Flat-Panel iMac

Let's take a look at the new iMac's face; I'll cover the different look of the vintage or Classic iMac in the next section:

- At the lower left of your flat-panel iMac is a tiny hole. It's not a keyhole; there's actually a microphone inside, and it enables you to record sounds on your iMac. And yes, after a fashion, you can give it commands (not like they do in those *Star Trek* movies, but good enough for simple functions). However, the real value is to add narration to home videos. You'll learn how to edit a home video in Hour 14, "Using iMovie, iDVD, and iPhoto."

- The flat-panel iMac has a tiny built-in speaker, but some units also ship with external plug-in speakers known as the Apple Pro Speaker. If you didn't get a set, you can buy one from your favorite Mac dealer.

FIGURE 1.2

The iMac's original form factor put the screen and the electronics in a single box.

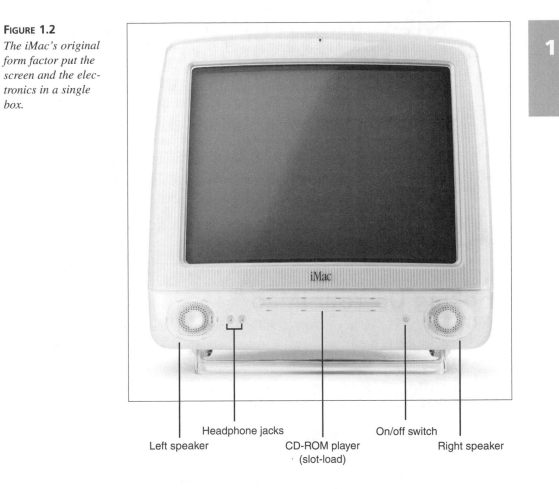

Left speaker
Headphone jacks
CD-ROM player
(slot-load)
On/off switch
Right speaker

- The base of the flat-panel iMac has the optical drive just below the Apple logo. Press the Eject key at the upper right of your keyboard, and the tray will pop right out.

- Where's the power switch? It's at the left rear, but I'll get to that shortly (and please, don't ask me why they put it there).

A Look at the Face of the Classic iMac

This section is devoted to the face presented by the Classic iMac:

- The microphone is found behind tiny hole at the top of the vintage iMac. Similar to the one in the flat-panel model, it's good for spoken word, and not much else.

- The speaker grills are located at the lower left and right. Earphones can be connected to either of the two jacks at the left of this model. They enable you (and a friend) to listen to your iMac in silence.

- The optical drive is located at the bottom center. On slot-load iMacs, just insert the CD (label up) partway into the slot, and the drive will grab it and pull it on. If you have an older iMac with slide-out CD drive, just press the little rectangular green button to open the CD tray. To close the drive, press the tray in gently.

- At the right of the CD drive is the on/off switch. We'll get to that in a moment (after you've plugged everything in of course).

The earphone jacks are located next to the right speaker on the first-generation iMacs.

Hooking Up Your iMac

I know you're excited to turn on your iMac. I remember when I bought my first new car (I think we had to use a crank to get it started in those days) and just wanted to go out and cruise the highways and try out the engine and handling.

However, you can't just turn on your iMac and browse the Internet. You have to hook up a few things first. So let's go through the steps:

Hooking Up Your iMac

1. Place your iMac on a desk.

2. Follow the suggestions in the previous section, entitled "Unpacking the iMac," to position your computer correctly.

3. Plug in the power cord, and take the other end and plug it into a convenient AC jack. *Don't turn it on yet! You need to do a few more things before it will work properly!*

4. How do you plug things into your iMac? On the flat-panel model, take a look at the rear (see Figure 1.3).

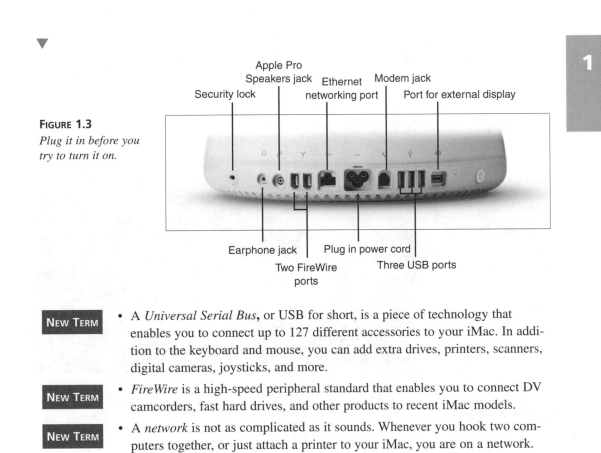

FIGURE 1.3
Plug it in before you try to turn it on.

Security lock
Apple Pro Speakers jack
Ethernet networking port
Modem jack
Port for external display

Earphone jack
Two FireWire ports
Plug in power cord
Three USB ports

NEW TERM • A *Universal Serial Bus,* or USB for short, is a piece of technology that enables you to connect up to 127 different accessories to your iMac. In addition to the keyboard and mouse, you can add extra drives, printers, scanners, digital cameras, joysticks, and more.

NEW TERM • *FireWire* is a high-speed peripheral standard that enables you to connect DV camcorders, fast hard drives, and other products to recent iMac models.

NEW TERM • A *network* is not as complicated as it sounds. Whenever you hook two computers together, or just attach a printer to your iMac, you are on a network. Just as in your office, when you try to make new friends or business contacts.

NEW TERM • *Ethernet* is a popular networking technique that offers high performance and easy setup.

You'll find the connection panel for your vintage iMac at the right. Figure 1.4 shows the view of the first-generation iMac's connection panel (you have to open the plastic cover to get to it).

5. Take the keyboard's cable and connect to one of the Universal Serial Bus jacks (it really makes no difference). Don't force the plug, it only connects in one direction (the side with the special symbol on it is at the top).

6. Plug the mouse into either jack on the keyboard. It really doesn't matter if you use your mouse left-handed or right-handed. I'm a southpaw myself, but I learned the mouse with my right hand. Go figure!

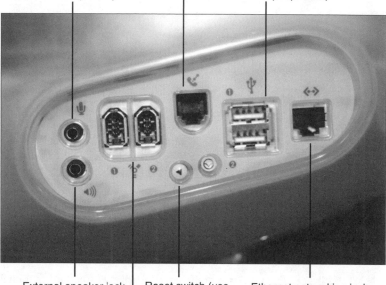

External microphone jack

Built-in modem jack

Universal Serial Bus
jacks for keyboard
and mouse (and
other peripherals)

FIGURE 1.4
*This photo shows
connection panel for
a Classic iMac,
which includes
hookup jacks for
FireWire.*

External speaker jack

Reset switch (use
only in emergencies)

Ethernet networking jack

FireWire jacks
(only on certain models)

A mouse is the pointing device you use to point to items on your iMac's display and to click them (which is the act of selecting them). Although a mouse or similar device is used on all personal computers, the Mac is unique because only one button is needed. In contrast, computers supporting other computer operating systems, such as Windows, require at least two buttons.

7. If you want to use your iMac's built-in modem, connect a modular phone plug into the modem jack (the one labeled with the phone receiver icon). Put the other end in your phone jack, or connect to the second jack (if any) on a telephone.

8. To connect your iMac to a regular Ethernet network, a cable modem or just to a single printer with an Ethernet connection, plug in the network cable to the jack on your iMac.

1

Although the modem and Ethernet jacks look almost the same, they serve different purposes. The smaller jack, for your modem, is used to dial up the Internet or send faxes. The thicker jack, for Ethernet, is used to connect your iMac to a network printer, to another computer to share files, or to access a high-performance Internet connection (we computer geeks call it "broadband."

9. If you have an iMac with a FireWire port, you can hook up a FireWire hard drive, DV camcorder, or other high performance device to either of the two FireWire ports. I'll tell you some more about FireWire in Hours 14 and 20, "Adding More Goodies to Your iMac."

10. Turn your iMac on. Where's the power switch? On the flat-panel iMac, it's at the rear left (you might have to grope a few times to find it until you're accustomed to its location). The power switch on a vintage iMac is on the front, at the left.

Your iMac's Startup Routine

As soon as you start up, the iMac will make a little sound. (I'll talk about that a bit more in the Question & Answer session at the end of this lesson.)

For the next minute or two, your iMac will go through a startup process during which several screens will appear. The first, whether you have an old or new model, is the famous Happy Mac icon. Under Mac OS X, you'll see an introductory screen where the components that are loading will be identified. The older Mac operating system will display various and sundry icons; little square pictures that identify a specific startup program.

NEW TERM The *operating system* is the fuel that feeds the engine or processor that runs your Mac. It's software that makes all the disparate components of your iMac run in harmony and controls how the various programs you run on your iMac operate. Without an operating system, your iMac would be like a car without gas.

All iMacs shipping since May, 2001 have two operating systems. One, Mac OS X, is Apple's Unix-based operating system. The other, Mac OS 9.1 or later, is the older operating system that enables you to use your vintage Mac programs. You can easily switch from one operating system to the other. Hour 2 covers the subject in more detail.

Questions, Questions!

The first time you start a new Mac, you'll have a close encounter with Apple's Setup Assistant.

The Setup Assistant's layout frequently changes, so I'm not going to show what it looks like here. I will, however, give you an idea of the sort of information that's requested, so you can be ready to respond.

If you decide to take the quiz offered by the Setup Assistant, just read the questions you see on the screen before answering. (You can always change the answers later if you come up with a better one.) Click the Continue button to move ahead, on older iMacs you'll see right arrows to move ahead and left arrows to return to a previous setup screen.

That little pointer you see on your screen when you move the mouse around is the mouse *cursor*. Its shape changes for different functions. For example, it will become a blinking vertical bar if you click an area where you enter text, and it will switch to a little hand if you point the cursor at something that can be activated with a single mouse click. When your computer is thinking over an operation you activated, the cursor changes to a little spinning watch.

I'll list most of the types of questions the Assistant will ask you. Not all the information listed will be covered, so don't be surprised if the precise topic isn't dealt with. Just read the directions carefully and the answers will come easily.

To fill in information, point the mouse cursor in the little text area and click. You'll see a blinking insertion point to signify that you are in the right text area. To move from one text area to another, press the Tab key on your iMac's keyboard.

Actually, you don't have to answer any of the Setup Assistant's questions. You can dismiss the Assistant whenever you want and answer the questions later. The Setup routine is needed to prepare your registration information on your new computer, set up Internet access, and to set the correct time for your computer's clock.

Here's a list of the sort of questions you'll be asked as the Mac OS X Setup Assistant progresses (but remember, some of this might change as Apple updates the way it runs):

- **Welcome**: Choose your country from the list.
- **Registration**: At the end of the setup process, your information will be sent on to Apple. Click Continue to progress through the screens. And, yes, you can opt out of receiving email offers from Apple.
- **Create Your Account**: Mac OS X is a multiple-user system, which means that you can set up a separate account for every person who will be using your iMac. But the initial setup is for you, as owner (or administrator) of your iMac. Now you have a title! Hour 21, "Backup, Backup, Backup...How to Protect Your Files," will tell you how to set up those other accounts.

Does the Setup Assistant and startup process look totally different to you? It's possible your iMac was set to start up in Mac OS 9. If that's the case, don't be concerned. Just read the instructions carefully in the Setup Assistant and supply the requested information where you can and you'll do just fine.

- **Get Internet Ready**: Do you have an Internet account. You can take this opportunity to sign up with EarthLink, Apple's default service and get a free trial, or add information from your previous ISP. You'll also have to select the means by which you connect. You can use your iMac's built-in modem, a network connection, a cable modem, or DSL. Not sure what to do? Check with the service you're using about what connection method you're using. Or just leave it alone and worry about getting on the Internet later (see Hour 4, "Getting on the Net," for more information).

If you're an AOL member, you can't set up your account here. Just tell the assistant you're not going to connect to the Internet right now. I'll tell you how to set up AOL in Hour 4.

- **Get iTools**: What's this about? Apple has a special service for Mac users at its Web site where you can have an exclusive mac.com address, get your own personal storage space, create a personal Web site, and send custom greeting cards to your friends and business contacts. It costs you nothing if you opt to take the service. Just click the setup button to register and answer a few simple questions. Or do it later, no problem.

- **Now You're Ready to Connect**: If you set up your Internet connection, you'll sit back for a moment now, as your registration information is sent to Apple. Just be patient, and you'll see be ready to move to the next setup screen.

- **Set Up Mail**: Mac OS X includes a neat little email program, simply called Mail. Here's where you need to set it up to work with your service. If you're not sure what to put here, just bypass the screen for now. You can set it up later.

> Not sure what information to enter to access the Internet? If you're not setting up a new or existing service with EarthLink, you need to use the information given to you by your current service or copied from another Mac. If you're not sure, call the service and ask what to do next. For now, you can bypass this setting and do it later.

- **Select Time Zone**: Where do you live? Just pick the time zone so that your Mac's click is correct, and your messages and files will have the proper time stamping.

- **Thank You**: You're welcome. This is just the final Setup Assistant screen. There, that wasn't so bad, was it? In just moments, you'll see your iMac's desktop, ready and waiting for you to begin using your computer (see Figure 1.5).

FIGURE 1.5

Here's the Mac OS X desktop. Click twice rapidly (double-click) on the icon at the upper right to see what's on your computer's hard drive.

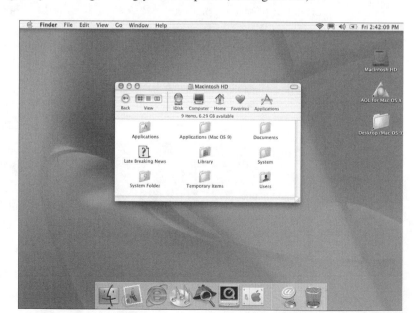

Turning It All Off

All Macs, including the iMac, have to do a little internal housekeeping whenever you shut them down. Here's how to turn off your computer:

- Take your mouse and point to the Apple menu (that thing on the top of the screen with an Apple icon), then click and hold. Then move the cursor to Shut Down and release the button, to select it. Within a few seconds, the iMac will comply and turn itself off.

> Using Mac OS 9? The procedure is the same except that the Shut Down command is in the Special menu. Point the mouse at the top of your iMac's screen, at Special, click and hold. Choose Shut Down and release the button and the iMac will soon close down.

If you listen carefully after the Shut Down command is engaged, you'll hear the hard drive on your computer churning a little bit. That's normal. The Mac OS is designed to do a few chores with the drive before the computer is ready to turn itself off.

> The Sleep function is used to put your computer into a low-power mode. The screen will darken, but the computer will still be on, and a simple press of any key on the keyboard will restore it to life. Anything you worked on before it went to sleep will still be there, ready to be worked on again. If you're planning on using your iMac later that day, Sleep is fine and your computer will be up and running a lot faster than shutting it down and turning it on again.

> If you accidentally shut the computer off by pulling the power cord, or there's a power failure, in most cases it will work just fine the next time you start it up. If you happened to be working with a file at the time, there's always the possibility the file might have become damaged, or there might be minor damage to the hard drive's catalog directory, so just be careful. I'll tell you how to fix common problems in Hours 23, "Crashin' Away: What to Do?" and 24, "An iMac Safety Net."

Discovering the Help Menus

Are you new to the Macintosh world? Or to computers in general? Well, take it from me, the mouse takes a little while to get used to, but after a couple of exercises you'll be working it like a pro.

Unfortunately, to learn to work with the mouse you have to use it to get to a tutorial. It's sort of like that old joke, "If you don't know how to spell the word, how do you look it up?"

Apple has a Help menu where you can receive tips and information. To get there, just point the mouse to the Help label and hold the mouse switch. Choose Mac OS from the menu to open a list of help topics.

To get from one to the other, just click the underlined link, known as a *hyperlink*. That click will open an information screen explaining what the function is all about. When you get the basics, choose the section in this book that covers the topic for a complete tutorial.

If you're having a bit of trouble getting to the Help menu, here's a fast tip. Just point the mouse to the item on the menu bar labeled Help and click the mouse button once. The Help menu will sit there until you pick a command (or about 15 seconds if you don't make a selection).

Keyboard Power

Don't feel that using your computer will confine you to the mouse. As you'll see throughout this book, there are many ways to use the keyboard (see Figure 1.6) to help you get around.

If you haven't used a computer before, you'll find a few odd keys surrounding the normal range of letters and numbers.

Here's what they do (from left to right, top to bottom, and so on):

- **Esc**: This is similar to the option on a Windows-based computer. It enables you to stop a function for some programs.
- **F1 through F15**: These are function keys. For some programs, you'll find they activate additional features. The manuals or online help for those programs will explain what they do.
- **Help**: Opens the Help menu for some (but not all) programs.

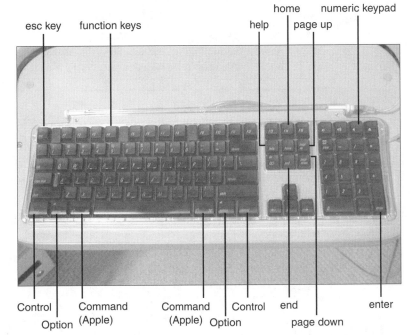

FIGURE 1.6
Here's the Apple Pro keyboard, which comes with all iMacs shipping since the summer of 2000.

- **Home**: They say you can't go home again, but the purpose of this is to take you to the top of a document page or directory window.
- **Page Up**: This keystroke takes you up a page or single screen in a program (but not all software supports the feature).
- **Page Down**: The reverse of Page Up. It takes you down a page or single screen in a program that supports the feature.
- **End:** Not available on the compact iMac keyboards, this command moves you right to the end of a document page or window.
- **Numeric keypad**: It's similar to a calculator, and you might find it convenient to enter numbers in a program.
- **Enter**: Used to activate a function. In many programs, the Return key and the Enter keys each trigger the start of a function, but only the Return key is used to end a paragraph when you write text in a program.
- **Control**: This is a modifier key. You press Control along with an alphanumeric character to activate a special function in some programs.

You can also use the Control key and a mouse click (pressed at the same time) to activate a special feature called Contextual menus. This feature opens a menu of command functions that apply to the item you're working on. If you've used Windows, the result is much the same as a right click.

- **Option**: Another modifier key. It's often used (along with an alphanumeric key) to get you a special character when you're typing a document (such as a foreign accent or symbol). This key is identical to the Alt key on a Windows keyboard.
- **Command**: It's sometimes called the Apple key because some keyboards show the Apple symbol there instead of the cloverleaf. It's another modifier key, used along with an alphanumeric key, to activate a command.
- **Media Keys**: The four keys at the left control both sound and drive media. The first three do precisely what the icons show, reduce volume, raise volume, or mute your iMac's speakers. The last is used to eject a selected CD or open and close the CD tray on the flat-panel model.

Summary

In Hour 1, you unpacked your brand new iMac. Then you connected everything together and turned it on for the first time. From here, you ran through Apple's setup assistants to get your computer set up and connected to the Internet. You also got a quick primer on the purpose behind those extra keys on the iMac's keyboard.

In Hour 2, you'll learn how to navigate between two operating systems, and then explore the two versions of the computer's desktop to see how to invoke simple commands to make your computer do things for you.

Q&A

Q What's that startup sound?

A Your iMac (and all new Macs) begins with a startup chime. On most current models, the sound resembles a G chord played on a synthesizer. Don't be alarmed; it's very normal. Don't be concerned if it takes a few moments for the screen to light up. Your computer has to do a self-diagnostic routine before it's ready to roll.

Q What's the *i* in iMac stand for?

A It's not a play on the old movie line, "Me Tarzan, You Jane." The iMac is meant as a convenient computer to connect to the Internet—hence the i in its name. And it sounds cute in all those ads.

Q Okay, tell me the truth: Was the first-generation iMac blue or green?

A According to Apple, the color is bondi blue. It's based on the color of the surf at Bondi Beach in Australia. Not having been down under, I can't confirm this. The lighter color is called ice.

The later generations of iMacs used a huge range of colors, from fruit-flavored, such as grape and strawberry to such 1960s-inspired shades as Blue Dalmatian and Flower Power.

Q The cute plastic exterior on a vintage iMac doesn't look terribly sturdy. What's the real skinny about it?

A The Classic iMac is made of polycarbonate plastic, similar to the material used for Apple's PowerBook line. It's pretty sturdy under normal circumstances, but you have to treat it with a bit of care. Don't scratch it with a sharp object, or rub on it with an abrasive cloth or other material. Keep liquids elsewhere. If you need to clean your iMac, shut it down, and use a slightly damp, lint free cloth.

And if you drop the iMac, it can definitely break. The same is true for the flat-panel version, which has a metal base.

Q Isn't the LCD display on my iMac delicate?

A Yes, so treat it gently. Apple supplies a convenient chamois cloth that you can use to clean it. A soft paper towel can also be used. Just don't pour any liquids onto the screen. At worst, spray a little water or a mild glass cleaner onto the cloth and wipe the screen gently. Don't press.

Q Can I expand the iMac to make it run better or add things to it?

A Yes to both. You can install additional random access memory (RAM), which enables you to add more memory to a program or run more at the same time. I'll tell you more about hardware expansion in Hour 22, "Giving Your iMac New Software, More RAM, and Other Things," but if you're not mechanically inclined, you might want to let your friendly, neighborhood Apple dealer do it for you.

You can also add a wide variety of extras to your computer, such as printers, additional drives (such as the famous Zip drive, which you can use to backup your files for safety), joysticks (for games), digital cameras, and a lot more. The iMac DV series can also be used to edit videos from your digital camcorder. Your favorite computer store no doubt has a lot of great products to expand the horizons of your iMac. I'll cover some possibilities for you in Hours 20 and 21.

Q A friend of mine is an illustrator, and she has two displays hooked up to her Mac? Can I connect a second or a larger display to my iMac.

A Yes, but only if you have a flat-panel model or an older model equipped with FireWire. The flat-panel iMac has a special jack at the rear, and you need an Apple adapter to hook up a standard display to it (called VGA). Older iMacs use a standard monitor jack at the bottom just above the access panel where you add a memory upgrade or an AirPort wireless networking card, to which you can connect a regular display. Normally, it's hidden away or covered by a little plastic cover (you'll find a replacement cover with an opening for the jack in your iMac Accessory Kit). Just pry off the original cover, snap on the replacement, and the jack will be accessible.

One thing, though, when you hook up a second display to your iMac (and this feature doesn't apply to the earliest iMacs), it will only duplicate or mirror the contents of your regular iMac display. It won't enable you to see a wider desktop. Don't forget to turn off your iMac before you attach that second display.

Q What operating system should I use?

A If you're new to the Mac and perhaps to personal computing, I'd vote for Mac OS X every time. The look and feel is easier on the eyes, and it's a lot easier to learn. But stay tuned, I'll be guiding you through both operating systems throughout this book, so you can decide which one to use; remember you can easily switch back and forth anyway.

Hour 2

Exploring the iMac Desktop

You know, it seems like only yesterday to old-timers like me, but in the very old days of personal computing the screen was just plain text. You had to type the instructions on the keyboard to tell your computer to do something. There wasn't even a mouse to click.

When Apple created the Mac they did it differently (and, no doubt, that's where the idea for the commercial—Think Different—was first spawned, although it came years later).

The Mac was designed to relate to you in a way that was familiar to anyone who works in an office, using a desktop. Common elements on the computer are shown as little pictures (icons) to serve as illustrations of the purpose of a specific item.

It's very true that there are still computers today that are set up to work with a text (command line) interface. There's of course DOS on the PC side of the personal-computer arena, and Unix, the industrial-strength operating system that forms the foundation of Mac OS X, which can work with either a text or a graphical user interface.

The iMac is the direct descendant of that original Mac. For Hour 2, you'll take a tour around your iMac's desktop. You'll see that there are actually two desktops to view (I'll explain this shortly). You'll learn

- Why there are two different desktops
- What all those little icons represent and what they're used for
- What the menu bar is all about
- How to select menu commands
- About your iMac's desktop folders and what they contain

Why Two Desktops?

If you've purchased a new iMac, you might have noticed a little note that explains that you have a computer with not one but two operating systems installed.

One of those operating systems, Mac OS 9.2.2, shown in Figure 2.1, is a direct descendant of the Mac Operating System that first debuted in 1984. If you put that original Mac side by side with your iMac, you'll see that the look of the operating system is very, very similar, even though color has replaced black and white, and there are richer textures and shadings to the various desktop elements.

The other operating system is Mac OS X (see Figure 2.2), which represents the future of the Mac platform. Mac OS X is based on Unix, an industrial-strength operating system, which has been around for more than 20 years in one form or another. Apple calls Mac OS X "the world's greatest operating system" because it takes an incredibly stable operating system and gives it an advanced Macintosh look and feel, called Aqua.

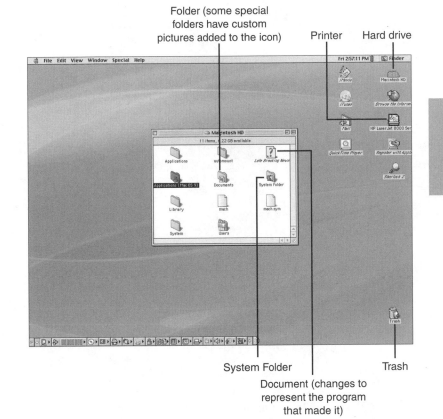

Folder (some special
folders have custom
pictures added to the icon)

Printer   Hard drive

FIGURE 2.1

*The traditional or
Classic Mac OS
offers an update to
the traditional Mac
look and feel.*

2

System Folder   Trash

Document (changes to
represent the program
that made it)

All right, I keep referring to Unix? So what is it. Well, the original version of
Unix was developed in 1969 at AT&T Bell Laboratories. It's an industrial
operating system with sophisticated multitasking and stability. The original
version of Unix, in fact, used a command line, like DOS and other older systems, and many Unix users still prefer it that way. Apple's Aqua user interface hides the complexity of Unix, but seasoned PC users can still examine
the command line by virtue of a little application Apple provides, called
Terminal, which you'll find in your Utilities folder.

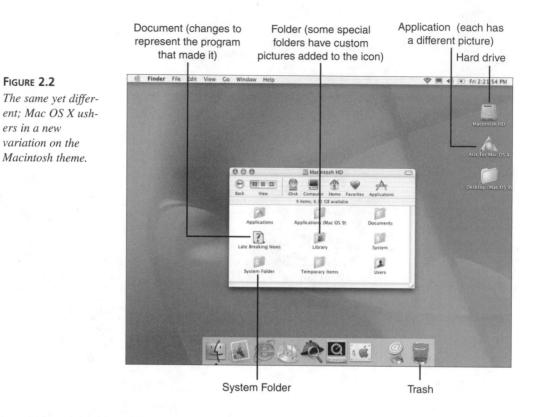

Document (changes to represent the program that made it)

Folder (some special folders have custom pictures added to the icon)

Application (each has a different picture)

Hard drive

System Folder

Trash

FIGURE 2.2
The same yet different; Mac OS X ushers in a new variation on the Macintosh theme.

Although highly reminiscent of the original Mac Operating System in basic respects, as you can see it is strikingly attractive, with a lot of attention focused on fit and finish. If you compare one against the other, it looks as if some highly skilled graphic artists went to work making everything look prettier, with no loss of functionality.

Because this book looks to the future, I'll focus, first, on Mac OS X, but I'll also give you a brief tour of the Mac OS 9.x desktop so you can see the differences.

Don't have Mac OS X yet? Well, Apple's new operating system will run on any iMac, with 128MB of built-in memory (check Hour 22, "Giving Your iMac and iBook New Software, More RAM, and Other Things," for more information on this subject). You can get a copy from your favorite Apple dealer. It's easy to install and, as you'll see in this book, easy to learn. After you've discovered the power of Mac OS X, you'll still be able to easily return to Mac OS 9.x without getting confused because many of the applications are very much the same. If you have a late model Classic iMac or the newest flat-panel version, you already have Mac OS X installed. With the latest models, your computer starts with that operating system, so you're ready to go.

If your iMac is running the older Mac OS (which I'll be calling Classic for the most part) it's very easy to switch to Mac OS X, assuming it's on your iMac. Here's what to do (consider this your first lesson):

Switching Startup Disks

▼ To Do

1. Move the mouse to the Apple menu, click and hold.
2. With the mouse button held down, move the mouse to Control Panels, which opens a submenu.

> If your iMac came with Mac OS X as the default operating system, go ahead and skip this section. You don't need it. Now how many book authors actually tell you *not* to read something?

3. Scroll through the submenu until you've selected Startup Disk (see Figure 2.3).

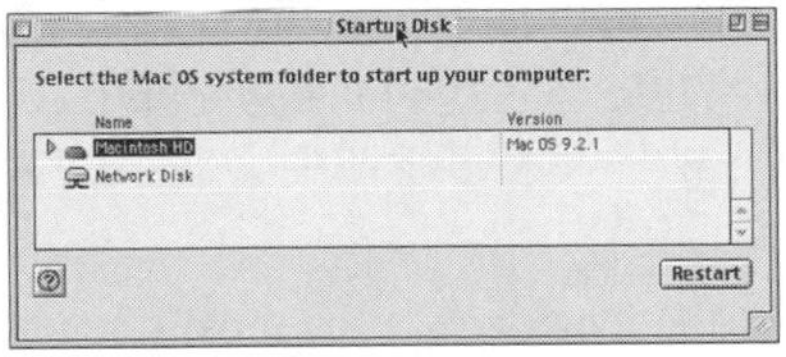

FIGURE 2.3
Startup Disk enables you to switch from one operating system to the other.

> Yes you can go back. After you've switched to Mac OS X, you'll find a Startup Disk function in a program called System Preferences that enables you to easily switch back to the Classic operating system. It's definitely *not* a one-way trip.

4. With the Startup Disk Control Panel open, click the little triangle to the left of the name of your iMac's drive, so it points down. You'll see the name of the two operating systems you have.
5. Click the listing for Mac OS X.
6. Now click Restart. Over the next few moments, your iMac will restart under the Mac OS X environment.

2

Remember the Setup Assistant I guided you through in Hour 1, "Setting Up Your iMac." Well, the first time you run Mac OS X, you'll see the equivalent. You'll be asked to enter your name and address all over again, so your copy of Mac OS X is registered with Apple. Then you'll be asked a couple of questions about whether you want Internet access and how your network is set up. I'll cover some of the basics of Internet access in Hour 4, "Getting on the Net" (you can bypass all those questions unless you just want to use your existing account).

Now that you're up and running OS X, I'll give you a tour of the landscape, the desktop, and you'll learn many of the functions available. After I've done that, we'll move on to Mac OS 9.x, so you can see what has changed.

What Do the Icons Stand For?

The items on your iMac are identified by little pictures, or *icons*, that tell you their function. This is one of the great features of a graphical operating system because, as they say, a picture tells a thousand words, or in this case, gives you a fast clue as to what kind of file you're looking at.

Here's a quick look at some of the icons you'll see most often and what they represent:

The iMac's Menu Bar

Your TV's remote control has buttons that turn the TV on or change channels. On the iMac, there are several ways to give the computer instructions to do something. The first one I'll talk about is the menu bar, that long, gray-shaded strip with thin horizontal lines that lies at the top of your iMac's screen.

If you've used Windows, you'll see one big difference between the way the menu bar works on the *other* side and on the Mac. With Windows, each program you use has its own menu bar, so you might find several menu bars across your computer's screen. On a Mac, however, there's only one menu bar, at the very top, which changes to reflect the features of the program currently in use. The advantage is that you only have to point your mouse in one specific place for it to work properly.

Document (changes to
represent the program
that made it)

Folder (some special
folders have custom
pictures added to the icon)

Hard drive

FIGURE 2.4
*Each icon accesses
a specific item or
feature.*

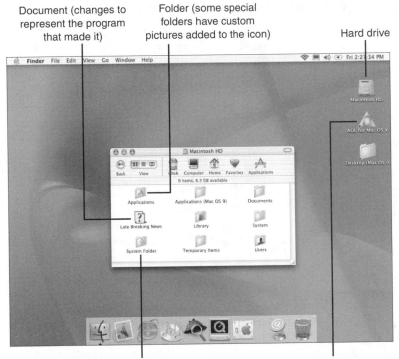

2

Mac OS 9.x System Folder

Application program
(each has a different picture)

About the Menu Bar

The iMac's menu bar has a set of labels that you click to open a list of functions (commands). In the next few pages, I'll take you through the Finder's menu bar, where you'll discover what all those commands really accomplish. In later hours, you'll learn specifically how to use these commands in other applications.

As you explore menu bar commands, you'll see that many of them are common from one program to another. That's a reflection of how consistent the Mac OS interface is. So when you learn what these commands do for the Mac OS X Finder, you'll also see how they work in other programs, such as the ones I'll describe in Hour 4, "Getting on the Net," Hour 9, "Teach Yourself AppleWorks," Hour 10, "Managing Your Bucks with Quicken 2002," and Hour 11, "Faxing, Other Software." That knowledge goes a long way towards learning how to use those programs.

Touring the Application Menu

Each application you use for Mac OS X has its own menu to the right of the Apple icon (which refers to another menu I'll tell you about shortly, the Apple menu). The application menu will always have the name of the active application, such as the Finder (see Figure 2.5):

FIGURE 2.5

The application menu has a basic set of commands for a specific program.

Here's how to see the contents of this menu:

Although many of the menus you see will be the same or similar when you use other applications on your Mac, some will be quite different. Each program has a separate set of functions that require different menu bar labels.

Checking Out the Application Menu

1. Move your mouse cursor to the Application menu.

2. Click the Application menu and hold down the mouse button. A list of the commands that are available from that menu will pop up on your screen.

Actually, the pop-up menu drops down, and if you use Windows you are probably used to calling them drop-down menus. Because this is a Mac, I'll use the word pop-up or pull-down to be consistent with Apple's terms.

3. To activate a command, move the mouse cursor to that item. You'll see a dark rectangle around it to show it has been chosen (or *selected*).

4. Release the mouse button to activate the command.

If holding down the mouse button isn't comfortable for you, just release right after you click a menu bar label. The menu will just stay there so you can easily point to a specific command. After you've done that, click that command. The menu will disappear and the command will be activated. Under Mac OS 9.x, by the way, the interval is 15 seconds.

You'll notice that some items are gray (or *grayed out*). Those commands are only available under certain conditions (such as Eject, which is used to remove a selected disk's icon, such as that of a CD, from the desktop and eject it), or if you select a specific icon to which the command applies. If the command is grayed out, you won't be able to perform that function.

- **About the Finder**: Select this to learn something about the program you're using. Usually, you'll see the version number and the name of the publisher of the program.

- **Preferences**: This command opens a dialog box where you can make a few settings on Finder functions (see Figure 2.6). I'll cover more about this when you get to Hour 16. Feel free to play with the settings for now. You can always change them back.

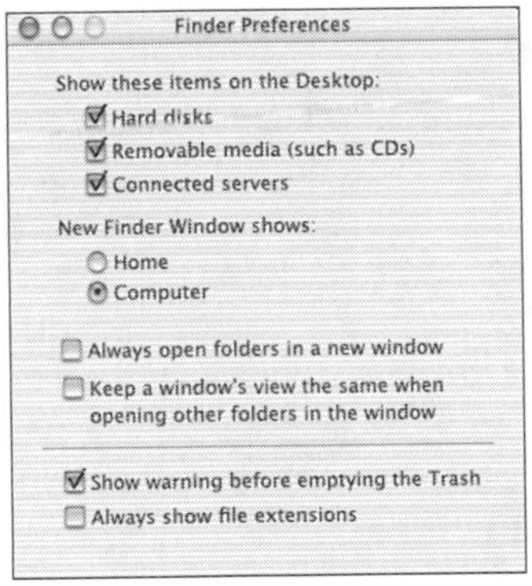

FIGURE 2.6

The Finder's preferences. Click an item to activate that feature or function.

Finder Preferences

Show these items on the Desktop:
- ☑ Hard disks
- ☑ Removable media (such as CDs)
- ☑ Connected servers

New Finder Window shows:
- ○ Home
- ⦿ Computer

- ☐ Always open folders in a new window
- ☐ Keep a window's view the same when opening other folders in the window

- ☑ Show warning before emptying the Trash
- ☐ Always show file extensions

- **Empty Trash**: When you drag an item to the trash can at the bottom of your iMac's screen, on the Dock, you can remove the item permanently with this command.

Did you put the wrong item in the Trash? Click on the Trash icon in the Dock, and a folder will open showing its contents. Now you can drag the items that you don't want to delete out of the Trash. When you activate the Empty Trash function, however, it's too late.

- **Services**: This is a clever Mac OS X feature that enables one program to call on the features of another to perform a function. A cool example would be to type the address of a Web site, copy it, then select a browser from the Services window and have it open that site.
- **Hide Finder**: Hides the window of the application, which helps reduce the clutter of windows on your desktop.
- **Hide Others:** Hides the windows for all other programs, so you can easily work with the one you're using.
- **Show All:** Reverses the previous two features.

Depending on the program you're using, an application menu might have additional functions. For example, other programs will include a Quit command that closes the program and all its documents in one operation.

Touring the File Menu

Now let's tour the File menu (see Figure 2.7). The following commands are available in the Finder's File menu:

FIGURE 2.7

The File menu controls basic file manipulation features of your computer.

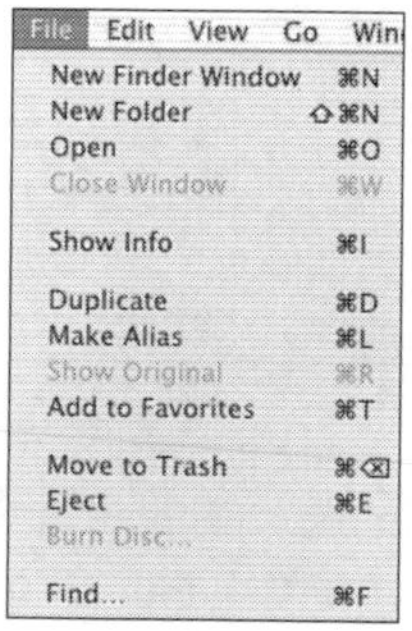

File	Edit	View	Go	Win
New Finder Window				⌘N
New Folder				⇧⌘N
Open				⌘O
Close Window				⌘W
Show Info				⌘I
Duplicate				⌘D
Make Alias				⌘L
Show Original				⌘R
Add to Favorites				⌘T
Move to Trash				⌘⌫
Eject				⌘E
Burn Disc...				
Find...				⌘F

2

- **New Finder Window**: Creates an Extra Finder window, which can help you work more easily with files from different locations. This way if you want to move files from different locations, you can get an easier handle on their exact positioning and not move the wrong file to the wrong place.

- **New Folder**: Creates a container to store files (or more folders). You can insert folders within folders to your heart's content (but don't overdo it) just by dragging one over to the folder you want to put it in. Wait for the target folder to highlight before releasing the mouse button.

 You don't have to use your mouse for all commands. Some functions have keyboard shortcuts, too. You'll see them listed at the right of the command label on a menu. The cloverleaf key stands for the Apple or Cmd key on your iMac's keyboard. If you hold down that key plus the second key listed, it will activate that function.

- **Open**: Opens a folder, or launches a program and brings a document to your screen.

- **Close Window**: Used to close the selected Finder window.

- **Show Info**: Use this command to learn more about a selected icon, apply access privileges to it, and, in the case of a document, even change the application used to open it.

- **Duplicate**: As it says, it will make a copy of the item you've selected.

- **Make Alias**: I'll cover this in more detail in Hour 6, "Files, Folders, Windows, and Other Things." An Alias in Mac OS parlance is an icon that points to the original (it's like running something on remote control). It has lots of cool uses, as you'll see later, the most important of which is to be able to access a file or application that's buried deep into a folder, without having to figure out where it is.

- **Show Original**: When you select the alias, or pointer to the original file, this command opens the original file, wherever it's located on your iMac's drive.

- **Add to Favorites**: If you want to call up a program or document often, you'll want to make it a Favorite, so you can get to it quickly. The selected item joins the list of Favorites that are accessed when you click the Favorites icon in the Finder's toolbar.

- **Move to Trash**: Puts a selected item in the trash can at the lower right of your iMac's Dock, that taskbar that sits along the bottom of the screen (the equivalent of the Hefty bags you keep in your garage).

Some commands in a menu have a right arrow next to them. If you see the right arrow, it means clicking on it will open a second menu (a *submenu*) showing additional functions that apply to that command.

- **Eject**: This command can be used to eject CDs, floppy disks, and so on.
- **Burn Disk**: If your iMac has a built-in CD burner, you can use this command to make a CD.

 Mac OS X's disk-burning software can also work with some external CD drives. I'll tell you more about the subject in Hour 15, "Managing Your Music Library with iTunes."

- **Find**: This command opens the great Sherlock search feature. You can use Sherlock to locate files on your iMac's drive or the text inside files and also on the Internet, all in one neat application.

 If you see three dots (an ellipsis) next to a menu command, you'll see another screen (a dialog box) when you select that function. You will have to make some choices from the dialog box to activate a function (that's why it's a dialog). I'll tell you more about this in Hour 6.

NEW TERM A *dialog box* is a screen or window where you can interact with your computer to make choices about a selected function. For example, if you want to print something you'll see a dialog box where you type how many copies you want of each page and what pages you want to print.

NEW TERM A *window* as described here is not that *other* platform, but a rectangular-shaped object that displays such things as a list of files, the contents of a folder, or the contents of a document (such as a letter to your mom). I'll explain more about how this all works in Hour 6.

Touring the Edit Menu

The next menu is called Edit (see Figure 2.8). It's used to make changes to a selected item.

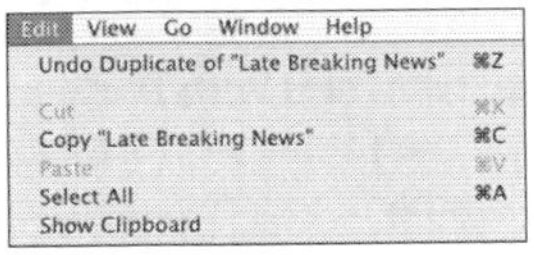

FIGURE 2.8

Use the iMac's Edit menu to make changes to a selected item.

Here's the list of commands that are used to Edit something. Once again, if something is grayed out, it means that command isn't available to work on the item you've selected.

The Edit menu includes the following items:

- **Undo**: They say there's no going back, but on the iMac this isn't always true. If this command is black, it means that the last action you took to edit something can be rescinded. Except for a very few programs, such as Microsoft Word, you can only do this sort of thing once. If it says Can't Undo, it simply means that function doesn't work for a particular item you've selected.

- **Cut**: This isn't used for removing files. It's designed to remove a text or picture you've selected and store it in a little invisible place called the Clipboard.

NEW TERM The *Clipboard* is a little cupboard or place in the iMac's memory where the item you copy is held in storage until replaced with another copied item—or until your computer is restarted or shut down. You use the clipboard whenever you copy or cut an item from your documents, such as a word, a phrase, or a picture.

> Be careful what you do after you Cut something. If you perform another operation (even typing a single letter), you won't be able to Undo the original function (except for a few applications that support multiple undo or redo, such as Microsoft Word X).

- **Copy**: This command makes a duplicate of the selected word or picture and stores it in the Clipboard. When an item is selected, the Copy command will include the name of the item (so you have a way to confirm your choice).

- **Paste**: Use this command to insert an item you've copied with the Copy command or removed with the Cut command.

Under Mac OS X, you can also copy files with these Edit commands. Just select a file, choose Copy, click the folder to which you want to copy the file, and select Paste. The Undo command will reverse the copy operation. This is one thing you just can't do with Mac OS 9.

- **Select All**: This command does precisely what the name implies. It highlights all the items in the selected window.
- **Show Clipboard**: This command opens a small document window showing the contents of the Clipboard.

Touring the View Menu

The next stop on our trip around the iMac's menu bar is the View menu (shown in Figure 2.9). It's used to control how items on your computer's desktop are displayed. The first three choices are either/or propositions with a checkmark to the left of the one you select.

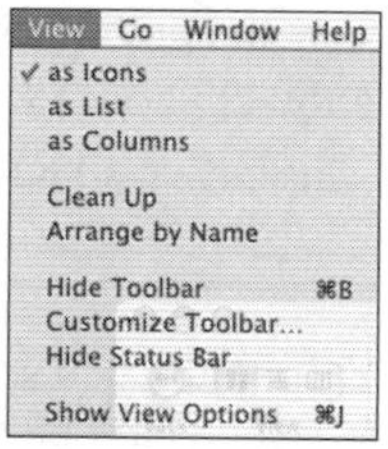

FIGURE 2.9
The View menu shows how items are displayed on the desktop.

View	Go	Window	Help

✓ as Icons
as List
as Columns

Clean Up
Arrange by Name

Hide Toolbar   ⌘B
Customize Toolbar...
Hide Status Bar

Show View Options   ⌘J

Here's a quick look at how the View settings work (adding the word View for clarity because it's not shown in the menu itself):

- **View as Icons**: This is the normal setup; everything is displayed as a colorful icon (shown in Figure 2.10).

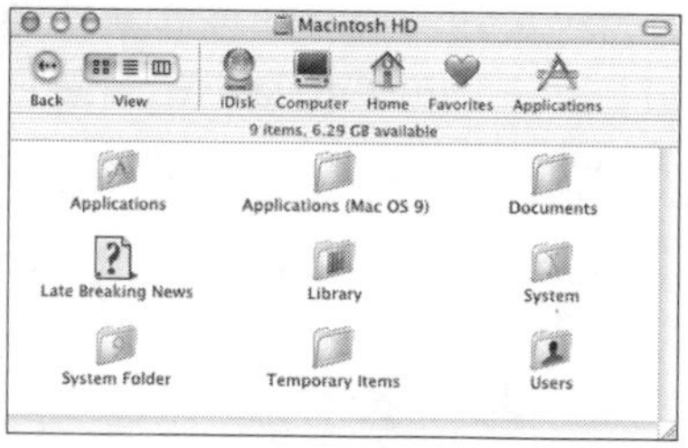

FIGURE 2.10
The normal display scheme for items on the desktop is the Icon view.

Macintosh HD

Back   View   iDisk Computer Home Favorites Applications
9 items, 6.29 GB available

Applications   Applications (Mac OS 9)   Documents

Late Breaking News   Library   System

System Folder   Temporary Items   Users

- **View as List**: Sometimes known as list view. It offers you a simple text listing or directory (see Figure 2.11). If you have a lot of items in a directory, this option makes them all take up a lot less screen space.

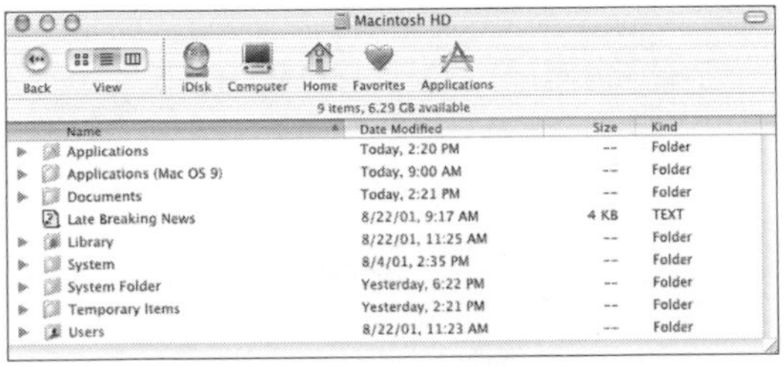

FIGURE 2.11

This is a simple text view of a directory.

- **View as Columns**: This function divides the Finder's listing into neat rows (see Figure 2.12). Click any item in any row, and you'll see the contents (or a preview icon) in the column to its right. When you click a folder in the right column, it will display the contents within that folder. The little resize handle at the bottom right can be used to make the Finder window smaller or larger (or just click the Maximize button to expand to the largest size to accommodate the contents).

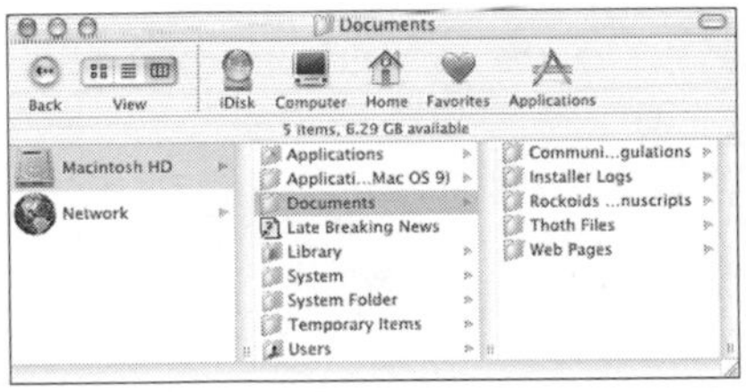

FIGURE 2.12

Column view, a new feature of Mac OS X, makes it easier to burrow deep down into the files on your iMac.

- **Clean Up**: If your icons are spread around, this helps clean them up with a neater arrangement. Now if it would only work that way in my office, I'd be all set.
- **Arrange by Name**: An easy way to sort the contents of a window.
- **Hide Toolbar**: The little row of icons at the top of a Finder window can be hidden this way (it changes to Show Toolbar after the toolbar is hidden).
- **Customize Toolbar**: Use this command to add or remove icons from the Finder's toolbar.
- **Show Status Bar**: Choose this command to see information about a folder or a drive, including the number of items and the amount of disk space available
- **Show View Options**: This will open a Setting dialog box (see Figure 2.13) that enables you to make further adjustments on how items on the desktop are set up.

FIGURE 2.13

Pick your View setup choices from this dialog box.

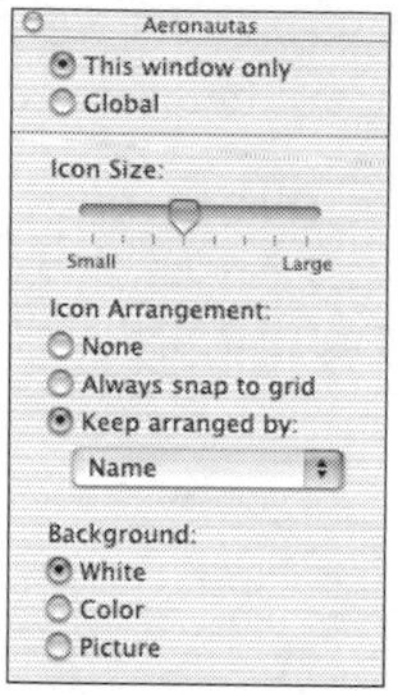

> What you see in the View Options window depends on what sort of Finder view you've selected. Some options, for example, don't appear in column or list view.

Touring the Go Menu

This menu (shown in Figure 2.14) is a speedy way to move from one folder or feature to another from the Finder.

FIGURE 2.14

A fast way to get from here to there, the Finder's Go menu.

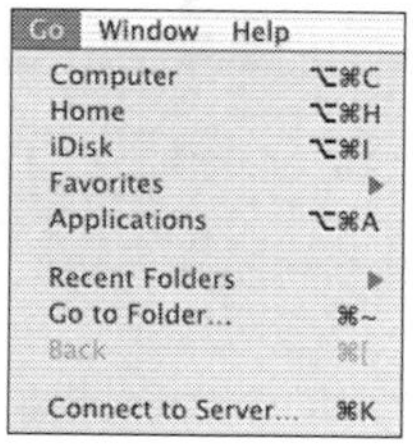

Let's take the Go menu items one by one:

> As you'll see, the bill of fare in the Go menu mirrors some of the standard Finder toolbar icons.

- **Computer**: This takes you to a Finder window that lists all your available drives plus your networking setup.

- **Home**: Under Mac OS X, this takes you to your personal user folder, the one that has your name. It enables you to easily view all your personal folders and files.
- **iDisk**: Use Apple Computer's convenient (and free) storage space reserved for every Mac user at its Web site. You just have to sign up for an iTools account (as explained in the Mac OS X Setup Assistant) to get your iDisk, which has 20MB of free personal storage space for you.

> Not yet an iTools member? No problem. Just launch the System Preferences application from the Dock, the Apple menu, or the Applications folder. Click the Internet icon, and then the iTools tab. Click the Sign Up button at the bottom right of the iTools screen to set up your iTools account.

- **Favorites**: This opens the folder that contains your Favorites list. Apple includes a list of their own, in addition to the ones you've selected.
- **Applications**: The Mac OS X programs that come with your iMac are included in this folder, plus the ones you've added.
- **Recent Folders**: Shows you a submenu displaying up to ten recently accessed folders. You can also access recent files and folders, but that feature is reserved for the Apple menu (I'll get to that shortly).
- **Go to Folder:** No searching needed. Choose this command and you'll see a little dialog box. Type the name of the folder and click Go, and you'll see that folder open in the selected Finder window. So, if you have selected the Applications folder, and want to go to the Utilities folder, enter Utilities in the Go to Folder window (it works on the top or active folder window).
- **Back:** Returns to the previously selected Finder window.
- **Connect to Server:** This is a very powerful feature. It enables you to easily network your iMac with other Macs. You can also network your Mac with computers running server versions of Windows or Unix.

NEW TERM A *server* is a computer that hosts files for distribution to other computers. For example, when you call up a site on the World Wide Web, you're actually connecting with a computer that stores the files for that Web site.

Touring the Window Menu

This is a fast way to manage the open Finder windows on your iMac. Here's a list of the available commands:

- **Zoom Window:** This command expands a window to the maximum size needed to contain its contents (up to the maximum available space on your iMac's screen).
- **Minimize Window:** This command reduces the window and sends it to the Dock, where it shows up as a colorful icon.
- **Bring All to Front:** Brings all open windows in the Finder to the front, for fast access (even if you hid them previously).

Beneath these commands will be a listing of all open windows for fast access.

Touring the Help Menu

When you run into a problem while working on your iMac, or if you just have a question, you'll want to keep this book at hand. But you'll also want to consult Apple's Help menu.

Each program will have its own set of Help choices. At the Finder, you'll see Mac Help, which opens a convenient window (see Figure 2.15) where you can learn more about functions and features of Mac OS X.

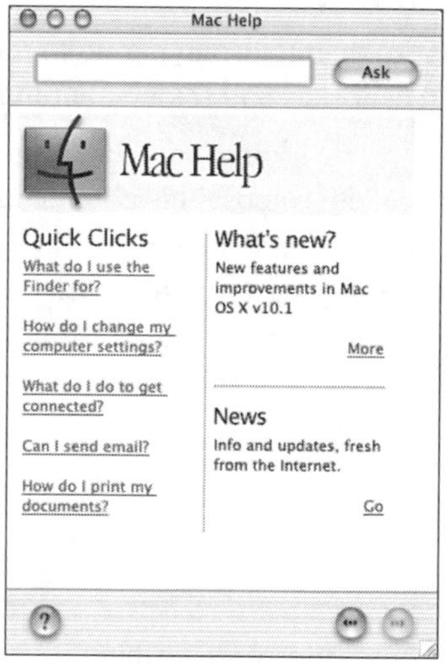

FIGURE 2.15

Click an item once to learn more about that feature.

> **Mac Help**
>
> **Ask**
>
> **Mac Help**
>
> **Quick Clicks**
>
> What do I use the Finder for?
>
> How do I change my computer settings?
>
> What do I do to get connected?
>
> Can I send email?
>
> How do I print my documents?
>
> **What's new?**
>
> New features and improvements in Mac OS X v10.1
>
> More
>
> **News**
>
> Info and updates, fresh from the Internet.
>
> Go

I'm not ignoring the right side of the menu bar. It contains your iMac's clock, plus one or more icons for quick access to some system functions, such as the settings for your iMac's display, speaker volume, and so on. You'll learn in Hour 16, "Using System Preferences to Customize Your iMac," that you can choose which of several icons show up here, and, if you want, you can even remove the clock.

Touring the Apple Menu

Our last menu bar option is actually the first on your screen, the Apple menu, which is, of course, identified simply by the symbol of an Apple (see Figure 2.16). The nice thing about the Apple menu is that the very same commands are available in every Mac OS X application you use on your Mac. That's why it has special commands.

If you've used a Mac before, you might recognize some of the following commands as the same ones that used to appear in the Finder's Special menu. I'll cover the Classic Mac OS Finder later in this chapter.

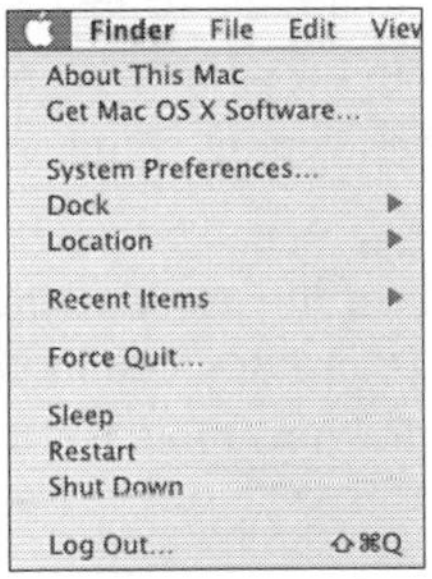

FIGURE **2.16**
The Apple menu offers quick access to more programs and documents.

Finder File Edit View
About This Mac
Get Mac OS X Software...
System Preferences...
Dock ▶
Location ▶
Recent Items ▶
Force Quit...
Sleep
Restart
Shut Down
Log Out...   ⇧⌘Q

- **About This Mac**: This one opens a screen that gives you some basic information about the Mac OS version you have, and the amount of memory installed.

If you run a program that is designed to run under the older or Classic Mac Operating System, you'll see a different Apple menu. There will be recent items, but a few more commands to choose from.

- **Get Mac OS X Software:** This selection shoots you over to Apple's Web site, where you learn about the latest software that runs under Mac OS X. All right, it's a commercial page, but it's a good way to learn about the latest and greatest Mac software.
- **System Preferences:** Use this command to launch an application to customize the way your iMac works under Mac OS X. I'll cover this subject in more detail in Hour 16.

- **Dock:** Use this command to customize the way the Dock, the colorful taskbar at the bottom of your iMac's screen, runs. You can, if you want, have it hang at the left or right of the iMac's screen. I'll cover the Dock in the next section and the settings you can make to change its look in Hour 16.

- **Location:** This is a feature of Mac OS X that enables you to set your iMac to automatically network with different setups in different places.

- **Recent Items:** Click this submenu to see a list of recent applications and documents for speedy access.

- **Force Quit:** This feature enables you to get out of trouble when a program freezes or stops working properly. I'll cover methods of dealing with such problems in Hour 23, "Crashin' Away: What to Do?"

- **Sleep**: This command puts your iMac into an idle or low-power mode. The screen will turn off, but the computer will remain on with anything you're working on still intact. Just press any key to awaken your sleeping computer. And it doesn't even snore.

- **Restart**: After installing a new program (or in case a program crashes or stops running for some reason), you should always use the Restart command. It causes the iMac to go through its normal shutting down routine, but then it starts up normally.

- **Shut Down**: Turns your computer off.

> Sleep, Restart, and Shut Down can also be activated by pressing the power button at the left rear of your flat-panel iMac, or below a Classic iMac's screen. It will open a menu giving these choices (plus the option to Cancel the operation). Clicking the appropriate function will activate it.

- **Logout**: Mac OS X is a multiple-user operating system, which means everyone who has access to your iMac can be set up with their own user account and their own Home folder. When you Logout, you'll be returned to a prompt where you can select a user name to log in again or choose the Restart or Shut Down functions. I'll cover this subject in more detail in Hour 21, "Backup, Backup, Backup...How to Protect Your Files."

What Is All That Stuff on My Desktop?

When you set up your new iMac, you'll see an icon labeled Macintosh HD near the upper-right corner of your screen (below the menu bar). Just double-click that icon to see the bill of fare (see Figure 2.17).

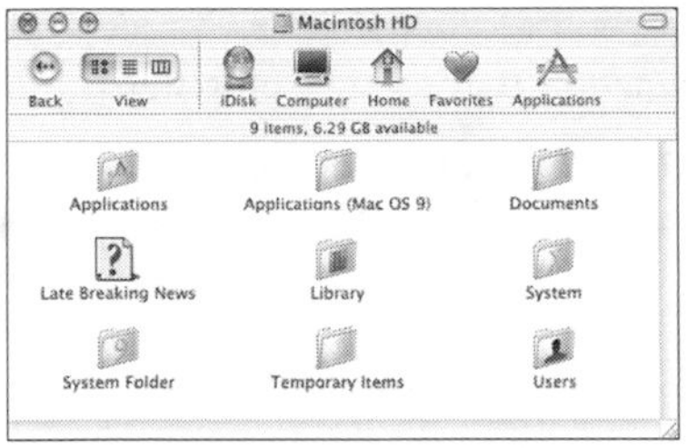

FIGURE 2.17

Most of the files stored on your new computer are in little containers (folders). This illustration only shows some of the folders you'll generally find on your iMac.

I'll assume that you've tried out the various settings in the Views menu to see what they do.

Here's a brief idea of the contents of those folder icons in the Macintosh HD window:

- **Applications**: This folder includes all the Mac OS X programs that were bundled with your iMac, plus new programs you might have installed. However, some programs put their own folders in the top level (root level) of your drive directory instead.

- **Applications (Mac OS 9)**: As the name implies, this folder is designed strictly for the applications that were designed to run with the older or Classic version of the Mac Operating System.

- **Documents**: The various documents that you create on your iMac can be located here.

> You also have a document's folder in your personal or user's folder, which is where you can put documents you might not want to share with others who might be using your iMac.

- **Late Breaking News**: Double-click this item to see information about your iMac or the Mac OS.

- **Library**: This is a folder that contains system-related files for Mac OS X. Feel free to look around, but don't mess with the contents because it might affect how your iMac works with Mac OS X.

- **System**: Another folder with system-related files. This one contains files that also relate to the way Mac OS X operates. These files are protected, however, so if you try to move one, it'll be copied, not moved.

- **System Folder**: This is the gut of your iMac's Classic system software. It contains the Mac OS software needed to make your computer run in that environment.
- **Temporary Files**: Sometimes an application creates special files that remain open while the application is open. They will be placed here.
- **Users:** Inside this folder is another folder bearing your name (and the names of any others that use your Mac). Inside the folder with your name are other folders with your personal documents, pictures, and settings files.

Introducing the Dock

At the bottom of your iMac's screen is a colorful banner of icons known as the Dock (again please go back to Figure 2.2). The Dock is used as a taskbar, to show which applications you're running, minimized or reduced versions of a document window, and programs you want to use frequently.

Whenever you launch an application, its icon will appear in the Dock (if it's not already there), and the icon will bounce up and down as it's opening. When opened, an upward-pointing triangle will show that it is open. When you quit or close the application, the triangle disappears.

To launch an item on the Dock, just click the icon once and the Dock will take it from there. As the application launches, you'll see the icon bounce up and down. When the Dock expands to the full width of the screen, it'll automatically get smaller as you add more icons to it.

Here's a fast overview of how the Dock works and how it's used:

- **Left Side:** There's a vertical bar on the Dock. At its left are icons for applications. The ones you've opened have a triangle below them.
- **Right Side:** At the right of the vertical bar are document icons representing the documents you've reduced or minimized. At the extreme right is the trash can, the place to drag files that you want to throw away.
- **Resizing the Dock:** To make the Dock larger or smaller, click the vertical line and then move the mouse up to increase the size or down to reduce it. If you hold down the Option key on your keyboard when you do this, the Dock stops at fixed sizes (in 64 pixel increments, to be technical about it).
- **Adding Icons:** If you want to get fast access to a document or application, just drag its icon to the Dock. It'll automatically go in the correct category, but the Dock doesn't organize by name. You can move items back and forth to reorder them.

- **Removing Icons:** You can remove an icon simply by dragging that icon away from the Dock. It'll disappear in a puff of smoke. You cannot, however, drag away icons for open applications.

That's it for now. I'll show you how to customize the Dock even further and move it to the left or right end of your iMac's display, in Hour 16.

> Why is a Dock icon suddenly bouncing up and down without letup? It means the program the icon represents is trying to tell you something with a notice or warning message. Just click the icon to move to the application and find out what it wants. In a Web browser, for example, you might see a message that a site cannot be retrieved.

Returning to Mac OS 9: Look at the Differences

Now that you've had a chance to see how Mac OS X is set up, let's return to Mac OS 9.x and see how it differs. You'll notice as we proceed that most things are very much the same, even though the user interface isn't quite as flashy.

> Why bother with Mac OS 9? Normally when you launch an older application, it runs Mac OS 9, or Classic, within the Mac OS X environment. But a few programs won't work this way, so you have to switch operating systems. Don't worry; you can easily switch back when you're finished using that program. One more thing, the reason I keep calling it Mac OS 9.x, is because several variations of Mac OS 9 work in the Classic environment, starting with Mac OS 9.1. You might have an iMac with 9.1, 9.2.1, 9.2.2, or a later version.

To return to Mac OS 9.x, follow these steps:

Returning to Mac OS X

1. Click the System Preferences icon on the Dock (or select it from the Apple menu). This launches an application used to customize Mac OS X (see Figure 2.18). Don't you worry about the rest of the available preferences. You can look at them later or see Hour 16 for more information on how to make more settings.

▼ To Do

▼

FIGURE 2.18
Customize Mac OS X with this application.

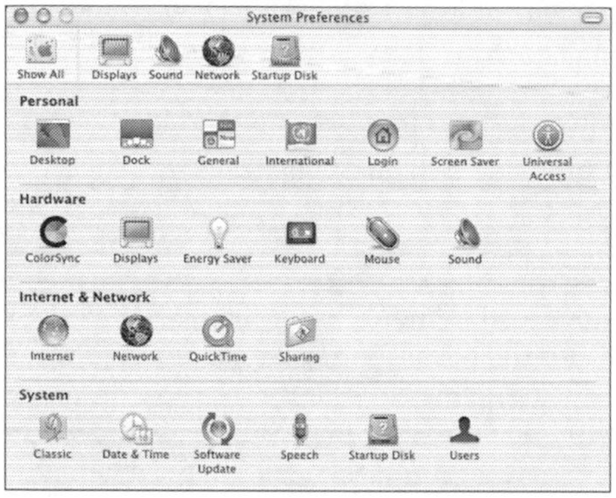

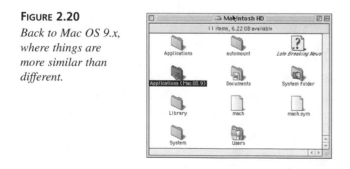

2. Select the Startup Disk icon and you'll see Figure 2.19.

FIGURE 2.19
Changing the startup system.

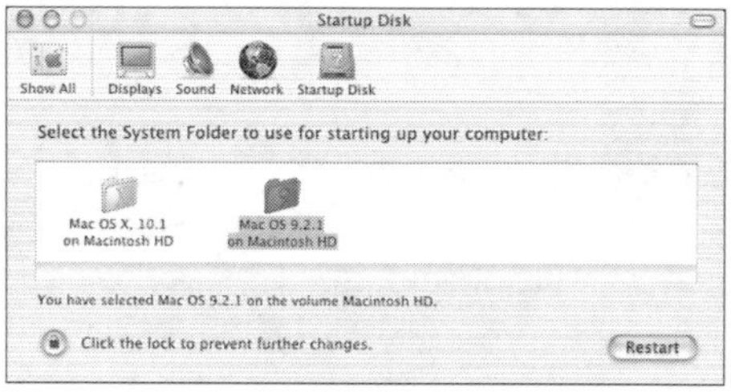

3. Click the folder that represents your Mac OS 9.x system version and click Restart. After you click Restart, you'll see an acknowledgement dialog box, where you

▲ click Save and Restart to begin the startup process.

Your iMac will now restart, and within a few minutes you'll return to the Mac OS 9.x environment (see Figure 2.20), where we can take a look at some of the differences. A list of the most significant differences follows:

FIGURE 2.20
Back to Mac OS 9.x, where things are more similar than different.

When you revert to Mac OS 9.x, you'll find some extra files with such mysterious names as mach and mach.sym. These files are required by Mac OS X to run. If you delete or even move those files you will not be able to return to the Mac OS X environment without reinstalling the operating system. So be careful.

- **Application menu:** For Mac OS 9, it's at the right end of the menu bar, and when you click it, you'll see a pull-down menu that lists all opened applications. The Preferences command for Classic applications is located in the Edit menu.

- **Apple Menu:** Under Mac OS 9, the system-wide commands to restart, shut down, or put your Mac to sleep aren't available (see Figure 2.21). Instead you have access to some commonly used applications, recent items, plus a submenu labeled Control Panels, where you can do system-wide settings. It's the equivalent of the System Preferences application for Mac OS X.

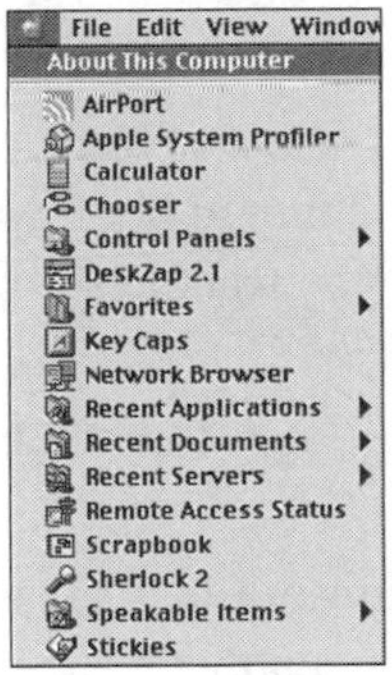

FIGURE 2.21

Mac OS 9.x has a totally different Apple menu.

File Edit View Window
About This Computer
AirPort
Apple System Profiler
Calculator
Chooser
Control Panels ▶
DeskZap 2.1
Favorites ▶
Key Caps
Network Browser
Recent Applications ▶
Recent Documents ▶
Recent Servers ▶
Remote Access Status
Scrapbook
Sherlock 2
Speakable Items ▶
Stickies

- **Special Menu:** The commands to empty the trash, eject a disk, sleep, restart, and shut down are only available from the Finder under Mac OS 9.x. This menu, as you saw previously, isn't part of Mac OS X; where some of these commands go to the Apple menu, the rest go to the Finder's application menu.

- **Missing Items:** Mac OS 9.x doesn't have a Go menu and, as you observed, no Dock either. In addition, the trash can sits at the bottom-right of the desktop, but it's a movable icon and you can move it elsewhere if you want. The Mac OS 9.x Finder has no toolbar and no Column view, but it does have a Button view, which reduces an icon to a large button that you click just once to activate.

I know you probably expected more, in light of the vast differences in user interface, but the devil is in the details. As you go through the menus, you'll also find some differences in the way commands are labeled, and you'll also find some are missing when you compare one to another.

Summary

In Hour 2, you began to discover how to make your iMac work for you. You toured the menu bar, and discovered the folders that contain all the great programs that Apple has thoughtfully provided for your computer. You also saw that, despite the surface variations between Mac OS X and Mac OS 9.x, many of the basic features are very similar. In Hour 3, "What's a System Folder and Why Do I Need Two," I'll explain to you why your iMac has two operating systems, and it's not there just to confuse you.

Q&A

Q I tried double-clicking an icon as you said and it doesn't work. What did I do wrong?

A Mouse skills take a bit of time to master. Double-clicking requires getting used to the right rhythm. You can also adjust the setting to fit in with your own taste. I'll tell you how when you get to Hour 16. If you want to see more, go ahead and turn the pages. I'll wait.

Q What happens when I double-click a file? Am I launching the file or a program?

A Well, both. When you double click a document file, such as one of those ReadMe files, first your computer launches the program that made it. Then the document itself is opened, so it's doing double duty. When you click a program's icon, just the program is opened. I'll cover this subject in more detail in Hour 7, "Opening, Saving, Finding, Moving, Etc."

Q My iMac's desktop doesn't look like the one in this book. What am I doing wrong?

A Probably nothing at all. If you are working on an iMac that has already been set up by someone else, perhaps the Views options are different, or a different desktop backdrop has been selected. It's even possible the folders that contain your computer's software have been organized in a different fashion (or have been placed within other folders). Maybe some of the programs my new computer contains aren't available on yours. I've tried to show typical desktops for Mac OS X and Mac OS 9.2.1 here. Your mileage may vary. The beauty of the Mac OS is that, like that fast-food restaurant you really can "have it your way."

Q I have Mac OS X, but some things you show in this chapter aren't there. What's wrong?

The answer is that you might not be using a current version of Apple's new operating system. This book is based on Mac OS X 10.1, which shipped in September of 2001. If you have an earlier version, you'll want to contact Apple about ordering the update CD, which runs a lot faster and more reliably on most Macs. You can find out by selecting About This Mac from the Apple menu, where the Mac OS X version number is shown.

There are a number of useful feature changes in Mac OS X 10.1. For example, the Finder looks somewhat different and columns, in Column view, can be resized. In addition, the System Preferences application has been redesigned and the Dock can be moved so that it hangs vertically at the left or right ends of your screen. Many features that weren't present in the original releases are available. These include the capability to burn a CD from the Finder, view DVDs (if your iMac is one of the models with a DVD drive), and network with Windows-based servers.

For those of you who have a flat-panel iMac, your computer already shipped with a recent version of Mac OS X, so don't worry.

Q Help—my iMac's keyboard and mouse won't work. What's up?

A Your iMac might have crashed (see Hour 23 and Hour 24, "An iMac Safety Net," for some help on dealing with such problems). For now, however, you should make sure that both your mouse and keyboard are plugged in securely. Don't feel shy about pulling out the plugs and putting them in again. The iMac's USB port is capable of hot swapping.

HOUR 3

What's a System Folder and Why Do I Need Two?

Are you used to the routine? The day-to-day use of your iMac involves a similar set of steps. You run some applications, such as your Web browser or word processing program, and you quit others.

But there is one set of software that runs every single moment that your iMac is turned on—your system software.

This is the operating system that gives your computer its special interface and offers the tools that enable your other programs to work. Without a working set of system software, your computer's incredibly fast G3 or G4 microprocessor would sit there and do absolutely nothing.

In this lesson, you'll learn

- The differences between Mac OS X and Mac OS 9
- What's inside those folders that contain system software

- What most of those files do
- The real definition of a clean system install

Why Two Operating Systems?

A new iMac contains a mixture of both old and new. The so-called Classic Mac Operating System is a descendant of the original system software that was included on the very first Macintosh computers in 1984. Although the look has been refined and features added, many of the elements that made the Mac unique are still there. All iMacs from the very first model include some version of the Classic system. The latest version shipping at the time this book was written is Mac OS 9.2.2.

Whether you buy a new iMac with it already installed or add it later, the other operating system, Mac OS X, represents the next generation. Mac OS X, as explained in Hour 1, "Opening the Box," offers advanced multitasking and memory management features that result in far greater stability. As you have already seen throughout this book, it also sports a new user interface, Aqua, that retains many of the familiar characteristics of the original Mac Operating System, but with a modified look and feel.

Superior multitasking and memory management counts for a lot on a personal computer. The combination means greatly improved performance when multiple applications are running, and it also means that your iMac will run much more reliably. Some Mac users keep their computers going for weeks under Mac OS X without a restart. I won't promise the same level of reliability, but it will be far superior to the Mac OS 9 environment. On the other hand, if you are much more familiar with the older Mac operating system, or your software isn't updated yet, you might want to stay with the tried and true for the time being.

You can easily switch from one operating system to the other using the Startup Disk panel in the System Preferences application under Mac OS X or the Startup Disk Control panel under Mac OS 9.x. When you need to run older applications that weren't modified for Mac OS X, yet stay in Mac OS X, the Mac OS 9.x system you're running opens in what's called the Classic Environment. In effect, two operating systems are running at the same time. Don't be confused by this, however, because the system software will sort it all out for you.

In a sense, you get the best of both worlds.

The two systems are organized somewhat differently, however, and you are going to find a number of strange folders on your iMac's hard drive. I'll cover the key elements of the two operating systems in the following pages, so you know what is going on with each.

Although it's easy to move files around in most of the system-related folders, you do so at your own peril. If the wrong file is removed or put in the wrong place, your iMac might refuse to start. Critical examples include the files labeled mach that you see on your hard drive when you return to Mac OS 9. Removing or moving those files will prevent your iMac from starting under Mac OS X. It's possible to remove applications from the Applications or Applications (Mac OS 9) folders or delete document files and system enhancements you might have added, but it's usually best to just leave the rest alone.

3

Welcome to the Mac OS X System Folders

Under Mac OS X, the components of the operating system are divided among several folders, each of which has files that perform a different purpose.

Here's a brief overview:

- **Library:** This folder, as shown in Figure 3.1, includes a number of files that extend the capabilities of Mac OS X. These include custom pictures for your iMac's desktop, fonts, plug-ins to add capabilities to your Web browser, the Internet search sites scanned by Sherlock, printer software, screen saver modules, and a number of other files that affect how programs look and are used. Anyone with administrator access to your iMac (such as you, as owner of your computer) can add and remove files to this folder. But, as I said, you should exercise caution and try to limit yourself only to components for non-Apple software that you've added to your system.

There is another Library folder inside your personal user's folder on your iMac. If you install anything there, such as a font in the Fonts folder, it'll only be available to you and not to other users of your iMac.

FIGURE 3.1

The Library is one of several folders containing system-related components for Mac OS X.

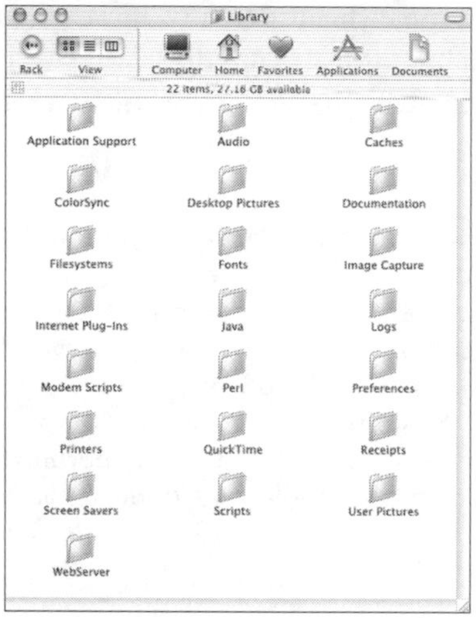

- **System:** Not to be confused with the System Folder under Mac OS 9.x, this folder also contains system components required for Mac OS X to run. Inside this folder, you'll see another folder labeled Library, and the various system files are divided into other folders inside. This folder is, in a sense, protected from user mistakes. You can't add anything to the folder, nor can you remove anything. If you try, all you get is a warning prompt for your efforts (see Figure 3.2). Any item you try to move is just copied, to prevent accidental removal of a key file that will prevent your iMac from operating.

FIGURE 3.2

The Mac OS X System folder cannot be modified.

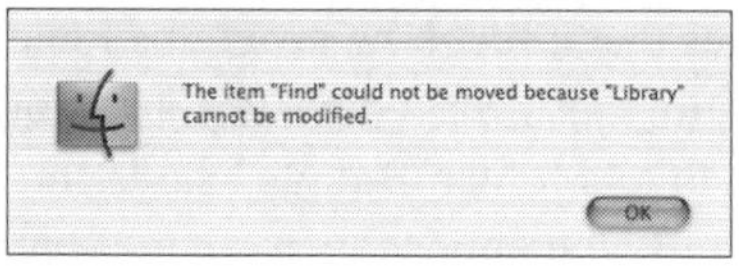

The protections for the Mac OS X System folder don't exist when you restart your Mac under Mac OS 9.x. You can then add and remove files without running up against a warning prompt. But don't try to experiment because you will make it impossible for your iMac to run Mac OS X without reinstalling the system.

- **Users:** Inside this folder is another folder with the name for each user who has set up an account on your iMac. The contents of those folders are only available to the administrator or owner of the iMac and to the individual users themselves (such as the Library folder mentioned previously). A Shared folder exists where the contents are available to anyone who uses your iMac. You'll find the Shared folder is a convenient place to leave files that are designed for access by everyone rather than one specific person.

You'll notice that there is also a Library folder in each user's folder. These Library folders store your personal program settings, fonts, and other files. Only you or another user with administrative access can start your iMac and look over this material, so here is a great way to keep your personal files.

If you restart your iMac under Mac OS 9.x, you'll find several more files with strange sounding names, such as Mach (no, that's not a far away place). These are also needed for Mac OS X to run and should be left intact. In fact, there are thousands of other files that are flagged as invisible, meaning they are not seen under Mac OS 9.x or Mac OS X, yet are crucial for your iMac to run. You needn't be concerned about them either. If you want to see them, however, you can install a shareware program, File Buddy, which enables you to view such files. Point your Web browser to http://www.skytag.com/ for more information about the program.

Welcome to the Mac OS 9.x System Folder

The other container for system-related components is strictly for Mac OS 9.x, and like all Mac Operating Systems that precede it, it's called, simply, System Folder (shown in Figure 3.3). Similar to the Mac OS X system-related folders, it's largely "a look but don't touch" area in terms of moving things around. Just about every one of the hundreds of files that lie there provides some essential function that your computer needs. From printing, to sharing files, to connecting to the Internet, or just your basic screen display, desktop appearance and file management functions, the System Folder is the heart and soul of all Mac OS computers running the Classic Mac OS.

I call it Mac OS 9.x because there are several variations out there that you might be using. As of the time this book was published, the latest version was Mac OS 9.2.2, but a later version might appear before you buy this book.

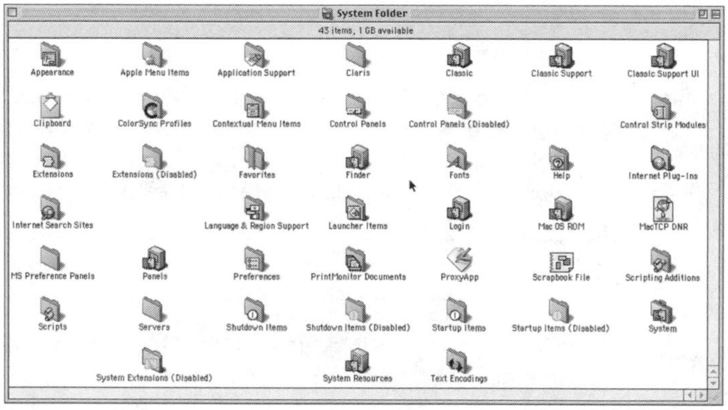

FIGURE 3.3

What are all those folders used for?

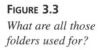

Over the next few pages I'll dissect the contents of the Mac OS 9.x System Folder, so you can see what most of those files are used for. You'll also have an idea what files you might safely remove without doing any harm to your computer's work capability.

You will find more files and folders in your computer's System Folder than the ones described here. I'm limiting this lesson to the files that are essential to the day-to-day use of your iMac's Mac OS 9.x System Folder. As you add more programs, additional files and folders will be placed there.

- **Appearance Folder:** This folder contains components used by the Appearance application to customize the look of your computer under the Classic Mac OS. The settings run the gamut from selecting a new desktop backdrop to choosing fonts and scrollbar enhancements. I'll tell you how to make these settings and others in Hour 16, "Using System Preferences to Customize Your iMac."

- **Apple Menu Items Folder:** This folder, shown in Figure 3.4, contains the files that are displayed in the Apple menu. Any file you drop in here will show up in that menu. In contrast, the Apple menu under Mac OS X can only be adjusted to display more Recent Items.

FIGURE **3.4**

The contents of the Apple menu.

Many of the files you install in your Classic Mac OS System Folder are automatically put in the right place. When you've booted your iMac under Mac OS 9.x, just drag them to the closed System Folder icon, and the Finder will figure out where they belong.

- **Classic Files:** Mac OS X's Classic environment works using your existing Mac OS 9.x System Folder. Several system components are installed that enable this clever marriage of the two systems to function. You'll find the various files hanging out loose in the System Folder and also in the Extensions folder (see following).

If you remove any of the files with the Classic prefix by mistake, they will be reinstalled (with a request prompt) next time you try to run Classic under Mac OS X (you'll have to OK a screen prompt, though). This isn't true about other system-related files you might accidentally delete, however.

- **Contextual Menu Items Folder:** These files support those clever little pop-up menus you see when you click an icon with the Control key held down.
- **Control Panels Folder:** Under Mac OS 9.x, a Control Panel (shown in Figure 3.5) is a program that is used to make settings. This folder gathers all those settings programs in one place, in a sense similar to your stereo or television remote control. Under Mac OS X, similar functions are offered by way of the System Preferences application, as you'll learn in Hour 16.

FIGURE 3.5

The Control Panel's folder contains applications that you can use to make different adjustments to your iMac.

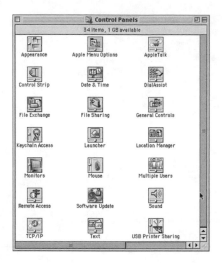

- **Control Strip Modules Folder:** The Control Strip is that cool palette that appears at the bottom of your computer's screen (or wherever you decide to put it) under Mac OS 9.x. Each little icon activates a different control function. Control Strips don't show up when you restart your iMac under Mac OS X; instead the Dock takes its place.

- **Extensions Folder:** A System Extension is used to add functions to your computer (hence the word *extension*) under the Classic Mac OS. The folder is really a catchall for files that do other things, such as drivers, shared libraries, and support files needed by some programs to work.

NEW TERM A *driver* is a file that communicates with one of your computer's components (or something attached to it) and makes that component run. A printer driver, many of which came with your computer, makes it possible for your printer to work.

NEW TERM A *shared library* is a file containing software-delivering features that can be shared by several different programs. Software publishers use these files to avoid having to duplicate efforts and features.

Let's now look over the contents of a typical computer's Extensions folder (mine), as shown in Figure 3.6, and see what the files are there for. If several programs are named similarly and offer similar functions, they're grouped together.

3

FIGURE 3.6

The Extensions folder enhances the functions of your computer.

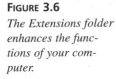

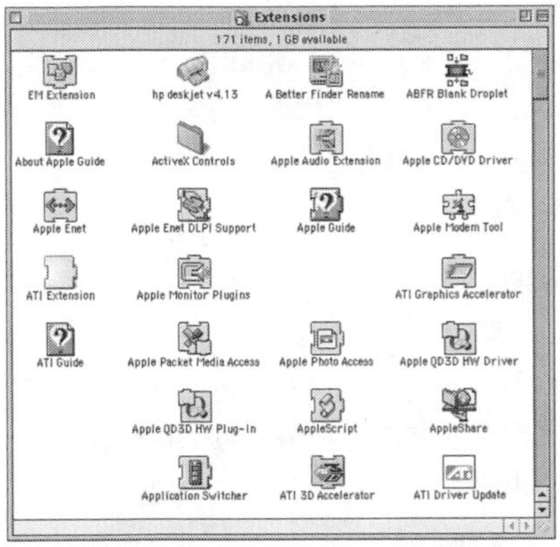

Let me remind you that a Mac OS 9.x System Folder might have a different range of contents, depending on how the computer is configured and what things might have been added courtesy of installers for some software.

- **Finder:** This is an application that runs all the time, offering your basic Mac OS desktop and disk management features. Whenever you open a directory, copy a file, or access a disk, the Finder is at work doing its thing. The Finder that works when you run your iMac under Mac OS 9.x is totally different from the one used under Mac OS X.

- **Fonts Folder:** The fonts you install on your computer reside here.

The fonts installed in this Fonts folder are available for both Classic Mac applications and Mac OS X applications. The reverse isn't true, however. If you install a font in one of the Fonts folders in a Mac OS X Library folder, those fonts are only available for Mac OS X applications.

- **Mac OS ROM:** In older Macs, the software needed to provide some basic functions at startup, was put on a little computer chip, called a ROM, located on your iMac's logic board. For newer Mac computers (such as your iMac), many of the functions are supported in this file, so they can be updated easily to fix problems or improve performance. There is, however, still a ROM chip inside your iMac, which performs basic startup functions.

NEW TERM A *ROM* (short for read-only memory) is a chip that offers permanent storage of computer data. The iMac has a very small ROM that doesn't do much more than enable it to start (boot). In essence, it's a "flash" ROM, which means it can be updated by software to fix bugs or add new features.

- **Preferences Folder:** When you change a setting in a program (or one of those Control Panels I'll discuss in the next lesson) it makes a little file that is stored inside this folder.

- **Startup Items Folder:** If you want a program to launch as soon as your computer has started, you put it here. A few files are already in this folder because some application software requires them.

- **System File:** This is the heart of your operating system software. In addition, the file stores keyboard layouts (used when working with foreign language programs) and system sounds that are heard when you restart your Mac under Mac OS 9.x.

- **System Resources:** Wouldn't it be nice if all the System file elements were put in one place? Alas, it is not to be for Mac OS 9.x. Part of the software required was put in a separate file.

- **Text Encodings:** This folder contains files needed for some foreign language functions and should be left intact (or some Mac OS 9.x programs won't work).

Did I miss a few things? Yes, you caught me! A number of other folders inside the Mac OS 9.x System Folder are used to work with some applications to make them run properly. Most of the names are fairly self-explanatory (such as the one for STF, for FAXstf, and Microsoft). Best thing to do is just leave them alone because they shouldn't affect the operation of your iMac, but might prevent a program from running if you remove them.

Summary

If your iMac has Mac OS X, it has several folders containing system-related files that are required for your iMac to run.

As you've seen, the files contained in those folders need to be treated with extreme care. One file moved to the wrong place can cause your iMac not to run. However, if you treat everything with care you shouldn't fear the presence of those folders. In some limited respects, especially with the Mac OS 9.x System Folder, some non-Apple files can be added or removed as needed.

Under Mac OS X, an application called System Preferences is used to modify the way your Mac runs. Mac OS 9.x offers a folder called Control Panels with little applications that perform similar functions. In the next hour, we'll look at both.

Q&A

Q I've heard about a *clean* system installation. What is it? Do I have to wipe my hard drive clean? Please explain.

A Settle down—you don't have to wipe out all your files. When you reinstall system software on your computer, the normal process is just to update your existing system files. Under Mac OS 9.x, a little button called Options on the first installer screen gives you the option of a *clean* install in which another brand new System Folder is created. The original one is renamed Previous System Folder (how original!).

Clean installs are done to help fix recurring performance problems, or constant crashes. Sometimes starting with a fresh slate is the way to go. And don't worry, you won't lose your old files.

Under Mac OS X, however, the process is a lot more complicated, and it's usually best just to reinstall, rather than to try and sort out ways to get rid of the original system files. The reason for this is, as I explained earlier, many of the Mac OS X files are invisible, which isn't something related to an old H.G. Wells novel. It means the files are set up in such a way that neither the Mac OS 9.x nor Mac OS X Finder can see them, so they can't easily be removed unless you get an application (such as File Buddy) that can locate such files.

Worse, if you've updated Mac OS X courtesy of Apple's Software Update feature, you can't just reinstall. That's because the old installer can't install the proper files. Apple says you need to back up your files and erase your drive to reinstall Mac OS X. But if you want to live a bit dangerously, you can go back to Mac OS 9, use that utility I mentioned earlier, File Buddy, to locate and eliminate both visible and invisible Mac OS X files, and start from scratch. Fortunately, you shouldn't have to concern yourself with this. The need to reinstall Mac OS X is a rare event, and you will probably never have to do it.

Q I want to reduce the amount of memory my computer uses. What Mac OS 9.x System Folder files can I remove?

A Under Mac OS X, memory use isn't an issue. The operating system allocates whatever memory is needed for a system-related function or application to run. Memory that isn't needed isn't wasted.

In addition, most of the files in the Mac OS 9.x System Folder actually don't use memory (or use very little) unless they are being used. Many of these files are drivers; software that communicates with your iMac and something connected to it to provide a specific function. For example, a printer driver is needed to process the information about your documents that goes to your printer. Unless you're printing, it just sits there and does nothing.

You should also be careful about what you attempt to remove from the System Folder. As you saw in this lesson, many of those files provide essential functions to make your iMac run properly. Without them, you'll find that CDs won't work, documents won't print, or you are suddenly unable to connect to the Internet.

Q All right, now I'm confused. I looked over my System Folder and the Mac OS X system-related folders and found many files that aren't part of your list. What do they do?

A Many programs scatter their own sets of support files around the Mac OS 9.x System Folder and even the system-related folders for Apple's new-generation operating system. I've only covered the standard files that ship with your iMac. As Apple updates its system software (or you install new programs), new components will be added and others will go away. If you're not sure what those files do, check the program's documentation or contact the publisher for the information.

However, it's usually perfectly all right to leave them around. If you remove the wrong file, one critical for a specific program to run, then that program will not function properly or at all.

Q Will all those extra files slow down my computer?

A No, not really. Some of those files might actually speed it up (such as those ATI drivers for your built-in graphic acceleration hardware). It really doesn't matter to your computer whether it has 125 files in the Extensions folder or 225. You just don't want to add files that have no purpose.

If you must remove a file, consider a printer driver that you aren't using. Because printer drivers are identified by manufacturer, this is probably not a problem. If you have an HP printer, for example, and you find files that identify a Canon printer you used to own, you can remove the latter without hurting anything.

Q Whenever I try to start my computer, I see a little disk icon with a flashing question mark. Is it broken?

A The most common cause of this problem is removing a file from the Mac OS 9.x System Folder that it needs to run. At the very minimum, you need the Finder, Mac OS ROM, System, and System Resources files to start your computer. You need the rest of the components of your System Folder for it to perform all its functions properly. A similar situation applies under Mac OS X, where the removal of a single file could also make the iMac unable to start properly.

If you encounter this problem, go get your copy of your computer's System (or Software Install) CD (or Mac OS X CD, whichever applies), place the CD inside the drive and force a restart with the little restart button on your iMac's connection panel. Then, hold down the C key to enable the iMac to boot from the CD.

After you're up and running, examine the System Folder on your computer's drive for missing items. If you can't find anything missing (or can't find the files to restore them), you should reinstall your system software. See Hour 22, "Giving your iMac New Software, More RAM, and Other Things," for more information.

3

HOUR 4

Getting on the Net

Why did you buy an iMac? One of the important reasons is probably its easy access to the Internet. The capability to get online in minutes rather than hours is a real plus.

So, in this lesson, you'll explore the subject of the Internet. You'll learn

- The differences between an Internet provider and an online service (and which to pick and why)
- How to sign up with EarthLink or a similar service
- How to join AOL and what it offers
- Some advice for getting started as an Internet surfer

The Internet is not a physical place to go (such as your corner deli). It's, well, a little more complicated than that. Remember that any time you connect even two computers together, you have a network.

The Internet is a network, too, only it doesn't contain just two computers, but millions of them, spread around the world. These computers not only share information but work as relay stations, forwarding the information they receive to other computers. Think of it as a gigantic relay race.

What's more, these computers aren't restricted to Macs or PCs. They run the gamut of many operating systems. Some are personal computers not much different in capability from your iMac. Others are huge mainframe computers, filling entire offices (similar to what you might have seen in some of those old science fiction movies showing computer systems). The Internet is, in a sense, a worldwide computer network that doesn't have any boundaries as to computer, operating system, or location.

EarthLink or AOL? What's the Difference?

Apple's default option for an ISP (Internet service provider) is EarthLink. However, you have, no doubt, seen all those TV ads talking about another service, AOL. AOL, part of the huge AOL Time Warner media conglomerate, bills itself (correctly of course) as the "world's largest Internet online service." But EarthLink is an Internet service, too, right?

Well, there *is* a difference. AOL, like EarthLink, does indeed give you an Internet connection and a Web browser to explore the Internet. Regardless, the only way to get on the Internet is to establish an account with a service provider, whether with these two or another company.

NEW TERM A *Web browser* is a program that calls up the information you want on the Internet, which is available at a Web site, and presents it on your computer with full-color animation and sometimes sound.

Although its custom content has expanded quite a bit, EarthLink primarily offers you a connection to the Internet, the same as your phone company offers you a connection to its phone network. There are additional features, such as some very nice Help pages and a well-integrated Personal Start Page (which you can customize to provide direct links to your favorite features). AOL, however, goes beyond an Internet connection. AOL is an outgrowth of what are sometimes called "bulletin board services" or BBS. It offers not only a connection, but has its own vast array of exclusive content available to members only. As you'll see (briefly) in the following pages, AOL has its own forums, chat rooms, discussion areas (message boards), software libraries, news centers, shopping centers, and other features that go way beyond just an Internet connection.

NEW TERM A *forum* is an online meeting place where folks of similar interests can get together, share information, and have discussions via their computers.

NEW TERM The *chat room* is the online equivalent of a meeting room, where you can talk in real time to other folks or listen to lectures. The talking, in this case, is done by typing on your iMac and sending the message to the chat room where others can see it.

NEW TERM A *message board* is similar to the bulletin board in your local supermarket. You can use it to leave little announcements, statements, or messages for others to see and reply to. Unlike a chat room, however, a message board is available to all users of a specific service, and messages remain available until a board moderator deletes them.

NEW TERM The *software library* is a place that stores files (such as software) that can be retrieved (downloaded) by others.

> Actually, AOL and EarthLink do share one other feature, instant messaging, the capability to communicate one-on-one in real-time with fellow Internet users. EarthLink is offering a special branded version of AOL's popular Instant Messenger software (which means it's the same software with EarthLink's name on it).

If you have children in your household, AOL has taken steps to make it kid safe. That is, they have special Parental Controls available to create a custom online setup for your children. This limits them to certain online forums and Web sites where the content is certified to be safe for them.

EarthLink also offers a page oriented towards Kids, the Kids channel, which provides a special online environment where children can find games and educational information (including homework help). It doesn't, however, restrict access by children to other Internet features.

> Higher speed options are available, too. In many cities, you can get connected with what is called a broadband ISP. Such ISPs use a cable modem or a system called DSL to provide super fast online speeds, sometimes up to 100 times faster than a regular modem. You will need to contact your ISP, local cable provider, or local phone company to see whether such services are available. What's more, both AOL and EarthLink offer similar high-speed options in some cities. I'll explain more about these worthy online alternatives at the end of this lesson.

Making the EarthLink Connection

When you first set up your iMac (in Hour 1, "Setting Up Your iMac"), you were interviewed by Apple's Setup Assistant and given a few questions to answer. One of the options was to sign up at EarthLink, Apple's default Internet provider.

But you don't have to take that route.

You can, if you prefer, use an installer CD from another ISP. In addition to AOL, services such as AT&T and Prodigy Internet also distribute Mac CDs that'll get you set up easily.

It's a sad fact that not all ISPs have Mac support. Most often they can set you up anyway, simply by showing you how to make a few settings on your iMac. Sometimes, as in the case of Microsoft Network (MSN), it requires special software that did not, as of the time this book was written, work on Macs.

Apple and EarthLink usually offer a free trial for the service, to give you a chance to see how it works for you. The usual period is 30 days (some AOL offers are for 45 days). During that time, you can cancel the service and owe nothing. You might also find similar offers from other ISPs.

In the next few pages I'll describe a typical ISP setup process. Do not expect the requirements to be the same for each one, but the general flavor of information needed to set you up is similar. As I said earlier, the only way for you to get on the Internet is to sign up with a service provider.

Before you set up an ISP account, you've connected a cable from your iMac's modem to the phone line (and make sure that nobody else is using that line during the setup process).

No matter what Internet service you want, have your credit card handy to enter your billing information. A few services can debit your checking account in payment instead (but will usually exact a slight monthly surcharge to do so), such as AOL and CompuServe. EarthLink will do it too, but you usually have to call their customer service department to set it up. Regardless, if you don't have a credit card handy, you might consider getting a MasterCard or Visa debit card that is attached to your checking account, but is accepted by companies same as a credit card.

Regardless of which ISP you choose, if you install special software you will be guided through a few simple setup screens that are designed to set up your account, pick a username, and get you online as quickly as possible. I'll just cover the basic categories of information required. Being forewarned will prepare you for the main event.

> Flat-panel iMacs include setup software for both AOL and EarthLink. Go to your Applications folder, and navigate to the folder labeled Utilities for EarthLink's setup application. AOL's software is located in the Installers folder, inside the Applications folder. If you have an older iMac, you won't find AOL on it, but the CDs are available at major stores all over the place, including Wal-Mart.

- **Pick Username:** When you join an ISP, you have to pick a username, the name by which you're known on the service. If you're lucky, you might be able to use your real name, or your favorite nickname. This name will become part of your email address. With millions of folks already online, however, more than likely you won't be able to get a preferred name. You'll have to take a second or a third choice. Most ISPs will give you a few options based on your name, and if you are willing to be patient and try out a few combinations, you'll soon find one you like.

- **Select a Password:** This is your lock and key, the way to protect your account from being accessed by someone else. You might be tempted to pick a password that's easy to remember, such as a child's name or birth date. The most secure password, however, is a collection of mixed uppercase and lowercase numbers and letters. Even something such as mY27ImAC would seem awfully simple, but it is reasonably secure, because the random combination of uppercase and lowercase letters might be difficult to guess.

- **Select an Access Number:** If the ISP uses your iMac's modem (and a few use high-speed cable modems or another high-speed feature called DSL), you will be asked to select one or more access phone numbers in your city. That way you can log into the service without having to pay long-distance fees.

> Not all ISPs have phone numbers in all cities. If you live in a small town, you might find that the first ISP you select requires a long distance call to get connected. If this is the case, and you can't find a national service that works, check your local phone company for a local ISP. If you find one, give them a call. If they know Macs, they can probably get you connected in just a few minutes, guiding you every step of the way.

4

- **Account Information:** Even if you get a free trial, the ISP wants to know who is going to pay the bills when they become due. Some ISPs give you a discount if you pay a year in advance, but most at least want to be able to bill a credit card or a checking account. So you'll have to give the service your contact and billing information. Before your account is set up, the ISP's computers will verify your billing information. This is done not just for their protection, but for yours, so they know that an invalid or stolen credit card isn't being used.

- **User Agreement:** When you install new software, you accept a software license, an agreement that covers use of the software on your computer. ISPs have rules of conduct that govern how you behave online. Although agreements can be written in simple English or complex legalese, they all share some things in common. You agree to respect others online, not to send offensive messages or junk email to strangers, that sort of thing. AOL, with its large number of chat rooms and message forums, has a somewhat more complicated agreement, but the end result is the same. Be nice online!

Take an ISP's user agreement seriously, particularly if you have children who will be going online, too. If they misbehave, even accidentally (and an over-enthusiastic teenager can sometimes cause trouble), you could lose your online account. So you should educate your children about proper online etiquette.

Try printing your setup information. Some ISPs give you the option to print a setup screen. If you see a print command, try it. If you haven't set up a printer yet (I tell you how in Hour 17, "Now That I Wrote It, How Do I Print It?"), try this command—Cmd-Shift-3. This action takes a picture of the screen on your iMac, and makes a file called Picture 1 (or 2, and so on) on your iMac's hard drive (on the desktop under Mac OS X). After you take pictures of what you see, you can print it later.

- **Behind the Scenes Configuration:** When you install software for an ISP, it'll go to work behind the scenes putting special settings on your iMac. This includes the network settings used to connect to the ISP's own computers, your username and password, plus the access number. After that's done you might have to restart your Mac (don't be concerned) before you connect for the first time. When you restart, your computer repeats its normal startup routine to enable special software to run at startup.

Where do the settings go? Well, under Mac OS X, the whole thing goes into the Network panel of the System Preferences application. If you are sticking with Mac OS 9, the phone numbers and login information go in the Remote Access Control Panel (available from the Control Panels submenu of the Apple menu). The rest go in the TCP/IP Control Panel. Feel free to browse to see what was done, but don't change anything or you'll lose your connection.

- **Browse the Internet**: Okay, what to do here? Under Mac OS X, click the Internet Explorer icon in the Dock (or from the Applications folder). Either way, you'll see an introductory page for your ISP (see Figure 4.1).

It didn't dial up? Locate Internet Connect from Mac OS X's Applications folder and launch it (your settings should already be stored there). Click Connect to begin the login process. When it's ready, you'll see a little screen at the bottom of Internet Connect showing connection status, and then you can launch your browser. For Mac OS 9 users, locate Remote Access in the Control Panels submenu (available from the Apple menu) and connect from there.

FIGURE 4.1

EarthLink's home page greets you when you first join the service.

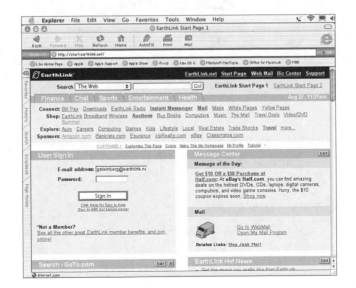

NEW TERM A *home page* is the introduction of a Web site. It will contain some brief information about the person or business running the site. You will find links to other pages and (no doubt) a few ads, too.

- **Personal Start Pages**: A great feature for EarthLink and other ISPs is the capability to create your very own customized start or home page for the service. To set it up, click the username or login icon or label. Enter the username and password that you established for your ISP. When you do that, you'll see options and instructions to customize your personal home page. EarthLink is not the only ISP that offers such a service. In Figure 4.2, you'll see my start page for another ISP, Cox Internet, a service that works with a number of cable TV providers to bring speedy service into millions of homes around the USA.

FIGURE 4.2

Yes, this is my real Cox Start Page.

No doubt you'll want to spend a little time exploring the vast frontiers of the Internet. You can just click any icon to start exploring (you'll learn more about navigating the Internet in Hour 12). When you're ready to sign off, here's what to do:

Getting Connected

▼ To Do

1. For a Mac OS X application, click the application menu of your Web browser and choose Quit. This will turn the program off. If you're using a Mac OS 9 application, it'll appear in the program's File menu.

2. To end your connection, open Internet Connect (see Figure 4.3) and click Disconnect. In a few seconds you'll be offline.

▼

FIGURE 4.3
*Click Disconnect to
log off.*

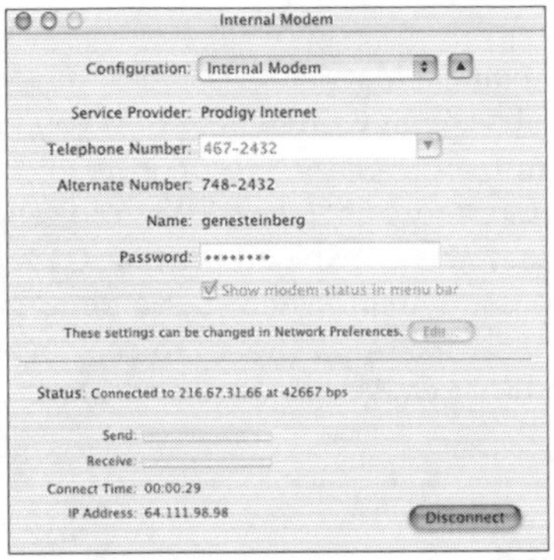

Internal Modem

Configuration: Internal Modem

Service Provider: Prodigy Internet

Telephone Number: 467-2432

Alternate Number: 748-2432

Name: genesteinberg

Password: ••••••••

☑ Show modem status in menu bar

These settings can be changed in Network Preferences. Edit

Status: Connected to 216.67.31.66 at 42667 bps

Send:

Receive:

Connect Time: 00:00:29

IP Address: 64.111.98.98   Disconnect

3. Quit Internet Connect to finish up.

If you're a Mac OS 9.x user, just use Remote Access to log off, the same way
got connected in the first place.

How to Join AOL

Don't have an AOL installer on your iMac. No problem. There are other ways to get the
software. You should be able to find an AOL CD at convenience stores, supermarkets,
electronics stores, and more. If you can't find a copy, call AOL at 1-800-827-6364 and
they'll get you a CD.

When you locate a copy of AOL's software follow these steps:

Getting Connected to AOL

▲ To Do

1. Insert the AOL software CD or locate the installer application on your iMac's hard
    drive (it's in the Installers folder, within the Applications folder, on the 2002
    model iMacs).

2. Double-click the installer icon and follow the prompts to complete the installation
    process. AOL will launch and you can proceed with the setup process from there.

AOL had begun shipping a Mac OS X version of its software only a few months before this book was written. If the CD you get doesn't say it's built for Mac OS X, it'll install the Classic version instead, which is not able to dial into AOL unless you restart from Mac OS 9.x. You can, however, set up your AOL account that way, then download the Mac OS X version and restart with the new operating system. When you've done that, you can install the new version and follow the setup screens to copy over your account information. Awkward, but it works.

First You Get Connected

The first time AOL's software launches, you'll see the first of several setup windows (see Figure 4.4). They might be different from the ones shown here, but as long as you read the instructions offered, you'll be able to get through it like a champ.

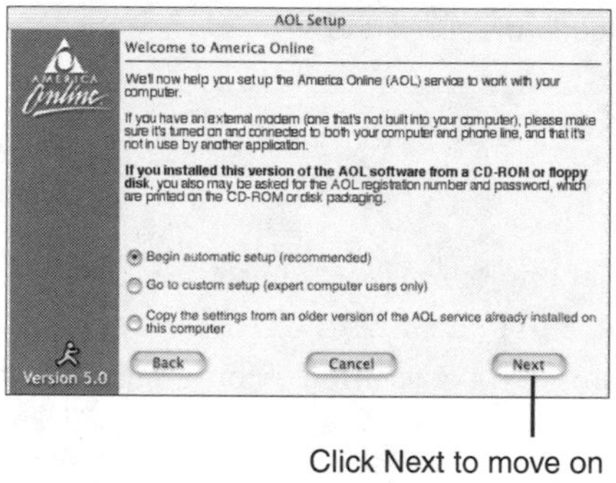

FIGURE 4.4

This is the beginning of the AOL sign-up process. Choose automatic setup.

Click Next to move on

Remember, you can always cancel if you change your mind. If you decide to try it again later, no problem. It'll start up right from the beginning.

There are three choices in your first AOL setup window, but the first, Begin automatic setup (recommended) is the one to pick.

Before continuing, be sure your computer's modem is connected to your phone line (and that nobody else is using that line during the setup process). If the line is busy, the AOL software won't be able to complete the sign-up process.

On the next setup screen, AOL Setup, the program will take a few moments to test your modem to determine what kind it is and set up the software to get the best possible connection. The software is designed to run on many different types of Mac computers, and there are a lot of modems out there.

The clever AOL software will soon get the message and report back to you that, yes, you are indeed using iMac's internal modem (see Figure 4.5). If AOL's software makes a mistake, click the pop-up menu and select the right type of modem from the list.

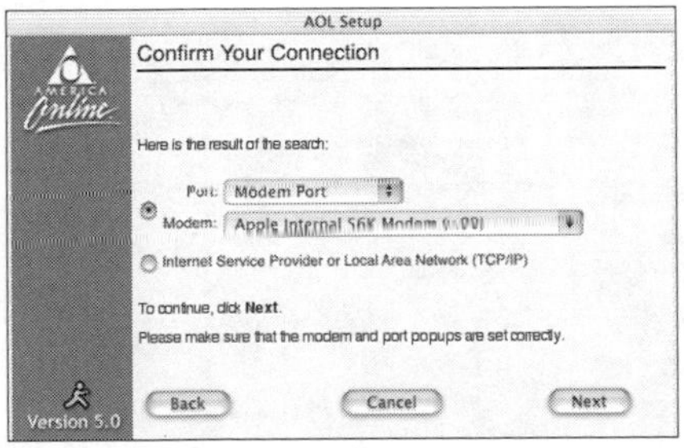

FIGURE 4.5

If this says it's an iMac internal modem (or an Apple internal), you're home free.

Okay, I know you're anxious to get going, but the software needs to do a few more things before you make that first connection as an AOL member. Next up is a dialog box where you confirm the dialing options (see Figure 4.6).

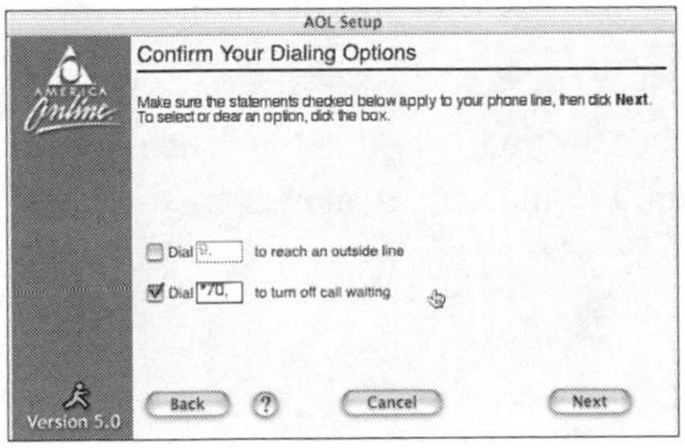

FIGURE 4.6

Read the screen carefully before moving on, in case you have to set it up for call waiting.

4

If you have call waiting service, be sure to click the second Dial option. The numbers shown, *70, are used by most phone companies to disable call waiting for the next call; this will prevent your AOL hookup from being interrupted if someone tries to call you while you're online. If you are located in an office or school environment, you might also need to enter a dialing out prefix to get connected, and this is set up in this dialog box.

After AOL software has decided how to connect to your computer's modem, it needs to determine where you are, so you'll dial up through a local number. On the next screen, you'll be asked to enter your area code (see Figure 4.7). As soon as your modem setup has been completed, type your area code in the appropriate text field so that America Online can hook you up to the closest and fastest (thus the cheapest) connection in your area.

FIGURE 4.7

AOL needs this infor-
mation to find a local
connection number
for you.

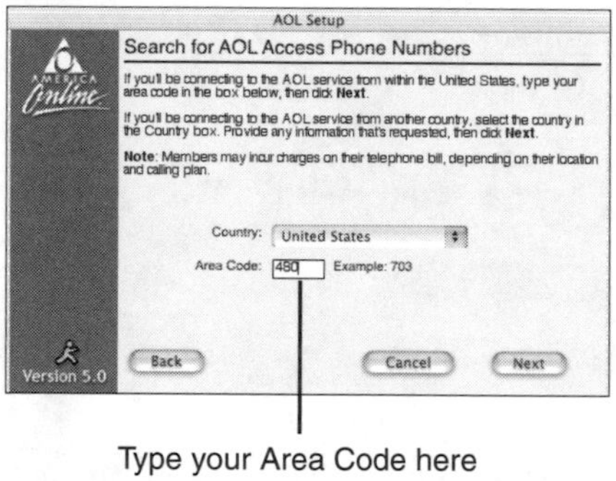

Type your Area Code here

After you've clicked Next, two things might happen. AOL will either consult its software database on your Mac for a number or it will dial up its host computer to check its directory. Don't be alarmed at the connection noises you hear on your computer's speaker. They're normal.

If AOL can't find a number for you, you'll get a chance to enter a different nearby area code and have it try again. For most cities, however, you'll get a result similar to the one shown in Figure 4.8.

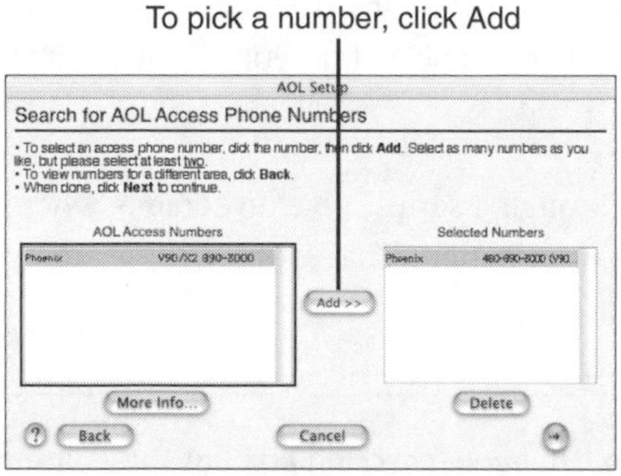

To pick a number, click Add

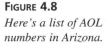
FIGURE 4.8
Here's a list of AOL numbers in Arizona.

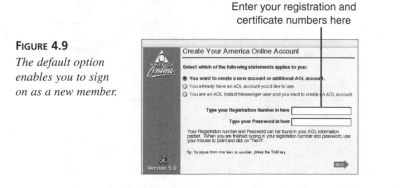

If more than one number is available in your city, pick at least two. AOL's access numbers are apt to get busy in the evening, so this gives you a chance to connect at the alternate number (AOL will switch automatically to the second number if it cannot connect the first time).

When you add a number, you'll see a confirmation screen (I won't show it here). Just click OK to move on.

Create Your America Online Account Now

AOL will now dial up your local number and take you to a screen where you begin to set up your online account (see Figure 4.9).

4

Enter your registration and certificate numbers here

FIGURE 4.9
The default option enables you to sign on as a new member.

If you're already an AOL member, click the second option in Figure 4.9 and place your present screen name and password in the text fields to pick up your account information.

Take out that insert from AOL (offering the free monthly trial) and enter the registration and password information where requested on your iMac's screen.

Click the Next button.

AOL will now guide you through a series of setup screens where you give them your name, address, and billing information. That's why I suggested you have a credit card ready.

> AOL can also debit your checking account for your monthly charges at a modest surcharge, but you might have to wait a day or two to get online, so they can set up the paperwork.

After your billing information has been set up, AOL will ask you to agree to its Terms of Service. These are the rules covering the service, and you'll want to check them. They're a little more involved than the standard software license. Basically, AOL expects you to be a good citizen online, and not bother others, that sort of thing.

What Do I Call Myself?

Folks who join an online service don't have to use their real names. Sometimes they can't because someone else is already using it. Instead you give yourself a handle, as they used to say when CB radios were popular. That's a nickname, which AOL calls a *screen name.* It's the equivalent of a username on EarthLink and other services).

> In the rare event you can actually use your real name, you might want to think twice. First and foremost, you make it easier for strangers to locate you, especially if you live in a small town where your name is unique. You might be better off using a nickname or a name that identifies a special character trait, such as "masterchef," a name that might be suitable for a person who does indeed perform that job at a restaurant.

After you've signed up, AOL will display a screen where you name yourself. At first, they'll suggest a name, based on your real name with perhaps a few numbers after it. Feel free to change it and try something else. Just remember that because no two AOL members can have the same screen name, you might have to endure a few moments of trying out names until one takes.

Please remember that you can't change your initial (master) screen name, so pick it with care. You can, however, add more screen names to your account (for your family or perhaps to give yourself another online identity like Superman and Clark Kent). At the time this book was written, AOL was setting up their system to allow for six extra screen names, with up to 16 characters each.

The First Connection

In a few seconds, you'll see AOL's opening screen and hear a "Welcome" message from that little man inside AOL's software (see Figure 4.10). Then you'll hear another announcement (just like on AOL's TV commercials and that Tom Hanks and Meg Ryan movie), "You've Got Mail."

FIGURE 4.10

Welcome to AOL.

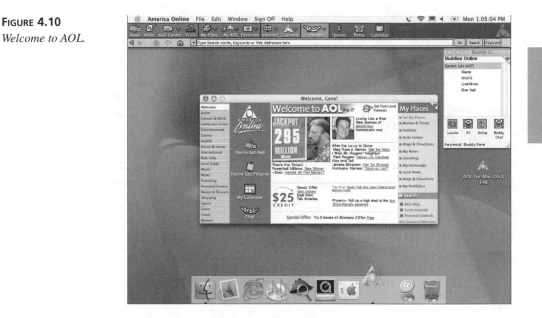

Yes indeed, there will be mail in your AOL mailbox. Click the You Have Mail icon and you'll see a letter on your computer's screen direct from AOL Time Warner's chief, Steve Case, welcoming you to the service. Well, don't take it as a personal greeting; every new AOL member gets one.

The Welcome screen (with your name in the title) is your gateway to the day's major features on AOL. If you want to see more of their range of services, click one of the items at the left-end of the Welcome screen (see Figure 4.11) to access one of those online departments.

FIGURE **4.11**

Here's AOL's Entertainment channel, one of the service's most popular features.

AOL members get around with keywords. You can enter the name of the area you want to visit in the bottom text field on the AOL toolbar shown at the top of Figure 4.10, click the Go button, and you're off to that location. As a new member, try the keyword, New Members.

Introducing Apple's iTools

When you first set up Mac OS X, Apple gave you an option: the capability to join its free iTools service (see Figure 4.12). This isn't an online service in the fashion of AOL or EarthLink, but a feature that more or less compliments those services.

FIGURE **4.12**

iTools is a set of free Mac user features courtesy of Apple.

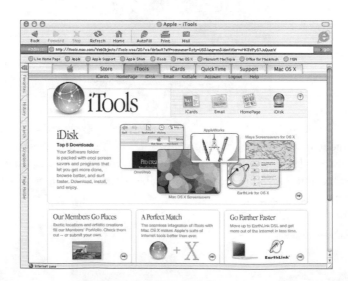

iTools offers several handy features that can extend your Mac user experience. These are

- **Email Service:** When you set up an iTools account, you can grab a 100% genuine mac.com email address. You can use that rather than your regular address (mine is genesteinberg@mac.com). When you set up your account under Mac OS X, Apple's Mail application is automatically configured to work with the account.

> Sorry, AOL members, but AOL's email software can't recognize a mac.com account. So even though you can set up the account, you won't be able to use AOL's software or an AOL connection to access your messages from other services, unless those services have an email system you can access from the Web.

- **iDisk:** This is one of the most useful features, 20MB of storage space on Apple's Web site. You can use it to store your files as backups, or even post files in a public folder for access by others. If you want, you can even order extra storage space at a modest charge.

- **Home Page:** Build a personal Web site in minutes following the simple instructions. When set up your Web site can be seen by anyone with Web access. Although not suitable for a business Web site, it's tailor made for resumes, personal sites, or just a place to show family photos.

- **iCard:** Using a set of cool-looking designs, iCard enables you to send online greeting cards to most anyone with Net access. As shown in Figure 4.13, you can choose from a number of colorful pictures in a number of categories (including pictures from popular movies), then select a text style and write your message. From here, the messages can be sent via email to your online friends.

Sound intriguing? Well, if you didn't set up an iTools account, there are two ways to go about it, depending on whether you're using Mac OS X or Mac OS 9.x:

- **Mac OS X:** Launch the System Preferences application from the Dock, the Apple menu, or the Applications. Click the Internet preference panel, and then the iTools tab. Click the Free Signup button and your Web browser will open. From here you'll be taken through a few setup screens, and finally you'll be all set up with your iTools user account. Similar to the username on an ISP, you'll probably have to go through several options to find one that works. You'll also want to make sure your password is secure, not easily remembered (but written down so you don't forget it).

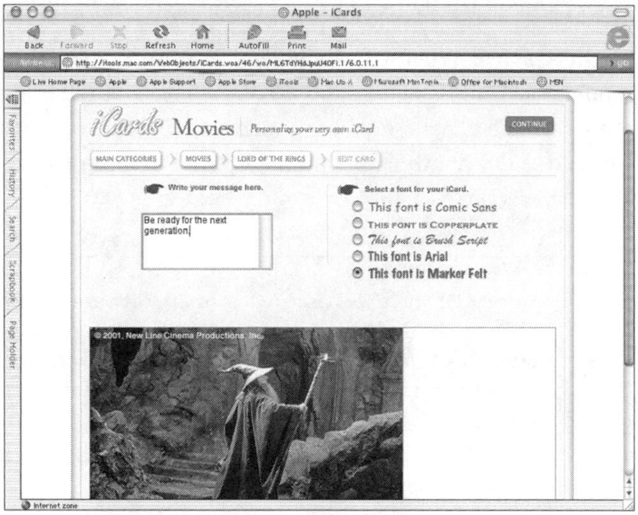

FIGURE 4.13

You can use iTools to send personal greeting cards to friends and business contacts.

- **Mac OS 9.x:** If you haven't established an account under Mac OS 9.x, just connect to Apple's iTools Web site at `http://www.apple.com/itools` and follow the simple instructions to set up the account. In moments you'll be up and running and ready to enjoy the features.

Summary

In this lesson, I introduced you to the incredible global-computer network, the Internet. You received instructions on joining an Internet service, such as EarthLink, and an online service, such as AOL. You learned the differences between the two, so you can make a decision about which to try (although many folks just use both).

One of the most important features of the Internet is email, and that forms the topic of the next lesson.

Q&A

Q I'm already a member of AOL. Do I have to join again?

A Not at all. When you run the AOL software that comes on your iMac, you'll see a screen where you specify whether you're joining as a new member, or you're an existing member. If you're already a member, just type your present screen name and password (if you have more than one on your account, any will do), and your membership settings will be transferred. And you'll still be able to use the AOL software on your other computer (just not at the same time).

Q You really don't show us any advantages to EarthLink. Are there any?

A Actually, yes. First off, it's cheaper than AOL (at least as of the time this book was written) and EarthLink is less affected by busy signals during the evening prime time access hours. In addition, you have more flexibility in terms of running software other than AOL as part of your Internet connection. Although you can use another browser and other Internet programs with your AOL connection, you cannot use other email software (except for Claris Emailer, a long-discontinued email program). Also, you cannot access AOL's Newsgroups feature with anything but AOL's software.

With EarthLink and other regular Internet services, you can choose from a number of different email programs. The same goes for such features as Internet newsgroups. I'll tell you about these and other Internet features in Hour 12, "The Internet: Learning the Ropes" and Hour 13, "The Wonderful World of Email."

Q Do I have to join EarthLink or AOL? What about another service?

A Although Apple made a deal with EarthLink and AOL discs are as ubiquitous as leaves, you are free to join any service you want, or just copy over the settings from the service.

In addition to EarthLink, there are thousands of Internet providers. Some are local, some are national in scope. Even local phone companies and long distance carriers have gotten into the act (and they often give you special deals if you take Internet service as part of a special service package). When picking a service, you'll want to compare prices and services. If you travel, you'll also want to know if you can connect in other cities without paying long distance charges.

Among online services, there's CompuServe, a service that's now owned by AOL and is often offered as a lower-cost alternative by electronics stores. There's also Prodigy Internet, which competes head on with AOL.

Q I already have a high-speed cable modem hookup. Can I use it with the iMac?

A Most likely, yes. Many cable modem services use an Ethernet port to connect to computers. Because you already have one with your iMac, hookups ought to be a piece of cake. But you'll need to contact the cable company directly about setting up your computer's Internet features to support their service.

The same holds true if you plan on trying out a DSL (Digital Subscriber Line) service, which enables you to get high-speed Internet connections direct from your regular phone lines.

In addition, if you have an existing account with AOL you can sign up for the lower cost "Bring Your Own Access Plan," which enables you to keep your screen name and avoid sending change of address notices, while connecting over you high-speed access hookup.

If you are already using another item on the Ethernet jack, say a printer or another Mac, you'll need a hub, a central connection device, to support multiple hookups (unless, of course, you already have one). Your computer dealer can help you purchase what you need. For a single hookup, a so-called Ethernet crossover cable can probably do the job. Hours 18 and 20 cover the subject in more detail.

HOUR 5

A Look at Your iMac's Software

Are you still attending school, or is it, like it is for me, a distant memory unless I visit one in connection with my son's education? Consider a personal computer similar to a blackboard. You need to write something on the blackboard to have something to read. And you need to run software for your iMac to have something to do.

Fortunately, when you buy an iMac, you don't have to go out and buy software to get it running. Some very nice programs are already installed on the hard drive, ready to run with a double-click of your mouse.

Of course, if you want to expand your horizons, thousands of Mac programs exist, covering different areas, from games to photo retouching.

In this lesson, I'll present

- The programs that came bundled with your new iMac
- A quick guide to what the programs do
- Some suggestions on how to get software if your dealer isn't friendly to iMac owners

Here's how to find the applications stored on your computer:

Two locations (called folders) contain the software that comes with your iMac. We'll start with the one that contains applications designed to run under Mac OS X, Apple's advanced operating system. To check those, double-click the Applications folder and take a gander at the contents.

After you've done that, locate the Applications (Mac OS 9) folder on your iMac's hard drive. Why two applications folders? Well, the first one contains all your native Mac OS X software and the second contains applications that, for the most part, are designed to run under Mac OS 9.x or in the Classic environment. However, regardless of where you get the software from, most of it will run just fine.

Over the next few pages, I'll highlight some of the most interesting programs that came with your iMac. Feel free to try out the others to see what they do.

A Fast, Cheap Guide to Your iMac's Software

The programs that come with your iMac cover a wide range of purposes. They do have a few things in common, however, the first of which is that they are easy to learn and use.

In this hour, we'll take a brief tour through the bill of fare, and in Hour 9, "Teach Yourself AppleWorks," Hour 10 "Managing Your Bucks with Quicken 2002," and Hour 11, "Faxing, Other Software," you'll get more detailed information about how to use these programs.

Let's look at what resides inside the Applications folder (the ones that are native to Mac OS X):

- **Adobe Acrobat Reader**: As you noticed when you opened your iMac's accessory box, there isn't much printed literature there. Most of your help information is available via the Help menu. Other reading material comes in the form of Acrobat documents (see Figure 5.1), which are exact electronic copies of the original printed book. You can actually print out these pages with good quality, but that defeats the purpose of having an electronic (rather than a hard copy) version of the manual.

Click to go to the next page

FIGURE 5.1

The manual for your iMac's fax software is typical of an electronic document you might open in Acrobat.

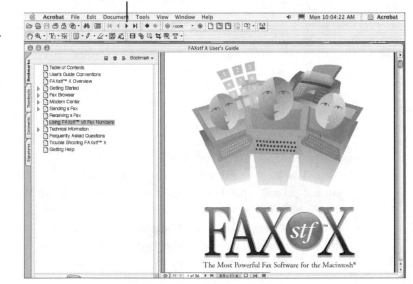

You can install your applications elsewhere!

One of the beauties of the Mac Operating System is that you don't have to install your programs all in one place. Over time, for example, you might decide to make new folders to cover different types of software, for example, Games. However, to keep things well organized many Mac users stick with the tried and true and let their applications stay put. This is especially true with Apple's own software because Apple's updaters expect those programs to be in the proper location and won't look anywhere else if they're trying to update you to a new version.

5

- **Address Book**: This program (see Figure 5.2) serves as your computer's variation on the Rolodex theme. It stores information about your personal contacts and is used with Apple's Mail application to store the addresses of the people you write to.

- **AOL**: The flat-panel iMac contains an Installers folder, which includes software for AOL, the world's largest online service. You can use this installer to establish a new account or just set up the one you have now in your new iMac.

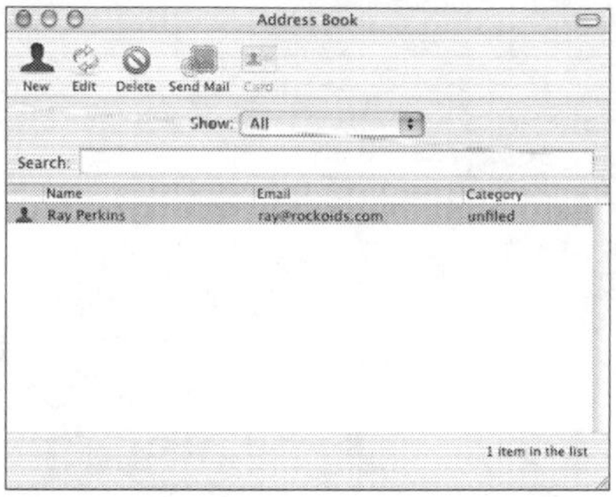

FIGURE 5.2

You can easily add your personal contacts to this program.

- **AppleWorks**: AppleWorks is a wonderful integrated program that serves the purpose of several separate programs (see Figure 5.3). It works as a word processor to handle your letters, novels, and so on. It can be used to draw pictures, set up business charts, keep a database of business contacts and (in the version shipping when this book was written) create simple online presentations (similar to a slide show). I'll give you a brief tutorial on how to use this program in Hour 9.

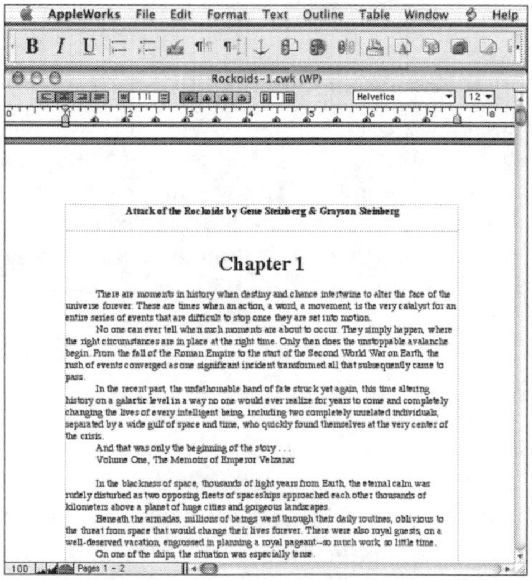

FIGURE 5.3

AppleWorks does a whole lot to spruce up your documents.

- **DVD Player**: If your iMac comes with a DVD player (and not all do), you can use this application to play your favorite movies. The functions mimic a home DVD player, so you can step through chapters or segments of your favorite flicks. You can also play a movie full screen, which means it expands to fill the full length and width of your iMac's display (with a black border around it). You can also reduce the movie's screen size and try to get some other work done while the movie is playing.

- **FAXstf**: Your iMac already has a built-in modem. So wouldn't it be nice if you could also use the modem to work as a fax machine, too? That way the documents that you write could be sent to your friends or clients without having to print a copy, and then run it through a separate machine. Well, it's possible, with FAXstf X, a well-known Mac fax software package. I'll give you a brief tutorial about sending faxes on your iMac in Hour 11. Briefly, the program also uses Apple's Address Book software to manage your regular contacts, and you can print faxes after you get them.

> If you aren't using Mac OS X, you'll find another version of FAXstf in your Applications (Mac OS 9) folder, which you can use with Apple's older operating systems. This version, however, won't work in the Classic environment of Mac OS X, which is designed to let you run most of your older applications under Apple's new operating system.

- **Image Capture**: Do you have a digital camera? Well, such devices are quickly replacing regular film for both personal photos and professional photography. Mac OS X's Image Capture application is designed to open automatically whenever you attach a supported camera, and then enable you to download the pictures in the camera to your iMac's hard drive. Really neat, but you'll want to read the following section about iPhoto, which does lots more than simply download your digital pictures.

> Not all digital cameras support Image Capture. If it works, you'll see a progress bar showing the picture capture process. If it doesn't work, you'll need to check with the camera maker for the right software (perhaps it's on the CD that came with the unit).

5

- **iDVD**: The DVD is the video medium that's taking over the prerecorded video world. A DVD is the same size as a regular CD, yet it holds a full length motion picture. If you have an iMac with a SuperDrive, you can easily make your own DVDs from a home video, a bunch of digital pictures, or a combination of the two. You'll learn more about this utlra-simple, ultra-smooth program in Hour 14, "Using iMovie, iDVD, and iPhoto."

- **iMovie**: One of the most thrilling pastimes is editing a home video, and Apple's iMovie software makes it easy as pie. If you have an iMac with a FireWire port, you can capture video clips from a DV camcorder, then add special effects, titles, transitions, and voiceovers. In a few minutes, you can produce professional-quality home videos that you can copy to your camcorder and play on a regular television. This subject is also covered in more detail in Hour 14.

- **Internet Connect**: This application (see Figure 5.4) is used to dial-up your Internet provider using your iMac's built-in modem and monitors the connection (except for AOL, which uses its own dialing software). I showed you how to get connected to the Internet in Hour 4, "Getting on the Net."

FIGURE 5.4

Click Connect to dial up your Internet service provider (ISP).

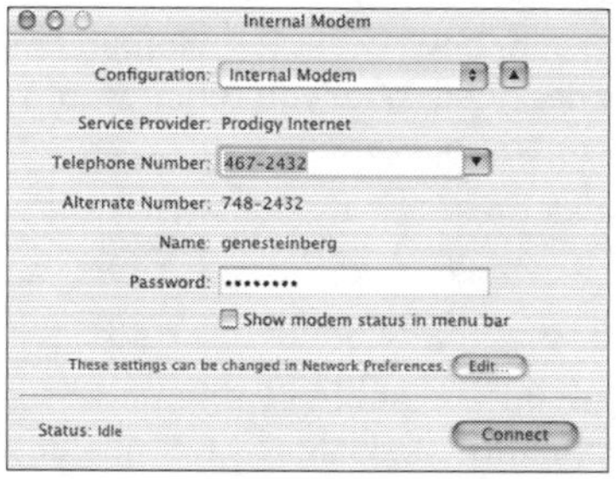

- **Internet Explorer**: From the folks at Microsoft, Internet Explorer is considered one of the best Web browsers on the planet. I cover Web access in Hour 12, "The Internet: Learning the Ropes." Briefly, Internet Explorer not only enables you to access your favorite Web site, but its convenient Favorites feature enables you to store the address of the site for fast retrieval.

- **iPhoto**: Taking Image Capture to another level, this handy application helps you manage your digital photo library. Special features allow you to upload a photo album to your iTools Web site, or even order high-quality prints or a complete hard cover book containing the best from your picture collection. I'll cover this subject further in Hour 14.

- **iTunes**: Steve Jobs, Apple's co-founder and CEO, says he regards the Mac as the center of a digital hub. One of those hub-management applications is iTunes, a jukebox application (see Figure 5.5). It enables you to copy music from an audio CD and build play lists from those songs, along with the ones you download from the Internet, and then play them back at your leisure. You can even use iTunes to burn a CD of your favorite tunes. Another feature of iTunes is Internet radio. You'll learn more in Hour 15, "Managing Your Music Library with iTunes."

FIGURE 5.5
Capture and listen to music with Apple's iTunes.

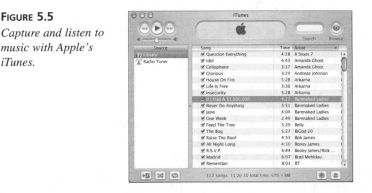

- **Mail**: Email is a huge part of the Internet landscape, and Apple's Mail application is a simple application that can easily manage all your mail (except for AOL, which uses its own software), even if you have several online accounts. I'll cover the complete world of email and how to harness the power of this marvelous application in Hour 13, "The Wonderful World of Email."

- **Otto Matic:** This outer space, action and adventure game (shown in Figure 5.6) exploits the capabilities of Mac OS X, providing great 3D performance in an exciting environment. You can spend hours enjoying this game, as I've done, but I have to get back to work now.

FIGURE 5.6
A simple, thrilling science-fiction adventure game.

5

- **PCalc 2:** This takes Apple's venerable calculator application one better and gives you all the tools of a high-quality scientific calculator. It's good for both simple calculations and the more complicated ones you might need for school or engineering use.

- **Quicken Deluxe 2002**: One great use of your iMac is to manage your finances. Quicken Deluxe 2002 (see Figure 5.7) is a popular program that serves as both a checkbook and bookkeeper. You can also use it to print your personal or business checks. You can use special checks supplied by the software's publisher Intuit, or other companies. You can also do financial planning and projections. I'll tell you how to set up this great program to manage your personal finances in Hour 9.

FIGURE 5.7

Track your personal or business finances with Quicken Deluxe 2002.

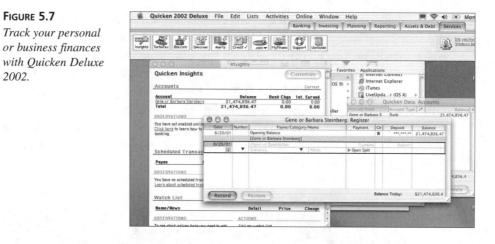

- **QuickTime Player**: QuickTime is Apple's multimedia viewing application. It can be used to do some simple video editing if you buy the more expensive Pro version from Apple. After you upgrade, you can easily play back films full screen (the maximum your iMac allows) and even save the ones you download from the Internet. I'll cover this subject in depth in Hour 14.

- **Sherlock**: No, this isn't the fellow with the strange hat who mutters "the game's afoot" when he plays detective. Sherlock is Mac OS X's search application that's equally at home finding files on your iMac's drive as it is finding information on the Internet. I'll cover the subject of finding things in Hour 8, "Opening, Saving, Finding, Moving, Etc."

- **System Preferences**: This is the application that Apple gives you to configure Mac OS X, so it works best for you (see Figure 5.8). You'll use settings panels to make the mouse move faster, change display resolution (see things are bigger or smaller on your iMac's screen), set up your network, activate Apple's screen saver, and set Universal Access options for folks who need a little extra help with the keyboard or mouse.

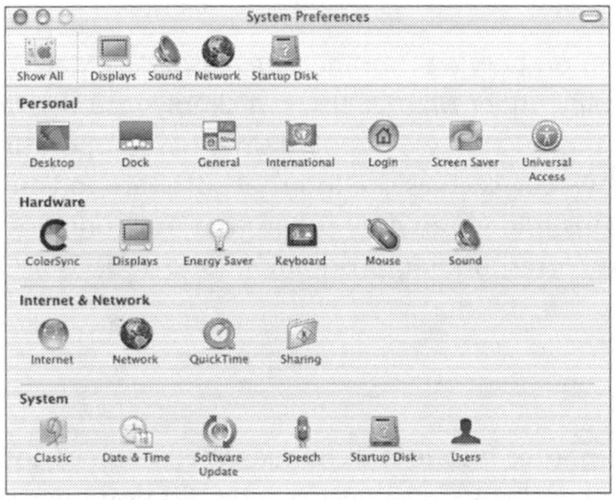

FIGURE 5.8

This application enables you to fine-tune Mac OS X to your needs.

- **TextEdit**: Almost every time you double-click a Read Me file with a .txt after it, you're opening a program called TextEdit. It's a simple, free word processor that Apple provides with all its computers. Although it won't do near as much as the integrated application, AppleWorks, which comes with your iMac, it's fine to jot down a quick note or a memo, not to mention reading those last-minute "Read Me" files that come with various software packages.
- **World Book Encyclopedia:** A great research tool, featuring an encyclopedia, dictionary, thesaurus, and more. When used in conjunction with the CD that's included in your iMac's disc packet, you can check out information on a variety of subjects. It's a useful tool for school or office.

5

There's actually another little word processor that comes with your iMac, SimpleText, which runs in the Classic Mac OS universe. SimpleText will open some of the text documents that you find on your iMac, or that come with various applications you might install.

NEW TERM   An *integrated* program is one that combines the functions of several programs into one. That's different from a program *suite*, which involves a number of separate programs put in one box. Examples of program suites include CorelDraw and Microsoft Office.

Are you sticking with Mac OS 9.x for now? Well, you'll find some corresponding applications in your Applications (Mac OS 9) folder. Feel free to check out the latest offerings.

Depending on how a program is developed, a Mac OS X application might run normally under Mac OS 9.x, but simply lose the fancy Aqua user interface and the reliability of Apple's Unix-based operating system. Some programs, however, such as the Internet software in your Mac OS X Applications folder, can only run in that environment. If it doesn't work, look for a corresponding program among your Mac OS 9.x collection.

Apple Computer frequently changes the lineup of software included with its consumer computers, such as the iMac. So don't be concerned if you have software I haven't described, or if one program or another described here isn't part of your package. The ones described here are strictly based on the bundle that shipped with the flat-panel iMac that was released in February 2002.

Summary

In Hour 5, you got a brief look at some of the software that Apple thoughtfully included with your iMac. I covered the basics and showed you some illustrations. When you get to Hours 9, 10, and 11, you'll learn more about the great features these programs offer.

For now, you'll want to spend a little time with each one. Look over at the Help menu, where you will find online tutorials that will assist you in getting started.

In Hour 6, "Files, Folders, Windows, and Other Things," I'll show you how to traverse the highways and byways of your iMac, how to manage folders, what all those little controls are on document windows, and so on.

Q&A

Q **I tried to open a program I retrieved from a friend. It had an .exe name at the end of it? But it won't run? What's wrong?**

A Programs designed for the PC platform use different programming code than the Mac version. So they won't run without a little help. There are ways, though, to use them. Virtual PC, from Connectix, can turn your iMac into a real Windows machine, enabling it to run any of several different PC operating systems. I'll tell you more about emulating Windows on your iMac in Hour 18.

Q I keep reading about computer viruses in the daily paper. Should I really be afraid of such things?

A I don't want to scare you unnecessarily, but it's quite true that a number of computer viruses are around. They are made by some nasty people who are playing practical jokes, or who just want to hurt people. Although some of them are not harmful, others are dangerous and can damage your personal files or even your programs.

Fortunately (for us, not them), most of the viruses infect users of that *other* platform, although some, the so-called Word and Excel macro viruses, might affect both platforms in some way. There are, however, a few of them on the Mac, too. If you plan on handling files from your friends and business associates, you'll want to get some virus protection software. I'll tell you more about that subject in Hour 24, "An iMac Safety Net."

Q I went to my local computer store to buy some Mac software. I couldn't find much. They tell me that only a few programs are made for the Mac, and that I bought the wrong platform when I purchased a Mac OS computer? I want the truth.

A I think about Jack Nicholson's scene-stealing cry in that great movie *A Few Good Men*. The fact is, however, you can definitely handle the truth, and the truth is that thousands of Mac programs are available, and more are released almost every day. You can find games, programs for retouching photos, programs for desktop publishing, programs to run a doctor's office, a dentist's office, and a lot more.

The CompUSA store chain, The Apple Store (both online and in the burgeoning retail chain), and some other retailers have special Mac areas where you're bound to find a reasonable number of titles. Other dealers tend to give the Mac short shrift, and if they have any Mac software, it's just a few popular selections. However, dealers can order them for you. In addition, some programs actually come in on a CD that carries both a Mac and Windows version (check the box to see), but more often than not the package is in the Windows aisle.

You'll also want to check one of the Macintosh magazines on your newsstand for suggestions; for example, *MacAddict*, *MacHome*, or *Macworld*. Look at these magazines for ads from mail-order houses that do stock Mac software. You'll be surprised at the variety of programs out there for your iMac. Some of them don't even have a Windows equivalent, which means some of your friends who use the *other* platform can even envy you now. One interesting example is a very unusual word processing program known as Nisus Writer.

Nisus Writer is an incredibly flexible word processor, one that excels at multilin-gual work and also sports a highly sophisticated search function that can even check documents created in the program that aren't even open. You can learn more about Nisus Writer and download a fully functional demonstration version at the publisher's Web site, `http://www.nisus.com`. You can also discover the latest Mac OS X software at VersionTracker.com (`http://www.versiontracker.com/macosx/`).

Q **The iMac sounds okay to me, but I'd like something better. Can I buy better speakers for it?**

A Absolutely. The flat-panel iMac has a special jack for the Apple Pro Speakers, which are included in some models, and optional on the lowest-cost version. It's a fine system, lacking only good bass to be complete. In addition, there are lots of really good computer speakers out there. Some even include Dolby Surround Sound and special digital effects. The best products are the ones made by the well-known stereo speaker makers such as Advent, Bose, Boston Acoustics, Cambridge SoundWorks, JBL, and Monsoon, just to name a few. Similar to regular audio speakers, the more expensive models tend to sound better. Some are even good enough to do double duty as a small stereo system.

Strangely enough, I've even managed to get the widely advertised Bose Wave Radio to handle the sounds from my iMac, because it has convenient jacks for external audio sources. Just keep the radio at least a foot away from your iMac, because the radio's speakers are not magnetically shielded and might affect the color purity of the monitor.

PART II
Making It All Happen

Hour

HOUR **6**

Files, Folders, Windows, and Other Things

Have you kept up with me so far? In the first five hours, you've discovered the neat, orderly iMac desktop, which is designed to mimic a typical office desk in terms of layout.

What you see is one of the great inventions of modern personal computing. Before the Mac Operating System came out, the typical computer presented itself to you with a text interface. There were just letters and numbers; white letters on black, black letters on white, and so on.

To tell that computer to do something, you had to type instructions on the keyboard and, usually, use the Enter or Return keys to send the command to the computer's brain or microprocessor.

With your iMac, you see a visual representation of what you want (an icon), and you use your mouse to select and click that item. (If you prefer, you can even use the keyboard for a lot of this.)

In this lesson, I'll tell you

- How to manage your iMac's files
- What folders do and how to move from one to the other
- How to work with document and directory Finder windows and what the little doo-dads surrounding them do
- How to get rid of the files you don't want (with some precautions)
- How to use your iMac's keyboard to give the mouse (and your hand) a rest

A Folder Is a Container

In the Mac OS, whether you're using Mac OS 9 or X, a folder is the computer equivalent to your file folder in your office, and it has a similar look, as shown in Figure 6.1.

Double-click a folder icon
to see what's inside

FIGURE 6.1

A folder on your iMac's desktop can hold a file or simply another folder (or many of each).

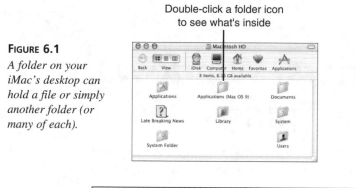

A fast way to find the folder you want among those listed is to type the first letter of the icon's name on your iMac's keyboard. The first folder with that letter in it will be selected (highlighted) and will appear bright as day. Who said you always need a mouse?

You can easily reorganize your iMac's desktop simply by clicking and dragging on a folder and putting it inside another folder (or pulling it out of one).

A Variety of Folders

No doubt you've noticed that some folders have different icons on them than others. Some of these are strictly custom jobs from the publishers of some programs who want to give their folders a special look with distinctive artwork.

Others, however, are designed to reflect the special nature of their contents. Here are some of the more common folder styles and what they're used for.

- **Applications folder**: This folder stores all your applications that are native to Mac OS X.

- **Applications (Mac OS 9)**: In turn, this folder contains the applications that are designed to run in the older or Classic Mac OS environment.

- **Library:** This folder contains files needed for Mac OS X. Examples include modem and printer-related files, add-ons (plug-ins) for your Web browser and fonts for your documents.

- **System**: The folder that contains a number of your Mac OS X system-related files. This is a look but don't touch location, so don't be concerned about it.

- **System Folder**: The contents of the software required to operate your computer under Mac OS 9.x is in the System Folder.

- **Users:** Under Mac OS X, each person who uses your Mac can have a custom place to store files and personal settings. This is both a convenience and a method of protection. Hour 21, "Backup, Backup, Backup…How to Protect Your Files," has more information on the subject.

Why two folders containing system files? Your iMac has two operating systems installed, so you can use older programs on your computer. Each requires a separate set of files to run. The one for Mac OS X has an icon with a distinctive X on it.

- **Alias to a file or folder**: The little arrow at the lower left indicates that this is not the actual folder or file, but a reference or pointer to it (hence the arrow). Double-click this icon and you'll see the contents of the original folder (it's similar to accessing your files via remote control). Under Mac OS 9.x, the name is also italicized.

6

It's so easy to move folder and file icons around that you can easily move things that shouldn't be moved. Don't move the files that are within an application's folder because the program might not run if all its files aren't in place. Don't touch any of the files in the Mac OS X Library folder or System folder until you've read Hour 3, "What's A System Folder and Why Do I Need Two." Moving the wrong file to the wrong place might prevent

your iMac from running or starting properly. Fortunately, you cannot move
files from the Mac OS X System folder (they are copied instead). If you accidentally move a file, the only solution is to put it back where you found it
(otherwise, you might have to undergo a reinstallation of the application or
the Mac OS itself).

Selecting and Opening Folders

Working with folders is simple. You click it once, and then drag the icon to move it
somewhere. You double-click it to view its contents.

In addition, there are some neat ways to move things around using the keyboard.

Here are some of the things you can do without ever touching a mouse. The techniques
work for both folder and file icons (way cool):

- Use the arrow keys on the keyboard to move from icon to icon. Movement is in the
  direction the arrow points (up, down, left, right).
- Use the Tab key to move from one icon to the next in alphabetical order.
- Hold down the Shift key if you want to select more than one consecutive folder at
  a time.
- Hold down the Option key when you double-click a folder icon to open that icon,
  and also close the parent folder the icon is in. So, if you double-click an icon
  inside the Applications folder, while holding down the Option key, the Applications
  folder is itself closed.
- Hold down the Option key when you drag a file or folder icon to another folder's
  icon, and you'll make a copy of the original. The original will just stay where it is.
- Hold down the Cmd key when you want to separately select two or more folders
  that aren't next to each other.
- Press the Return key to highlight the name of an icon you've selected. You can then
  rename the icon something else if you want. There's nothing to prevent you from
  calling your Applications folder "the den of inequity," if you prefer.
- Press Cmd-L (Cmd-M under Mac OS 9.x, and don't ask me to explain the reason
  for the change!) when you select an icon, and you'll create an alias to it (see
  Figure 6.2). You can also click the File menu and choose the Make Alias command, or hold down Cmd-Option while dragging a folder, to accomplish the same
  thing. As I mentioned in Hour 1, "Opening the Box," an alias is a reference to the
  original file, folder, application (or disk, for that matter). It's a great feature that

enables you, in effect, to have a number of ways to get to a folder without having to make extra copies.

All right, so what does Cmd-M do under Mac OS X? It minimizes a window and reduces it to an icon on the right side of the Dock (M = minimize). To make a minimized icon larger again, just click once on that icon in the Dock.

A fast way to know if an icon is an alias is the icon itself. If it's an alias, it'll always have a little upward-pointed arrow at the lower left, and under Mac OS 9, it'll also be *italicized*. Another way to see whether it's an alias is to select the icon and choose Show Info from the Finder's File menu. Under Kind, it'll say it's an Alias.

Double-click an alias icon to open the original

FIGURE 6.2

Not live, but Memorex, or rather an alias or pointer to the original icon.

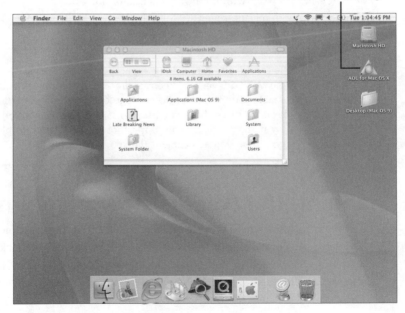

• Press Cmd-Delete to move a selected item to the trash.

If you move the alias of a file to the trash, the original is not deleted, just the alias. If you really want to delete the original, too, you need to drag both icons to the trash. If you trash the original and not the alias, the latter becomes nonfunctional, although the Finder will usually give you the chance to pick another file for it to point to when it's double-clicked.

A File Isn't a Container

Compared to a folder, the file icon actually does something other than just function as a container. If you double-click a program's icon, you open the program itself. When you open a file, it does two things: launch the program that made the file, and then open the folder and bring it onto your screen. I'll cover the elements of a directory and document window a bit later in this lesson.

The great thing about the Mac Operating System is that many of the skills you use to handle folder icons work in the very same way as file icons. So, you don't have to learn anything new to work with them. This is one of the wonderful features that makes the system so easy to master, regardless of whether you're using Mac OS X or Mac OS 9.x.

Be careful about renaming application icons. The Mac OS Finder (especially the Mac OS 9 version) keeps a directory of document and program links that enable you to double-click a file to open the program. If you rename the program's icon, however, (such as calling your AppleWorks software "The Great Starship"), it might upset those links. There's nothing to prevent you from changing a document file's name, though.

Changing the Folder/File Viewpoint

In the previous sections, I covered file and folder icons in their standard state, as icons. You don't have to view them that way, however. As I explained back in Hour 2, "Exploring Your iMac Desktop," you can view your icons as a list if you prefer (see Figure 6.3), just by choosing the View as List option from the Finder's View menu. There are two advantages to this arrangement:

FIGURE 6.3

You sacrifice appearance for speed and convenience with the list view.

- You save space, which is great if you have a lot of icons to work with.
- It takes a little longer for your iMac's screen to display the fancy artwork in a regular icon (although the delay is less under Mac OS X), so things might slow down a bit if you have lots of icons in a folder.

Click the left arrow next to a folder to see the contents (it will point down). Hold down the Option key to open all the folders inside that folder (this can take a bit of time). If you click the arrow again, it closes the folder (and with the Option key held down, all the open folders inside it). Isn't that Option key great?

The disadvantage: Well, it doesn't look quite as pretty.

To select all your files and folders at once, press Cmd-A.

I'll Take One from Column A, One from Column B

6

The third method of viewing icons under Mac OS X is the column view (one you might come to prefer when you try it), and it's also selected from the Finder's View menu, as shown in Figure 6.4.

The Column view is exclusive to Mac OS X, and it's great for looking at a folder with a lot of folders (or nested folders) inside it. When you click a folder's name, the column jumps to the left and the contents are shown at the right. If you click an icon representing a file (application or document) you see a preview image in the column at the right. Nifty!

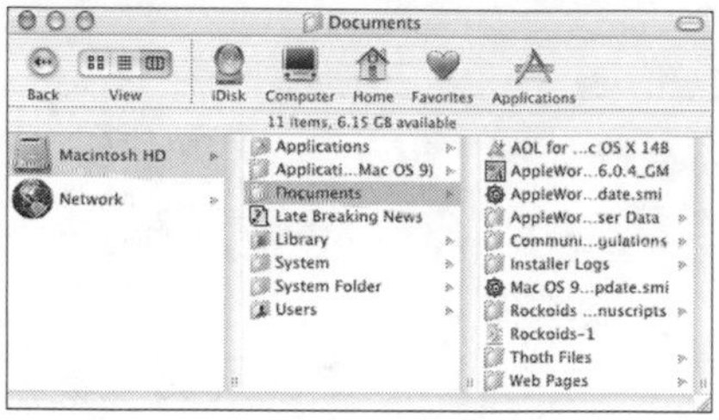

Figure 6.4

The column view is a convenient way to view folder levels side by side.

How do you get back to where you were? Just click and drag the scroll arrow at the bottom.

What's that Back arrow for? As the label implies, it takes you back to the folders or items you previously checked, one by one. It does so regardless of the order you checked them. So, at least in the case of Mac OS X, you can truly go back.

Under Mac OS 9, there is no column view. The third view option is the Button view, which turns all items into large buttons. All you have to do is click once on any button to open the item, but it takes up a lot more space. And not everyone likes large buttons; maybe that's why Mac OS X doesn't offer this view option.

Working with Windows, Doors, and...

For this section, it's just windows, and not the kind that you use on that *other* computing platform. To make a window active, you click it (it makes the title black and brings it to the front). Every time you open a directory of any kind by double-clicking it (a disk, folder, or a file), it opens a Finder display window (see Figure 6.5 for the Mac OS X version and Figure 6.6 for the Mac OS 9 variation). The one I'm showing here is the icon view.

As you it's can see, although the Mac OS X and Mac OS 9.x Finder windows look different, they share many functions. The features I'll describe here apply to document windows also (although document windows might have a few more icons and displays to cover a particular feature), and I'm concentrating on the Mac OS X version here. I'll refer to the 9 version in each item.

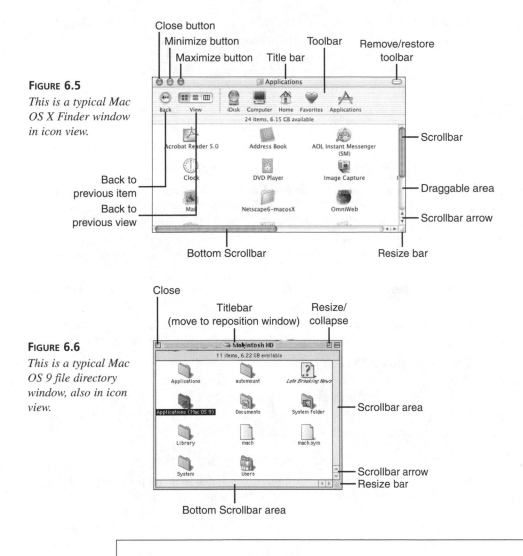

FIGURE 6.5

This is a typical Mac OS X Finder window in icon view.

FIGURE 6.6

This is a typical Mac OS 9 file directory window, also in icon view.

Okay, there's another difference. Under Mac OS X, you can only move a Finder (or document) window by dragging the top. For Mac OS 9 and older Mac systems, you can click any area of a window and move it. Don't ask me why this changed, but that's the way it is.

6

- **Close button**: Click the red button to close your document. The little square box at the left of a Mac OS 9.x window performs the same function.

When you close a document window, you aren't closing the program. The program remains active until you choose Quit from the application menu—or the File menu in a Classic Mac OS application—or press Cmd-Q.

To close all open windows (whether two or 20) hold down the Option key when you click the close button. This works with directory windows, but might not work with all programs (some don't recognize all the keyboard tricks).

- **Minimize button:** Click the yellow or middle button and the window is reduced to an icon at the lower left of the Dock, with a little visual flourish. To restore the icon to its original size, just click the icon from the Dock. Under Mac OS 9.x, the minimize box (at the extreme right), reduces the item to just its title bar.

- **Maximize button:** Click once on the green or right button to make the window as large as possible to fill the contents inside. If the contents exceed the size of your iMac's screen, you'll be able to use scrollbars (see following) to look at more. Click again and it reverts to its previous size. Under Mac OS 9.x, the button second from right performs the same function.

If you choose the Graphite appearance option in the General panel in the System Preferences icon, you won't see the colors. Regardless of the appearance choice you make, when you move your mouse over a button, you'll see an "X" appear in the Close button, a "-" in the Minimize button and a "+" in the Maximize button to remind you of what it does.

- **Title bar**: This contains the name of your folder list or document. Click the title bar (or on any of the other three borders of the window) to move the window around. Just click and drag on the title bar of a window to move it around the screen.

Just hold down the Cmd key and click a title and you'll see a little pop-up menu that shows you a list of all the folders where the item is located (sometimes called a folder hierarchy).

- **Remove/restore toolbar (Mac OS X only)**: Click the clear button at the upper right of a window and the Finder's toolbar will disappear. Click again and it returns. There's also another effect of this little feature. When you dispatch the toolbar, that is when you click a folder, it opens a brand new Finder window (the same effect occurs in Mac OS 9.x). With the toolbar displayed opening an item simply shows its contents in the same window. This is one of Mac OS X's better ways to reduce window clutter.

- **Back arrow:** Click this arrow to return to the previous Finder window, and click again to see the one before that. This feature works the same regardless of the sequence of windows you went through.

- **View icon:** A single click and you can change the view of a Mac OS X Finder window, switching from the icon to list to column view, as you prefer.

- **Toolbar:** The Mac OS X Finder's toolbar gives you one-click access to important functions. It can also be customized, using the Customize Toolbar command in the View menu, so you can add or remove icons.

You can also customize the Mac OS X Finder's toolbar by dragging an icon to it. The icon will appear in approximately the position you placed it. Clicking and dragging the icon off the toolbar removes it (except for the default toolbars, which can only be removed via the Customize Toolbar command found in the View menu).

- **Scroll arrow**: Click it to move up or down slightly through a directory or document window. Hold down the mouse when clicking an arrow to get a continuous motion.

- **Scrollbar**: Click and drag on this bar to move back and forth through your folder list or document. The distance you can move depends on how big the listing or document is.

- **Draggable area**: This is the place where you can drag the scrollbar (see following). If the area is white rather than blue (and the scrollbar isn't there), it means that the entire window is displayed on your screen and there's nothing to scroll to. You'll notice that there's both a horizontal and vertical draggable area.

6

Normally, you can only work on a window if you select it (to make it active). But if you hold down the command key, you can move around a window without bringing it to the front.

 Click the draggable area above the scrollbar to jump rapidly upward through a list or document, a page or screen at a time. Click below the scrollbar to move downward through the document at the same rate. This is the equivalent of the Page Up and Page Down keys on your iMac's keyboard.

- **Size bar**: Click this bar and drag it to resize a document window the way you want (see Figure 6.7). It resizes in the direction you drag the mouse (up, down, sideways).

FIGURE 6.7

Drag to the right and the window gets bigger.

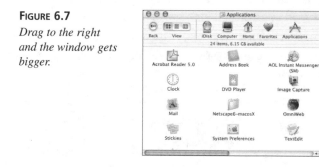

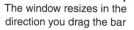
The window resizes in the direction you drag the bar

 Under Mac OS X, when you resize a window in the Finder, and most (but not all) other applications, you'll see the contents displayed as the size changes (with maybe a brief hesitation). Under Mac OS 9.x, and a few Mac OS X applications (such as AppleWorks, AOL, and most applications from Adobe, Corel, Macromedia, and Microsoft), instead you will see a faint bounding box showing the area you've resized. The actual size of the window doesn't change until you release the mouse.

- **Window options**: As I said earlier, some programs add a few features to the window to reflect special functions. In the picture shown in Figure 6.8, you'll see the extra options offered for AppleWorks. I'll tell you more about them in Hour 9, "Teach Yourself AppleWorks."

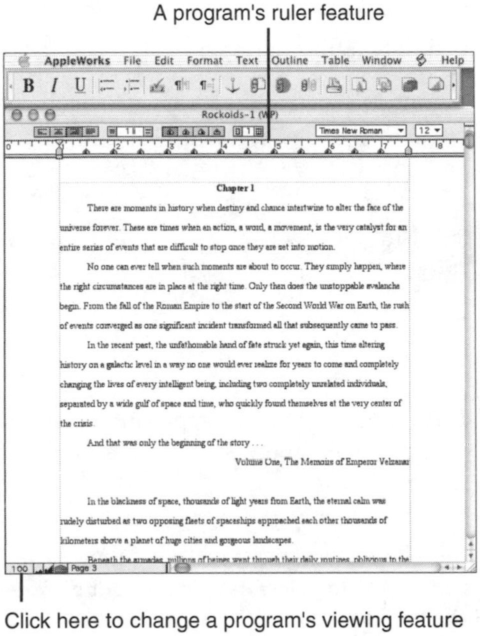

A program's ruler feature

FIGURE 6.8

A document window offers additional features that control some program features.

Click here to change a program's viewing feature

The ruler at the top of Figure 6.8 is used to show the width of the area where you enter text. At the bottom left you'll see icons that you click to change the way you view your document or the size of the text on the screen. Each program will have its own particular set of added features.

Trashing It for Good

The final icon management feature I'll discuss is the trash can (see Figure 6.9 for the Mac OS X version that appears on the Dock). That's the place you send your files and folders when you decide you no longer need them. The first figure shows the trash is empty. The second, shown in Figure 6.10, shows the trash filled with one or more files.

FIGURE 6.9

This trash can is empty.

6

Figure 6.10

The trash is full, and the files are ready to be zapped.

Removing Trashed Files

To get rid of your files, simply follow these steps:

1. Click and drag a program's icon to the trash can, which will be highlighted as soon as the icon is brought atop it. See Figure 6.11 for the effect.

Figure 6.11

When you release the mouse, the file is placed inside the trash can.

2. Choose Empty Trash from the Finder's application menu, which opens the request for confirmation, as shown in Figure 6.12.

> When you click and hold the trash icon, you'll see an Empty Trash command, which is a fast way to delete its contents. But be forewarned: There is no second chance, no warning. When you choose this command, the contents of the trash are gone.

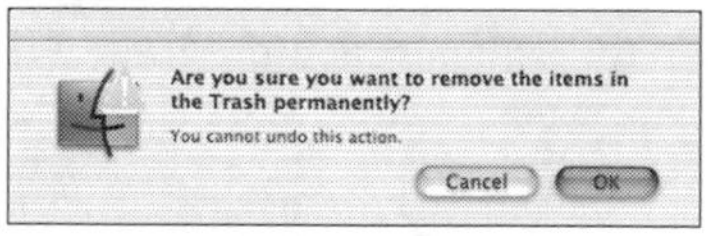

Figure 6.12

Do you really want to zap that file?

Are you sure you want to remove the items in the Trash permanently?
You cannot undo this action.

Cancel   OK

When you OK the message, the file will be history.

> Before you empty the trash, be sure you really want to get rid of those files. If you're not certain, click Cancel. When you dump those files, they are gone, probably for good (although there are a few programs that might recover them if you make a mistake).

The trash can works like a folder. If you're not sure what's inside, just double-click it to open the directory list. If you decide not to trash something, click and drag that icon from it.

The trash can under Mac OS 9.x appears as a movable icon on the desktop. For the most part, it works the same as the Mac OS X version, except that the Empty Trash command is found in the Mac OS 9.x Finder's Special menu.

Summary

In this lesson, you learned how to use the elements on your iMac's desktop. You worked with folders, files, directory, and document windows, and you discovered how your computer's Trash feature enables you to remove unwanted items.

I also showed you some of the key differences between the Mac OS X Finder and the Mac OS 9.x Finder, so you can easily move between the two operating systems and feel comfortable with the user environments.

In addition, you discovered how to use your iMac's keyboard to do many of the same tasks that the mouse is used for.

In Hour 7, "Making Documents, Editing Documents," we'll get deep into document management. You'll learn how to use your computer's file management and editing tools to create brand new documents and store them on your hard drive.

Q&A

Q How many folders can I place within another folder?

A You can nest hundreds of folders within other folders. The practical limit is one of organization and speed. The more files you have to look through in the Open dialog box (something you'll discover in Hour 7), the longer it takes to display them. Just to be practical, I'd recommend you keep the number of items in a folder to 100 or less, although I've done well with a few hundred.

Q Can I protect my files from others who might have access to my computer?

A Hour 21 has more information on protecting your files. But under Mac OS X, there is a User's option in the System Preferences application that enables you to create an account for each user of your Mac. This can limit access to certain files and folders.

6

A similar feature, called Multiple Users, appears in Mac OS 9.x, as a Control Panel. It's similar in approach, but offers highly customized and simplified environments for beginners.

Some separate security products offer much greater levels of protection. Among the more popular examples are SubRosa from FWB Software, DiskGuard and FileGuard from Intego, and DiskLock and OnGuard from Power On Software. Before you buy a copy, though, it's important to check to be sure you are buying a version that runs under Mac OS X. In fact, it's essential, because using an older security software application could cause more trouble than it's worth.

Q I installed a new program on my computer, but it wasn't put in the Applications folder. What did I do wrong?

A Those program installers don't always put things quite where you want them. When you install a new program, you might see a dialog box on your computer's screen where you can specify what folder you want them placed. But sometimes you won't. In this case, the program's folder will sit on your hard drive (top level). But there's nothing to stop you from dragging that folder to the Applications folder to keep everything neatly organized. And, in fact, nothing to prevent you from moving the folders inside the Applications folder to another place on your hard drive. The great thing about the Mac Operating System is that you can move some things around (except for system-related files) and the programs will run normally. Just be careful about the files inside an application's folder (as I explained earlier in this lesson).

There is an exception to this rule, though, and that's Apple's own applications as installed on your iMac. When Apple wants to update those applications, the updater doesn't always look for an application in another location and won't update properly. So be careful.

Q I'm really impressed with all the great things you can do on the iMac with the keyboard. But what about all those pictures of the screen you have in this book? Did you sit in front of your computer with a camera to get them?

A I love photography, but there are very few real photos in this book—such as the ones that show the exterior of the iMac's case in Hour 1 and Appendix A, "Using Your Vintage iMac." Some of those pictures were made with a digital camera (others were supplied to us by Apple). You can also make pictures of your computer's actual screen without a camera. To shoot your screen, just press the following:

- **Cmd-Shift-3**: This keystroke combination gets you a picture file of the entire screen. When you type it, you'll hear a distinct camera click in your computer's speaker, and you'll see a file named Picture 1 on your iMac's desktop. The second picture will be Picture 2, and so on.

- **Cmd-Shift-4**: After you press this keyboard combination, just take the mouse and click the screen. The cursor will change to a plus (+). Then move (drag) the mouse around the area of the screen you want to capture. When you release the mouse switch, the picture will be taken. Click.

The same features come in Mac OS 9.x, but the files are placed on the top level of your iMac's hard drive.

Another option for capturing the screen of your iMac is Grab, a utility that is present in the Utilities folder under Mac OS X. But the most flexible screen capture application of all is Snapz Pro X, a shareware program from Ambrosia Software (http://www.ambrosiasw.com), which can save your captured images in many formats, with custom backgrounds and custom filenames (and that's only a small part of the available features). There's even an extra cost option that lets you capture a QuickTime movie. This is the application I used to capture most of the screen images used in this book.

Q Help! My keyboard and mouse are dead? What do I do?

A First, make sure that both items are plugged into your iMac.

If they are, it might just mean that your computer has crashed because of a problem with a particular program. Although this doesn't happen too often, Mac OS computers can crash on occasion. Here's how you can get your computer to run again:

NEW TERM In computer-ese, a *crash* means that a problem with your software has caused your computer to freeze, or stop working. It doesn't mean you dropped it by mistake. There's also such a thing as a hard drive crash, which means something has caused the drive to fail. But that's a rare occurrence (see Hour 24, "An iMac Safety Net," for more troubleshooting help).

Recovering from a Crash

▼ To Do

1. Press Cmd-Option-Esc. If this works, you'll get a message listing applications to force quit, the one you were using when the problem occurred will be selected. Just click the Force Quit button to make it happen (you can repeat the process for other programs if necessary). Under Mac OS 9.x, you'll just get a Force Quit prompt, with no options other than Force Quit and Cancel. With luck, the program will close gracefully. Under Mac OS X, the operating system's resilient memory protection enables you to continue to use your Mac. However, with Mac OS 9.x, you should then restart your computer (using Restart from the Special menu) before you continue to use it because a force quit can leave your system a little unstable and might cause more crashes with other programs.

▼

6

▼
2. If the force quit fix doesn't work, you'll need to reset the iMac, which forces it to restart. On the flat-panel iMac, reach over to the power button at the left rear, and press and hold for five seconds. This will turn your iMac off. Wait a few seconds, then press it again to start it up again.

3. On the slot-loading iMac's just press the tiny button with a triangle on it, located on the jack panel at the right side of the computer.

▲
4. Press it in just slightly and release. You should see your iMac's screen darken and hear the startup chord sound.

For additional help on dealing with such problems, check Hour 24.

HOUR 7

Making Documents, Editing Documents

You're making great progress. When you finished with Hour 6, "Files, Folders, Windows, and Other Things," you could manage icons and windows on your iMac's desktop like a pro. You also discovered some of the differences in the way things are done under Mac OS X and Mac OS 9.x. Really, the Mac OS is simple enough to master very fast.

Now it's time to put all that information to work.

In this lesson, you'll have the chance to work on a project using your iMac. You'll make a brand new document, containing the text of your first novel. Then, you'll edit the document to make everything just perfect.

You'll learn

- How to open a brand new document
- How to change the text style
- How to move text around
- How to move back and forth between one program and another to work on more than one task (called *multitasking*)

Multitasking is the capability to run more than one application or function on your computer, such as writing a letter and printing another document at the same time.

Creating a New Document

In this lesson, I'll introduce you to Apple's integrated productivity program—AppleWorks. You'll have a chance to create a brand new word processing document, perhaps your first novel. Then, you'll see how to change things around to make the text flow better or to remove parts you don't like.

Do you have an older version of AppleWorks. If you have 6.0 or later, look for the latest upgrade, free from Apple's Web site. That's the one that works best with Mac OS X. If you have a flat-panel iMac, you already have that version. Hour 12, "The Internet: Learning the Ropes," explains how to retrieve files when you're online.

In short, you'll do some of the very same things I did when I wrote this book. Word processing is only one of the things AppleWorks does well; I'll cover more in Hour 9, "Teach Yourself AppleWorks."

To start your new document:

1. Double-click the Applications folder on your computer's desktop.

On some iMacs, you have to check the Applications (Mac OS 9) folder instead for your copy of AppleWorks.

2. Locate the AppleWorks folder and double-click that to open it.
3. The AppleWorks program icon ought to be near the top. If not, look through the folder to find it, then double-click it. You'll see a small introductory screen (it's sometimes called a *splash* screen), which identifies the program and version number, and then you'll see a little dialog box asking what sort of document you want to create (see Figure 7.1).

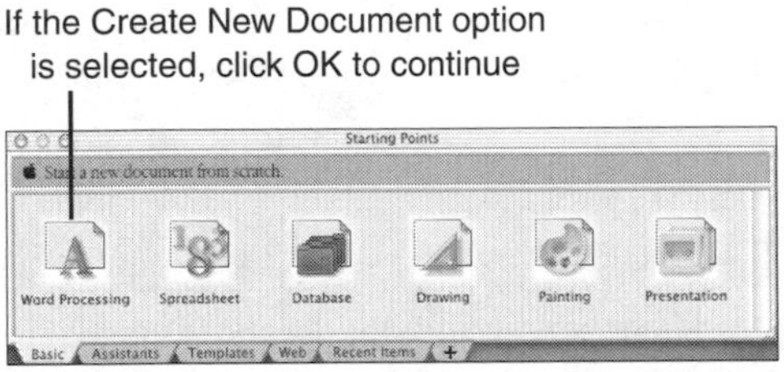

FIGURE **7.1**

Choose the type of document you want to make.

If the Create New Document option
is selected, click OK to continue

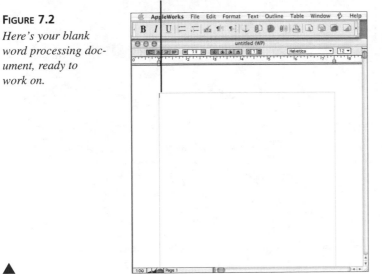

AppleWorks has a setting that turns off the New Document screen when
you launch the program. If it's not there, just press Cmd-N (or choose New
from the File menu) to open it.

4. Select Word Processing from the list.

5. Click the button labeled Create New Document.

6. Click OK, and you'll see an empty document on your computer screen (see
   Figure 7.2).

FIGURE **7.2**

Here's your blank word processing document, ready to work on.

Click here to enter text

7

The second option in Figure 7.1, Assistants, enables you to use the assistants in AppleWorks to help you set up the style of your new word processing document. Go ahead and try it out; I'll tell you more about it in Hour 9.

Entering Text

The next step is simple. The text area of your document page is surrounded with a dotted rectangle. Click anywhere on it, and start typing (see Figure 7.3). You'll see the letters you type appear on your screen, and the mouse cursor will change to a blinking vertical line.

FIGURE 7.3

That's more like it. The creation process begins.

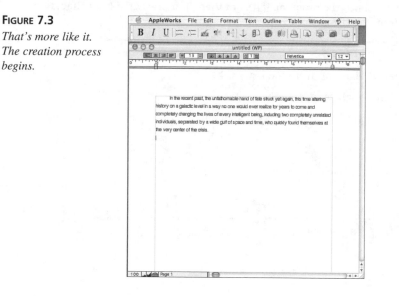

Some basic functions are common to all Mac programs that involve editing text, and those are the ones I'll concentrate on here. So you'll be able to apply the things you learn in this lesson to other software, too, with a few changes.

Go ahead and write your material. For the purpose of this exercise, I'm going to include the text of an actual novel (one my son and I wrote), so you can get the flavor of a real writing session on your computer.

A computer isn't like a typewriter. You don't need to press the Return key after every line. Just continue to type a single stream of words and only press Return at the end of a paragraph.

Formatting Text

After you've written a few words, maybe you've decided that some of this text ought to be different, or the words are too small. Perhaps you want to make the next word bold text to have it stand out.

Making Text Bold

To make the next word or words bold, do the following:

1. Click the Text menu, choose Style and select Bold from the submenu (or press Cmd-B).

2. Type the word or words you want to emphasize.

You can also restore plain text after typing bold text simply by pressing Cmd-B a second time.

3. When you're done, click the Style menu and choose Plain Text (or press Cmd-T). The result is shown in Figure 7.4.

Here are some of the choices available to alter the look of the text in most word processing programs (you can combine two or more for a specific effect):

- **bold**
- *italic*
- ***bold italic***
- underlined
- ~~strikethrough~~
- ~~double strikethrough~~
- Outline
- Shadow

7

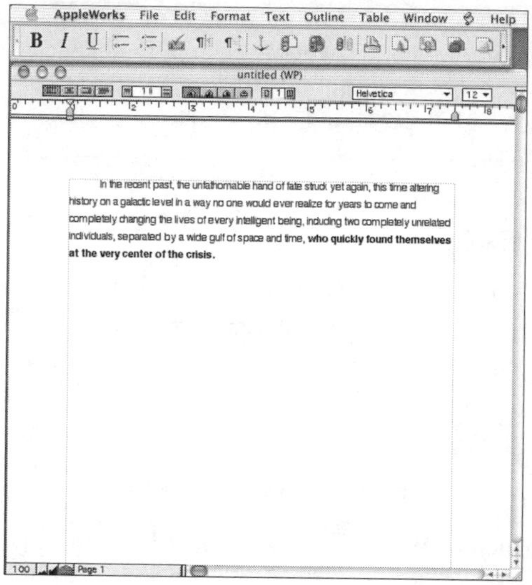

FIGURE 7.4
You can make words bold for emphasis.

No, wait a minute! Maybe the letters are just too small. So the next option is to change the size of a paragraph or headline to give it emphasis.

Let's add a headline to the letter and make it larger:

Increasing Letter Size

1. Click the Text menu, choose Size from the submenu and select 24 Point.

2. Type the word or words you want to use as a headline.

3. Press the Return key to end the line or paragraph.

4. When you're done, click the Size menu and pick the previous size (in this case 12 Point.) The result is shown in Figure 7.5

You can also style the larger text bold to make it stand out even better. Or you can even change the typeface (or font).

NEW TERM   A *font* is a collection of letters and numbers that come in a specific artistic style. Literally thousands and thousands of fonts are available for your computer.

Your iMac comes with a small number of fonts to pick from under Mac OS 9.x and a greater number to use in your Mac OS X applications. As you get accustomed to using the iMac you'll begin to locate sources for other fonts. Some programs, such as those from publishers such as Adobe Systems, Corel, and Macromedia, actually include a number of free fonts with their software. You can also buy fonts from your favorite software dealer.

FIGURE 7.5

There you go. A big headline to spruce things up.

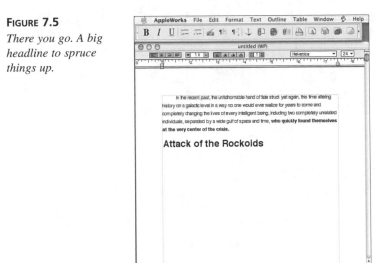

To change the font you're using in your document, do the following:

Changing the Font

1. Click Text and choose Font from the submenu, which opens the screen shown in Figure 7.6.

FIGURE 7.6

Here are the fonts that came with your new iMac. The styled Font menu is a special feature of AppleWorks.

▼   2. Pick the font you want to use by dragging the cursor and highlighting the one you
          want. The text you type next will be changed to the new face (see Figure 7.7).

FIGURE 7.7

*The remaining text is
now in a different
typeface.*

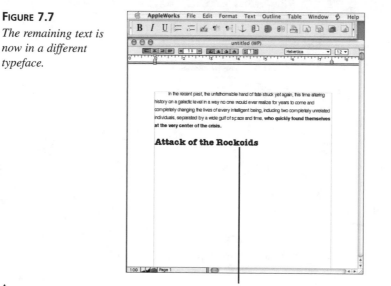

▲

This is the new font you've just selected

You can also change the font or style of the words you've already typed by
selecting that text and making your changes just as I described. I'll tell you
more in the next section.

Text styles and size changes are designed to enhance the look of a document, but use the features with care. Putting too many styles and sizes
together can make your letter or novel look like a ransom note.

Aligning Text

The usual setting for text in a new document is flush left, which means the text is aligned
at the left, and staggered at the right. Just like the text in this book.

Most programs offer a set of icons above a document's title bar (see Figure 7.8) that
enable you to line up text differently. Here's how they work:

Click one of these icons to align text as shown

FIGURE 7.8
The standard four text alignment choices are shown in the icons at the upper left.

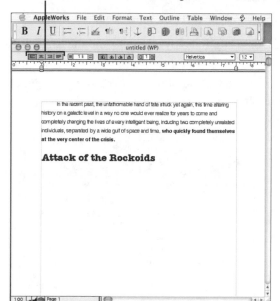

- **Flush Left**: This is the standard format. The left side of text is aligned, and the right side is staggered.
- **Centered**: The lines are put smack in the middle of the page, and the right and left lines are indented identically. You'll usually center the text used for a headline.
- **Flush Right**: The right side of the text is aligned, and the left side staggered. This style is sometimes used for a photo caption or advertisement.
- **Justified**: This style commonly occurs just as you see it in your daily newspaper and many books and magazines. Both the right and left sides of the paragraph are aligned, except for the last line, which (if short) aligns at the left.

Editing Text

After you've written some material, no doubt you'll look it over and make a change. Perhaps you need to move some words around, or convert the regular text to bold and vice versa, or make it smaller. For this part of the lesson, I'll take you through the words you've already typed and show you how to select them for further changes.

7

Selecting Text

Here's one way to select the text you want to edit:

1. Click the mouse key and move the cursor to the beginning of the area you want to select.

2. Drag the mouse to the end of the area you want to highlight, and then release the key. The result is shown in Figure 7.9.

FIGURE 7.9

The highlighted text is selected, ready for you to edit.

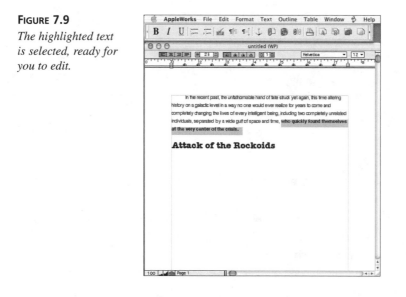

3. Change the style of your text as you want, and it will be applied to the selected area.

Another Way to Select Text

As with many Mac OS features, there's more than one way to skin a cat, as it were. Here's another way to select an area of text:

1. Click the mouse button and move the cursor to the beginning of the area you want to select.

2. Press and hold the Shift key.

3. While holding down the Shift key, click the mouse cursor at the end of the area you want to select.

4. After making changes to the text, click the selected area again to deselect it.

In addition, some mouse shortcuts for selecting specific amounts of text exist. Here are the common ones that apply to AppleWorks and similar programs:

- To select a single word, double-click anywhere on that word.
- To select an entire line, click three times anywhere on the line.
- To select an entire paragraph, click four times anywhere in the paragraph.

The options I'm describing here for selecting words, lines, and paragraphs apply strictly to AppleWorks. Some programs enable you to select an entire paragraph with three clicks, an entire document with four. You'll want to check the instructions that come with a program to see how such things differ.

- To select all the text in the document, press Cmd-A or choose Select All from the Edit menu.

After you've selected text, be careful what you do next. You have only one chance to Undo what you've changed. If you press a single letter, that one letter will replace what is there on your screen (even if you selected an entire long document). That will constitute your single Undo option. Your only other choice, then, other than to manually edit the text, is to choose Revert from the File menu. This choice changes things to the way they were when you last saved your document (and that might change too many things).

Using the Edit Menu to Adjust Text

In addition to selecting an item, you have several commands in the Edit menu that will work with all Mac programs. I listed them in Hour 2, "Exploring the iMac Desktop," so you'll want to recheck that hour as a reminder.

That's not all the functions available. Some programs add the capability to insert special characters, numbers, or dates. Others enable you to check the spelling or fiddle with a program's settings (preferences).

In Hour 9, I'll cover some of the special Edit menu features that you'll find in AppleWorks, so stay tuned. Each Mac program has a different range of choices there, you'll want to explore the menu bar commands of each program and try them out before getting to work.

7

Many of your iMac programs have common names for functions, but they might work differently. If you don't have the chance to read an entire manual, look over the Help menu for advice.

Secrets of Moving, Dragging, and Dropping

The are several ways to move text around. One is simply to use the Cut and Paste commands from the File menu. Here's how it's done:

Moving Text with Cut and Paste

1. Select the text you want to move.

2. Choose Cut from the Edit menu to remove it from its first locale.

3. Click the area of your document where you want the text to be placed.

4. Choose Paste from the Edit menu to put it there.

The Mac's clipboard only holds one item at a time. That means if you Cut something else from your document before you paste the first item, the first item will be gone—history. Some programs out there make multiple clipboards, but that's not the standard way it's set up.

You don't have to visit the Edit menu to use the basic editing commands; your keyboard will do just fine. Cmd-X will Cut text, Cmd-C will Copy text, Cmd-V will Paste text, and Cmd-Z will Undo the previous operation.

Many Mac programs, such as AppleWorks, offer yet another great feature to move things around. It also makes it possible to bypass the cumbersome Cut and Paste routine.

It's called drag and drop. And here's how you do it:

Dragging and Dropping Text

1. Select the text you want to move.

2. Click the text and drag it to the place where you want to move it. You will see (depending on the program) a small rectangle surrounding the mouse cursor.

   3. Release the mouse key. Presto! The text is moved to its new location.

You can also make a clipping of the text you want to move by dragging the selected text away from your document and clicking on your computer's desktop. When you do it this way the original text stays where it was. You can then take your desktop clipping and drag it to another document. Cool!

Some Mac OS X applications only work with drag and drop if you click and hold the mouse down about a second before attempting to move a selected item. An example of such a program is Mail. If drag and drop doesn't work the first time you try it, be a little more patient and hold the mouse for a full second, and then, if the program supports the feature, it should function the way you want.

Switching Applications

When you are working in a specific program, its name will appear in the Application menu, located at the right of the Apple menu. To switch to another application that might be open, just do this:

To Do

Switching Applications

1. Locate the application's icon on the Dock. If it's open, a vertical arrow will be below it. If the application icon is not in the Dock, go to the Applications folder.

FIGURE 7.10
These are the programs you're now running on the iMac.

2. Click the application's icon. If you're not sure what the icon stands for, don't worry. The name appears right above the icon on the Dock when you pass your mouse over it.

▲

Summary

7

You've now had an opportunity to create something all new on your computer, the beginning of your novel or letter. You learned how to use the iMac's text editing tools (many of which are common from program to program) to manipulate the words in the document, to change things, to remove things, and to move things around.

In Hour 8, "Opening, Saving, Finding, Moving, Etc.," I'll show you what to do next—save the document. You'll also learn how to open new documents and locate other files on your computer's drive.

Q&A

Q I tried to open a document, but now I can't find it. What do I do?

A Call on Sherlock. Nope, not the dude who runs around with that Watson fellow, but Apple's search program, which (among other things) locates files on your computer's drive (or any other drive hooked up to it).

To use it just click the Sherlock icon in the Dock (or check the Applications folder if it's not on the Dock. Figure 7.11 shows Sherlock. Click the File Names button (the one at left) and enter the name of the file you want to locate. This program is terrific, and it can find a lot more than just filenames. I'll cover Sherlock 2 in more detail in Hour 8.

Type the file's name (or part of the name) here

FIGURE 7.11

Sherlock is at your beck and call to find the files or information you want.

If you happen to be using Mac OS 9.x, don't fret. There's a version of Sherlock for the older or Classic Mac OS, too. It's in the Finder's File menu, under Find, or the Apple menu (where it's called Sherlock 2, because two times a charm).

You have another option—Contents, which enables you to find text in a document, but only if you've indexed the folder first. You can do that with your Users folder, plus another folder by choosing Add Folder from the Find menu. When the folder's name is selected and appears on the Sherlock list, select it and choose Index Now from the Find menu. Indexing is a process of storing information about the documents, so Sherlock can find the text inside those documents.

Q **I like this concept of multitasking, but whenever I try to type something while printing, everything is so sluggish. I'm using an older application that runs in Classic.**

A Multitasking on the Classic Mac OS is called cooperative. That means that the programs are set up to get out of the way, or at least reduce their activities when other programs are working. The process isn't perfect, however, and you can divide up tasks in several ways. It's normal for performance to be somewhat sluggish when two or more things are happening at the same time. Under Mac OS X, a different multitasking scheme, called preemptive, is used. In this case, the operating system acts as the traffic cop, so to speak, and performance when running multiple applications is a lot better.

Q **How many programs can I run on my computer at the same time?**

A Each program you use takes a chunk of memory (or RAM). As you open a new program, you have less available for other programs. If you hit the limit, you'll get a warning if you're using Mac OS 9.x. Under Mac OS X, the operating system uses an advanced memory management setup that automatically gives an application the amount of memory it needs. If you run out of real RAM, it uses virtual memory. Virtual memory is a process that uses a part of your hard drive in place of RAM, to extend memory. But it's not perfect, or even virtually perfect. It can slow things down a bit, but it helps make your iMac do more and run more programs at the same time.

7

PART III

Being Productive on Your iMac

Hour

Hour **8**

Opening, Saving, Finding, Moving, Etc.

I realize many of you read book chapters out of sequence, as you need the information. But if you've been going through all the lessons in sequence so far, you now have a new document on your iMac's screen ready to do—well—something with. If you are satisfied with the document you re-created, you'll want to store it for safekeeping and later retrieval.

In this lesson, I'll show you how to open existing files, save files, and locate files on your hard drive (when you don't know where they are).

You'll learn

- How to use Apple's Open dialog boxes
- How to save files
- How to use Sherlock, a great tool to find the files you want

Using the Open Dialog Box

There are two ways to open a file. The first, discussed in previous lessons, is to just double-click it or its alias. This process does double duty: It opens the application that made the document, and then opens the document.

If you've already launched a program that you want to use to work on another document, however, it's a little awkward to switch back to the Finder's desktop, locate, and double-click another document.

Instead you can use the Open dialog box. But, depending on the Mac OS version you're running, there are different types of Open dialog boxes. We're going to start with the Mac OS X version, because that's the one you'll use most often:

> Actually, three different types of Open dialog boxes are available. There's the original version, used with older programs (and even some that come with your iMac). I'll show you the second style, used with more recent software, called *Navigation Services*, which is designed to work better. Best of all is the Mac OS X version, which is sometimes labeled a "sheet" because it drops down from a document window for convenience.

Opening a File

▲ To Do ▼

1. With a Mac OS X application open, choose Open from the File menu, or press Cmd-O. Either step will produce a dialog box similar to the one shown in Figure 8.1.

Click this pop-up menu
to select a folder or disk

FIGURE 8.1
This is the super-spiffy Mac OS X Open dialog box.

```
Open: AppleWorks 6
From: ☐ Documents

📁 Applications          ▶   AOL for Mac OS X 148
📁 Applicatio...(Mac OS 9) ▶  AppleWorks_6.0.4_GM
📁 Documents                  AppleWork...Update.smi
📁 Late Breaking News        AppleWorks User Data  ▶
📁 Library              ▶   Communi...egulations  ▶
📁 System               ▶   Installer Logs        ▶
📁 System Folder        ▶   Mac OS 9.2.1 Update.smi
📁 Users                ▶   Rockoids Manuscripts  ▶
                             Rockoids-1
                             Thoth Files

Document Type          File Format
All Types          ▾   AppleWorks       ▾

Go to:

Add to Favorites          Cancel      Open
```

— Drag scrollbars to see more

— Click file to select

— Click to choose a file format

— Type folder name here

Click to choose a document type

8

2. If the correct folder isn't shown, click the pop-up menu at the top to locate the folder that contains the file you want to open.

3. Scroll through the file list to find your file. You can use either the scrollbar or the Page Up and Page Down keys.

> To locate a folder by its name, type the name in the Go to column.

4. Click a file once to select it.

5. Click the Open button to open the file. (Double-clicking on the filename itself does the same thing.) The result is shown in Figure 8.2. You can press Cmd-W or click the close box to close the open file.

FIGURE 8.2
Here's the file you chose to open.

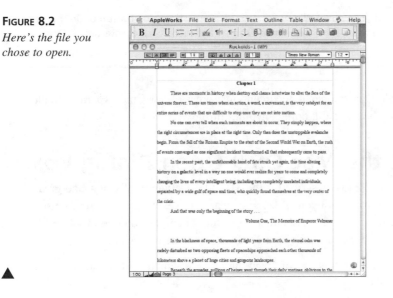

> Apple has set up the Open dialog box so the folks who write the software can customize it for their own purposes. The example shown in Figure 8.1 comes from AppleWorks, and you'll see they've added Document Type and File Type options. Other Open dialog boxes might have different options or show nothing extra.

Manipulating Files Via the Keyboard

You can minimize the amount of mouse clicking and perform many Mac OS operations from your iMac's keyboard.

In addition to using Cmd-O to invoke the Open dialog box, here's a list of other keyboard timesavers that work within that dialog box:

- Press Ctrl-↑ to move up one folder level.
- Press Ctrl-↓ to move down one folder level.
- Press Ctrl-D or Cmd-Shift-↑ to switch to the desktop's file list.
- Press Ctrl-O or Cmd-↓ when an Open dialog box is up to open a selected folder or disk.
- Press the Return or Enter key to open a selected file. It works the same as the Open button.

 No it's not alive! Whenever you see a pulsating blue button under Mac OS X, it means that its command can be activated with the Return or Enter keys.

- If you don't want to open a document, just press esc or Cmd-. (period) to close the Open dialog box without doing anything further.

Looking at the Mac OS 9 Open Dialog Box

The Open dialog box I just described is the Mac OS X style, totally new and greatly simplified. As you work with your iMac's software, however, you'll begin to discover another sort of Open dialog box, one that shows up when you run one of your older or Classic applications or restart with your Mac OS 9.x system version.

Let's take a quick look at this sort of Open dialog box, which is also known as Navigation Services.

You can invoke it the same way as other dialog boxes, by choosing Open from the File menu or pressing Cmd-O. But what you see is very, very different, as shown in Figure 8.3.

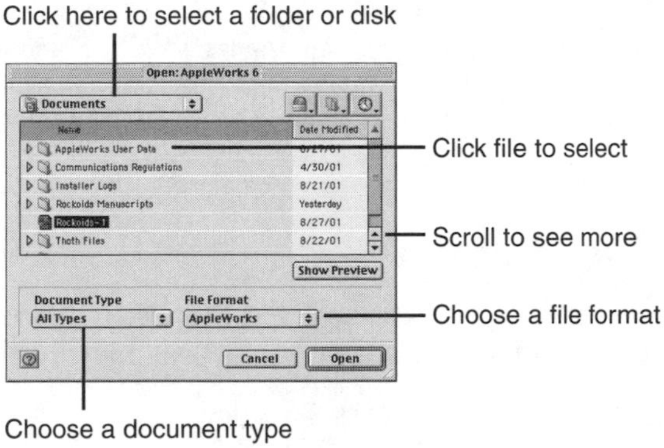

FIGURE 8.3

Apple's navigation services give the Open dialog box some great new features.

Click here to select a folder or disk

Click file to select

Scroll to see more

Choose a file format

Choose a document type

Well, it sure looks different, although many of the functions are the same.

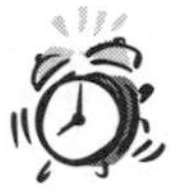

> Be careful about how many files you open in a program. Each open document might use a big portion of the memory available to the program. If you open too many files at once, the program might freeze or stop working, or the application might quit, which means you'll have to restart Mac OS 9.x or the Classic environment. A handful of files at a time is usually enough. Hour 22, "Giving Your iMac New Software, More RAM, and Other Things," covers the subject of adding more memory to your computer.

> You can make the Open and Save dialog boxes larger. Just click the resize bar at the bottom right and drag it to make the box larger (or smaller if it has already been enlarged). You can also drag the dialog box to another position in the screen.

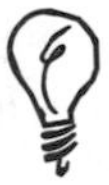

Saving Your Files

When you make a new document, as I described in Hour 7, "Making Documents, Editing Documents," you have a file that lives only in your iMac's memory. When you shut down or restart your iMac, the file is gone, history.

If you want to keep that file, you need to save it first. This puts a copy of the file on your iMac's hard drive.

> As you will see in the next few pages, Mac OS X and Mac OS 9 have different Save As dialog boxes, too. Many functions are similar, but Apple tried to make the saving process easier in its newest operating system.

Saving a File in Mac OS X

1. If the file has not yet been saved, choose Save As (or Save) from the File menu, or press Cmd-S. This opens the dialog box shown in Figure 8.4.

Name your file

Choose a folder

FIGURE 8.4

Get ready to name and save your file.

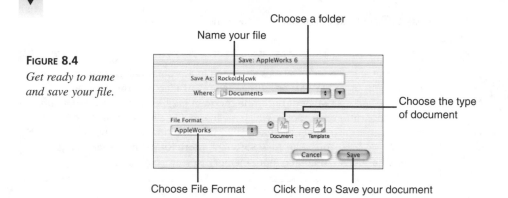

Choose the type of document

Choose File Format

Click here to Save your document

2. Choose the folder where you want to save your file from the pop-up menu.

3. Type the name of your file in the highlighted text box. You'll want to give it a name that makes it easy to recall later.

> Filenames were limited to 31 characters under Mac OS 9, but a file's name can be up to 254 characters with Mac OS X, far longer than you can read in a file list. If you plan on sharing files with others who aren't using Mac OS X, you'll want to play by the rules and keep filenames short. In addition, if you give a file the same name as one already in the folder, you'll see a dialog box asking if you want to replace the other file. Be careful! If you replace the other file, that file is gone for good! It's best to give your new file a unique name.

▼ 4. Click the Save button to store your file.

Before you save your file, double-check the name of the folder shown in the pop-up menu, to make sure it's going to the right place. Otherwise, you might end up with little bits and pieces of a long project, spread haphazardly around your computer's drive.

8

The Expanded Mac OS X Save As Dialog Box

Believe it or not, Mac OS X gives you another Save As dialog box, hidden away but at your beck and call when you need it. All it takes to get there is the click of an arrow.

With the Save As dialog box visible, simply click the little down arrow next to the Where pop-up menu. The result is shown in Figure 8.5.

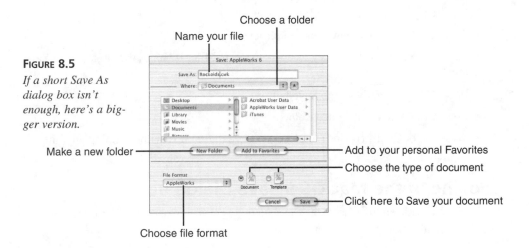

Choose a folder

Name your file

FIGURE 8.5
If a short Save As dialog box isn't enough, here's a bigger version.

Make a new folder

Add to your personal Favorites
Choose the type of document

Click here to Save your document

Choose file format

With the expanded Save As dialog box, you gain a full Finder-type column view of the contents of your drive, same as in the Open dialog box. You also gain a New Folder button, which enables you to create and name a folder in which to store a file. The third option is Add to Favorites, which takes the selected file and makes it a favorite. When it becomes a favorite, it'll be available when you click the Favorites icon in the Mac OS X Finder or Favorites from the Go menu.

If you don't need the extra options in this expanded Save As dialog box, click the little up arrow at the right of the Where pop-up menu and it'll revert to its reduced size.

Which Save As dialog box do you get? That depends on what you selected last time. If it was the short one, that's what you get this time around, and vice versa. If you expand or collapse the dialog box, the setting is remembered the next time you use it.

Save Dialog Box Keyboard Shortcuts

The Save dialog box has its own share of keyboard shortcuts. And, as you'll see, they are very similar to the ones I described for the Open dialog box. Consistency rules!

Here's the list, which works primarily in the expanded Save As view:

- Use the up and down arrow keys to move to the item above and below the selected file.
- Press Ctrl-↑ to move up one folder level.
- Press Ctrl-↓ to move down one folder level.
- Press the Return or Enter key to open a selected file. It works the same as the Save button.
- Press Cmd-S to activate the Save button.
- Press Cmd-N to create a new folder.
- Press esc or Cmd-. (period) to close the Save dialog box without doing anything further.

Looking at the Mac OS 9 Save Dialog Box

Back in the Classic environment, the Save As dialog box mirrors the Open dialog box with its special features, so I'll just cover it briefly.

You summon it the same way, by choosing Save or Save As from the File menu in your unsaved document. The dialog box shown in Figure 8.6 will appear.

Save, Save, and Save Again

After you've made a copy of your file on your computer's drive, you can go ahead and continue working on it.

What you do on your screen doesn't change the file you're storing. To do that, choose Save from the File menu or press Cmd-S.

Shortcuts to access other networked Macs
List of folders or disks │ List of Favorites
List of available files │ List of recent files

FIGURE 8.6
*Name your file where
indicated.*

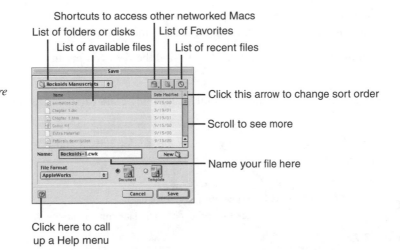

Click this arrow to change sort order

Scroll to see more

Name your file here

Click here to call
up a Help menu

8

 You should get in the habit of saving your document every five or 10 minutes. If your computer crashes, or there's a power outage, the only part of the file you'll be able to retrieve is what you've saved (even if a later version is on your screen). Some programs even offer automatic saving options so a file is always saved at regular intervals. First, look at the program's preferences dialog boxes for the option. If you don't see it, refer to the manual or Help menu to see if such a feature is available.

 If you quit a program without saving, you'll see a dialog box asking if you want to save the changes. Unless you're absolutely sure you don't want to keep the changes, click the Save button in the dialog box to record the latest version of your file for posterity.

Where's That File? Only Sherlock Knows for Sure

When I first learned how to use a Mac, I quickly got in the habit of saving my work at regular intervals. But I always had a problem finding the stuff I'd saved. The files were all over the place, a real mess, like the desk in my home office (which still looks that way, despite my wife's best efforts to straighten it out).

Naturally, I could never find the files I needed, when I needed them. So, I had to keep searching for them and moving them all to the right place.

Fortunately, Apple has a great way to find the files you put in the wrong place (or just misplaced).

It's called Sherlock, and it puts the magnifying glass to your iMac in search of files.

To call up Sherlock, just click the Sherlock icon in the Dock, choose Find from the Finder's File menu or, while you're in the Finder, press Cmd-F to open the screen shown in Figure 8.7.

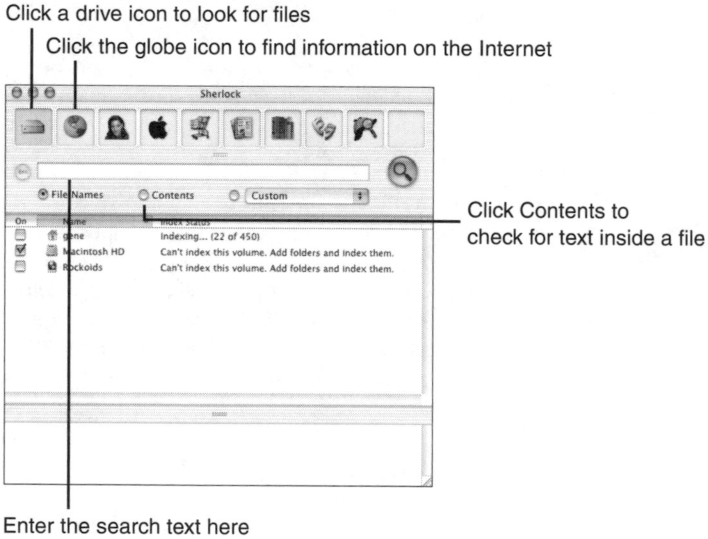

Click a drive icon to look for files

Click the globe icon to find information on the Internet

FIGURE 8.7

Sherlock is your iMac's file detective.

Click Contents to check for text inside a file

Enter the search text here

Sherlock has three ways of locating something.

We'll start with the first, by filename. To locate the file by its filename:

Finding Files with Sherlock

1. Click the disk icon in Sherlock's toolbar to select the drive to be searched.

2. Enter the file's name (or part of the name) in the text field.

You'll want to be as specific as possible about the search request. If you keep the string too short, you might be rewarded with a huge list of files that have those letters in the filenames, which will only make it harder to find the one you want.

3. Click Custom if you want to search for a file by date, or some other criteria.

4. Click the Find button (the magnifying glass). Within seconds you'll see a screen similar to the one shown in Figure 8.8.

Double-click a filename to open it

FIGURE 8.8

The game's afoot! Sherlock has found your file.

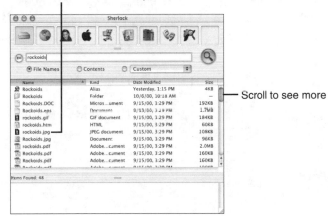

Scroll to see more

Click once on a file's name, and you'll see its exact location listed at the bottom half of the Sherlock screen. You can also use Sherlock to reorganize your files; just drag the file onto your iMac's desktop or into another visible folder from the search window. Talk about spring cleaning!

After you find the file you want, double-click it to open it.

Selecting More than One File

1. Click the first file.

2. Hold down the Shift key and click the last file in the group.

3. To open the selected files, choose Open Item from the File menu.

> If you want to select two or more files that aren't consecutive, use the Cmd key instead of the Shift key while you select each one.

Locating Text Inside a File

Sherlock can dig down really deep to find the stuff you want. For example, maybe you need to find a file with a certain word in it, but you can't recall the file's name. You can call up the second option in Sherlock's bag of tricks, Contents (see Figure 8.9).

Enter the text you want to search for here

FIGURE 8.9

Like a good detective, Sherlock has many tricks up its sleeve, such as finding the text inside a file.

>
>
> Sherlock needs to make an index of your computer's drive before it can search for the text inside a file. To make the index, click the Find menu, choose Index Volumes, and then select the name of the drive you want to index on the following screen. The cataloging process can take anywhere from a few minutes to an hour or two to complete, so you might want to be prepared for a long lunch break before you get started. Your startup disk can't be indexed, but if you choose Add Folder from the Find menu, you can select one or more folders to be searched directly (such as the Documents folder).

If you've already selected Sherlock's file search option (the standard setting), you can press Cmd-G to pick to the Contents option and press Cmd-H to search the Internet.

8

Locating Material on the Internet

Clicking the Globe icon accesses Sherlock's next feature, which selects the Internet channel (we'll get to the others shortly). This great feature enables Sherlock to log on to the Internet, and then call up any of several search engines to find the information you want.

Sherlock's Internet search feature only works if you've signed up for an Internet account, as I described in Hour 1, "Opening the Box" and Hour 4, "Getting On the Net." In addition, if you use AOL, you have to log onto that service first before invoking the Sherlock's Internet feature. AOL won't connect you automatically; ditto for AOL's affiliate service, CompuServe.

The Internet has a huge amount of information on all sorts of subjects, and Sherlock is tapping huge databases to find the information you want. Here's how it works:

Searching the Internet with Sherlock

1. Open Sherlock.
2. Click the Globe icon (or press Cmd-K).
3. Enter a word or phrase that describes what you want.
4. Click the Find (magnifying glass) button.

Within a few seconds, Sherlock will dial up your Internet service (if you're not already connected), and then seek out the information you want. See Figure 8.10 for an example.

If you find a likely match among the list, just click once on the item to see additional information in the bottom half of the screen.

Click once to open the actual reference (see Figure 8.11). The information will show up in a Web browser window.

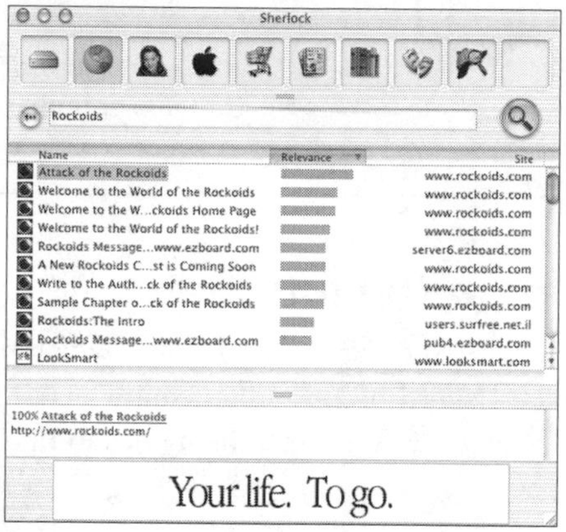

FIGURE 8.10

Sherlock is ranking its results to show which ones are the closest matches to your request.

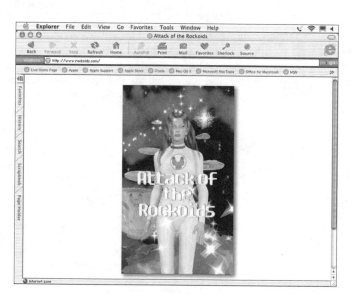

FIGURE 8.11

At last! The information you sought, courtesy of Sherlock.

Some More Sherlock Channels

In addition to searching for files on your hard drive and Internet sites, Sherlock comes with seven additional channels that are used to seek Internet information in various fields. To access any of these, just click the appropriate icon in the Sherlock search screen.

These include

- **People:** You can search for the email addresses and phone numbers of your friends and business contacts.

- **Apple**: This option opens Apple's product information and support Web sites.

8

- **Shopping**: A handy choice. You'll be able to pick from a list of vendors and check products and pricing. In time, many online merchants will provide Sherlock plug-in modules so you can search their offerings as well.

> Yes, you do have another version of Sherlock, called Sherlock 2, for Mac OS 9.x. When you've restarted under Apple's Classic Operating System, just choose Find from the Finder's File menu, or Sherlock 2 from the Apple menu to launch the application. You'll find the features are quite similar to the ones available in the Mac OS X version, similar enough that you can read this section and be able to easily perform all your searches.

- **News**: Read the latest news and views from major news services around the world.
- **Reference**: A great place for you to do online research for homework, a special office project, or to simply learn more about a topic.
- **Entertainment**: Check on the latest news, views, and gossip from the show business world. One of the standard search tools, Internet Movie Database, is bound to make you a trivia expert. You'll learn plenty of cool stuff about the latest flicks and early movies going back to the silent era.
- **My Channel**: Be creative. You can simply drag and drop search modules from your Internet Search Sites folder and build your own custom channel that searches the information you want.

Summary

Making sense of Apple's various flavors of Open and Save dialog boxes isn't always easy. There are a lot of detours, and it's very easy to put a file in the wrong place. This lesson taught you how to deal with those detours. You discovered handy keyboard short-cuts to get around those dialog boxes in quick order.

In Hour 9, "Teach Yourself AppleWorks," you'll learn about one of the best productivity programs out there. With it, you'll be able to write letters, keep a database of business contacts, make simple charts, and draw pictures. It's called AppleWorks, the program I've been using so far to demonstrate your computer's file-handling features.

Q&A

Q **After I saved my new document, I used the Save command again, but I didn't see the dialog box. Where is it?**

A It's not necessary after your file has been saved the very first time. Each successive Save command will simply update the file that's on your computer's drive. You only need to open that Save As dialog box when you want to make another copy of the file with a new name. Then you use the Save As command instead.

Q **I use the Save command over and over again but nothing happens. What's wrong?**

A The Save command works only if something is changed in your document (even a single letter or number). Otherwise, well, nothing happens. Some programs will sound a beep if you attempt to Save a saved document without making any changes.

Q **I tried to open a file from the Favorites list of that Mac OS 9 Open dialog box, but it didn't work. What happened?**

A It could be that you deleted the file. After a file is gone, there's no going back (unless you follow the steps I will describe in Hour 24, "An iMac Safety Net").

Q **I need to work on some files from my office. But they come on floppy disks. Can I install a floppy drive on the iMac?**

A Yes, you can. There are external drives for your computer that will do the trick. They come from Imation and other companies and they can read the floppy disks with the HD label on them. Another type of drive, bearing the name SuperDisk (as opposed to SuperDrive, which is the combo DVD-R drive offered in some flat-panel iMacs and Power Mac G4's from Apple), can also read HD floppies, plus a special breed of media, SuperDisk, which holds 120MB or 240MB of data (about the equivalent of 85 or 190 regular floppies). I'll tell you more about the various extended storage options in Hour 21, "Backup, Backup, Backup...How to Protect Your Files."

There are ways to get those files without buying another product, however. If you have another Mac on the network, you can use file sharing to exchange files. Hour 21 will cover that, too. You can also exchange files via modem, if both you and the other Mac user have an Internet or AOL connection. I'll cover the technique of attaching files to email in Hour 13, "The Wonderful World of Email."

HOUR 9

Teach Yourself AppleWorks

You bought your iMac to run applications, not to stare at a pretty face. Fortunately, there are thousands of Mac programs available. They run the gamut from games to financial management programs. You can explore the stars, run a doctor's office, and learn how to cook.

Most often, however, the sort of things you'll be doing can be accomplished with very few programs. This lesson is devoted to one of those programs, considered the best of its kind. It does several things quite well, and best of all you don't have to buy it. It's already available as part of the software bundled with your computer.

It's AppleWorks.

In this lesson, you'll get a fast and dirty (well, not too dirty) tutorial on

- How to put together a simple brochure in AppleWorks
- How to make drawings for your documents
- How to make business reports and charts
- How to create a database of business and personal contacts

Introducing AppleWorks

AppleWorks is a "Swiss Army Knife" sort of program. It serves in place of several programs. More importantly, however, it does those functions well—well enough to make professional-looking documents without having to spend lots of time to page through a long, complex manual.

> Just to remind you, on a number of first-generation iMacs, AppleWorks was known by its former name, ClarisWorks. But the program, past the label, is the same. In addition, the version I'm showing here, for Mac OS X, is essentially the same as AppleWorks 6 for the older or Classic version of the Mac OS except for the Aqua look. If you have the older version, you need to buy a new copy to keep up-to-date; there is no upgrade program for those using older editions.

The Bill of Fare

You can consider AppleWorks to be the functional equivalent of six different programs. You can also combine the functions, which delivers an even greater variety of potential uses. Here's what AppleWorks does

- **Word processing**: Creates text-based documents for ads, brochures, letters, novels, reports, and more.
- **Drawing**: Does simple line drawings, using lines, circles, and rectangles.
- **Painting**: It won't help with the garage or the den, but the AppleWorks paint module enables you to add color and shading to your drawings. It's great for making simple illustrations for your documents, and when you get the hang of it, you might discover you have a flair for computer art.
- **Spreadsheets**: Creates a document with numerical data, useful for business reports, financial summaries, or charts. The program even does the calculations for you (so you can put the pocket calculator back in the closet).
- **Database**: Makes a record of your business and personal contacts. Then uses the information for a computerized Rolodex, customer or billing records, or to print out mailing labels.
- **Presentation**: This is the newest feature of this handy program. You can create slide shows on your iMac, using this module. The feature is great for a small business, where you can give a demonstration about a new sales policy or a new product. You can even put in a set of family photos and move from one to the other on your iMac's screen.

Making Your First Document

I already covered the basics of making and formatting a word-processing document in Hour 7, "Making Documents, Editing Documents." So for this lesson I'll cover the document creation process from a different angle. Rather than have you build your document from scratch, we'll allow the software to do most of the work for you. You just have to make a few choices and click a few buttons. (Of course, you still have to write the content of the document; computers haven't quite gotten around to replacing writers yet, thank heavens!)

To guide you along, we'll call on one of the AppleWorks Assistants.

Creating a Document

Here's how it works:

1. Locate the AppleWorks folder in your Applications folder.

2. Open the folder and double-click the AppleWorks icon to open the Starting Points screen (see Figure 9.1).

FIGURE 9.1

Choose the kind of document you want to make by clicking one of the icons.

If you don't see the Starting Points screen, choose Show Starting Points from the File menu and it'll show up in a jiffy.

3. Because you're going to let AppleWorks guide you through the document setup process, click the Assistants tab at the bottom of the Starting Points screen. Here you will see the available assistants.

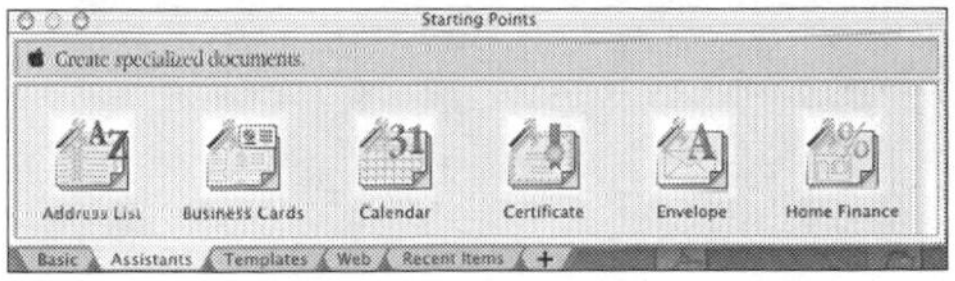

FIGURE 9.2

Here is the brief list of available Assistants offered by AppleWorks.

▼

Another way to ease the document setup process is to use a template. A template is a file that contains all the special formatting and layout needed for a particular type of document. All you have to do is put in your text and pictures. Click the Templates tab on the Starting Points screen to see a selection of templates.

4. For this lesson, you will be using the Home Finance Assistant, which enables you to create a chart showing your financial picture. To get started, click the Home Finance icon, which creates the dialog box shown in Figure 9.3.

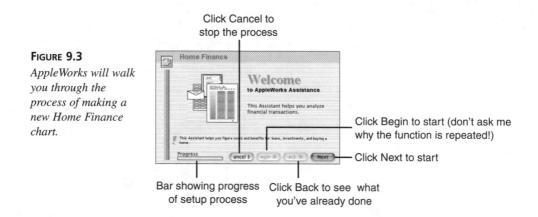

FIGURE 9.3
AppleWorks will walk you through the process of making a new Home Finance chart.

Click Cancel to stop the process

Click Begin to start (don't ask me why the function is repeated!)

Click Next to start

Bar showing progress of setup process

Click Back to see what you've already done

5. To move through the Assistant, just click the Next button. Don't fret if you make a mistake or aren't sure what you did previously. Just click the Back button at any time to fix or check a prior setup. Click Next to get started (see Figure 9.4).

FIGURE 9.4
What kind of Home Finance chart do you want to make? Make a selection here.

▼

6. For this example, I'll be doing an investment analysis (the topic entitled "What will my investments be worth in the future?"). Now this might not be a pleasant thing to display, considering how stock prices tanked in 2001, but it will at least show you how you can make such a chart in a minute or so. So click the last option on the Assistant, then click Next to continue and you'll see the screen shown in Figure 9.5.

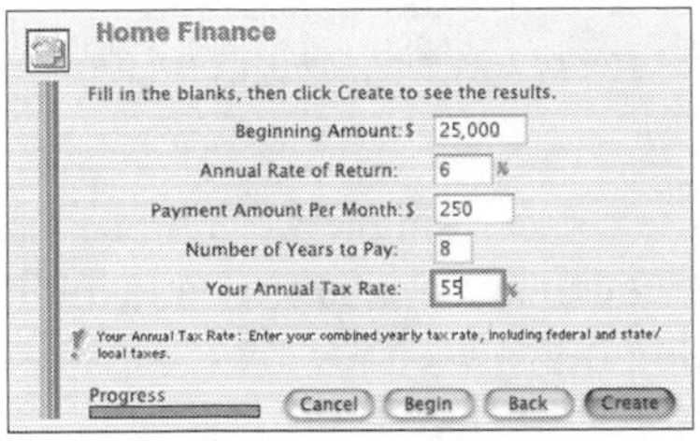

FIGURE 9.5

This is not the author's investment profile; it's too high. But it gives you a sample of how to set up this chart.

Feel free to toggle between the Next and Back buttons to review your work before you finish it.

7. Click a text field, and type the figures requested. Use the Tab key to move down through the fields (Shift-Tab to go back up). Or just click the text field directly.

8. When all the financial information is entered, click the Create button to produce your chart (see Figure 9.6). What you see here is a spreadsheet displaying the status of your investment profile in an easy-to-read chart. You'll be able to make other Home Finance charts just as quickly.

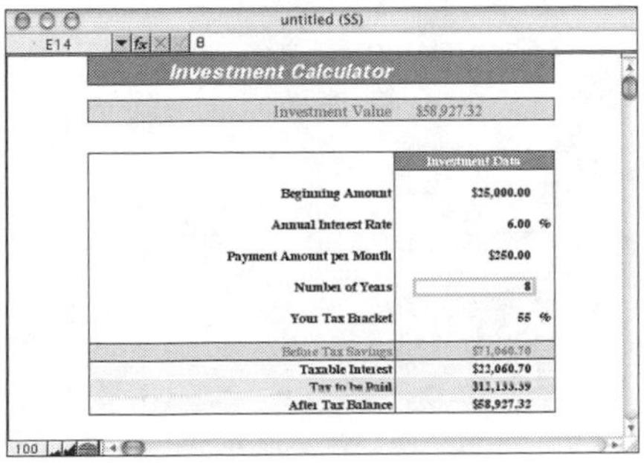

FIGURE 9.6

A completed chart, fully formatted, made in just a minute with AppleWorks.

The Assistants feature I've described here is used to create many forms of documents; it's not just limited to home finance. What's more you can modify the formatting of your documents in many ways to fine-tune them to your needs.

Now that wasn't so hard, was it? In about a minute, you made a fully formatted spreadsheet chart showing some element of your financial status. Now maybe the news won't be as good as you want, but it's a way to track your portfolio so you can find ways to make it better.

The next thing we'll try is just to create a simple word processing document, containing the text for a novel. To do that, click the close button on that little chart you just created. (You will see a dialog box asking if you want to save it, say yes if you want to and no if it was just a sample.)

With the chart closed, the Starting Points screen will reappear like magic. If it doesn't just choose Show Starting Points from the File menu, and click the Word Processing icon. This will produce a blank word processing document (see Figure 9.7).

FIGURE 9.7

As simple as pie, click the text area and write your great American science fiction novel, or a letter.

In the previous Hour, you learned how to use the Save As dialog box. Now you will want to put it into practice. Before you progress with your word-processing document, choose Save As from the File menu and name it. As you continue to type, choose Save from the File menu every five or ten minutes to preserve what you have written on disk. That way, if something happens that causes your Mac to freeze (if you have one of those rolling power blackouts), you won't lose all your hard work.

All ready (see Figure 9.8)? Now it's time to spell check your document to make sure that "the" is spelled "the" and not "hte."

FIGURE 9.8

Here's the text of the "Great American Novel" written by the author and his son, ready for spell checking.

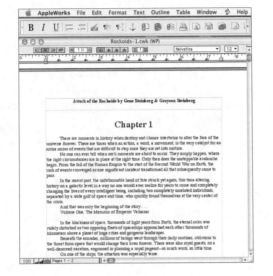

9

The spell-check feature in AppleWorks isn't limited to word processing. You can use it with the other AppleWorks components, too. That's why I'm describing it in extra detail here.

 Spell Checking Your Document

1. Choose Writing Tools from the Edit menu.
2. Select Check Document Spelling from the submenu, which opens the dialog box shown in Figure 9.9.

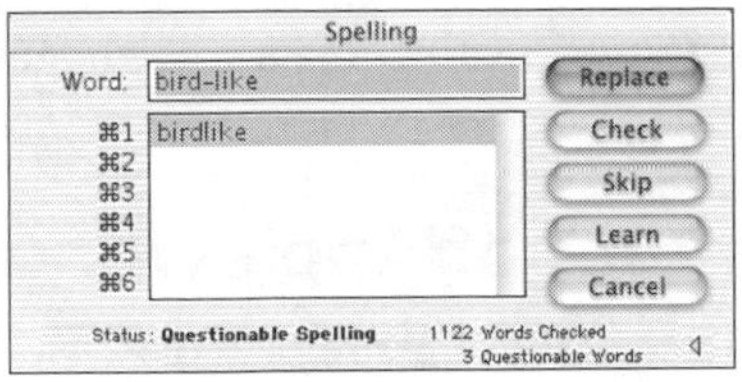

FIGURE 9.9

Check your spelling first before you print.

▲

Save mousing around and use the keyboard shortcut Cmd-= to open the spell-check screen.

Spell checking isn't perfect. It won't pick out a word that is spelled differently to convey a different meaning, or one that is incorrectly used. So you still want to proofread your document carefully before you print it. That way you can save trees and make sure that the hard copy is as good as it can be.

Here's what those little buttons in the spell-check window do:

- **Replace**: Substitutes the selected word for the one in your document.
- **Check**: Click here to find the spelling for the selected word.
- **Skip**: Don't bother checking this word; move to the next one.
- **Learn**: If the spelling is correct, but it's not in the program's dictionary, click this button to record it.
- **Cancel**: Click here to stop the spell check.

You can use the keystroke shortcut Cmd-. (that's Cmd-[period]) to stop your spell check. You'll be pleased to know that this very same shortcut is the standard command to halt an operation (though it doesn't work in all programs or all the time).

The numbered buttons at the left in Figure 9.9 enable you to quickly select a word to replace the one selected. Just type the Cmd key plus the number and click Replace to substitute the selected word.

Now that you've gotten a brief start in creating a fancy document in AppleWorks, we'll move on to the next module.

File Translation Features of AppleWorks

Do you have a document made in Microsoft Word or Excel? Do you want to read those documents, but you don't have either program around? Well, let me save you a few bucks. AppleWorks 6.2 and later can read and save files in a number of formats. This makes it ultra simple to get most or all the information from documents made in other programs.

Don't have AppleWorks 6.2? No problem. It's a free download to all AppleWorks 6 users from Apple's Web site (but check the online instructions about possibly having to do two updates if you're using 6.0.4 or earlier). If you have a version of AppleWorks older than version 6, or ClarisWorks, you'll need to buy the newest version from Apple or your favorite software dealer (regular USA resale price is $79.95).

9

What formats? Well, in addition to the Microsoft Word and Excel files, AppleWorks uses Apple's QuickTime to open image files in a variety of formats. So there's a great possibility that you'll be able to read many of the files you get that defy description. How do you know? Just give it a try; it only takes a minute to find out.

Translating Files in AppleWorks

▲ To Do

1. Locate the file you want to open and drag the file's icon and drop it right atop the icon for AppleWorks. If AppleWorks is already opened, you can drag it directly to the AppleWorks icon in the Dock (the application icon can be moved to the Dock even when it's not open). You will see a couple of progress bar windows, and then the document should open.

2. If the first step fails, make sure that AppleWorks is open; then go to the File menu and choose Open.

3. In the Open dialog box choose All Available from the File format pop-up menu (see Figure 9.10).

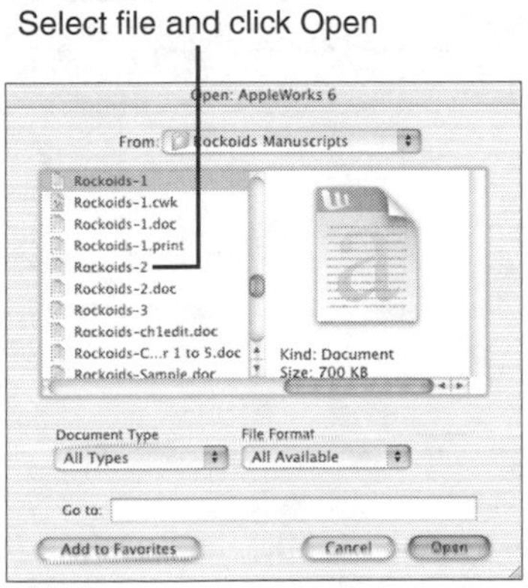

Select file and click Open

FIGURE 9.10

The files shown were all done Microsoft Word, but can be opened by AppleWorks 6.

▼   4. Locate and select the file you want to open.

5. If you want to save your AppleWorks document in a different format, choose Save As from the File menu.

6. Select the format from the File Format pop-up menu.

The file translation process is by no means perfect. It will handle most Word and Excel documents made in recent versions of these two programs (Word 97, Word 98, Excel 97, Excel 98, and later), but might not work with older versions. In addition, some special features of these programs might not carry over. One example is the Track Changes feature of Word (used by book authors and publishers and other groups working on a single document) won't translate properly. But all the text will be there.

Learning to Draw in AppleWorks

The phrase "a picture is worth a thousand words," is such a cliché that I hesitate to use it. Better to say that you don't have to be an artist to do a creditable job of drawing pictures with your computer.

Let's begin by creating a new document, just as shown way back there in Figure 9.2. But this time, you'll choose the fourth icon, Drawing, which will produce the screen shown in Figure 9.11.

FIGURE 9.11

This is your canvas for your homegrown artwork.

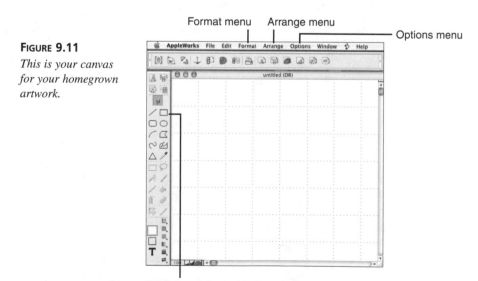

Click one of the tool icons to begin

You'll notice the menu bar changed when you went to the AppleWorks draw module. Feel free to look over the new set of commands and try them out.

Don't worry if you can't draw a straight line with pen and ink; I have trouble with that also (and please don't say anything about my handwriting). Drawing illustrations on a computer is different in many ways. For example, making simple shapes is easy because the basic tools require just a click and a drag.

I don't want to mislead you about doing computer art. Doing simple drawings might seem very easy, but complex artwork, whether on a computer or an ordinary canvas, requires imagination, talent, and training. But you can certainly get by with the basics. In addition, AppleWorks offers some packaged artwork that you can adapt to your needs. Click the Templates or Web tabs of the AppleWorks Starting Points screen for more choices.

Before you begin, take a look at the AppleWorks bag of tricks, the toolbar; there's not a screwdriver or wrench in the bunch. But take a look at Figure 9.12, and you'll see what that toolbar can do for you. Don't concern yourself about the tools that are grayed out; they are used strictly for the AppleWorks Paint module.

FIGURE 9.12

Click a tool icon to activate it.

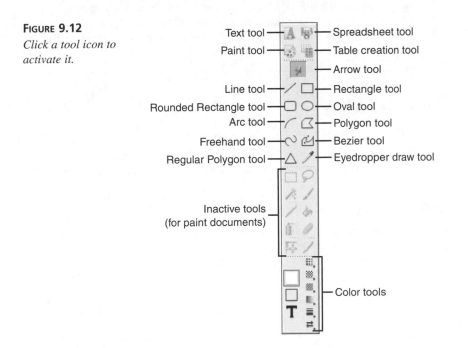

Not sure what a tool does? Just hold the mouse cursor above the tool and a label will appear showing what the tool is used for and how to apply it.

I know that you're anxious to start, but I just want to add a couple of bits of information about the pieces of artwork that you're going to create:

- Each element of your artwork is called an *object.*
- When you draw one object atop another, it's stacked, like putting sheets of paper atop a desk (graphic artists call it layers). To switch the stacking order (to get at something underneath), you use the commands in the Arrange menu, such as Move Forward, Move Backward, and so on.
- You can size up objects as you desire on your computer's screen, but use the Object Size command in the Options menu to specify them exactly.
- To change the thickness of a rule or border, use the little tool with the stacked rectangles on it as previously shown in Figure 9.12.

You can open a big floating color palette this way: Click a color tool in the toolbar and drag it away from the toolbar. Presto! You have a floating palette. To choose a color, just click it, and then click the object on which you want to insert the color. Just click the close button at the upper left of the palette to send it away.

Creating a Drawing

▼ To Do

1. Click the rectangle tool to select it.
2. Then click the blank canvas shown back in Figure 9.12 and drag the mouse to the right. You'll see a small rectangle, getting larger as you continue to drag it to the right.
3. To make the rectangle longer, drag it downward.
4. When it's the size you want, release the mouse button. See Figure 9.13 for the result.

▼

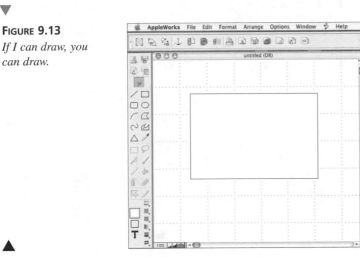

FIGURE 9.13
If I can draw, you can draw.

After your object is drawn, you can click it and move it around your screen. When the object is selected, you'll see little dark squares at each corner. If it's not selected, just click the arrow tool (shown back in Figure 9.12). Then click the object itself to move it where you want.

> When drawing a shape, hold down the Shift key to keep it in proportion. This makes a perfect circle or square, depending on the tool you're using.

Using the Paint Module

After you've become accustomed to drawing in AppleWorks, you'll want to try another component of the program, one that enables you to extend your drawing abilities. The next module enables you to add color and various shading effects to your artwork. So let's return to the Starting Points New Document window; now choose the Painting icon, which produces the screen shown in Figure 9.14

Okay, it's very close to the drawing module, but no cigar. There are a few differences, such as the addition of the Transform menu, which adds a set of commands to manipulate your illustrations.

The other is the toolbar (see Figure 9.15), which resembles the drawing toolbar, but adds a few extras, the very tools that were grayed out in the drawing toolbar.

Transform

Format menu   Options menu

FIGURE 9.14

A painting adds color and style to your drawings.

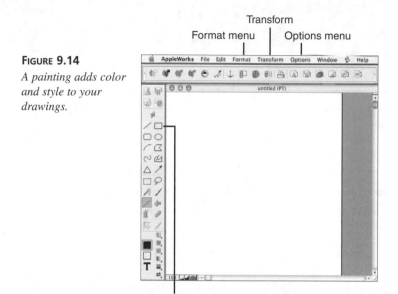

Click one of the tool icons to begin

FIGURE 9.15

There are some extra tools in the AppleWorks paint component.

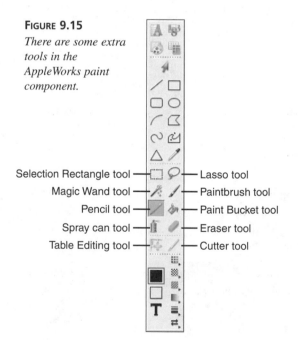

Selection Rectangle tool ——   —— Lasso tool

Magic Wand tool ——   —— Paintbrush tool

Pencil tool ——   —— Paint Bucket tool

Spray can tool ——   —— Eraser tool

Table Editing tool ——   —— Cutter tool

The new tools do precisely what their labels say they do. You can use the pencil tool to perform some of the same functions as a regular pencil, although it takes a little while to make your mouse act like one. The eraser tool can be used to wipe out the element you drag it over.

To see the difference between the drawing and paint functions, first make a rectangle just as you did in the previous section. The result, shown in Figure 9.16, shows a big difference.

FIGURE 9.16

A painting adds some color to your drawings.

This rectangle is filled with black. To change the color, just click one of the color tools before you make your drawing. You can also insert elements of color by using the paintbrush tool.

The possibilities are almost endless.

Creating a Spreadsheet

The AppleWorks spreadsheet component enables you to track financial information and prepare business reports and charts. Let's do one and see how easy it is to set up.

First, open your Starting Points window and click the Spreadsheet icon.

As you see, your AppleWorks spreadsheet document somewhat resembles graph paper (Figure 9.17).

FIGURE 9.17

Enter your financial information here.

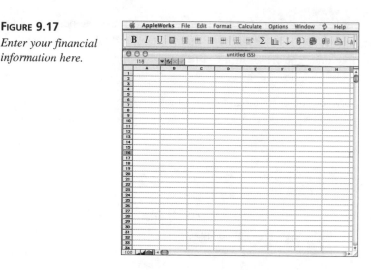

Here are the components you'll be working with:

- **Cells**: A cell is the compartment in which a bit of information is placed. Each rectangle shown in Figure 9.17 is another cell, and AppleWorks enables you to work with thousands of them.
- **Grids**: The dotted lines between the cells are grid lines.
- **Rows**: The horizontal lineup of cells is called a row.
- **Columns**: The vertical lineup of cells is called a column.
- **Headings**: The letters across the top of the spreadsheet are column headings. The numbers at the left are row headings.

> When you make a printout of your spreadsheet, you have the option to remove the headings and grid lines. When you open the print dialog box, simply choose AppleWorks 6 from the pop-up menu labeled Copies & Pages, and you'll be able to uncheck various options so they don't appear in the printouts.

Creating a Spreadsheet

▼ To Do

1. Click the first cell in your spreadsheet to select it.
2. Click the text entry field above the column levels to enter your information.
3. After entering the information, press the Tab key on your computer's keyboard to move to the next horizontal cell. Press the Return key to move to the cell right below it.

4. When you're finished entering your horizontal numbers, click the first cell in the second row.

5. Click the text entry field to insert your information.

> If your spreadsheet cell is too narrow just put your mouse between any two columns. The mouse cursor will change to a horizontal line with an arrow at each end. Click and drag the mouse to the right to make the cell at the left larger. You can do the same trick between rows.

9

After you've entered all your data, here are some of the things you can do with it:

- **Calculate the Math**: Check the calculate menu for the various choices.
- **Decorate It**: Use the options in the format menu to make it look the way you want.
- **Make a Chart**: This setting is available from the Options menu. You have a choice of pie charts, scatter charts, and more. Check out Figure 9.18 for a sample.

FIGURE 9.18
This chart is built from a few rows and columns of numbers.

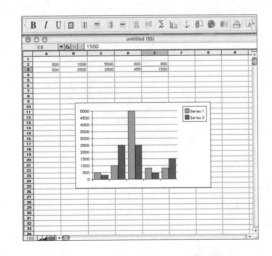

> Whenever you change the figures in your spreadsheet, the chart will automatically update itself to reflect those changes. Way cool!

AppleWorks 6's Database Module: Your Computerized Rolodex File

I used to keep information about my business contacts on index cards, and I used a typewriter to update the entries. (Now this dates me, I suppose.) With AppleWorks, you can create your personal index card file with your computer, using the database component. And you don't just have a set of cards (or records).

You can do lots of interesting stuff with them, such as

- **Sorting**: You can organize your records by date, name, location, and so on.
- **Mailing Labels**: You can set up and print out labels for business promotions, or to send out your club newsletter.
- **Invoices**: You can use the information to send bills to your clients.

To get started with your interactive Rolodex file, you need to make a new database document. Just invoke that Starting Points screen and then choose the Database icon. This opens a new database document window and one labeled Define Database Fields (see Figure 9.19).

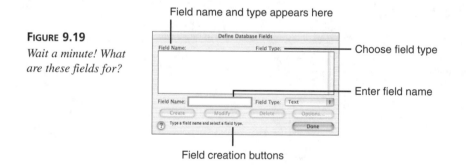

Field name and type appears here

FIGURE 9.19
Wait a minute! What are these fields for?

Choose field type

Enter field name

Field creation buttons

To create your little Rolodex file, you need to first tell AppleWorks what sort of information is going to appear on the index card. We'll start with a simple list of names. Here's how it's done:

Creating a Database

1. Choose Name from the Field Type pop-up menu.
2. Type **First Name** as the Field Name.
3. Click the Create button. You'll see the label and type of field entered on the list.
4. Type **Last Name** as the second Field Name.

5. Click the Create button again. This adds the second field to the list (see Figure 9.20). The Options button opens a list of choices for a particular field, such as whether a name is automatically entered in the field, whether a blank entry is allowed and whether duplicate entries are acceptable.

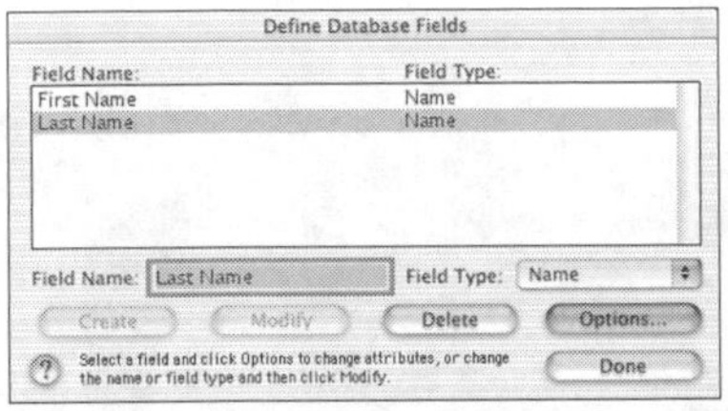

FIGURE 9.20
This listing shows two fields to enter first and last name.

9

6. When you're finished, click Done to create your simple index card. See Figure 9.21 for the result.

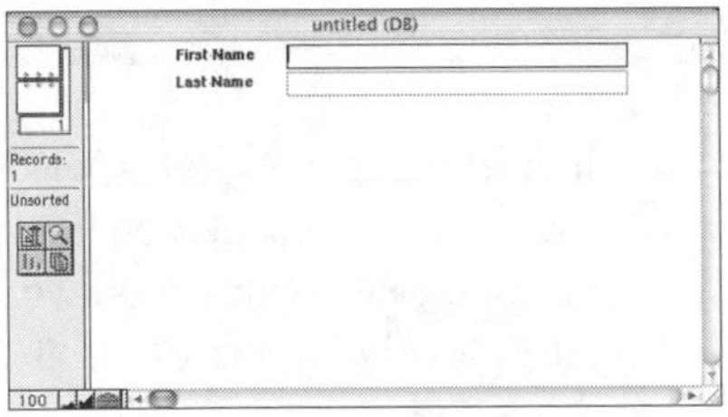

FIGURE 9.21
There you have it the beginnings of your address book.

To change the design of your database, simply choose Layout from the Layout menu. Then you can click and drag elements around as you prefer.

This is just the beginning of what you can do with your database. There are a wide variety of setups you can make for your records. And a single set of records can be used for a number of purposes, from that address book, to complete business reports, along with a chart or two from your spreadsheet to enhance the appearance.

Creating a Slide Show

The final component of AppleWorks looks almost the same as the drawing module, with one significant difference. There's also a Control palette that enables you set up separate drawings to run in sequence. This is the Presentation module, which enables you create simple slide shows.

You can use text, pictures, or any combination of the tools (including pictures you've brought over to your iMac courtesy of your scanner) to make a business presentation or even a home slide show (see Figure 9.22).

The Presentation module is, like all other components of AppleWorks, available via the Starting Points palette. After you open a blank presentation document, you can add text and elements the same as in a document created with the drawing module. Adding a slide is a simple matter of clicking the plus sign in the Controls palette. In a few moments, your slide show will be ready to roll.

The Sum of the Parts

You can share data between components in AppleWorks. You'll notice, for example, that the ever-present toolbar (shown back in Figure 9.12) has a spreadsheet tool you can use to insert tables in all sorts of documents. In addition, you can use the program's Insert feature (available from the File menu) to bring the contents of one document into another. That way you can spruce up your documents with illustrations you make your-self or with photos that you bring into your iMac with a scanner. I'll cover scanners and other devices you can add to your computer in Hour 20, "Adding More Goodies to Your iMac."

Summary

The great thing about AppleWorks is not just that it rolls a number of software packages into one program, or even that it's easy to use. The fact is that AppleWorks gets rave reviews from the computing magazines because it does so many things so well.

In the next lesson, I'll cover one of the premiere Mac financial management programs, Quicken 2002.

Q&A

Q **Something is wrong. The version of AppleWorks I have doesn't look anything like the one you have. For one thing, there's no Starting Points feature. How do I fix it?**

A Maybe you need to upgrade to AppleWorks 6. To find out, click the icon for AppleWorks, and choose Show Info from the Finder's File menu. This will open a little screen that displays the version number you have. If it's not AppleWorks 6, you'll need to order a copy from your Apple dealer. After you buy and install the new version, you'll want to go to Apple's Web site (`http://www.apple.com/software/`) and look for the latest AppleWorks updates among the list of updates at the right side of the screen.

When you locate the title, click the link and follow the information screens about updating your version of AppleWorks to the Mac OS X version. After you upgrade, you will be using the very same version I used when I wrote this book.

Q **When I launch AppleWorks, I don't see the New Document or the Starting Points dialog boxes. Where are they?**

A No doubt somewhere along the line you (or someone using your computer) has changed the application's preference setting. When you choose the Preferences command from the AppleWorks application menu, there are a number of settings you can make to the program. Choose General from the submenu that appears to the right. At the left of the dialog box, is a list of options under the label On Startup, Show and here's where you can decide whether to display the Starting Points dialog box and what the default new application you make will be.

The option you pick depends on your work habits. One specific setting isn't necessarily better than another.

If you don't see anything on your screen, just choose New from the File menu and specify the kind of document you want to create from the submenu.

Q **I'm already using another integrated program, Microsoft Works. Is there any reason to switch?**

A I suggest caution. Microsoft Works was never updated for the latest version of the Classic Mac Operating System and certainly not for Mac OS X. Although it's possible to use many older applications in the Classic environment with good performance, you might want to consider changing.

Because you already have AppleWorks on your iMac (even if it's an older version), it might be time to consider a switch. If this helps, you can read your Works documents in the latest version of AppleWorks if you first convert them to Microsoft Word or Excel format in that program's Save As dialog box. The reason? AppleWorks includes a set of MacLink Plus translators from DataViz that handles the conversion process. It's not perfect in retaining special document formats, but at least you'll get all the data or text from the original document. You'll want to refer to the instructions earlier in this chapter on how to use this feature.

Q Just one more question: Where's the manual?

A A friend used to say to me, "Manuals? Manuals? I don't need no ------- manuals." Sounds like a line from a movie. Anyway, there really is an AppleWorks User's Guide file inside the AppleWorks folder on your computer. Just look for a folder called AppleWorks Extras, and then one inside that called documentation. Two documents, AppleWorks Getting Started, and AppleWorks Install Manual are provided. The two files are in PDF format. Just double-click the documents and you'll see them open in a compatible program (such as Mac OS X's Preview).

After the document has been opened, you can use the Print command from the File menu to have a regular printed version. And to think, they once said we wouldn't need paper. Just make sure your printer has enough for the entire document.

Q Tell me the truth: Is AppleWorks 6 Better than Microsoft Office?

A That depends on what you want to do with these programs. The capability of AppleWorks to translate Word and Excel files enables you to share documents with users of those two programs with most formatting intact. In addition, AppleWorks offers a reasonably large set of features that should than meet the needs of many users.

But Microsoft Office is an extremely powerful software suite. The Mac OS X version looks just great and will do most anything you might want of word processor, spreadsheet, and presentation applications. Word, for example, is tailor made for workgroups, where many eyes might need to read and make changes or comments on a single document. There's a Track Changes feature that shows you who made a change and when. Just about every book I've written is done this way, and it makes the editing process go a whole lot smoother.

There's also another component of Office, Entourage, a terrific email and contact manager, and that's something for which there's no equivalent in AppleWorks.

Then again, AppleWorks came free with your iMac, so you have plenty of time to look it over and see whether it does what you want, or whether what you really need is Office. I highly recommend both packages; it just depends on your particular requirements.

Managing Your Bucks with Quicken 2002 Deluxe

In this day and age, financial transactions have taken on a new level of complexity. Of course, money management has always been difficult. It's not just reconciling a checkbook or two. You have to keep track of monthly bills, figure out budgets, track your financial worth, and decide whether an investment is a good idea.

Even if you're just a working stiff like me, you need more accurate tools than ever to keep up with the world of personal finance.

In this lesson, I'll introduce you to a program that works not only with your personal finances, but also with small businesses. It's another great program included with your iMac—Quicken 2002 Deluxe.

In this lesson, you'll discover

- How to set up your own checkbook on your iMac
- How to track your monthly expenses
- How to get started with financial planning
- How to make reports and charts showing your financial picture
- The advantages of online banking

Getting Started with Quicken 2002 Deluxe

Quicken 2002 Deluxe begins with a simple checkbook and adds to that the capability of keeping a wide range of financial records. You can even keep both business and personal accounts, check your investments portfolio, and use your Internet service to track your finances while online.

Here's a brief look at the things you can do with Quicken 2002 Deluxe:

> Have a Classic iMac? Don't be concerned if your iMac came with either Quicken 98 Deluxe or Quicken 2001 Deluxe. Although the look of this application changed when it was brought over to Mac OS X, most of the features I'm describing will apply to all these versions. You can stick with what you have, or just contact the publisher, Intuit, about buying an upgrade. You can get information on the upgrade from the publisher's Web site at http://www.intuit.com.

- **Bank accounts**: Manage your personal and business checking accounts, and automatically reconcile your checks as they are written. You can also print checks if you have a printer attached to your computer.
- **Investment tracking**: Whether it's one stock or a large portfolio, Quicken 2002 Deluxe helps you keep tabs on all your investments. You can track transactions, compare market values, and see just how much profit you've earned. This particular version also enables you to download your transactions from many online stockbrokers, so you can make sure your financial data is absolutely up to date.
- **Track your net worth**: Keep a complete record of all your debts and assets. You can record loan transactions, real estate loans, personal possessions, and more.

- **Financial planning**: This feature isn't just for your business. You can use Quicken 2002 Deluxe to examine your personal finances, help you figure out where your money is going, assist you in making plans for the future, and track your possible tax liabilities.

- **Online banking**: If your financial institution supports this feature, you can log on to your Internet account and use Quicken 2002 Deluxe to handle your transactions.

> Intuit, publisher of Quicken 2002 Deluxe, also publishes a tax preparation program called TurboTax (originally it was called MacInTax, but the publisher decided to keep names consistent between the Mac OS and Windows platforms), which can help you prepare your return with professional results. It can also read your financial information from Quicken 2002 Deluxe to simplify the usually complex process of entering your critical data.

10

- **Reports and charts**: You can use Quicken 2002 Deluxe to make detailed reports and charts to give you a far-ranging picture of the present status of your finances, and how things might change in the future if you try different approaches.

> If others have access to your computer, you might want to use Mac OS X's multiple users feature. You'll want to create separate user accounts for others who might access your iMac. This way, after you log out, they can't read your personal documents. I'll cover the subject of security in more detail in Hour 21, "Backup, Backup, Backup...How to Protect Your Files."

Managing Your Bank Account

Because most of you will probably use a program such as Quicken 2002 Deluxe to handle your checkbook, I'll begin with that feature.

Getting Started with Quicken

▼ To Do

1. Locate the Quicken application inside the Quicken folder on your computer (it should be in the Applications folder).

2. Double-click the Quicken 2002 Deluxe folder to launch it. The first time it opens you'll be asked to personalize your copy. Enter your name in the text field and click the OK button.

3. After you've personalized the program, you'll see a prompt to register Quicken 2002 Deluxe (see Figure 10.1).

▼

FIGURE 10.1

Choose your registration option.

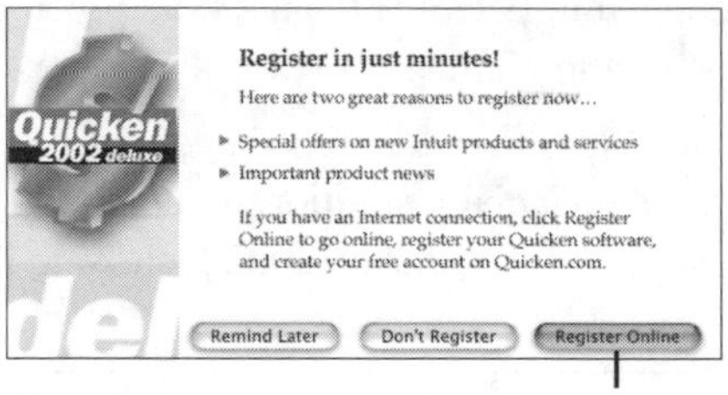

Choose Register Online if you have an Internet account

I recommend that you register Quicken 2002 Deluxe as soon as you can. That way you can contact the publisher for support if you run into a problem using the program.

4. After you've registered Quicken 2002 Deluxe, you'll tell the program whether you're upgrading or setting up your initial account (see Figure 10.2). Assuming you're using Quicken for the first time, click the New User button to continue.

FIGURE 10.2

Specify New User to get going.

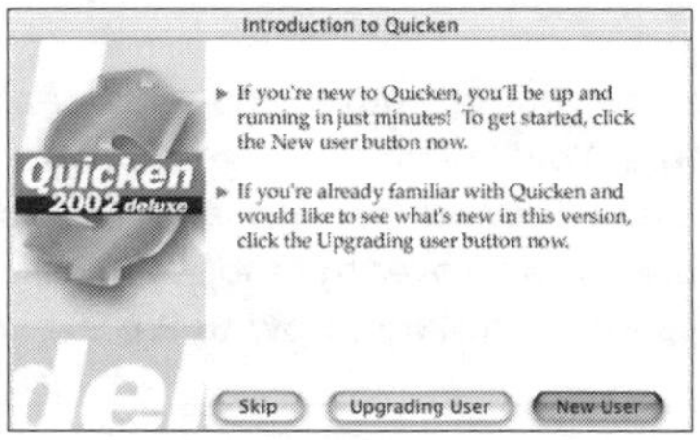

5. Now the publishers of Quicken will help guide you the rest of the way, with the Quicken Assistant (see Figure 10.3).

FIGURE 10.3

Are you a new Quicken user?

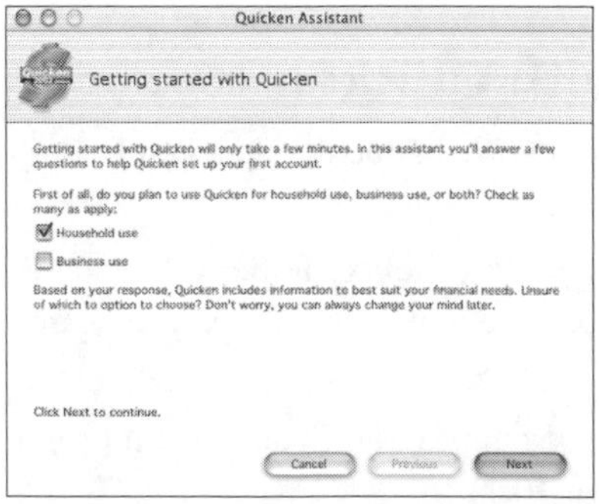

If you're updating from a previous version of Quicken click Upgrading User, and the program's assistant will take you the rest of the way. If your previous version of Quicken was installed on another Mac you'll have to copy the file to your new iMac, double-click the file to launch Quicken Deluxe 2002, and then continue the upgrade process. Hour 20, "Adding More Goodies to Your iMac," contains information on how you can add extra drives to copy the data over (or use your iMac's Ethernet port if your other Mac has one, to transfer the files via file sharing).

6. Your first step is to specify the type of account you want to create. You can make an account for Home or Business use (we'll use Home for this lesson). Click Next to continue. The first time you click an option, Quicken will create a file called Quicken Data, where all your financial information will be stored for you in a summary file called Quicken Insights. That, along with your personal account window, will appear on your Mac behind the Assistant.

None of your choices are set in stone. Click Previous to review a setting, and Next to go on. Or just click Cancel if you prefer to finish later.

7. Click and read a couple of information screens and you'll soon come to a screen labeled Choose an account type. Click the pop-up menu and make your selection, as shown in Figure 10.4. Let's pick Bank because that's the most common account that'll be used with Quicken 2002 Deluxe. Click Next.

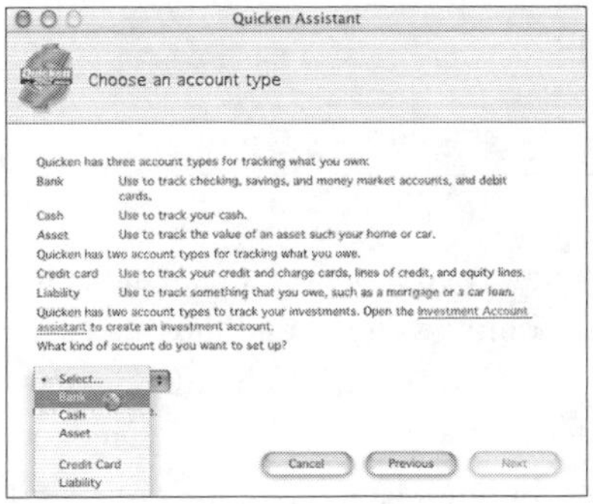

FIGURE 10.4
Select the kind of account you want to configure?

> If you're going to bring over the transactions from your existing checking account, you'll want to dig out your checkbook for the remainder of the setup process.

8. On the next Quicken Assistant screen, you'll be asked to give your account a name. The easiest method here is to use the same name as you use for your account (such as Gene Steinberg or Gene or Barbara Steinberg, which would include a joint account with my wife). Click Next.

> If the letters stop entering, it means you've made the account name too long. Just shorten it.

9. On this setup screen enter the date and balance of your last bank statement, and then click Next.

10. All ready? Review your settings on the Create the account screen (see Figure 10.5), then click Go Ahead to set up your account with the present balance.

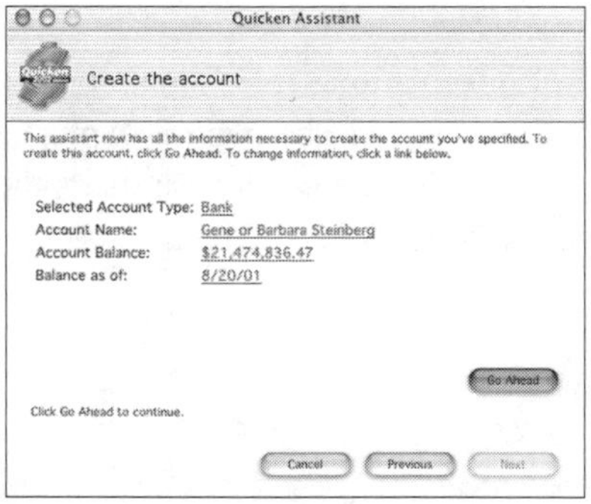

FIGURE **10.5**

No folks, this isn't my real account balance. I'm just dreaming!

11. On the next screen, you have two more options. One is to configure your account to work with your bank's online system, and the other is to set up another account category. Click one choice or the other or click OK to exit the Assistant and get on with the business of entering transactions in your Quicken 2002 checkbook.

12. To actually access the account register, click the Quicken Data: Accounts screen, and select your account.

13. Click Open to open the check register (see Figure 10.6). From here just click a text field under a category to enter information. The arrows signify a pop-up menu with additional choices.

Click the pop-up menus for entry shortcuts

FIGURE 10.6

Click the pop-up menus for entry shortcuts.

Click Record to store the information

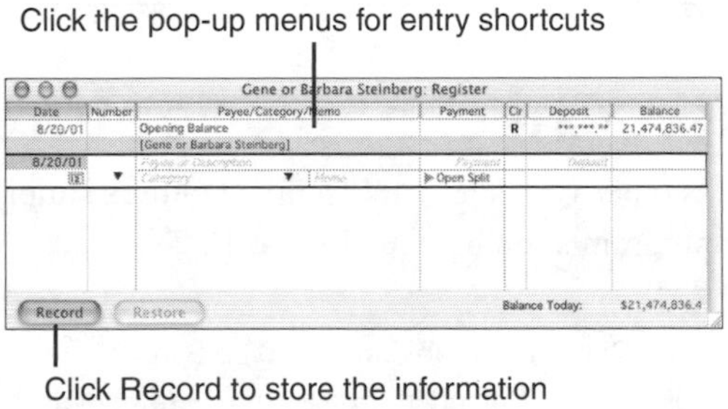

14. Click Record to store the information

You must click the Record button to store a transaction before you can move on to the next one.

15. For better organization you can click the pop-up menus and assign a category such as Auto Insurance, Home Repair, and so forth, to a transaction.

Any time you enter a payee's name for the first time without assigning it to a category, Quicken will give you one of two options: a Go Back option to pick a category, or a Record Without option to continue without the category.

16. Continue to enter your transactions until your account register is finished. Notice that your balance is adjusted automatically every time you Record a new transaction. You can put away that calculator. Reconciling your checkbook couldn't be easier.

> Press the plus key (+) in the Number field to enter the next consecutive check number. You can also use that keystroke in a date field to move to the next dates or the minus (–) key to move to previous dates. Pressing it will return you to today's date.

Other Quicken Checkbook Features

You can easily access other Quicken 2002 Deluxe features simply by clicking the appropriate labels on the program's toolbar (see Figure 10.7).

FIGURE 10.7
These are the tools for Quicken's Banking category.

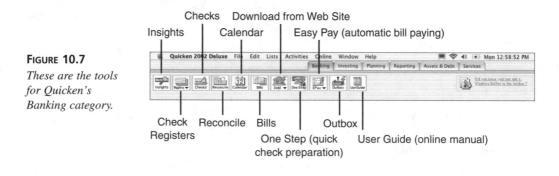

> What are all those tabs for? Well, rather than make a toolbar that's long and complex, Quicken 2002 divides it all into categories. Just click a tab and you'll see the tools that apply.

Writing a Check

Not only can you keep a checkbook register with Quicken 2002 Deluxe, you can write checks, too. All you need is a set of special checks from Intuit and a printer to make checks that look as good as those made by large companies.

Writing a Check with Quicken

1. Click the Check icon on Quicken 2002 Deluxe's program toolbar, which opens the blank check screen shown in Figure 10.8.

Click a text field to enter the information

FIGURE 10.8

Here's a blank check, ready for your information.

Click the pop-up menu to choose the category

When you write a check in Quicken 2002 Deluxe, the information is automatically recorded on your account register. No more need for double entries.

10

2. Click a text entry field to enter the payee and the amount. Use the Tab key to move through the fields.

Quicken 2002 Deluxe will automatically insert the information from the last transaction with the same payee to save you time, but you can change it if necessary.

3. Click Record to store the transaction and open another blank check screen.

4. Close the Write Checks window to finish writing checks.

You can manage your finances in many ways with Quicken 2002 Deluxe. For example, some folks prefer to write checks directly from the check register.

5. After your checks are written you can use the Print Checks command in the File menu to get your completed check.

> Quicken 2002 Deluxe includes a special feature, Billminder, which gives you an onscreen reminder about payments that are due. To set it up, choose Preferences from the application menu and scroll through the list to the Billminder option.

Tracking Your Investment Portfolio

In addition to managing your checkbook, Quicken 2002 Deluxe can also keep tabs on your investment portfolio. That way you can track whether the money you've spent on those investments is really helping your bottom line, or reducing it.

To set up a financial portfolio in Quicken 2002 Deluxe, first click the Investing tab on the program's toolbar (again refer to Figure 9.7). You'll see some new button options across the top; click the one labeled Portfolio (see Figure 10.9).

Enter current security information here
Portfolio
Customize
Record
Detail
Add Security
Click Customize to add more account categories

FIGURE 10.9
Enter your investment accounts in this register.

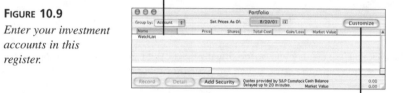

After you've typed all the information, Quicken 2002 Deluxe will dial up your Internet service and receive the latest price information (if you're using an "always on" service, such as cable or DSL, the site will be accessed immediately). That way you can easily see where your money is going or how much you've profited from the investment.

Checking Your Net Worth

After you've set up your checkbook and investment portfolio, you'll want to consider setting up a complete financial statement. Whether you just want to see how much money you have, or you need the information for a business or personal loan, you'll find that Quicken 2002 Deluxe can help guide you through the rough spots of recording the information in short order.

Setting Up Your Net Worth Statement

▼ To Do

1. Click the Assets & Debt tab on the Quicken 2002 Deluxe program toolbar (it's second from the right).

2. This will change the icons at the top. Choose Insights, which will open the screen showing all your existing Quicken account summaries.

3. Now click Customize and you'll see the Customize Insights screen (see Figure 10.10).

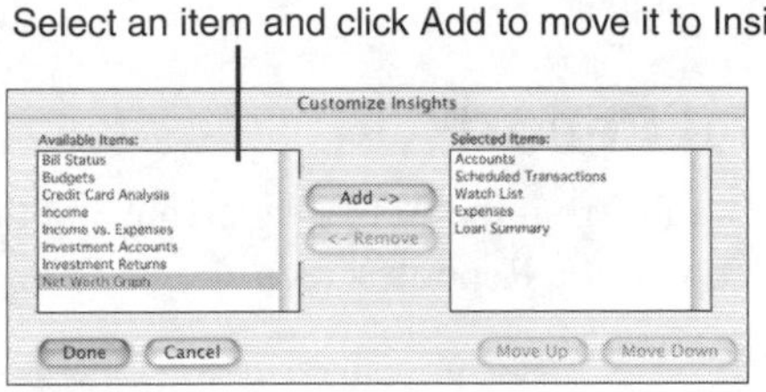

Select an item and click Add to move it to Insights

FIGURE 10.10

You can add several categories to your Insights report here.

10

4. Click the Net Worth Graphic to select it, and then Add to include it in your Insights summary.

5. All ready? Click Done to proceed and update Insights.

6. Your net worth will be automatically calculated by Quicken (see Figure 10.11), depending on the information you've entered in the various information categories.

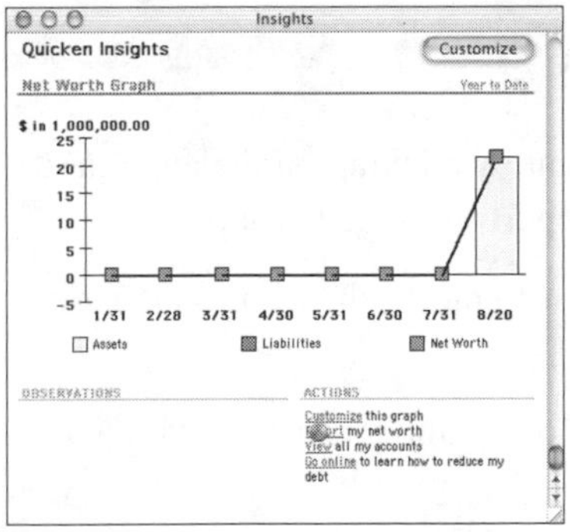

FIGURE 10.11

Quicken automatically updates your net worth depending on the data you enter into the program.

To see a table of your net worth rather than a graphic, just click Report at the bottom part of the Insights chart for your net worth. Piece of cake!

When you're done you'll be able to view a graphic display of your financial picture and print a copy for your review or to hand over to your financial analyst.

Creating Financial Reports

Now that you've set up a checkbook, done your monthly payments, and tracked your investment portfolio and net worth, no doubt you'll want to see what all this means to you.

Quicken 2002 Deluxe can make a professional report and set of charts to show you your entire financial picture.

Creating Financial Reports

To Do

1. Choose Reports & Graphs from the Activities menu, and then select Reports from the submenu, which opens the Reports screen shown in Figure 10.12.

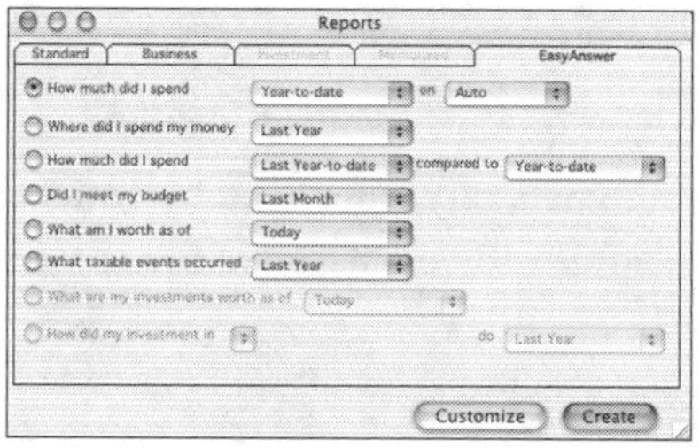

FIGURE 10.12

Tell Quicken what sort of financial report you want.

2. Select the items you want by clicking on the appropriate buttons, and then choose the timeframe for the report from the pop-up menus.

3. When you're finished customizing the information, click the Create button to make your report.

You can also create a professional caliber chart showing your financial information. To access this feature:

Creating a Financial Chart

To Do

1. Click Reports & Graphs from the Activities menu and select Graphics from the submenu, which opens the Graphs setup screen shown in Figure 10.13.

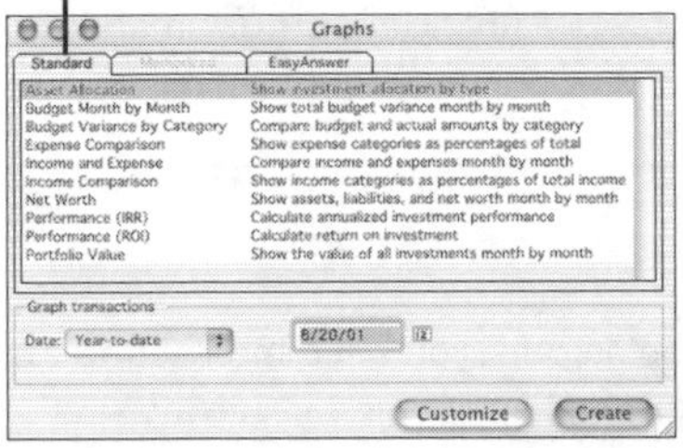

Click the tab at the top to change the setup option

FIGURE 10.13
Choose a Standard business graphic or the EasyAnswer variety.

2. Choose the range of information you want to provide in your graph.

3. When you're finished click Create to open the chart.

Your completed graph can be viewed on the screen or printed for later review. After a few hours of this, you'll feel like an expert.

10

> It's never a bad idea to have a backup copy of your financial data in case something goes wrong with the original file. To make one or more backups, choose Preferences from the Edit menu and scroll to the Save a Copy command.

Online Financial Transactions

More and more financial institutions have set up an online banking feature so you can handle your bank transactions without ever visiting a branch.

Online banking enables you to do the following:

- Update Quicken 2002 Deluxe with information received directly from your bank.
- Pay your bills electronically and regularly. No more envelopes, stamps, or checks getting lost in the mail. And no more past due statements from your creditors.
- Transfer funds between one account and another at the same bank.
- Get up-to-date account balances for your checking account and your credit accounts in seconds.
- Handle scheduled payments, such as a car payment or mortgage, automatically.

The online accounts you establish with financial information are encrypted. That way they are kept secure from prying eyes and potential thieves. You might want to contact a financial institution about their safety measures before you set up your online account there.

To set up an online account you need Internet access. Please check Hour 1, "Setting Up Your iMac," and Hour 4, "Getting on the Net," for information about how to get connected with an online service.

Summary

I don't want to pretend that I've done much more than scratch the surface of financial management possibilities you can explore with Quicken 2002 Deluxe. As you can see from the brief tour in this lesson, the program has a surprising array of features.

If you want to learn more about the program click the UserGuide icon in the toolbar, which will launch your online manual. Although some might prefer a printed manual, you can print out your own copy if you want to refer to some material later.

Q&A

Q I got the hang of writing my checks on my computer. But what do I do with checks that I write at my supermarket?

A I often wonder what it would be like if folks went and unpacked their computers and printers at the checkout counter (well, I guess it's not too difficult with an iBook, especially the newest model, which is so small). But all you have to do is write a check by hand and enter it in the Quicken 2002 Deluxe account register when you get home.

If you're printing your checks through Quicken 2002 Deluxe you can just prepare checks made out to the stores you're visiting, leaving the figures blank. Then you can reconcile your register later (but don't forget to do it).

Q You say I can use Quicken 2002 Deluxe to print checks. How's that done?

A Well, first you need a printer, and then you need to order checks from Quicken 2002 Deluxe's publisher, Intuit (or through one of the check vendors you see in the computing magazines). I'll tell you more about connecting your computer to a printer in Hour 17, "Now That I Wrote It, How Do I Print It."

Q I deleted Quicken 2002 Deluxe by mistake. Can I reinstall it without having to restore all my other software?

A It depends on the version you have. For most iMacs you'll find a separate CD for Quicken 2002 Deluxe in your iMac's accessory box or a copy on a CD labeled Applications. Either will have the installer application on it, so you can reinstall this program all by itself. It just requires double-clicking the installer icon, clicking a few buttons, and it will be done in short order. You'll have to restart your computer to complete the process, though.

Q What's "Deluxe " about Quicken 2002 Deluxe?

A The CD-ROM that comes with it. It contains additional financial information resources.

Q I have another computer here. I own the software, right? Why can't I install Quicken 2002 Deluxe on that one, too?

A When you purchase software, whether bundled with a computer or separately, you're not buying the software itself, but a license to use it. Most software licenses limit you to installing the program on a single computer and maybe making a backup copy for safekeeping.

Some programs enable you to install one copy on a desktop computer and another on a laptop, so long as both copies aren't being used at the same time. That would mean, if the license allows it, that you could install the same program on both an iMac and iBook.

The best thing to do is to read the software license that comes with the software to see what is covered. If you need to run more than one copy, you'll want to contact the publisher about additional software licenses. Usually, additional copies cost less than the first.

Q Help! I lost my Quicken data? What now?

A By default, Quicken automatically creates backup files of your financial data, bearing the clear identification "backup" in the file's name. This is one way to get around this problem, but the safest approach is to copy your important files to another storage device, such as a Zip drive, so you will always have another copy in the event something happens to the original. You'll learn more about the subject in Hour 21, "Backup, Backup, Backup…How to Protect Your Files."

Q Why can't I use Quicken at my bank's Web site?

A Unfortunately, some financial institutions design sites that are hostile to Macs. Some, such as Bank of America, offer you the opportunity to handle financial transactions direct from the Web site, which means you'll have to manually enter

10

the information in Quicken. If in doubt, contact your bank or Intuit's technical support for assistance. I'm not about to suggest you choose a more Mac-friendly financial institution, but be aware there might be problems integrating Quicken 2002 with such Web facilities.

HOUR 11

Faxing, Stickies, and Other Software

You'll find virtually unlimited prospects for creativity on your iMac. As you've seen in previous chapters, you can use it to connect to the Internet, do word processing, draw pictures, prepare financial reports, assemble a Rolodex file, manage your checkbook and investment portfolio, and figure out your net worth.

In this lesson, we'll look at some of the other programs that are packaged with your iMac.

Don't be surprised if the software you get in your iMac differs from what is described here. Apple might occasionally change the software package that ships with its consumer models. The flat-panel, for example, includes extra software for Mac OS X, including the version of FAXstf described in this chapter.

One of the programs you receive with your iMac can turn it into a fax machine, another program will show you how to create little sticky notes on your desktop to remind you of special events, and another will help you make simple documents without having to open a full-fledged word processor, such as AppleWorks.

In this lesson, you'll discover

- How to fax your documents without having to first make a printout
- How to put little sticky notes on your Mac's desktop
- How to read and create simple text documents

Getting Started with FAXstf X

If you've signed up with an Internet service or joined AOL, no doubt you've spent a little time learning how the modem inside your computer can open up a new world to you, a world filled with possibilities for communication.

That modem can do more than surf the Internet. It can double as a fax machine, using a clever program from a company known as Smith Micro, FAXstf.

There are actually two versions of FAXstf. One, FAXstf X, will work with your Mac OS X native programs. The other version of FAXstf, located in your Applications (Mac OS 9) folder, will work strictly with your Classic Mac OS software, but you can only run it after rebooting your iMac into the older operating system. Why? Well, that's partly a hardware limitation of Mac OS X, which prevents fax software from working in the Classic environment.

Here are a few of the things you can do with FAXstf. After this you might just want to ditch that old-fashioned fax machine:

- **Fax directly from any Mac OS X application**: Using a simple keyboard shortcut, you can call up FAXstf from within the program you're using, and then fax your documents directly to one or more recipients.

- **Assemble an address book**: You can store information about your personal and business contacts, making it easy to send them a fax when you need to. Because FAXstf uses the very same Address Book application supported by Apple's Mail application, you can use a single set of contacts for both faxing and email. What a time saver!

- **Receive and print faxes**: As long as your iMac is running, it can be set to receive faxes, just like that regular fax machine. The received fax can be viewed on the screen or printed.

- **Custom cover pages**: You can create a page that identifies you and your business and provides information about the fax that you're sending.

Installing FAXstf X

All right, where is it? The Mac OS X version of FAXstf X is available on new iMacs, but not installed. You'll find it in the Installers folder inside the Applications folder.

When you locate the installer, follow these steps:

Running the FAXstf Installer

1. Double-click the FAXstf X 10.0 Installer icon.

2. Click Continue on the first screen, accept the user license on the second, and click continue on the third.

3. When the main installation screen appears, click Install. Over the next minute or so, the software will be installed on your iMac.

4. Click the final prompt to quit the installer when the process is done. You won't have to restart your iMac to use FAXstf X.

Setting Up Your Modem

All right, it would be great if you could just send a fax and get going, but with many programs you have to do a few preliminaries. First, you have to add the fax driver to Mac OS X's Print Center software.

Configuring FAXstf X

1. Go to the Utilities folder and launch Print Center.

2. In the Printer List window, click Add Printer.

3. From the Printer List pop-up menu, locate and select FAXstf (see Figure 11.1).

▼

FIGURE 11.1

Choose FAXstf from the list.

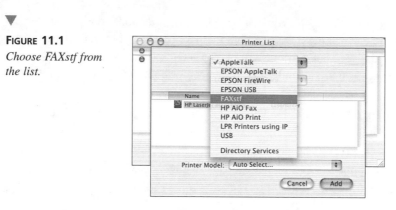

4. We're almost there, but not quite. Now select Apple Internal Modem in the list window and click Add.

> Print Center is a little peculiar about making your last selected printer or fax driver the default printer. So when you've added your modem, click the name of the printer you use most often in the Printer List, then choose Make Default from the Printers menu. Otherwise, the fax modem becomes your default printer.

▲   5. Quit Print Center. Now you're ready to create your cover page.

Sending Your First Fax

Before you send your first fax, you'll want to set up the cover pages for them. For FAXstf X, you'll be using Apple's Address Book application to store your personal address information.

Setting Up Your Personal Information

To Do ▼

1. Pay a visit to the FAXstf X folder, located inside your computer's Applications folder.

2. Double-click the Fax Browser application.

3. When Fax Browser opens, choose Preferences from the application window.

4. Under Identity, click the Address icon, which opens Apple's Address Book application.

5. If you haven't done so already, create your own vCard (contact listing) in Address Book by clicking on the New icon.

▼

▼

6. Enter your personal information, part of which will be used in the page header and cover page information for the faxes you send, just as I've done in Figure 11.2.

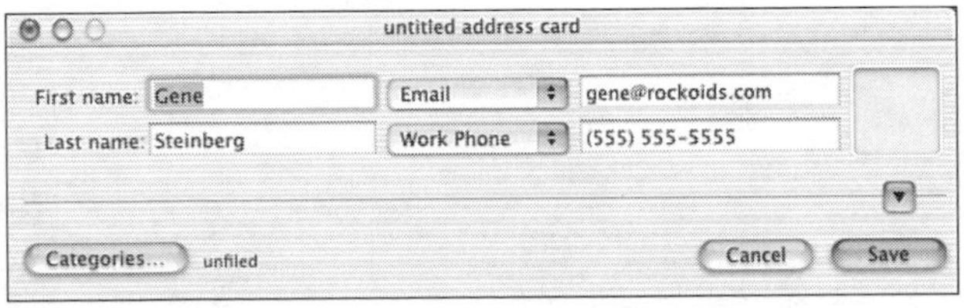

FIGURE 11.2

Click the down arrow at the right to enter your address and other information.

As you know, the Tab key is used to move from one text field in a dialog box to the next. To move to the previous text field, press Shift-Tab instead.

7. We're almost there. Click Save to store the entry and locate your vCard icon from the Address Book window and drag it to the tiny field located at the very top of the Identity window in the Fax Browser preference box.

▲   8. Click OK to store the settings.

Now you're ready to send your first fax. As a test, perhaps you can have a friend or business colleague who is willing to serve as guinea pig for your little experiment. You'll want to ask that person if he is willing to receive a fax, and then send one right back to you. Just be prepared to offer a lunch or dinner as payment for that person's time.

To get started, make sure you have an entry in Apple's Address Book application for the recipient of your fax and that the entry includes the fax number. Take your time; I'll be here when you're ready.

With the preliminaries out of the way, open up a word processing document you've made with AppleWorks (as described in Hour 9, "Teach Yourself AppleWorks"), as I've done in Figure 11.3.

If you haven't gotten around to writing a full-fledged document with any of your computer's software yet, you can open one of your Read Me files instead and fax that. Remember that this is only a test and you can always fax just one page of a document for your test or open a short document.

11

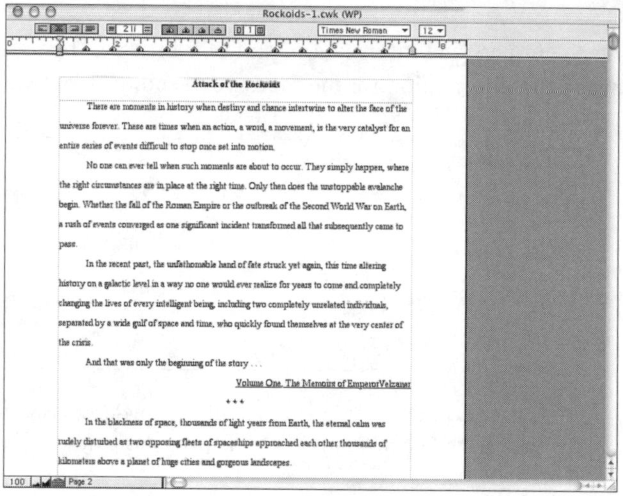

FIGURE **11.3**

This is the actual document I wrote in AppleWorks.

Sending a Fax

▼ To Do

1. With your document open, choose Print from the File menu.
2. Under the Printer category, choose Apple Internal Modem from the pop-up menu (see Figure 11.4).

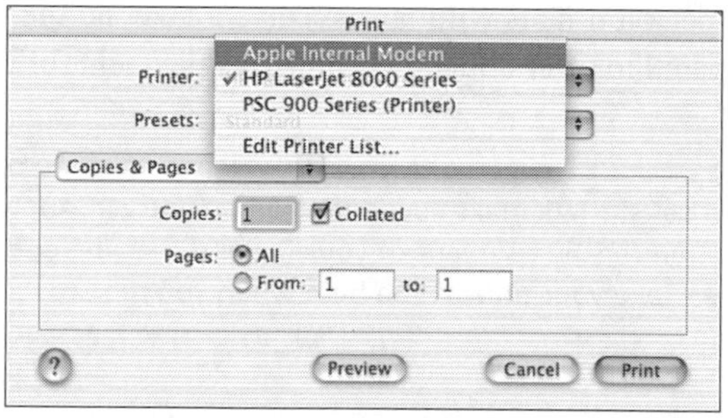

FIGURE **11.4**

Use this dialog box to begin the faxing process.

3. Click the printer options pop-up menu, the one that says Copies & Pages, and choose Addresses.
4. In the Addresses dialog box, click the Address Book icon, then locate and drag the vCard or contact icon of the recipient of the fax and drag it into the destinations or To: window (see Figure 11.5 for the result).

▼

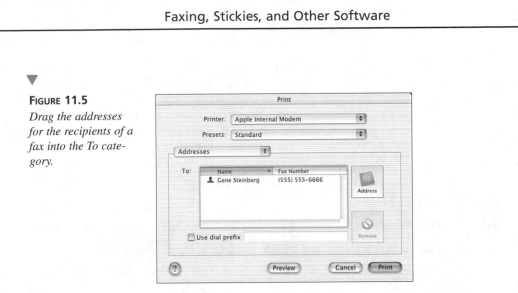

FIGURE 11.5

Drag the addresses for the recipients of a fax into the To category.

5. Repeat the previous step for each recipient of the fax or just select and drag several addresses at once.

6. To change the quality of the fax, choose Fax Quality from the printer options menu. The normal setting is Standard, but you can use Fine if you want to send a fax with sharper text and pictures.

7. If you want to include a cover page, pick Cover Page from the printer options pop-up menu.

8. In the Cover Note field, enter a short note about the fax, if this is necessary (you can skip this step if you want). Figure 11.6 has an example of a typical note you might send to a business contact.

FIGURE 11.6

If you want, you can include a note on your cover page to help direct a fax to its proper source or identify what it contains.

| Print |
| Printer: Apple Internal Modem |
| Presets: Standard |
| Cover Page |
| ☑ Include Cover Page |
| Cover Note: This is the fax to end all faxes, a fax that exists out of time and space and will change your life forever for the better. |
| Preview   Cancel   Print |

9. To speed the fax on its way, click Print. Over the next moment, your fax document will be converted to a file, then your modem will dial the recipient's fax machine, after which your fax will be sent.

11

▼

> FAXstf X has a few limitations, which might be addressed by the time you read this book. For example, if the fax doesn't reach its destination, there's no automatic redial; you'll have to redo the process.

▲

Receiving a Fax

To receive faxes automatically, you'll need to configure FAXstf to run in receive mode.

1. Go to the FAXstf X folder, and launch the Modem Center application.

2. In the Modem Center window, click the Setup button to open the preferences dialogs.

3. In the category labeled Answer after, put in a number from 1 to 9 (see Figure 11.7); the default setting, 0, tells the program not to receive faxes automatically. A good rule of thumb is 2 rings. If the number is shared with your telephone, you might want to set it to 4 rings, to give you a chance to answer the phone for a voice communication.

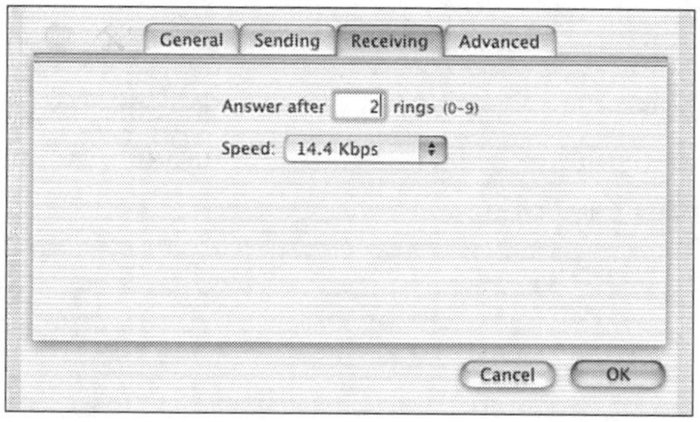

FIGURE 11.7

Enter the number of rings before the fax is answered.

| General | Sending | Receiving | Advanced |

Answer after [2] rings (0-9)

Speed: [14.4 Kbps ▼]

[Cancel] [OK]

▲   4. Click OK and quit Modem Center.

When FAXstf X detects a call Modem Center will be opened automatically and show the progress of your fax transmission. To see the fax you've received, launch Fax Browser and click In Box in the Trays window.

Similar to Apple's Mail application, whose interface Fax Browser resembles, unread faxes will be flagged with a blue button. Click the title of the fax to see its contents in the lower window.

To print a fax, simply choose Print from the file menu and click the Print command.

Making Sticky Notes on Your iMac

One of the most interesting Mac software utilities is the outgrowth of a little program that's been present for years. Are you a fan of sticky notes, those little sheets of paper with light adhesive at the top? I've been to homes and offices were the little notes are found on refrigerators, closets, and around the edges of computer monitors.

There is yet another way to make those sticky notes without having to worry about clutter or wasting trees. It's a program that has been with the Mac for years, called Stickies (see Figure 11.8).

FIGURE 11.8

Put little notes on your iMac as reminders or places to store text for reuse.

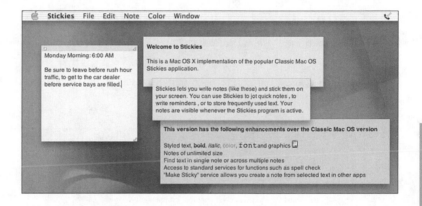

Setting Up Stickies

1. Go to the Application folder and double-click Stickies.
2. To create your first note, click the File menu and choose New Note (see Figure 11.9).

To Do

FIGURE 11.9

Begin a new note from here.

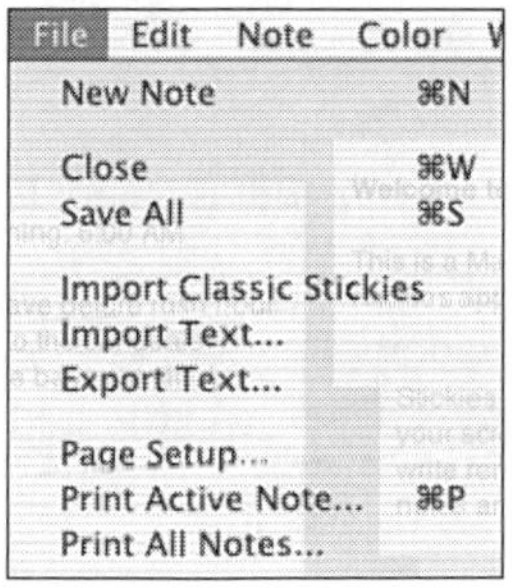

11

▼

3. When a blank note appears on your iMac's screen, just click it and type. You don't have to save the note because it'll be saved as you type.

▲ 4. Just follow the previous two steps if you want to create more notes.

Making Stickies a Startup Application

One minor shortcoming with Stickies is that you have to launch it each time you restart your iMac, or just login. Here's a little trick that you can use to make Stickies (and any other Mac application for that matter).

Setting Up Startup Applications

To Do

1. Open the System preferences application from the Dock, the Apple menu, or the Applications folder.

2. Click the Login preference panel, which opens the screen shown in Figure 11.10.

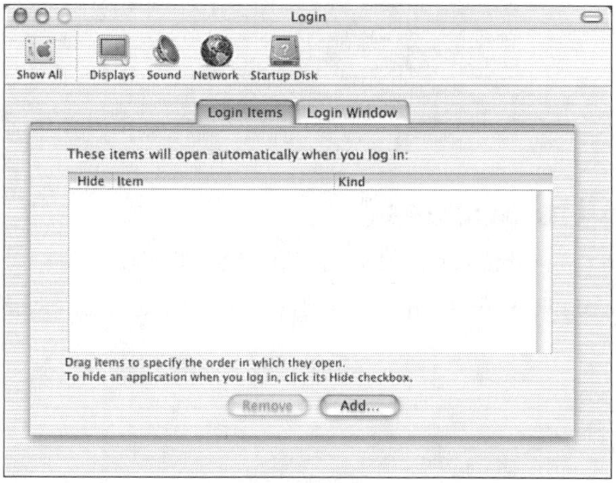

FIGURE 11.10

Add Login or startup applications here.

3. Click the Add button and, in the dialog box that appears (see Figure 11.11), select Stickies.

4. Click the Open button and the selected application will be added as a Login application. You can repeat these same steps if you want to add more startup applications to your iMac.

▼

FIGURE 11.11

Choose a startup application here.

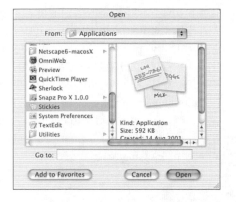

Want to remove a Login application? No problem. With the Login panel of System Preferences opened, just click any application, and then the Remove button and the application will be removed from the list.

5. Quit System Preferences when you're finished. From here on whenever your iMac starts, or you log in, the applications you've added to the Login preference panel will start, too.

A separate Classic Stickies exists, by the way, for Mac OS 9.x. The features are similar to the ones in the Mac OS X version, and it is available from the Classic Apple menu if you want to look it over. One big difference, however, is the way it becomes a startup application. All you have to do is choose Preferences from the Classic Stickies Edit menu and click the checkbox labeled Launch at System Startup; yes, that's all.

Reviewing Stickies Features

After you've played with Stickies for a bit, you might want to look at some of its more interesting features. It does more than simply enable you to put sticky notes up on your iMac's screen.

Here's a list of some of those features:

- **Import Classic Stickies:** If you've been using Stickies for your Classic Mac OS, don't fret over losing any of them. Just choose Import Classic Stickies from the Edit menu of the Mac OS X version to bring them over. Selecting this command will call up an Open dialog box where you must select your Stickies file, which is located inside the Preferences folder of the Mac OS 9.x System Folder.

11

- **Import and Export Text:** You can use this feature to grab text from other applications or save the text from your Stickies notes and make it possible for other applications to use them later. You can use plain text, or a format called RTF (Rich Text Format), which enables the text to retain all the size and text styles you've selected. RTF works with Apple's TextEdit application AppleWorks (which is described in the next section), Microsoft Word, and many other applications.

- **Text Formatting:** The Note menu in Stickies (see Figure 11.12) enables you to choose the font and size for your notes, and also change the color of the text. The Use as Default option means that whatever format you make can be set as the one that works with all the new notes you create.

FIGURE 11.12

Pick a font and style for your little notes.

- **Search:** As you begin to expand your repertoire of little notes, it might get a little difficult to find a word or phrase right away. Stickies has a solution, however. Just choose Find from the Edit menu and pick a search option from the submenu to a word or phrase from a current note or all the notes you've written.

Using TextEdit for Simple Word Processing

Aside from email and surfing the Internet, one of the most popular pursuits on a personal computer is word processing. From simple memos to complete novels, a word processing application is usually essential.

As you learned in Hour 9, your iMac comes with AppleWorks, a powerful, yet simple-to-use application that includes a word processor. What if you really don't want to mess with a lot of formatting, all you want to do is write a simple text document and limit fonts and format selection to the bare minimum?

Apple's alternative is TextEdit (see Figure 11.13), an application that might be what you're looking for. In this exercise, you'll learn how to make a basic TextEdit document.

FIGURE 11.13

TextEdit can handle simple text documents with ease.

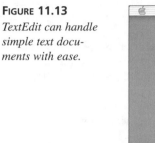

Remember SimpleText or TeachText? If you've used a Mac before, you might remember one of those two applications, which are used to open ReadMe files, those little documents that come with a new application and tell you, basically, what doesn't work and what to do about it. TextEdit is a grown-up descendant of these two, and you'll find that your iMac still has SimpleText in the Applications (Mac OS 9) folder.

Running TextEdit

1. Launch TextEdit from the Mac OS X Applications folder, which will create, as you saw in Figure 11.12, a blank, untitled document.

2. To get started, just click the document window and start typing. But before you go too far, choose Save As from the File menu and, in the Save As dialog box, name your file and choose a place to store it.

3. When you're document is done, choose Spelling from the Edit menu to double-check your spelling.

Would you like TextEdit to check your spelling as you type your document? Just choose Preferences from the Edit menu and look at the bottom-left of the Preferences box. Click the Check Spelling As You Type checkbox. Now click the close button to dismiss Preferences (feel free to look at some of the other options, such as setting a default font). From here on, whenever you make a spelling mistake, a little squiggly line will appear under that word to warn you of the error.

4. After you're finished, you can start another document or just print the document you have. I cover your iMac's printing features in Hour 17, "Now That I Wrote It, How Do I Print It?"

5. All done? Choose Quit from the application menu to close TextEdit.

Here are some more useful TextEdit features:

- **Formatting Features:** Check out the Format menu (see Figure 11.14). You can pick a font and size for your documents, but also make it plain text (which means what you write can be read by any program that reads text). The Make Read Only option means that the document you create cannot be changed by someone else unless they go the extra mile and revisit the Format menu and choose Make Editable.

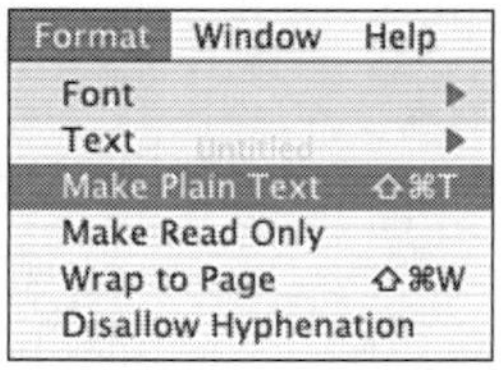

FIGURE 11.14

You can use this menu to change formatting for your TextEdit documents.

Format	Window	Help
Font		▶
Text		▶
Make Plain Text		⇧⌘T
Make Read Only		
Wrap to Page		⇧⌘W
Disallow Hyphenation		

- **Speech Support:** After you've written a document, go to the Edit menu, click Speech, and choose Start Speaking from the submenu. Your iMac will begin to read the document back to you in a computer-type voice. You can pick additional voices in the Speech panel of the System Preferences application. Don't expect miracles, however. The speech system sometimes gets words wrong (or they sound strange), but it's something worth trying out, or just useful if your eyes are tired and you don't want to stare at a long document on your iMac's display.

- **Search Feature:** As with Stickies, there's a search feature, in the Edit menu, that enables you to find a word or phrase in a document.

As you see with Stickies, Text Edit, and other Mac applications, there's a lot of consistency from one program to another. Most have a File or Edit menu, many have a Format or a Window menu. Although commands might differ in these menus, many perform the same or similar functions. When you learn how to do something in one application, you can usually take that skill and apply it to another application.

Summary

In this lesson, you discovered how to use your iMac as a fax machine, to send and receive faxes using a clever program called FAXstf X. You also discovered the Stickies application, which puts little post-it notes on your desktop and TextEdit, a simple word processor for short memos.

Next up, you'll learn the ins and outs of navigating the Internet. See you online.

Q&A

Q I sent a fax of a drawing with the EPS label on it and the recipient complained that the quality was awful. What went wrong?

A EPS files come in a language called PostScript, which is used by publishers to get high-quality illustrations. Fax software doesn't support PostScript and can only send the low-resolution screen preview of the illustration. That's the limitation of this process. I've seen attempts to support PostScript in fax software from time to time, but so far, it hasn't succeeded.

Just about any other text or picture can be faxed without trouble with pretty decent quality, however.

Q I tried to send a fax, but nothing happened. I didn't hear the phone dial on my iMac. What went wrong?

A It's a good idea to double-check your modem hookup. Make sure that your phone cable is plugged into your wall jack and your computer's modem jack before you send a fax.

Just because you don't hear the dialing up process on your iMac, don't assume the connection wasn't made. Maybe the volume was just turned down.

Q There's a busy signal. Will FAXstf dial again?

A The Mac OS X version doesn't support this feature, so you have to start from
scratch. The Mac OS 9.x version of FAXstf has this feature, along with a few others that are not available under Mac OS X, such as sending faxes on a preset
schedule.

**Q The FAXstf software in the Applications (Mac OS 9) folder looks and works a
little different. Why?**

A The publisher built a whole new application from the ground up when moving over
to Mac OS X; they didn't just port or bring over the previous version. Many of the
functions are the same, however, such as setting up a cover page, choosing how
many rings before a fax is answered under the program's preferences, and using
the Print command to open a dialog box to send a fax. But for the Classic Mac version, you also need to hold down the Command and Option keys to trigger the fax
driver. It's not automatic as it is under Mac OS X.

Q I turn off my iMac at night. How do I receive faxes then?

A Okay, you've got me there. This is one limitation of a fax modem. Your computer
must be on for it to work. Otherwise, you might really want to think about getting
a regular fax machine (they aren't quite obsolete yet).

Q My iMac has some software you didn't discuss in this book. Why?

A Apple Computer, naturally, reserves the right to change the software package as
they want; for special promotions or because they've made new agreements with
software publishers.

The programs covered in this book are, in various versions, present on virtually all
iMacs. Some programs have been taken out of this edition because they are no
longer supported or available (that certainly doesn't mean you can't use them if
you have them). Over time you'll see other programs added to the list. For example, some iMacs come with Palm Desktop, a program that enables you to work
with Palm OS handheld computers from such makers as Handspring, Palm, and
Sony.

And, though I hate to say it, some of those changes might mean that some of the
software packages I'm describing won't be there at all. But there's nothing to stop
you from visiting your software dealer and buying a copy of any of these programs
if you like what you see.

In addition, some dealers might offer custom software packages at a slight additional cost. The possibilities are endless.

PART IV
Discovering the Internet

Hour

HOUR 12

The Internet: Learning the Ropes

True, networking might seem to be an alien concept if you're using your iMac in your home or a small office. But, even if you don't think your iMac is on a network, it's very likely that it is. When you connect to another computer or a networked printer, you're on a network. The Internet is a network, too, only much larger. To the tune of millions of computers, sending and receiving information all day long, every day, all across the world.

I suppose when humans are regularly exploring the far reaches of the universe, the scope of the Internet will be similarly expanded.

In this lesson, you'll get a chance to exercise your Internet surfing skills. You'll discover

- What some of that weird Internet jargon means
- How to change your home page
- How to make a list of favorite sites
- How to search for information on the Internet (with a little help from Sherlock)

- How to download files
- Whether Internet cookies really are something to be feared
- Web caches and how to get rid of them

Getting Started on the Internet

The first time you open your Web browser on your iMac it goes to a special location called a home page. For this lesson, you'll need to have your Internet connection established to be able to take advantage of the information.

NEW TERM   A *home page* is similar to the cover of a book. It's the introductory page of a Web site. A typical home page will tell you about the site and offer fast access to other parts of the site (or to other sites with similar content).

> If you're using America Online, you can still take advantage of the information here. A Web browser, based on Microsoft's Internet Explorer, is built in AOL's software. I'll cover some of the minor differences as we continue.

Running Your Browser

▼ To Do

1. Click the Internet Explorer icon on the Dock to launch Apple's default browser (if it's not there, check the Applications folder). This will launch the Microsoft browser and start your Internet connection. If everything is set up properly you'll see Internet Connect, your iMac's Internet dialing machine, doing its thing and connecting you to your Internet provider. When connected, your home page will appear (see Figure 12.1).

2. Click any title or button where the mouse cursor changes to a hand to see another page. For this example, I'll select the Entertainment channel (see Figure 12.2).

3. To return to the previous page (whatever it is), click the Back arrow on the toolbar. The Forward arrow takes you back to the page you visited before clicking Back (if there is one). Click the Home icon to go back to the home page you selected.

▼

FIGURE 12.1

Here's Apple's default home page, which is powered by AOL Time Warner's Netscape division.

FIGURE 12.2

A single click takes you to another Web page or even another site altogether.

Feel free to spend a little time clicking here and there to see whatever information suits your fancy. A quick click of the Home icon on the toolbar gets you back where you started. Your browser will track your visits via a history file.

NEW TERM A *history* file simply records the sites you visited with your Web browser during your session, so you can get to them again easily.

> If you've visited a lot of sites during your session, you can access any one of them quickly by clicking the Go menu and selecting that site from the list. You can also access the history and other features by clicking the tabs at the left of your browser window.

Making Sense of URLs

The clever folks who designed the World Wide Web devised a way to summon a site quickly without knowing the exact route. Unfortunately, it's not in plain English, so it might seem a little confusing. You call up a Web site by its URL.

NEW TERM *URL* is short for Uniform Resource Locator, and it's the syntax used to identify a Web site so that it can be accessed. I'll dissect a URL in the upcoming pages, so you can see the stuff from which they're made.

Let's see what all those little letters and numbers mean by calling up a common, garden-variety Web site—Apple's. You can access it this way:

Accessing a Web Site

▲ To Do

1. Click the Address field below your browser's toolbar.
2. Enter the following: `http://www.apple.com` (do it exactly as I have written it).
3. Press the Return or Enter key on your iMac's keyboard. Your Web browser will send the request for the site across the Internet, and then retrieve the information to display in your computer. In a few seconds, you'll see Apple Computer's home page, just as you see in Figure 12.3.

> When you open your Internet Explorer browser, you'll find there's already an icon for Apple Computer and other Apple Web pages right below the Address field. To add a site to the toolbar just access the site, click the icon next to its address, and drag it to the toolbar. You can also drag URLs right to the Dock and have them a click away from access. If you want to remove an item from the toolbar, Cmd-click the item and choose Delete from the pop-up (Contextual) menu. You can even drag the URL to the trash to accomplish the same result.

▼

FIGURE 12.3

Welcome to the home of the "Think Different" folks, Apple Computer, Inc.

4. To see more information at Apple's site just click any of the colorful pictures.

> Not all pictures you see at a Web site can be clicked to take you to another destination. You'll know you can access such a destination (or link) with a picture when your mouse cursor changes to a hand whenever you point it over the picture.

12

Let's dissect Apple's URL to see what the information means:

- **http://**   This prefix, short for hypertext transfer protocol, tells the browser that you're asking for a Web site. If it has an ftp:// prefix, it means you're accessing a file transfer site instead (it stands for file transfer protocol).

- **www**   This information tells the browser this is the URL for a Web site, though a number of URLs don't include it. Rather than guess, just use whatever address is given for the site to be sure you get the right one.

> If a site's URL has the telltale www letters in it (and not all do), you can skip the http:// prefix and just enter the rest of address. The Web browser is clever enough to know what you want.

- **apple**   This is the first part of the site's domain name.

 NEW TERM A *domain* is the online equivalent of the Web site's street address. It tells the browser where to go to get what you want.

> Each part of a URL, except for the prefix, is separated by a period (referred to as a "dot" in the computer universe) or a slash. Don't forget to enter the correct character where needed to get to the right place.

- **com**   This identifies the site as commercial. The suffix **edu** means the site is an educational institution, **org** represents an organization of some sort (usually a charitable organization or club), and **gov** represents a U.S. government agency. If you see **be** as the suffix the site is located in Belgium. When the suffix is **ca** the site is located in Canada, whereas **uk** represents the United Kingdom (and **co** identifies a commercial site from that country). Additional suffixes are found in other parts of the world, and others are added from time to time.

> If you've visited a site before, you'll notice your Web browser will try to fill (or autofill) the missing information when you begin to enter the URL, by putting up a pop-up menu. Just move the mouse to select the site you want, if you see the correct one, and press Return or Enter to get to where you want. Otherwise, continue to enter the proper address.

> URLs are usually not case sensitive, so it really shouldn't matter whether you enter the address with uppercase or lowercase letters. But if a site has a password as part of a URL, you'll need to type that perfectly (uppercase and lowercase, as required).

Making Your Own List of Web Favorites

Over time, you'll visit Web sites you want to return to again and again, but the Go menu's history file is only good for a few dozen sites. The older sites are automatically removed from the list.

What to do?

Fortunately, your browser has a way to store the URLs of sites for quick retrieval. You can take advantage of this feature by using the Favorites menu. It's the best trick this side of *Star Trek's* "beam me up Scotty" routine to quickly get where you want to go.

Storing URLs

1. Access the site you want to revisit regularly. For this lesson, I've chosen my own entertainment Web site, Attack of the Rockoids (see Figure 12.4).

▼ To Do

FIGURE 12.4

If you like this place, you can make it a Favorite for quick return visits.

2. Click the Favorites menu (see Figure 12.5) and choose the first option, Add Page to Favorites. The site you've opened will immediately become a part of this menu. Real neat!

FIGURE 12.5

Your Favorites menu can be quickly customized to your taste.

▼

12

> You can save a trip to the Favorites menu by typing Cmd-D to add the page to the list.

3. If you want to check the sites you've added to change or remove them choose the second command in the Favorites menu, Open Favorites, instead. Or choose the Favorite button on the toolbar.

4. To remove a site, simply select it from your Favorites directory and press the Delete key. Acknowledge your decision to delete on the next screen and zap—it's gone. Once again, you can also access your Favorites by clicking on the tab at the left of the browser window.

> AOL members have a different way to store sites for fast retrieval, and it works with any area you access on that service. It's called a Favorite Place. If the area or site can be added to your Favorite Place directory, you'll see a small, heart-shaped icon at the upper right of the title bar. Just click it to add that location (or insert the location in your email). AOL's Favorites feature covers their forums plus Web sites.

Searching the Internet

There are literally millions of sites on the Web. Some are run by large commercial enterprises, such as Apple Computer, or government institutions, such as the CIA or IRS. Each and every site might have hundreds or even thousands of pages to access.

The possibilities are mind-boggling. Fortunately, with easy Web access and easy ways to make sites there are also easy ways to find the information you want.

In Hour 8, "Opening, Saving, Finding, Moving, Etc.," I introduced you to Apple's clever Sherlock search tool. To briefly recap, Sherlock enables you to

- Find files on your computer's drive
- Find text inside a file
- Search for information on the Internet

Sherlock is a great way to automate Web searching. It works behind the scenes to access huge Web search tools to locate something.

Sherlock can be updated to store additional search sites (but quit the program first before trying). Some Web sites offer search modules (or plug-ins), which bear a filename with the extension .src. Where do you put them? Locate the Library folder inside your Users folder. Inside, you'll find a folder called Internet Search sites, and separate folders for each search category inside. Just place the .src file within the appropriate category and that search icon will appear next time you launch Sherlock.

You'll often find that a direct visit to those search sites can provide a more leisurely way to explore the Internet. To see the possibilities, click the Search icon on your Web browser, which will open a screen similar to the one shown in Figure 12.6.

FIGURE 12.6

I've set my Web browser to access Yahoo (`http://www.yahoo.com`*) as the search locale, but you can pick another if you want.*

When you set up your Web access, you might find that a different search site is selected. No problem. You can try that site or change it to another site by entering the URL in your Internet preference panel in Mac OS X's System Preferences application. I'll tell you more about making such settings in Hour 16, "Using System Preferences to Customize Your iMac."

12

You'll see that Web search sites do a lot more than just search. Here are other things you'll often find at these locales:

- **News and financial information**: The search site links to a news service, such as CNN or Reuters, to offer hourly updates on the day's events.

- **Recommended sites**: The search site's management reviews new places, often every day, and will recommend popular watering holes for further review.

- **Ads**: You can often place personal and business ads at a Web search site or find fast links to such places.

- **Free Email**: Sites such as Yahoo enable you to create your own personal email account (although you already got one when you joined an Internet service).

- **Custom Settings**: You can set up a search site front page to look the way you want (very much similar to the start page for many ISPs). When you click the My icon at Yahoo's home page, for example, you'll see a sample Front Page that you can tailor to your own needs (see Figure 12.7). Check the Personalize This Site screen to customize the page.

FIGURE 12.7

This is my personalized front page at Yahoo's Web site.

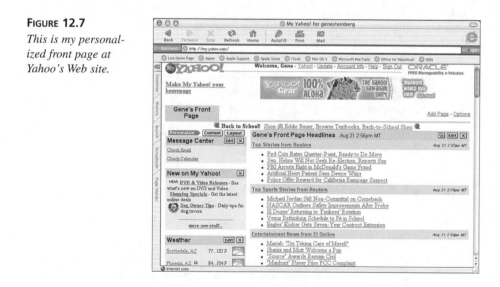

There are several large Web sites that compete with Yahoo. The best thing to do is to try out a few for size and see which one works best for you. Here are some of the others:

- **AltaVista**: http://www.altavista.com
- **AOL Search**: http://www.search.aol.com. Nope, you don't have to be an AOL: member to use this search tool (although it's similar in many respects to Excite because it uses Excite's search capabilities).

- **GoCom**: http://www.go.com

- **Google**: http://www.google.com. This search site is ultra-fast and ultra-cool. You might make it your favorite after you try it; I have.

- **LookSmart**: http://www.looksmart.com

- **Lycos**: http://www.lycos.com

- **Netscape Netcenter**: http://home.netscape.com

The Web search sites shown use different techniques to ferret out information, so what you find at one site might be different from another. Don't forget, Apple's Sherlock search program can check a number of search engines to find what you want.

Downloading Files from the Internet

The Internet is not just a place for information, but a place where you can get pictures and software, too. As you explore various sites, you'll find download areas and other places where you can retrieve files and transfer them to your computer.

Before I show you how to download a file from a Web site, here are two points to consider:

- **Compatibility**: If you're downloading software, check the information at the Web site on whether the software can run on your iMac. Look for something that specifies compatibility with a Macintosh. If it says Windows or DOS, you won't be able to use the program, unless you buy a PC-emulator program (see Hour 18, "Coping with the Windows World").

- **Computer Viruses**: Movies such as *The Net* and *Independence Day* have romanticized the unlikely notion of using a computer virus to beat the bad guys. In the real world, however, a computer virus is something vicious. It can cause your computer to crash, or even damage your files. Although major online areas will check their files to be sure they're virus free before putting them up, you should arm yourself with virus protection software before you attempt to get these files. See Hour 24, "An iMac Safety Net," for advice.

With the preliminaries out of the way, let's find a file to download and see how it's done:

12

Downloading a File

1. For this lesson, first access Apple's support Web site at `http://www.apple.com/support`, which opens the screen shown in Figure 12.8.

FIGURE 12.8

Apple's support Web site has files and troubleshooting information for all users of their products.

2. Look for the Downloads label and click it. In a few seconds you'll see Apple's software updates page.

3. Locate a file title under Featured Software and click the Get button.

4. On the next window, click the name of the file you want to retrieve. In a few seconds you'll see the Internet Explorer Download Manager window (see Figure 12.9). If you want to stop the download just click the filename, press the Delete key, OK your decision on the following screen, and the process stops.

> If the file list says form, it means you have to fill out an online form (usually with your name and address) to get the file. In addition to the actual file you want to download, most sites will offer a link to an instruction file or a page that explains how to install the software. Look for telltale references to such titles as Instructions, Read, or Text for this information.

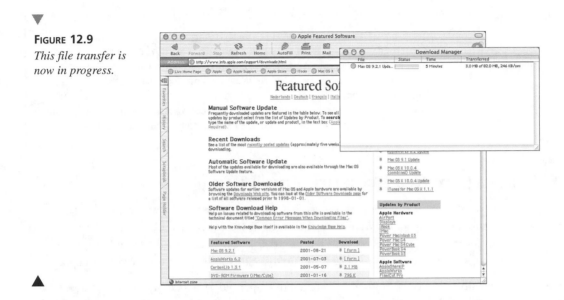

FIGURE 12.9
This file transfer is now in progress.

The Low-Down on Internet Cookies

You've heard the warnings. When you visit a Web site they are apt to send you a danger-ous thing called a *cookie* that can ferret out the secrets of your hard drive, damage your files, or just cause general annoyance. Don't take such warnings seriously!

NEW TERM In the online world a *cookie* is not something that tastes better with milk. It's actually a small file that is sent to your computer when you visit a Web site. It saves information about the places that you visited at the site, so you can access them more efficiently the next time you go there.

When you visit a Web site for the first time, perhaps you signed a guest book or you took a certain route through the various pages that made up the site. Maybe you had to estab-lish a password to get in.

When you visit that site, it sends a small file to your computer. This file, the cookie, is designed to track that information, so the folks who run the site can see which areas are visited most frequently (it helps them sell ads, frankly). The cookie also helps you get where you want quickly.

I suppose that it's possible to imagine there's some insidious purpose behind those cook-ies, and that someone out there really wants to steal your financial information or what-ever. But in the real world, cookies aren't really anything to worry about.

Now death and taxes—well, that's something else altogether.

12

The words "it's a jungle out there" were never truer where the Internet is concerned. Although most sites are safe there is a lot of content out there that might offend you. And, if your kids access the Internet, you'll want to put some safety measures in place. With Internet Explorer, just choose Preferences from the application menu and select the Ratings option. You'll then be able to set custom settings to stop access to sites with unacceptable content. AOL members can also use a feature called Parental Controls.

Take that Cache and Zap It

The word cache has several meanings, but for our purposes it's a secret place where you store things. I suppose a Web browser's cache is secret because it's not visible unless you look for it. But, it's a place where recent artwork you've accessed from a Web site is stored, so you can revisit the place and not have to wait as long for the page to appear.

Normally, your Web browser is designed to empty older cached artwork, so it doesn't get too large and slow down performance. At times, though, things still bog down anyway.

What to do? The easiest step to take is simply to empty the cache, which means your browser will have to build it again. But, more often than not, it makes your computer seem faster when accessing the Internet.

Here's how it's done with Internet Explorer (just check the preferences of other browsers to look for delete cache options):

Emptying the Cache

1. With Internet Explorer running, choose Preferences from the application menu.
2. Click the arrow next to Web Browser to make sure it points down.
3. Now click Advanced and look for the Cache category and click the Empty Now button (see Figure 12.10).
4. To finish up, click the OK button. This action will clear the contents of the cache file used by Internet Explorer.

If you're an AOL member, choose Preferences from the application (America Online) menu. Scroll down to the WWW icon and click the Empty Cache Now button. Click OK and the deed will be done.

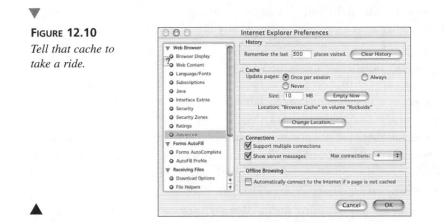

FIGURE 12.10
Tell that cache to take a ride.

Summary

This lesson offered you a tutorial on Internet use. You learned how to change your browser settings to point to a different Web site when you start up, how to locate information, and how to transfer files to your computer. You also discovered how to store a list of your favorite Web sites, so you can get back to them in seconds.

Many of you join an Internet service just to send email, and I'll cover that subject in Hour 12, "The Wonderful World of Email."

Q&A

Q I tried to access a Web site. But the attempt to load it failed. What's wrong?

A Numerous reasons can keep you from accessing a site. Here's what to check:

- Make sure that you are still connected to your Internet service. Sometimes a poor connection will result in getting disconnected, but usually Internet Connect, Mac OS X's connection software, will report that after a short time.

- Double-check the URL to that site. If you enter even one letter or number incorrectly when specifying the address, you won't be able to connect to the site (or you'll get the wrong place).

- Web sites might be run by no more than a single computer, perhaps one not much different from your iMac. If that computer crashes (or is down for maintenance), you won't be able to connect. There's nothing you can do but try again at a later time.

12

Q I notice you're using Microsoft's Internet Explorer for this lesson. Do I really have to use Microsoft's product? Is there any alternative?

A Absolutely. You have several choices of browsers for Mac OS X. A quick way to find out what's available is to visit the VersionTracker.com Web site (`http://www.versiontracker.com/macosx`), where you can find a choice selection of software. Click the search field and enter browser. You'll be able to choose from such browsers as iCab, Netscape, Opera, and OmniWeb. When this book was written, some of these programs were in public preview form, which means prerelease. Thus, you might find that they do not run as well as you might expect, but if you really want to avoid a Microsoft product, it's worth a trial. My personal experience has shown that OmniWeb is one of the best alternatives.

If you leave off the macosx suffix for the VersionTracker.com site, by the way, you'll see a list of the latest Classic applications, most of which will run just fine under Mac OS X's Classic environment (you can continue to use Classic browsers, too). You have plenty of options.

Q I started downloading a file from the Internet, but then I got disconnected. How do I get it back?

A If you're using Internet Explorer, you can sometimes resume the file download (but it's not 100% dependable). Just choose Download Manager from the File menu and double-click the listing for the file you tried to retrieve. Then choose your downloading option. You'll be connected back to that site and, if all goes well, the file download will continue where it left off. But as I said, the process isn't perfect and sometimes it'll just try and try and not succeed. In that event, you'll just need to start the file download from scratch.

Q Okay, I downloaded a file. Now where is it and what do I do with it?

A Your iMac comes with StuffIt Expander, a little program that can process the file after you get it and convert it to a form that you can use. After that's done, take a look at your computer's desktop. You'll see the file there. If you double-click it, it'll either open the file or start the installation process. If you're not sure what to do, go back to the site and see if there's a text or instruction page there with further instructions.

HOUR 13

The Wonderful World of Email

Letter carriers seem to bear lighter loads these days. It's not because folks have stopped sending mail. Far from it. It's the result of sending mail via a different method, email.

In this lesson, you'll learn how to use email to communicate quickly with millions of people around the world.

You'll discover

- How to address your email so it gets to the right destination
- How to send files over the Internet
- How AOL's email setup differs from the rest of the world
- Introducing Entourage X for email and contact management
- What email spam is all about and how to deal with it
- The truth about those email hoaxes

Learning How to Send Email

You don't need an envelope, a stamp, or even a piece of paper to send email. After you establish your Internet account, sending email is really quite simple. You don't even need to buy any special software. Your iMac already has a Mac OS X program called Mail that will do the job just fine for you.

You aren't stuck with Mail. Netscape 6 for Mac OS X includes an email component, and there are other options, such as Qualcomm's Eudora, to consider. Microsoft's Entourage X, part of Office, not only manages email, as you'll see later in this chapter, but also features a calendar and reminder feature. In addition, you can use email software from the Classic environment, such as Microsoft's Outlook Express, which is also included on your iMac. If you're an AOL member, you have to use either AOL's own software, visit the service's Web site, or use Netscape 6 to access your messages.

Here's How to Get Started with Internet Email:

Getting Started with Internet Email

1. Click the Mail icon on the Dock (the one that looks like a postage stamp). If it's not there, you can launch the program right from the Applications folder. Either result will launch Mail (see Figure 13.1).

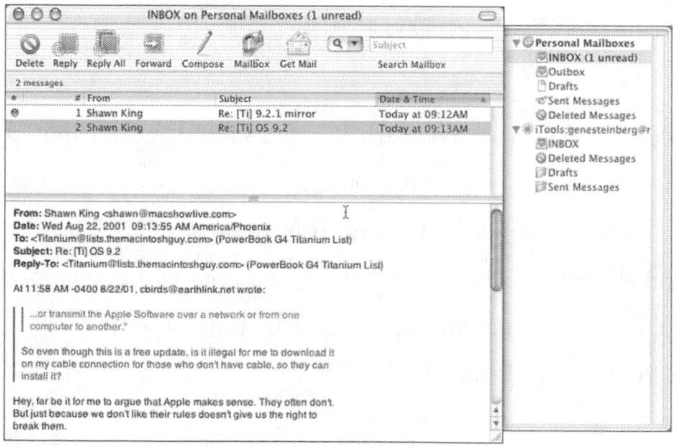

FIGURE 13.1

Use Mail to send and receive email.

I'm assuming here that you've already set up an account with an ISP, and that Mail has been configured as part of the setup process. I described the process in Hour 4, "Getting on the Net." If Mail hasn't been set up for you choose Preferences from the application menu, click the Accounts icon, and then click the Create Account button. Then, in the Account Information dialog box, enter the information required by your ISP to access its email system and click OK to store the settings. How do you get that information? Ask your ISP or check the settings on your older Mac, if you have one. It differs from one to the next.

2. To send a new message, click the Compose icon, which opens a blank message window (see Figure 13.2).

FIGURE 13.2

Write your email on this form.

```
┌─────────────────────────────────────────────────────────┐
│ ○ ○ ○              New Message                    ○      │
│  ✐    ⊘    @    A    ○    ▯                              │
│ Send Attach Address Fonts Colors Save As Draft           │
│     To: ┌──────────────────────────────────────────┐     │
│     Cc: ├──────────────────────────────────────────┤     │
│ Subject: ├──────────────────────────────────────────┤    │
│ Account: [Gene Steinberg <gene@macnightowl.com>  ⬦]      │
│                                                          │
│                                                          │
│                                                          │
│                                                          │
│                                                          │
│                                                          │
│                                                          │
│                                                          │
│                                                          │
│                                                          │
└─────────────────────────────────────────────────────────┘
```

If you prefer to use the keyboard to open a new message window, type Cmd-N instead. You can also click tab to move through the text fields.

13

3. If you don't know of anyone to send a message to, just enter your own email address in the To field. This is, after all, only a test.

The Cc field is used to send a courtesy copy (or carbon copy) to someone else.

4. Use the Tab key to step through to the subject line and give your message a topic name.

5. Click Tab to move to the message window and write your message.

The toolbar in the message window is used to set up and format your email document. Formatting options are similar to those of a word processor. You can change fonts and the color of your text.

6. When you're finished writing your message, you'll notice the Send button has darkened (it remains grayed out until you enter the email address, by the way). Click Send to mail it. Your Internet provider will be dialed and when you're connected your email will be on its way.

Be careful about applying text formats (such as bold or italic) to your email message. Unless you know for sure that the person who gets your message is using a program that can read formatted text, it's possible that the formatting you set so diligently might look like plain-old, unvarnished text when opened.

After your email is sent, open the Internet Connect application (located in the Applications folder) and click Disconnect to end your session. Or click the modem icon on your menu bar (if present) and choose Disconnect. If you're connected to a high-speed or broadband ISP using cable or DSL you're always online, so you don't have to disconnect.

A Fast Guide to Internet Addresses

As you saw in Hour 12, "The Internet: Learning the Ropes," Internet communications have to follow a strict format to work. The same is true with email. Here's how to address your email so that it gets to the right place without any problem.

For this example, I'll dissect an email address I use with my AOL account, gene@aol.com (cards and letters welcome):

> If you're on AOL and you're sending email to another member on the service, you don't have to add the domain information (@aol.com). AOL's email system will figure that out automatically.

- **gene**: This is my Internet name or screen name.
- **@aol.com**: This is the domain name, the location where the email account is located. As I explained in Hour 12, "The Internet: Learning the Ropes," a designation of .com means it's a commercial site, .org refers to an organization, and so on. You'll also find the suffix .net for some Internet services, such as @prodigy.net. My Prodigy address, by the way, is genesteinberg@prodigy.net.
- **Don't use the spacebar!** The Internet doesn't recognize an empty space and will ignore everything before it. If the email address has two names in it separated by a space, use an underscore (_) instead, such as gene_steinberg. Quite often eliminating the space entirely will work just as well.
- **Caps don't matter!** Uppercase, lowercase, makes no difference.

Sending Files with Your Email

Your email isn't limited to just a message. You can transfer files that way, too. If you want to include a file with your email message, just follow these steps:

Sending Files with Email

1. Address and write your email as described previously. Before sending it click the Attach button on your Mail email form, which opens the dialog box shown in Figure 12.3.
2. Locate the file you want to send in the dialog box (using the information you learned in Hour 7, "Opening, Saving, Finding, Moving, Etc.") and click Open. The file you've attached will appear in the bottom pane (half) of the dialog box.

▼ To Do

13

> To attach all the files in the opened folder type Cmd-A to select them all and click Open. You can select individual files by pressing the Cmd key and clicking on each file until all the ones you want have been selected.

▼

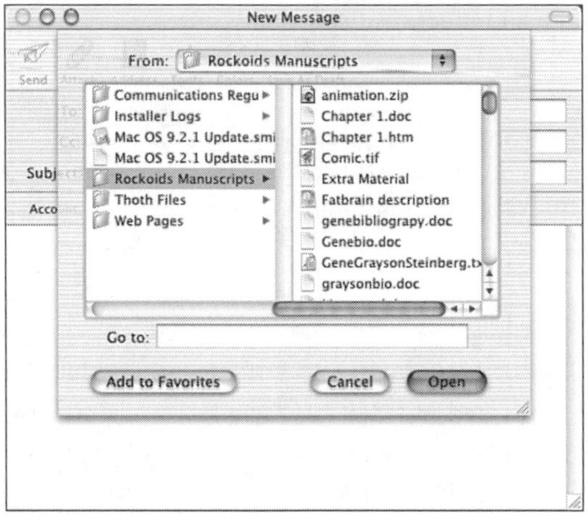

▼

FIGURE 13.3

Choose the file or files you want to send.

New Message

From: Rockoids Manuscripts

- Communications Regu ▶
- Installer Logs ▶
- Mac OS 9.2.1 Update.smi
- Mac OS 9.2.1 Update.smi
- Rockoids Manuscripts ▶
- Thoth Files ▶
- Web Pages ▶

- animation.zip
- Chapter 1.doc
- Chapter 1.htm
- Comic.tif
- Extra Material
- Fatbrain description
- genebibliograpy.doc
- Genebio.doc
- GeneGraysonSteinberg.t
- graysonbio.doc

Go to:

Add to Favorites   Cancel   Open

3. When you're finished, click Open to return to the email form (see Figure 12.4). Icons for document files and the actual picture you're sending will appear. Click Send to send the email, complete with attached files.

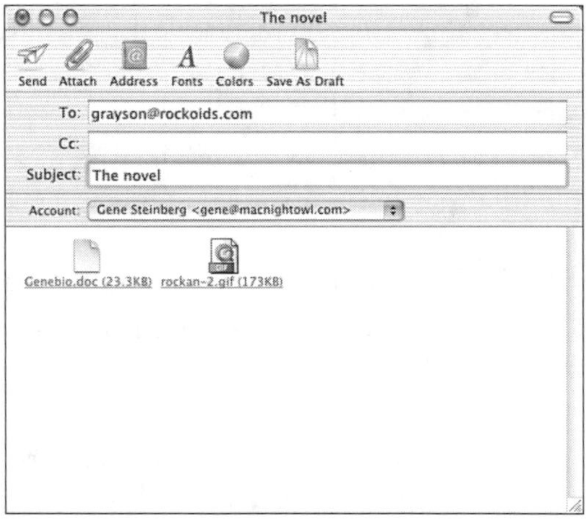

▲

FIGURE 13.4

Your completed email with files attached is ready to ship.

The novel

Send Attach Address Fonts Colors Save As Draft

To: grayson@rockoids.com

Cc:

Subject: The novel

Account: Gene Steinberg <gene@macnightowl.com>

Genebio.doc (23.3KB)   rockan-2.gif (173KB)

If you add a file by mistake to your message, just point the cursor to the right of the item (just as you do with text) and press the Delete key on your iMac's keyboard to detach the file. Also please bear in mind that Internet services often restrict the size of file attachments to a few megabytes (check with your service). If files are too large, the email will be bounced (returned)

back to you without reaching its destination. If you need to send a large file, you might consider buying a program that can compress files to make them smaller, such as Aladdin's StuffIt Deluxe.

Some More Great Email Features

As you saw back in Figure 13.4, there are some other features in your email software you'll want to use from time to time.

Here's what they do:

- **Save As Draft**: If you don't want to send your email right away, click this button to keep a copy for later shipment. If you have lots of email to write you might want to build up a collection (queue) and send them later in one operation. The email will be stored in the Drafts folder in Mail. To send it, you'll need to open it from there after you are connected.

- **Signature**: This feature enables you to add your personalized signature to all your email (automatically), by the click of a button. To set it up, just choose Preferences from the application menu and click the Signatures tab. From here click Create Signature and enter it. After it's saved it'll show up as an entry in the Signature pop-up mail of your email message form.

- **Address**: This feature enables you to store the email address and other contact information for your friends and business associates in a separate application that works with Mail, called Address Book (see Figure 13.5 for a sample). Click New in the Address Book window to store the address.

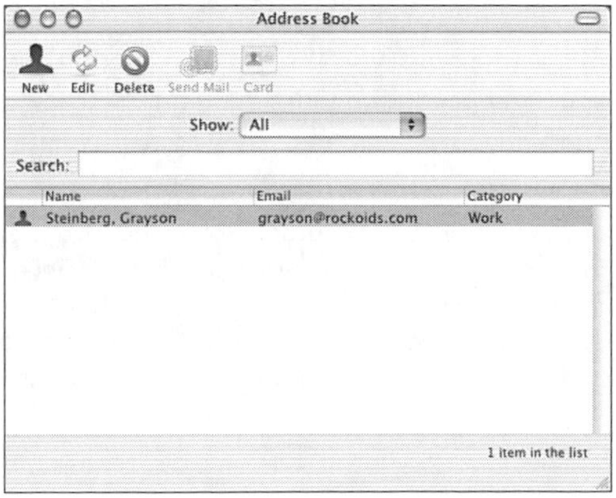

FIGURE 13.5

Here is a contact that I've added to my address book.

13

- **Favorites**: When you click this button, it opens a side panel (or sidecar) in Mail where you can enter and add a list of your favorite email addresses, sort of a second Address Book.

- **Search:** This feature allows you to look for messages in a message folder by sender, recipient, subject, or contents.

- **Forward:** If you want to send a message you've received to another recipient, open the message, click Forward, and the contents will show up in a new message form. Address the message, add your comments, and send it on its way.

Mail has an automatic complete feature similar to the one available in Microsoft Internet Explorer. When you begin to type someone's email address, the program will offer options to complete the address. It stores not just the contacts in your Address Book, but the recent names you've used.

How to Receive Email

After you write some email to your friends and business contacts, you'll probably want to check your Internet mailbox regularly to see what's there. Unlike the postal service, deliveries occur at any hour of the day or night, even on weekends and holidays and when it sleets, snows, and rains.

1. Launch Mail from the Dock or the Applications menu.

2. Click the Get Mail button. This operation will log you on to your Internet service (if you're not already connected), ship the email you've written, and then retrieve the email that's waiting for you.

3. If there's email awaiting you, you'll see it displayed in the inbox (see Figure 13.6). New messages will be identified with a blue dot.

You can configure Mail to automatically check your email at a regular interval. The option is available when you choose Preferences from the application menu and click the Accounts icon. By default, the Check Accounts for New Mail pop-up menu is set to Every 5 minutes. If you choose Manually, the application will only check for messages when you click Get Mail or type Cmd-Shift-N.

FIGURE **13.6**

You've got mail! No, wait, that's the announcement from the other online service.

Click the email listing to see the message

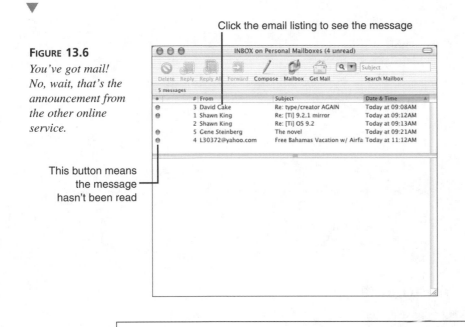

This button means the message hasn't been read

Got new messages? Just look at the Mail icon in the Dock and you'll see a little red postmark that shows the number of messages awaiting you.

4. To read the message, just click once on the title, same as you do with a link at a Web site (see Figure 13.7). If the email message has an attachment you can click the attachment to open it. If you want to dispose of the message after reading it just press the Delete button (or the Delete key on your keyboard) and it'll move it to the Deleted Messages folder where it can be emptied (zapped) at will (choose Empty Deleted Messages from the Mailbox menu) or when the Mail application has quit.

13

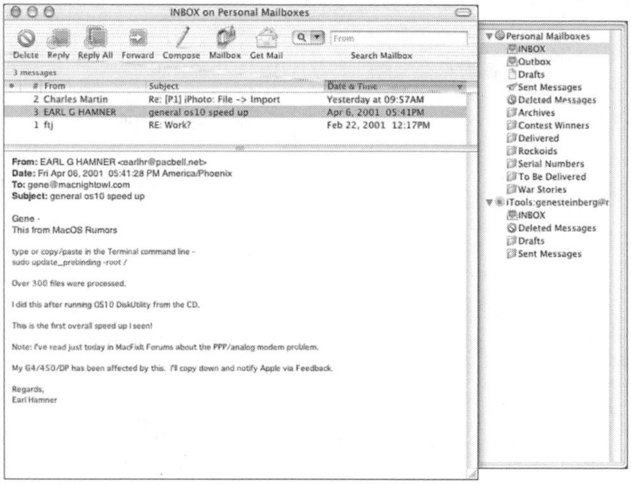

▼

FIGURE 13.7
Here's my first email message (to myself).

▲

Replying to Email

If you want to answer the message, just follow these steps:

1. To reply to a particular passage in the message, click and drag on that passage to select it. Then click the Reply button, which opens the screen shown in Figure 13.8.

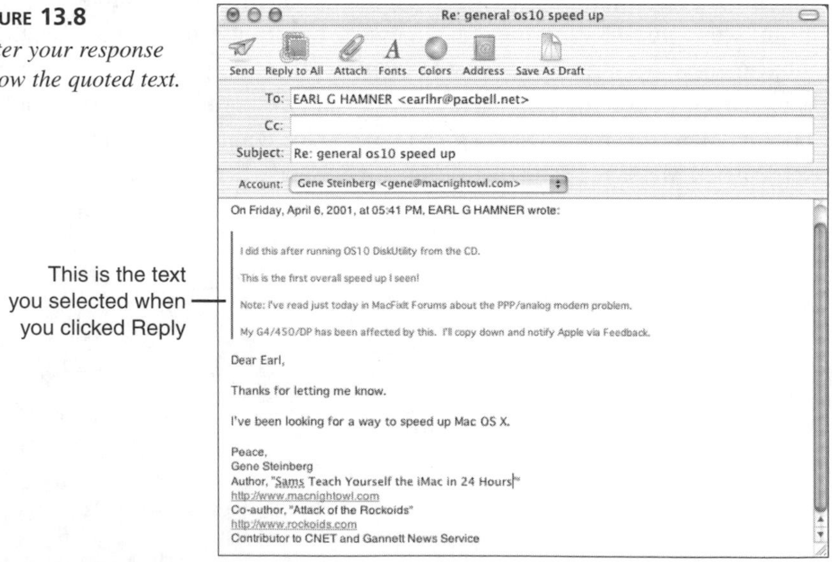

FIGURE 13.8
Enter your response below the quoted text.

This is the text
you selected when ——
you clicked Reply

▼

If the email was sent to multiple recipients, use the Reply All feature if you want your response to go to the same people. Remember, however, that some folks might not want to get copies of everyone's response, so use the Reply All function with care.

On the Internet it's customary to quote the relevant portions of a message when you respond. That way a busy recipient knows what you're talking about without having to refer to an older message. If you want to just say you agree to something, only quote enough of the message to show what you're agreeing to (not all of it, which just wastes everyone's time). Either way, it might also be a good idea to explain why you agree. You quote a portion of the message simply by selecting it before you click either the Reply or Reply All button. If you quote too much you can always delete the extra text in your response before you send it.

2. Type your message and click Send to ship it.

AOL Email Is Different

If you're an AOL member, you'll find that the same email features described previously (except for stored signatures) are there, but they look rather different.

Sending Email on AOL

1. Log on to AOL.

2. Click the Mail icon on the AOL program toolbar (which opens the screen shown in Figure 13.9).

To Do

13

Unfortunately, AOL doesn't work with separate email programs, except for two, Claris Emailer, which was discontinued several years ago, and Netscape 6. You can get the latest version of Netscape, which includes the browser and an instant messaging feature, from http://www.netscape.com. The other alternative is to log onto AOL's Web site, http://www.aol.com, where you can send and receive email directly.

FIGURE 13.9
*AOL's email form
might look different,
but you can generally
use it the same as
you use Mail.*

3. Address your email.

4. Enter the subject.

> If you fail to enter a subject in the proper field, the email will usually go out
> without a subject in the subject line, but that might be confusing to the
> recipient. Best thing to do is enter a subject description that applies to the
> message being sent, so the recipient can organize it properly if a lot of mes-
> sages are being received.

5. If you want to attach a file, click the Attach Files icon and locate the file or files
   you want to send.

6. Click the Send button to ship it.

> AOL users can take advantage of a special feature called Automatic AOL to
> send and receive email and other messages at predetermined times (so long
> as your computer stays on). To set up the feature, click the Mail Center icon
> and choose the Set up Automatic AOL command.

When you receive email on AOL, you'll hear that famous "You've Got Mail" announcement when it arrives (yes, just like that movie with Tom Hanks and Meg Ryan).

Accessing the email is simply a matter of clicking on the You've Got Mail icon and
selecting the messages you want to read. Piece of cake!

Entourage X: An Email Alternative

Microsoft's Encourage X, part of its Office software suite, is another useful email alternative (see Figure 13.10). In addition to managing your messages you can also use the program's Calendar feature to set up reminders, and even a tasks list, so you can organize your busy schedule as efficiently as possible.

FIGURE 13.10

There are an infinite number of possibilities to help you organize your life with Entourage X.

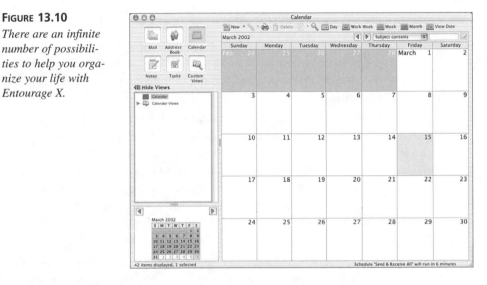

In addition, Entourage X can also handle newsgroups, those Internet-based discussion boards where you can read and share information about a wealth of topics. Unlike the other programs mentioned in this chapter, though, it doesn't come free. You have to purchase Microsoft Office v. X to obtain your copy. If you have an older version of any of Microsoft's popular business applications, though, you're eligible for a discount. Check with your dealer or Microsoft's MacTopia Web site (`http://www.Microsoft.com/mactopia`) for the specifics.

How to Combat Internet Spam!

When I was young (definitely in prehistoric times), SPAM referred to that famous lunch-meat concoction from Hormel.

If you're interested in learning more about the product, access the company's Web site, at `http://www.spam.com`. Seriously! There's even a fan club and SPAM-oriented merchandise.

13

Today, spam is the commonly used term for the Internet variation of the junk mail that fills your regular mailbox. It comes in the form of offers for get rich quick schemes, porn sites, cheap software, and more.

No doubt some of it might consist of legitimate offers from real companies trying to generate business on the cheap (sending bulk email costs a fraction of what it costs to mount a real direct-mailing campaign), most of it is downright annoying.

Here's some tips on how to deal with this growing torrent of annoying material:

- **Don't respond to it!** Even if the message contains an address where you can ask to be removed from the list, ignore the message. When you send them email, you're only confirming that your email address is correct, and you make yourself vulnerable to getting more of it.

- **Complain to the Internet provider who sends it!** It's true that many of the addresses you see are forged, but that's your first line of attack. Forward the message (using that function in your email program) to the service from which the email might have originated. The usual address would be postmaster@*[domain]* (the material in the bracket would represent the part of the address that follows the @ symbol, such as aol.com. Another is abuse@*[domain]*. Even if the email address is a fake, the major Internet services can examine the email for telltale information (called headers) to see where it originally came from.

- **Don't expect miracles!** Services such as America Online have legal eagles on staff to combat this problem. They've even gone to court to get injunctions against the worst abusers. The reality is that spam won't stop completely. But if you report the problem to the appropriate parties it can be reduced.

- **Look for compliance messages!** Legitimate bulk emailers are supposed to include their actual contact information in response to proposed government regulations. If you see this information you'll have a source to complain to if you want to stop those mailings.

If you get a lot of email from specific sources, you can use AOL's Parental Controls feature to block that mail. Apple's Mail application has a feature called Rules (available from the Preferences dialog box) where you can specify what to do with messages from a specific source (such as trashing those messages).

The Low-Down on Email Virus Hoaxes

After you've been exchanging email for a while, no doubt you'll receive messages warning you not to open certain messages because they'll destroy your computer. You are asked to forward the email to everyone you know, to inform them of this great danger.

One infamous example of this sort of tomfoolery was the fake warnings about the so-called Good Times virus, which was forwarded to millions of people. Similar fake threats come from time to time. Here's some advice to consider:

- **Don't forward the message!** Spreading fear and confusion to others might be the actual virus here. Besides, sending chain letters (the ones that say to pass it on to someone else) is not allowed on AOL, EarthLink, or most other Internet services. If you forward those messages you can only cause problems between yourself and the service to which you subscribe.

- **Opening an email message won't give you the virus!** Aside from a rare bug that appeared in email programs a while back, you cannot get a computer virus just by reading a message. A file that you can launch can only spread a virus.

- **Watch out for unsolicited files from strangers!** You get them from time to time. A message from someone who writes, "here's that photo you asked me for" with a few enticing lines. Then you see that there's a file attached to your email. Fortunately (for us, not them), most of the dangerous files sent this way only work with users of the *other* platform. They'll have .exe or .shs file extensions (to cover two examples). The folks who run those files (and again they're Windows-based files) can risk activating a real virus, or a program designed to steal the password they use for their online service. Because of the proliferation of so-called email viruses (which steal or mine the address books of the affected users), you should even be cautious about opening files from someone you do know. If you didn't expect a file from someone, write to them and confirm they really sent it before you open the file.

- **Practice safe computing!** An old friend used to say in his public pronouncements, "practice safe hex," which is a play on the code entered into a computer program. But the meaning is the same. If you do a lot of Internet visiting, you should definitely buy a virus protection program for your computer. Check out Hour 24, "An iMac Safety Net," for more information about this subject.

13

Summary

You might never use a stamp again after you get the hang of email. It enables you to communicate to millions around the world without worry of rain, sleet, snow, or time of day. In fact, this entire book was written using email to transfer the completed manuscript files between my publisher and myself.

In Hour 14, "Using iMovie, iDVD, and iPhoto," I'll introduce you to the wonderful world of multimedia, Apple style. You'll learn that you don't have to go to film school to create and edit professional looking videos, record DVDs, and manage your digital photo library, so stay tuned.

Q&A

Q **Every time I try to send someone email from AOL it gets bounced back to me by some dude called MAILER-DAEMON@aol.com. Who is that person and what does he want with me?**

A That's just AOL's automated notification name (and you might see it on other services, too). You need to read the message to see why your email couldn't be delivered. Usually, it's because the email address was incorrect, or the recipient is no longer an AOL member.

Q **I know the email address is correct. I've sent email to that recipient before and the account is still current. But the email gets rejected. Why?**

A Internet services will, from time to time, shut down their service for maintenance. Sometimes there's an equipment failure that prevents email from getting to its destination. By virtue of their huge size, email providers such as Hotmail and AOL handle more Internet email transactions than any other services and they've had some notable, well-publicized failures of the system on rare occasions. If your email is returned to you, just send it again. More than likely, by the time you send it the problem will be fixed and your email will get through.

Q **The message I sent to a friend was sent back, saying the person's mailbox was filled up. What do I do now?**

A Services usually put limits on the number of unread messages a single subscriber is allowed. It's 550 on AOL, for example. If your friend hasn't read email in a while, the cup may indeed be overflowing. If you can contact your friend in another fashion, perhaps the old-fashioned telephone, explain that messages need to be read periodically, so other messages can get through.

Q **Every time I send email to someone, I keep getting an angry response that I've reached the wrong party. Why is that person mad at me?**

A Email addresses are very literal, and it's possible you just got the wrong number there. Please remember to check the address carefully before you send the message. A single character or number incorrectly entered will send it to the wrong party (just as you press the wrong number on your phone-dialing pad).

One of the consequences of having an easily remembered email address (such as the one I use on AOL, Gene) is that you become a target for misdirected email. I cannot tell you how often I get mail from folks thinking I am their long-lost uncle, brother, or son. Some have even sent me their resumes, tax returns, and more (really!).

Fortunately, a gentle reminder that they have made a mistake is enough to deal with the situation.

Q **I notice you are recommending Microsoft software. Isn't Microsoft supposed to be the enemy of Mac users?**

A The technology business makes strange bedfellows. On the one hand, Microsoft and Apple have competing operating systems. However, Microsoft also has a special division devoted strictly to producing Mac software; one that has proved to be a profitable division for the company.

What's more, Microsoft's Mac applications have been big sellers and highly praised by both users and product reviewers. So they're definitely worth consideration, if you can ignore the politics.

13

PART V

Using the iMac for Multimedia

Hour

Using iMovie, iDVD, and iPhoto

There is good reason to believe that the Mac is, as Apple's marketing team says, the hub of your digital lifestyle. From early on, Macs were touted as multimedia computers.

Multimedia is an overused term, however. At its heart, it means the marriage of animation, audio, and video. Just about every personal computer is advertised as having multimedia capabilities, so I'm going to focus this lesson on what multimedia means to you, and how the iMac can exploit this great capability.

In this lesson, you'll learn about the Apple technology, called QuickTime, which is so good it's being used by professional movie studios to create their products. You'll also learn about a program that exploits QuickTime to make it possible for you to make home videos with a professional spit and polish. It's none other than iMovie.

You'll learn

- What QuickTime is (and isn't)
- How to view videos on your computer
- How to use iMovie to edit your home videos on an iMac
- How to make a DVD from your videos
- Introducing iPhoto, Apple's digital photo organizer

What QuickTime Can Do for You

First and foremost, let's talk about Apple's core technology that makes desktop video possible, QuickTime. By itself, QuickTime isn't a program that you run. It's a set of tools that Apple developed that enable you to create, edit, and view multimedia presentations on your Mac. Windows even has a version, so your friends using the *other* platform don't have to feel left out in the cold.

The actual viewing and editing is done with programs that support the QuickTime technology. They range from the simple QuickTime Player application that comes with your iMac to sophisticated video-editing software that commercial broadcasters use to create the programs you see every day on TV.

Very briefly, here's what the current version of QuickTime provides for you:

- **Digital Video**: QuickTime offers techniques to compress video productions, so they don't overwhelm your computer with their storage space needs. Without this compression, long video files (such as a movie or even a TV commercial) would be huge, far bigger than most computers could handle on any ordinary drive.

NEW TERM

Compression is a technique designed to make things smaller. The usual way is to find redundant data and reduce it to a shortcut that identifies the original. Two types of compression are *lossless*, which means that the data compressed is not altered in any way and *lossy*, where the information needed the least is removed. The new DVD-video format uses a lossy-compression technique that reduces the file size to a fraction of the original with minimal loss in quality.

- **Audio**: QuickTime gives you the capability to view, process, and edit audio presentations.
- **Streaming Audio and Video**: Working with your Web browser, QuickTime can deliver live audio and video on your iMac. You can watch programs delivered by major entertainment and news services such as ABC News, Disney, HBO, and more.

Viewing QuickTime Movies

If QuickTime is just a set of tools, what do you use to see a movie? Fortunately, your computer has several programs that are QuickTime-aware and enable you to see such productions. These include AppleWorks (described back in Hour 9, "Teach Yourself AppleWorks,") and your Web browser.

To start this off, I'll introduce you to Apple's QuickTime Player application, which not only enables you to view QuickTime productions and image files in such formats as GIF and JPEG (common on Web sites), but do some very basic sound and video editing.

However, if you really want to get down and dirty with video editing, you'll want to explore Apple's marvelous iMovie software, which will be described later in this chapter.

Viewing a QuickTime Movie

To Do ▼

1. Launch QuickTime Player from the Dock or the Applications folder.
2. Go to the QTV menu and choose one of the video sources. For the sake of this exercise, I'm using TechTV.
3. Click the Play button to begin playing the video (See Figure 14.1)

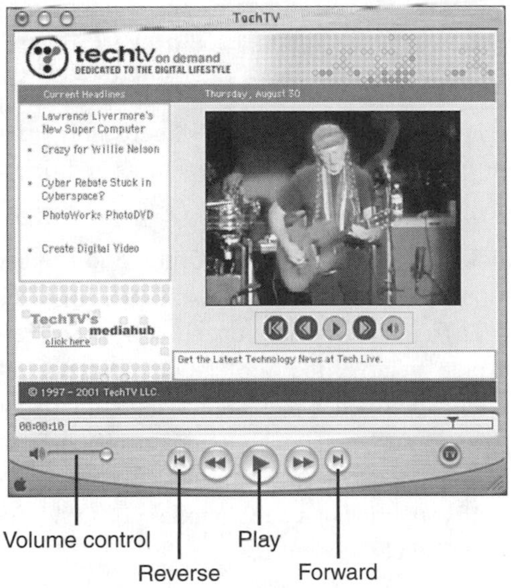

FIGURE 14.1
This is a video interview with country artist Willie Nelson, courtesy of QuickTime.

Volume control   Play
Reverse   Forward

4. When it finishes running, the movie will stop all by itself, but a press of the Play button will start it again. You can change volume with the volume slider, and use the forward and reverse buttons to shuttle through the video.

▲

14

> You can play a movie clip over and over again without stopping. Just open the movie file and choose Loop from the Movie menu before you play it (or press Cmd-L). The next time you play the movie, it will continue over and over again until you stop it.

> I'm showing both QuickTime Player and iMovie under Mac OS X. But both programs work pretty much the same way under Mac OS 9.x, so you can follow these instructions even if you're using Apple's Classic operating system.

Seeing Movie Trailers on the Web

When *Star Wars Episode I: The Phantom Menace* was being promoted, millions of computer users got a chance to see the trailer on their own computers, courtesy of Apple's QuickTime technology. Since then, trailers have been released for the sequel, *Star Wars Episode II: The Clone Wars, Spider-Man,* and many others.

In fact, Apple keeps a big list of movie trailers at its QuickTime Web site (`http://www.apple.com/trailers`), so you can catch up on movies you're planning to see and learn what films will be hitting the local theaters in the future. You can do all this without leaving your home or office.

Those movie trailers, however, can be positively huge, and you might have problems viewing them on your browser. So here are a few hints and tips to make the process as much fun as possible:

- **Configure QuickTime for the Correct Connection Speed:** The QuickTime Player application works best when you configure it for the correct Internet-connection speed. To do that, simply open the System Preferences application from the Dock, the Apple menu, or the Applications folder. Click the QuickTime icon. With the QuickTime preference panel open, click the Connection tab, and click the Connection Speed pop-up menu, where you specify how fast your iMac connects. For a regular dial-up connection, specify 56 Kbps modem/ISDN (this is usually the default setting). If you're using a cable modem or DSL, you'll want to choose whatever speed is listed by your ISP.

- **Get a Small Video for Dial-Up:** It can take several hours to access a large movie trailer, so if you don't want to waste a lot of time online getting your favorite, choose the smallest available size. When there's a choice, it's small, medium, and large, and the image size will be listed. You have to weigh the disadvantage of seeing the trailer on a small window against the time it takes to retrieve.

- **Don't Expect Miracles:** Sound and video quality on video feeds isn't perfect, though quality is better if you have a really fast Internet connection. But don't give up your cable TV or satellite TV connection just yet.

- **You Need QuickTime Pro to Save a Trailer:** Although QuickTime is free with your iMac, a few functions are unavailable. One of them is the capability to save a movie trailer you download (so you can only see it during your online session). If you opt to buy the QuickTime Pro upgrade from Apple's Web site (and you'll see a screen message about it every so often when you run QuickTime), you can not only save files, but also perform simple video edits. However, in some cases, the capability to save a movie trailer might (depending on its source) still be turned off.

Introducing iMovie

At one time, editing a home video was a chore. You had to sit and copy each section separately from your camcorder to your VCR in the order that it was to be viewed. Pros call this *linear* editing because everything is put in place in the exact sequence.

You could, if you wanted, buy a video-editing device that would control the camcorder, specify the edit points, and then enable the contraption to play back everything in the order you selected as your VCR recorded the video as one project. Of course, quality suffers because the copy is never as sharp as the original. Some devices even enable you to add simple titles and other transition effects (the little fades and screen movements that separate one scene from the next).

Being able to edit a video on a computer is a revelation because you can copy the clips or segments in any order you want. Then, during the editing process, you put things in order. This process is called *nonlinear,* and it's a lot more flexible.

At one time, editing videos on a personal computer required expensive software and expensive peripheral cards that would interface the camcorder with the computer. Then came FireWire, Apple's Emmy award-winning technology that enables you to attach such devices as a DV camcorder right to the computer by a simple cable, without having to add a peripheral card.

That's just dandy for an iMac because you can't add a peripheral card to an iMac. But what about the software? That was still an expensive proposition, unless you wanted something cheap and with limited features, until Apple's iMovie came along (see Figure 14.2).

14

To use iMovie on your iMac, you must have a model that came with FireWire ports. If you're not sure, check the connection panel and see if you have a pair of FireWire connectors there. You can identify them by their peculiar shape. Thin, oval at one end, squared off at the other. If you don't have FireWire, the only alternative available when this book was written was the Sonnet HARMONi, a logic board upgrade kit that includes a faster processor (up to 600Mhz), plus a FireWire port.

FIGURE 14.2

iMovie makes video editing a joy.

Click to control camcorder or see work in progress

Choose clips and effects here

Drop your clips and effects here

Where's Mac OS X's Dock? When you launch iMovie, the Dock goes into its hide mode, but you can bring it up simply by moving the mouse down to the bottom of your screen (or wherever it last appeared if you've moved it to the side of the screen). Like magic, it'll pop up again. When you quit iMovie, the Dock reverts to its former state.

Frank 1:30 - 3:00 Rm.? M-W
Music
Bldg.

Don's Tree Service   689-5244

~~Stormsman   240-6397~~

Tree Tech Services   386-1780
      2/27 between 8-12p

+ 0100   + 0117   - 0127   0167
+ 0102   + 0119   + 0133
- 0110   + 0120   ~~0137~~
+ 0111   - 0121   + 0140
+ 0112   + 0122   ~~0147~~
- 0115   + 0123   + 0153
- 0116   + 0124   ~~0163~~

To use iMovie, you must first make sure it's installed on your iMac. The Mac OS X version ought to be in your Applications folder; the Mac OS 9.x version is in the Applications (Mac OS 9) folder.

If it's not installed, check the CD package that came with your iMac. If it's not there, pay a visit to Apple's support Web site (http://www.apple.com/support) check the software downloads area for the latest version.

> If you don't have a DV camcorder and FireWire connection, you can still use iMovie for purposes such as editing movie files copied to your iMac's drive, or making slide shows from still photos.

Capturing Video Clips with iMovie

When iMovie is present and accounted for, you need a DV camcorder to take your home videos and copy to your iMac's hard drive. Let's get started.

> If you have an old (non-DV or Digital8) camcorder, you might be able to use a converter box to change the output to FireWire so you can connect it to your iMac. One such converter product is the Formac Studio. Check out http://www.formac.com for more information on the product, which can also be used with a regular VCR to transfer clips to your iMac. Another site to check is http://www.apple.com/imovie/compatibility.html, which lists compatible camcorders and other products.

Using iMovie to Capture a Video

1. Prepare your camcorder by inserting the tape you want to edit.
2. Connect the camcorder to the iMac's FireWire port using the cable supplied with the camcorder.

> The FireWire connector on your camcorder might be known by a different name. Some call it an IEEE 1394 or 1394 port (that's the technical name for FireWire). Sony refers to the feature as i.Link. But FireWire by any other name is still FireWire.

▲ To Do ▼

14

▼

3. Locate iMovie on your iMac (most likely in the Applications folder), and then launch the application. You see a little multimedia dialog box with buttons on it (see Figure 14.3) where you choose whether to start a new project, open an existing project, or view the tutorial. Click New Project.

The first time you launch iMovie, you might prefer just to look at the tutorial to get a good visual idea of how the program works. But actually, as you'll see in the following pages, everything you have to do to edit a video is pretty clear, and the skills you've already learned while using your iMac work fine here.

FIGURE 14.3
Choose New Project to get started.

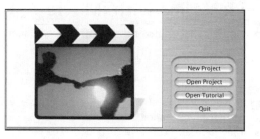

4. When you select New Project, you'll see a standard Save As dialog box. Here you'll name your video project, and then specify where to save it on your iMac's drive.

5. Turn on your camcorder, and then click the little switch next to the controls in the main preview window and slide it towards the DV icon (see Figure 14.4).

If you see a message that your camcorder is disconnected when you move the control button to the camcorder position, make sure the unit is properly connected. Then turn it off and on again and make sure its in the playback or VCR mode. You might have to move that slider switch back and forth for it to realize the camcorder is really connected and working.

6. Click the Play button. Your video will appear in the large monitor window at the upper-left of the iMovie project window, and the sound will be heard on your iMac's speaker system. Let the playback continue until you reach the point where you want to start capturing a clip. You can use the Stop, Forward or Reverse buttons to shuttle the tape to the point you want.

▼

FIGURE 14.4
With your camcorder selected, you can click one of the play buttons to make it run.

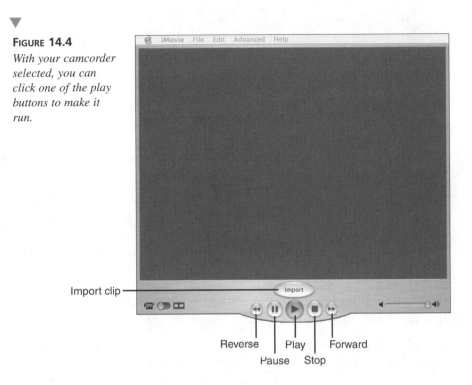

Import clip

Reverse | Play | Forward
Pause | Stop

7. When you've reached the point where you want to start copying a clip, click the Import button. When you're finished, click Import again to halt the process.

To avoid the possibility of dropped frames, don't try to do anything else on your iMac while a video clip is being retrieved.

Each scene on your video will be captured as a separate clip and included in your collection of clips. By default, they'll be labeled by clip number and time, but feel free to click the name and change it to something that's easier to identify later. Because they are separate clips, you can put them in any order you want in your finished product.

14

▼

8. You can record different segments from the same tape or different tapes and include them in your clip collection for editing. When you're finished, move the slider button towards the movie clip icon and you're ready for the actual editing process.

Video clips take up a lot of drive space. While you are capturing video, pay attention to the Free Space display at the lower right of the iMovie project window. That way you can see if you're running out of storage space. If you are, you can edit the segments you have and copy them back to tape. Then, trash the clips and capture some more. If you're doing a lot of video editing, you might want to buy a separate FireWire hard drive to store your clips.

▲

Editing Clips in iMovie

Now that you have a collection of video clips to edit, it's time to move on to step two, which is to actually edit the video and generate a finished movie.

You can simply copy the finished video back to your camcorder. From there, the tape can be played back through your TV or copied once again to a regular VCR. Your choice.

You can even convert your movie to a QuickTime movie file, same as those movie trailers you saw at Apple's Web site. That way you can send your finished masterpiece to your friends or business contacts as an email attachment (if it isn't too large), or just copy it onto a disk to send out.

If you or someone you know has a flat-panel iMac or Power Mac G4 with SuperDrive, you can actually copy your movie onto a DVD that can be played on just about all but the very earliest DVD players. I'll tell you how in the next section.

Before getting started, you'll want to take a look at the various parts from which you generate your movie. Each shelf or collection of elements for your movie is divided by category. Click a button to move from one to the other. Here's what you have available:

- **Clips:** These are the various scenes from which you'll create your finished movie. They're identified by name and duration.

- **Transitions:** A transition (see Figure 14.5) is a special effect that you insert between scenes, such as fading in, fading out or, as they did it in the old-time movie serials, have one frame slide left to replace the previous one. As with the other effects you add to your video, you can set its duration or speed with a slider, and preview an image to see how it looks.

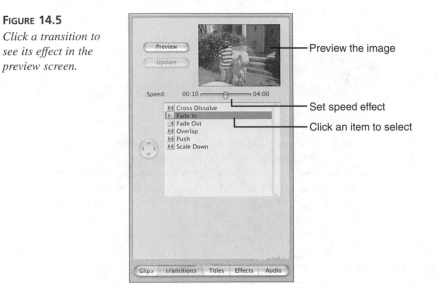

FIGURE 14.5

Click a transition to see its effect in the preview screen.

Now's your chance to show off your creativity. Let's begin.

- **Titles:** Give your movie a title. Choose the effect, whether it'll be centered, splashed across the screen, and so on. One of the neatest effects is Music View, which places the title of the clip and credit in a single unit at the lower left, the same way it's done on MTV. You can choose fonts and relative sizes for your title, and specify how fast the letters move across the screen. As with other effects you add to your videos, click Preview to see how it works before you use it.

- **Effects:** This option won't give you the ability to replace a special effects studio on your iMac. You can, however, do some simple things, such as change the picture to black-and-white (great for a dream sequence), and add effects, such as a water ripple (just as if you were scuba diving). In addition, brightness and contrast can be altered to make day into night or show the intensity of the sun, if you want to create a desert scene.

- **Audio:** If you want to add narrations or music, you can deposit them in the Audio try for later use.

14

Editing Your Video

1. If your project file isn't opened, locate and double-click it to launch iMovie.

2. Now it's time to assemble your clips. The window at the right is iMovie's shelf, which contains all the parts from which you make a video. To add an item to your movie, just click and drag the item to the Preview window at the lower left (see Figure 14.6). When you add a clip, its icon disappears from the Clips shelf.

FIGURE 14.6

Assemble the parts of your clip in iMovie's Preview window.

Yes, you can indeed add a clip from a commercial movie or commercial. But remember, such clips are protected by copyright. You are free to play with the file at your own leisure for your own amusement and education, but don't attempt to distribute an altered version of that or any other copyrighted file to anyone else. That would be a violation of the copyright and could get you in legal trouble.

3. When you're finished assembling your clips, it's time to add the spit and polish. In turn, click each shelf by its name (in whatever order you want) to add special effects, titles, and audio to your movie.

4. Before adding an effect, click the Preview screen to double-check the way it runs; then drag it to the proper location in the Preview window. Transitions are placed between clips, whereas effects that cover an image, such as Water Ripple, are placed on top of the clip.

5. To see how well you're doing, feel free to press the playback controls to see your work in progress. At any time during the editing process, you can click and drag clips or effects to different positions to change the sequence.

6. All finished? You'll want to play it all back one more time to be sure that everything is all right, and, if needed, make your last-minute corrections.

7. When you're finished, it's time to make the movie. To do that, choose Export Movie from the File menu (see Figure 14.7) to open the Export Movie dialog box.

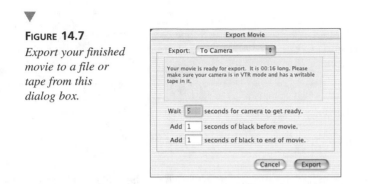

FIGURE 14.7
Export your finished movie to a file or tape from this dialog box.

8. To copy the finished production back to tape, use To Camera from the Export pop-up menu. You can also save your movie as a QuickTime movie or copy in iDVD format for use in making a DVD via Apple's iDVD software (this last option is only available on some iMovie versions). Click Export to complete the process.

If you're using the To Camera option to send the movie to tape on your camcorder, the playback will occur in real time. If you're copying to a QuickTime Movie or iDVD file, be prepared to wait a few minutes for rendering as the movie is encoded into the proper format for either of those file formats.

▲ All done? Yes, you've just made your first iMovie video. See you at the Oscars!

Converting Your Video to DVD

Are you still buying movies on videotape? Well, that's a technology that might eventually go the way of 8-track tape. The fastest growing consumer electronics product is a DVD player. A DVD puts the contents of an entire movie on a disc no bigger than a CD. What's more, you can now transfer your videos to DVD, and produce a professional quality disc, complete with navigation menus and motion (moving) menus.

You don't even need expensive gear to accomplish that task. Some iMacs and Power Mac G4s are equipped with a special optical drive that Apple dubs "SuperDrive." This drive, manufactured by Pioneer, the large Japanese consumer electronics company, can play CDs and DVDs, and burn both.

In the next lesson, I'll show you how to copy your data to DVD, but here we're just interested in transferring your movies. For that, you need a Mac with a SuperDrive, some DVD-R media, and, of course, Apple's iDVD software.

14

Macs with the SuperDrive usually come with one or two DVD-R discs for you to get started. You can buy more from your favorite Apple dealer or online at The Apple Store.

Here's a brief look how things work in iDVD:

- **Drag and Drop:** Select a QuickTime file or digital photo and drag into the iDVD window.
- **Build Slide Shows:** Assemble your digital photos and have them playback on your DVD player, complete with your narration and music track.
- **Build Menus:** Just like a commercial DVD, you can set up clickable menus, including motion menus that can use your own video clips and pictures as a backdrop.
- **Customize Themes and Menus:** Pick from a selection of built-in Themes, customize their look and actions, or build your own.
- **Easy Previews:** During each step of the process, you can preview your work so you won't waste DVD blanks and make a mistake.

When you're ready to roll, here's a brief summary of how to make your first DVD.

Want a practice tour. When you launch iDVD, you'll have the choice of opening the program's tutorial, a handy way to learn the ropes.

A Quick Guide to Making Your First DVD

All set? Well we're just about ready to begin, but there is one more step to consider first. If you're planning on making a DVD of the video you've just edited in iMovie, you'll need to export the movie in the proper format.

The DVD you make will play on most DVD players and the DVD drives on a personal computer. However, some of the oldest DVD players, made during the first year the format was introduced, cannot play DVD-R media. Check Apple's Web site, at http://www.apple.com/dvd/compatibility/, to see a list of the players that have been tested and found compatible. Newer players, even if not listed at the site, will likely work without any problem.

To do that, return to the previous section for information on exporting your video. When you choose Export Movie from iMovie's File menu, select For iDVD from the Export to pop-up menu.

> The capability to export your iMovie video to bring into iDVD requires iMovie version 2.0.3 or later. You'll find that version is already installed with Mac OS X Version 10.1 or later, however. If you have an earlier version of iMovie 2 on an older iMac, you can get the update from Apple's Web site.

Making a DVD

▼ To Do

1. Locate iDVD in your Mac OS X applications folder and launch it.
2. On the introductory screen, choose New Project and name your product in the Save As dialog box.
3. Locate and drag and drop your videos or stills into the iDVD project window (see Figure 14.8).

> Your DVD can contain up to 90 minutes of material, but Apple suggests you limit a movie to 60 minutes for the best picture quality. If your movie takes longer, you should divide it in half or at a convenient breaking point and make two or more DVDs.

> iDVD is a consumer-level application, so it's not designed to make commercial DVDs. It is fine for family videos or portfolios. In addition, you cannot copy a commercial DVD. It is not only illegal, but copy protection prevents you from doing so. You can, however, bring in segments from a commercial video courtesy of iMovie, but again copyright laws make it illegal to take it beyond your personal use.

4. Click the Theme button to open up the drawer containing the list of available Themes for your background and buttons.
5. If you want to make your own themes, just click the Customize tab in the Theme drawer (see Figure 14.9) and go through the categories to make shape your DVD the way you want.

14

▼

FIGURE 14.8
Place your movies or photos in iDVD's work area.

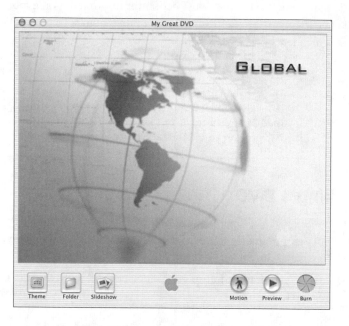

FIGURE 14.9
Customize a theme.

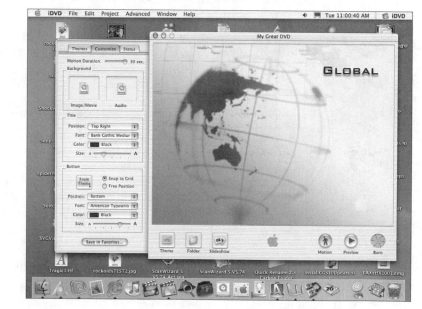

6. When you're finished, click the Preview button at the lower left of the iDVD project window and test every single function.

▼

7. When you're satisfied that your DVD works exactly as you want, you're ready to write a DVD. Just click the Burn button.

8. When you're prompted to insert a DVD, insert a blank disc into your iMac's SuperDrive.

9. Click Burn again for the process to begin. Expect it to take at least twice as long as the total time of the movie. So a 20 minute video will take roughly 40 minutes or more to write on a DVD.

> Do not move the source files until you've finished making your DVD. iDVD simply stores a link to the files, not the files themselves. If you move or delete those source files, your DVD will simply have blank spots where you expect your movie to be.

Introducing iPhoto

Film cameras might soon be history, replaced by digital cameras. As these clever devices get cheaper, and quality goes up, it becomes harder and harder to justify the trip to the supermarket to get that roll developed.

But like your physical photo library, perhaps you've reached the point where you can't begin to organize your library.

Enter iPhoto (see Figure 14.10), Apple's Mac OS X-only digital photo–management software. Your flat-panel iMac includes a copy on CD or already installed. You can also download a copy from Apple's Web site at `http://www.apple.com/iphoto/`.

> If iPhoto isn't on your iMac, you can install it from the CD or download it. When you have the installer, just double-click it and follow the prompts. The iPhoto installer will require that you authenticate yourself first, which means you enter the password for the administrator or owner of your iMac. When you do that, just OK the license agreement, click the various Continue and Install buttons and iPhoto will be set up on your iMac in short order.

14

FIGURE **14.10**

Manage your digital photo library easily with iPhoto.

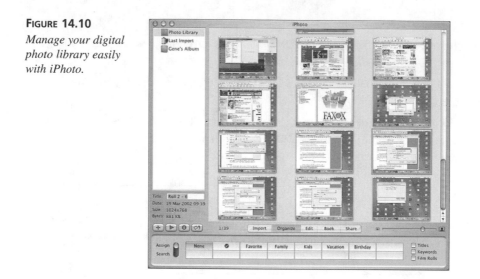

Here's a brief look at what iPhoto can do for your picture library:

- **Import Your Pictures Automatically:** It works with most digital cameras, from such companies as Epson, HP, Kodak, Olympus, and more. Just plug in your camera, and iPhoto launches. From here you can import all the pictures from your camera or just a selected few.

- **Organize Your Photos:** Separate the photos into categories, for example by a specific event or person, so you can easily locate the ones you want to see.

- **Edit Your Photos:** Get rid of the red-eye effect, which occurs sometimes when you use a camera with a flash (or perhaps the subject of the photo had a few too many the night before). You can also crop (reduce the visible area), scale, or rotate the picture without having to learn how to use an image-editing program.

- **Make a Printed Photo Album:** They are just beautiful, with high-quality paper and a hard cover. Of course, you have to pay for the album, using Apple's ordering system. But you might find the price is well worth having a permanent book with your favorite photos.

- **Buy Prints:** All right, you have a great color printer, but after waiting 5 or 10 minutes for a high-quality photo, maybe you'd rather just have a commercial supplier do the prints. Again this is a commercial offering from Apple's Web site.

- **Make an Online Photo Album:** Using the free Web site courtesy of Apple's iTools, you can make your pictures available to anyone with a Web browser. All you have to do is click the Share button at the bottom of the screen, and on the next window, click HomePage. Enter a description of your album on the Publish

HomePage window (see Figure 14.11) and click Publish. It'll appear on the HomePage, precisely as you made it.

FIGURE 14.11
Making an online photo album is a few clicks away with iPhoto.

- **Make a QuickTime Slide Show:** Yes, you can export your photos, and then bring them into iMovie or iDVD for a finished video production.

Summary

In this lesson, you discovered Apple's QuickTime technology. You also learned to capture or copy videos from a camcorder to your iMac and make professional-caliber videos courtesy of Apple's iMovie. You also discovered the magic of iDVD to make your own DVD copy of your video as well as Apple's photo library organizer, iPhoto.

In the next hour, you'll discover another snazzy Apple program, one you can use to play audio CDs, capture tracks from the CD or the Internet, and make your own custom music play lists. You can even use the play list to make your own custom music CDs. The program is called iTunes.

14

Q&A

Q **I love the clear and sharp pictures, but this is supposed to be a multimedia computer. Why are the sounds so, well, *tinny?***

A As I mentioned in Hour 5, "A Look at Your iMac Software," you can easily hook up another set of speakers to your computer to get better sound. There's only so much you can do with the tiny speakers that came with most of Apple's computers.

Q **Every time I start my computer under Mac OS 9, I get the message that QuickTime couldn't load because it was already installed. What's wrong?**

A The message signifies that you have two copies of the QuickTime extension in the Extensions folder (within the System Folder). The solution isn't hard. Simply open the System Folder and open the Extensions folder. You might want to change the Extensions folder window to the View as List option to enable you to quickly check for multiple copies.

Don't worry about all those strange files with strange-sounding names. I'll cover that subject in Hour 3, "What's a System Folder and Why Do I Need Two?" If you see more than one copy of QuickTime, you'll want to trash one of them. First you want to make sure that you have the latest version installed, so select one copy of QuickTime, choose Get Info from the Mac OS 9.x Finder's File menu, and see what the version is. Keep the latest one, toss the other, and restart your computer.

Q **I double-clicked on a QuickTime or sound file, and it won't open. The message says the application isn't available. What do I do?**

A QuickTime supports more than 50 multimedia formats. It doesn't just cover Mac multimedia formats, but Windows formats, too. They include formats such as WAV, AVI, and BMP files (all of which are part of that *other* platform). If you can't open a multimedia file, simply drag its icon to the QuickTime Player application icon and it should work.

Q **I began to play a movie, but the sound is suddenly gone. What's wrong?**

A First, check the volume icon on the movie player screen and make sure that the dial is moved all the way up. If it is, take a gander at the speaker (volume) setting in the Sound panel of the System Preferences application and check to be certain it's turned up, too. If you've attached a speaker system to your computer, make sure that the system is connected properly, that it is on, and that the level control is turned up.

Bear in mind that some QuickTime movies just don't have a soundtrack. To be certain your sounds are working, just click the sound slider on the Sound Level Control Strip, and it should produce a sound.

Q I keep hearing about another audio and video player, called RealPlayer. What's the difference? Is it better than QuickTime?

A RealPlayer is a competing streaming audio and video format from a firm called Real Networks. Because the formats aren't compatible, you cannot use QuickTime Player to run a Real Audio/Video production, or vice versa. If you want to try RealPlayer, you can download the latest version from the publisher's Web site at this URL: `http://www.real.com`.

However, when this book was written, I didn't see a Mac OS X version, so all I can suggest is that you check the company's Web site for updates (it might be out by the time you read this).

Another audio and video player to check out is the Windows Media Player, which, despite the name, is also available for Mac users at Microsoft's MacTopia Web site (`http://www.microsoft.com/mactopia`). This program accesses multimedia content that uses Microsoft's own special format; the same one, in fact, that is supported in Windows XP.

14

Hour **15**

Making Music and Making CDs on Your iMac

No, rip and burn have nothing to do with discarding secret documents in a fireplace. It's really all about music.

In the 21st century, ripping is the process of copying music tracks from an audio CD to a computer. Burning is the process of making a CD. Both pastimes are as popular today as making tape cassette copies of recorded music was a few years ago.

But making music CDs is just part of what you can do on a computer. You can also use a CD burner to copy data files that will preserve the items you save on a cheap and convenient CD.

In this lesson, you'll learn

- How to setup iTunes
- How to use iTunes to assemble a music library

- How to listen to Internet radio
- Using your iPod with iTunes
- How to record both music and data CDs

Introducing iTunes

The highly flexible MP3 format has taken the music world by storm. For better or worse, millions of music lovers are busy converting their existing music to the convenient, compact, MP3 format and listening to the music on both computers and special portable devices.

MP3s can also be used to edit music libraries, create custom play lists, or make collections of your favorite tracks. You can also copy them back on to a CD that can be played on most any CD player, a computer, or home music system.

NEW TERM   *MP3* is a compression system that reduces the size of a music file by a factor of 10 to 15, or more. How's this magic accomplished? By removing data that the human ear either cannot, or doesn't hear. Audio quality can be almost indistinguishable from a CD, or, if you opt for more compression, audibly different.

Apple's iTunes is an MP3 or jukebox application that (see Figure 15.1) comes preinstalled on new iMacs, and is available from Apple's Web site. Under Mac OS X, you'll find its icon in the Dock or in the Applications folder. When set up, you'll find that the Mac OS 9.x version and the Mac OS X version look almost identical and run essentially the same way, so let's start ripping.

FIGURE 15.1

iTunes helps you build an MP3 music library and hear Internet radio.

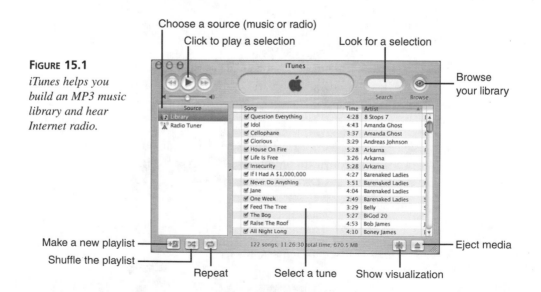

Setting Up iTunes

The first time you launch iTunes, there will be a short Setup Assistant, and then you can use the software. Let's see how it works.

Making a Music Library

1. Launch iTunes from the Dock or the Applications folder. The first time the program opens, you'll see the iTunes user license (you must agree to it, of course) and then the Setup Assistant. To get started, click Next (see Figure 15.2).

FIGURE 15.2

Set up iTunes using the Setup Assistant.

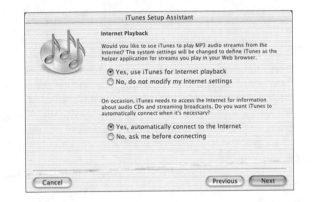

2. On the first screen, you'll want to decide whether to use iTunes for playing back Internet music or radio or not, and whether to connect to the Internet whenever information about music and radio access is needed. When you've made your selections, click Next to Continue (click Previous at any time to review your selections).

> If you use a dial-up connection to the Internet, such as AOL or EarthLink, you might prefer to choose the second selection about making the connection—No, ask me before connecting. Otherwise, the connection attempt will be made without warning, which could be a problem if you have only one phone line that shares voice and Internet access.

3. Do you want iTunes to seek out MP3 music files on your iMac's drive? On the next Setup Assistant screen (shown in Figure 15.3), you make your choice. It's easier to just enable the program to do it. Click Done to begin the music search process.

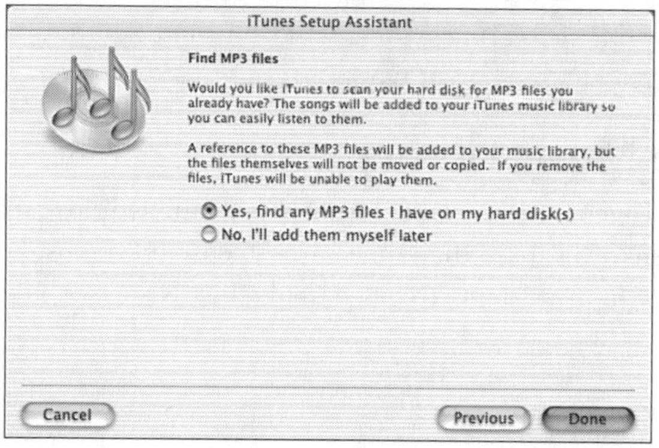

FIGURE 15.3
Decide whether iTunes should look over your iMac's drive for MP3 music.

Over the next few moments iTunes will look for music files already on your iMac's hard drive, and you'll see an Adding Files progress screen as it's happening. The actual files aren't moved; all iTunes does is add an index to the file, so it knows it's there and you can play the song without having to know where it is on your hard drive. If you've just installed a brand new iMac, by the way, you'll find that there are a number of music files already in your play list.

Have you copied more music to your iMac? iTunes will find it if you choose Add to Library from the File, and then locate the music file or files you want to add in the Choose Object dialog box.

Organizing a Music Library

Now that your play list is established, all you have to do to play a tune is select it from the iTunes window and click the play button. In this respect it works the same as an audio CD player.

As you'll notice back in Figure 15.1, there's even a little volume slider below the play buttons, in case you want to make the music louder, or you need to tone it down in case family members or coworkers don't appreciate your musical tastes.

You can also *rip* or encode music from your music CDs and add them to your iMac's music library. From here you can organize your play list or even make a custom CD containing the tracks you like.

Starting the Ripping Process

▲ To Do

1. With iTunes open and running, insert an audio CD into your iMac's CD drive. Over the next few seconds, the contents of the CD will be read and a play list bearing the CD's name and contents will appear in the iTunes window (shown in Figure 15.4).

FIGURE 15.4

Here's some tracks to rip.

The information for many of your music tracks comes from the CDDB database on the Internet. So, some of the information from a CD might not appear until you've made an Internet connection, and the information is retrieved from the database. Because the database isn't 100% complete, you might not see data for your CD, especially if it comes from an independent label or a local band that cut its own custom recording.

2. All the tracks on your CD will be selected by default. You can click the check box next to the track's title to unselect it. To begin the ripping process, simply click the Import button. As the progress bar at the top of the iTunes window shows what's being imported, the songs will play, in succession.

You can rip in silence. Just click the Stop button (which replaces the Play button) to halt playback. The selected tracks on your audio CD will still be copied and encoded.

▼

3. Repeat steps one and two for each CD you want to capture.

4. When you're finished, you're ready to make a custom CD of your favorite tracks. To begin the process, click the Create a Play List button at the bottom left of the iTunes window.

Don't want a track listed in your iTunes play list? No problem. Just select the item, and press the Delete key on your iMac's keyboard. You'll see a prompt asking if you really want to delete the entry. Click Yes to remove the items. This action just removes the listing for the track. The actual music files are still present and accounted for on your iMac's drive. Normally, the files you rip go into the iTunes folder, inside your Documents folder. But iTunes can recognize any tune on your iMac's drive.

5. A new entry with the title highlighted will appear in your Source list, called untitled play list. Now just give your play list a name (let's call it Mix) and a new, empty play list will be ready for you to populate with tracks.

6. To add tracks, click in the Library list, and, holding down the Cmd key, click each tune you want to add to the Mix play list.

7. Drag the tracks to your Mix play list (don't worry, the selections are just copied, not moved, so the original in your Library play list stays intact). The usual maximum is 74 minutes (the time will appear at the bottom of the iTunes window), though some CD blanks support up to 80 minutes. When you're done, you'll see your finished play list when you click Mix (shown in Figure 15.5).

You can modify the sequence of your tracks just by selecting and dragging a track's name and moving it to a new position in the play list. By default, it's copied in the order it was selected.

8. All set? From here you can just click the Play button to hear your music, or you can copy the selections to CD or to an MP3 music player. To make a CD, just insert a blank CD into your iMac's CD drive (if it came with a CD burner) or into a connected CD burner. Your MP3 music player's instructions will tell you how to copy music to one of these devices.

FIGURE 15.5
Here's your completed custom play list, ready to listen to or make a CD copy.

	Song	Time	Artist
1	The Supremes - Where Is It I B	3:59	artist
2	Go Your Own Way	3:40	Fleetwood Mac
3	Free Falling	4:10	Tom Petty
4	Stairway to Heaven	8:03	Led Zeppelin
5	Don't Tell Me	4:41	Madonna
6	Yesterday	2:07	The Beatles
7	Taxman	2:39	The Beatles
8	Eleanor Rigby	2:07	The Beatles
9	I'm Only Sleeping	3:01	The Beatles
10	Love You To	3:01	The Beatles
11	Here, There And Everywhere	2:26	The Beatles
12	Yellow Submarine	2:40	The Beatles
13	She Said She Said	2:37	The Beatles
14	Good Day Sunshine	2:09	The Beatles
15	And Your Bird Can Sing	2:01	The Beatles
16	For No One	2:01	The Beatles
17	Doctor Robert	2:15	The Beatles
18	I Want To Tell You	2:30	The Beatles
19	Got To Get You Into My Life	2:30	The Beatles
20	Tomorrow Never Knows	2:57	The Beatles
21	(I Can't Get No) Satisfaction	3:48	The Rolling Stones
22	Thank You - Dido	1:58	Various Artists
23	I Still Haven't Found What I'm ...	4:38	U2

23 songs, 1:11:58 total time, 88.2 MB

Not all iMacs have a built-in CD burner. If yours doesn't, you can add an external CD-burning drive. iTunes works with a number of makes and models from such companies as LaCie, Plextor, Que, Sony, VST, and other popular brands. You'll want to check with your dealer or Apple's iTunes Web site (http://www.apple.com/itunes) for the list of supported devices. Even if you can't burn a CD, you can still rip tracks from an audio CD using your iMac's CD drive.

9. With the CD in place, double-check your play list, and then click Burn CD to make your custom disc. Depending on the speed of your CD burner, making a CD can take up to half an hour. When you're done, you can eject the CD (pressing the Eject button at the lower right of the iTunes window). Repeat the previous steps to make more play lists and more CDs.

Reviewing iTunes Options

As you can see, building play lists in iTunes and making CD copies can be done in just a few minutes. Easy as pie! If you want to look at the power of the program, however, there are some useful options to get you better quality CDs and fine-tune the program.

You'll find them under Preferences in the iTunes application menu (it's in the Edit menu with the Mac OS 9.x version).

Here's a brief look at the three preference dialog boxes available with iTunes:

- **General:** When you click the General tab (see Figure 15.6), you have three categories of preferences you can set. Under Display, you can pick a text size from the two pop-up menus and whether the musical genre (such as Country or Rock) should be displayed in your play list. The Internet option simply enables you to select the same choices you made when the original iTunes Setup Assistant appeared. Under CD Insert, you indicate with the pop-up menu what to do when you insert a music CD. The default is Show Songs, but you can also decide to both play and import the contents of a CD automatically.

FIGURE 15.6

Choose various display options for iTunes here.

- **Importing:** Now click the Importing tab (shown in Figure 15.7) to decide how imported music is handled. The key setting here, the Configuration pop-up menu, enables you to choose the data rate in kilobits per second. The higher the data rate, the better the quality of the encoded music. Anything lower than 128 kbps is quite different (and inferior) to the quality of a regular audio CD. Above that figure and it gets mighty close and sometimes almost impossible to tell the difference. Remember also that the higher the data rate, the more disk space a music file occupies on your iMac's hard drive.

- **Advanced:** The final option isn't one that you'd see very often (shown in Figure 15.8). The first setting is where to place your play list, and the rest are specific to the kind of CD burner you are using and how you want the gap between musical tracks handled.

FIGURE 15.7
Pick the CD encoding rate here for best quality.

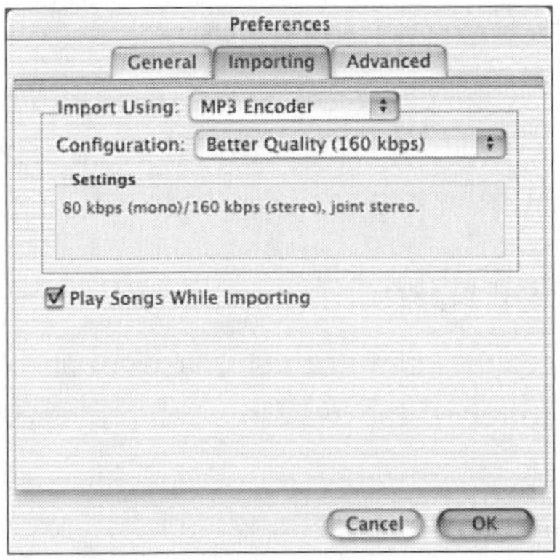

> **Preferences**
>
> General **Importing** Advanced
>
> Import Using: MP3 Encoder ▾
>
> Configuration: Better Quality (160 kbps) ▾
>
> **Settings**
> 80 kbps (mono)/160 kbps (stereo), joint stereo.
>
> ☑ Play Songs While Importing
>
> Cancel   OK

FIGURE 15.8
The location of your play lists and settings for your CD burner are shown here.

> **Preferences**
>
> General Importing **Advanced**
>
> **Music Folder Location**
> Macintosh
> HD:Users:gene:Documents:iTunes:iTune   Change...
>
> **CD Burning**
> CD Burner: TOSHIBA DVD-ROM SD-R2002
>
> Burn Speed: Maximum ▾
>
> Gap Between Tracks: 2 seconds ▾
>
> Streaming Buffer Size: Medium ▾
>
> Cancel   OK

There is yet another way to listen to music from your iMac, and that's with an MP3 player, a portable device, similar to a portable CD player or radio, which plays MP3 music. A number of current models can be connected to the USB port of your iMac, and you can use iTunes to download music directly to them. First you'll want to make sure you buy a player that is Mac OS compatible (it'll say so on the box or at the company's Web site). At the time this book was written, iTunes supported Apple's own iPod MP3 player, plus players from Creative Labs, Iomega, SONICBlue/S3, Nike, and Nakamichi. You'll want to check each product for its compatibility with various versions of the Mac OS. The iPod, for example, runs perfectly fine in either Mac OS 9 or X.

15

Listening to the Radio on iTunes

Another cool feature of iTunes is the capability to receive radio broadcasts from the Internet. When you click Radio Tuner in iTunes, you'll see a list of station formats available. The choices run the gamut from pop to classical to talk.

Using the Tuning Feature

▼ To Do

1. With iTunes open, scroll to the radio format you want and click the side-pointing arrow so it points down to reveal the available selections (see Figure 15.9).

FIGURE 15.9

Internet radio plays back on your iMac's speakers.

Stream	Bit Rate	Comment
▼ 50s/60s Pop (10 streams)		
⊚ 60s Music!	32 kbps	BEDANKT EN LEUK DAT JE LUISTERT!⊗-Zoa...
⊚ Beatles World	32 kbps	The Ol'm Telling Ya guide to 60's Cool
⊚ Bobby Rock	32 kbps	Bobbyrock loves all music of old. I grew u...
⊚ Bobby Rock T1	56 kbps	Every Number 1 Through 3 Song From 19...
⊚ Chart Boy	56 kbps	60's CHART TOPPERS-Every #1 & #2 Hit Of...
⊚ Goodtime Oldies	16 kbps	From Doowop to Motown to the Beachboy...
⊚ Rewind 69	56 kbps	Rewind69's Radio- The best of the 60s' an...
⊚ Sir Aragon	24 kbps	One of my first summer jobs was working ...
⊚ Vegas On The Air	24 kbps	Your online connection to live entertainme...
⊚ Vinyl Cobwebs	16 kbps	VINYL COBWEBS Radio: The Most Obscure ...
▶ 70s Pop		
▶ 80s Pop		
▶ Alt/Modern Rock		
▶ Americana		
▶ Blues		
▶ Christian		
▶ Classic Rock		
▶ Classical		

10 streams

The Bit Rate column shows how much data the station is sending. The higher the bit rate, the better the audio quality. If you have a regular dial-up connection to the Internet, you should restrict your selections to 32 kbps or lower. Otherwise, playback will occur in fits and starts, with gaps as additional data is downloaded to your iMac. The quality will be audible, but not nearly as good as an MP3 music track unless the bit rate is really high. You can also improve audio quality somewhat by selecting the Advanced tab under iTune's preferences and changing the Streaming Buffer Size to Large.

2. Select a station and double-click its name or click the Play button to start playback. There will be a short interval of silence as data is buffered to your iMac (extra data is sent to give you a safety margin, because Internet streaming speeds can be very inconsistent).

3. When you're finished listening to the station, click the Stop button or double-click another station to dial up that one instead.

> You can only get so much data from the Internet at a time. Unless you have a really fast Internet connection, don't try to download a file or browse a Web site while listening to an Internet broadcast. With all that data coming to your iMac, reception will stop or proceed with fits and starts.

Using Your iPod with iTunes

Apple's tiny digital music player, the iPod (see Figure 15.10) can serve double-duty. You can use it as an extra FireWire hard drive for your computer (see Hour 20, "Adding More Goodies to Your iMac") or you can just stick with its core function, which is a hand-held (or pocket-held) music device.

FIGURE 15.10
The iPod delivers digital music with style.

Making your iPod work with your iMac is an almost automatic process, so I'll be brief about it (aren't you glad?).

Updating Your iPod's Music Library

1. To dock your iPod to your iMac, first make sure your iMac is running.

2. Take the FireWire cable that comes with your iPod (or any regular FireWire cable for that matter) and plug it into your iPod and your iMac's FireWire port. When connects, you'll see a FireWire icon on your iPod's display. When set up, iTunes will open automatically and your iPod will automatically synchronize its music library with the one on your iMac.

> Some FireWire cables, especially those designed for DV camcorders, have a 4-pin cable at one end. These won't work with your iPod, which requires a 6-pin cable to enable it to draw current from your iMac, used for recharging its battery.

3. If you prefer to transfer music manually, connect your iPod as described previously and allow iTunes to launch.

4. Select your iPod in the iTunes source list (the list of music libraries), and click the iPod icon at the bottom right of the iTunes window, which opens the program's preferences box.

5. With preferences displayed on your iMac, check the item labeled Manually manage songs and play lists.

> You won't be able to use your iPod with other computers without it replacing your music library if you use the standard option to automatically update your play list when your iPod is attached to your computer. That's because it'll base its play list strictly on the Mac to which it's connected. If you feel you want to use the iPod on different Macs, use the manual song management option described previously.

Making a Data CD on Your iMac

Without a doubt, making a music CD is just one part of the equation. Depending on what kind of iMac or CD burner you have, you can also transfer regular data files (such as your documents) to a CD, using Apple's disk burning software.

The steps involved in copying files to a CD are hardly more difficult than copying files from one drive to another. Here's how it's done:

Burning a Data CD

▼ To Do

1. Insert a blank CD into your iMac's drive. Look for a dialog box about preparing the CD, as shown in Figure 15.11.

> Apple's disk-burning software works with the internal burner on any Apple computer and with a number of third-party devices. If you're not sure if your third-party device will work (and it should, but won't always, work either with iTunes or with Apple's regular disk-burning software), the simple thing to do is to try it. If it works, you'll be able to run through the entire process of preparing and burning a disc as described here. If it doesn't work, you can still use the software that came with the drive (but make sure you have a Mac OS X version to use it under. Mac OS X Classic CD burning applications won't function).

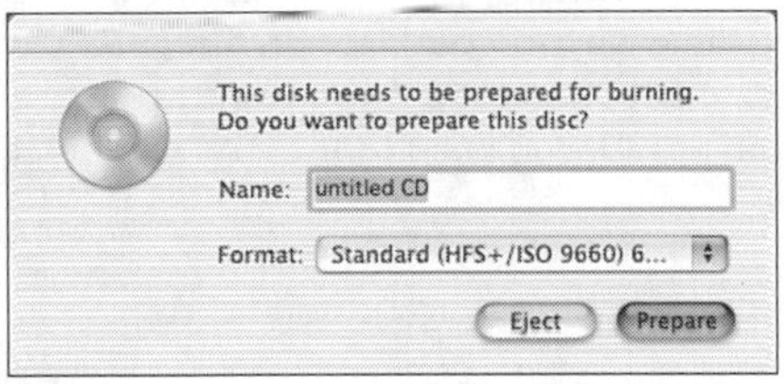

FIGURE 15.11

Get your CD ready to receive files via this dialog box.

This disk needs to be prepared for burning.
Do you want to prepare this disc?

Name: untitled CD

Format: Standard (HFS+/ISO 9660) 6...

Eject   Prepare

2. In the Name column, type a name that best describes the contents of your CD. An example might be Photo Files for a CD that contains the contents of a photo collection.

3. Click the Format pop-up menu and choose what sort of CD you want. The Standard option is for a data CD (there are options for MP3, too).

4. Click Prepare to finish the first stage of the process (or Eject if you decide not to burn a CD at this time). When you click Prepare, an icon with the name of the CD will appear on your iMac's desktop.

5. Now select and copy the files you want to add to the CD, up to the maximum of 700MB for a so-called 80-minute CD or 650MB for a 74-minute CD. You'll see a standard Finder process bar showing what you've copied, as shown in Figure 15.12.

▼

FIGURE 15.12

The file list is being copied to the CD icon.

> ○ ○ ○   Copy
>
> ▼ Copying 279 items to "Data CD"
>
> ▭▭▭▭▭▭▭▭▭▭▭▭▭▭▭▭▭▭   (Stop)
>
> Item: "Rockoids Document"
> Copied: 15.4 MB of 52.1 MB
> Time remaining: Less than a minute

When you copy files to the CD icon, you aren't actually transferring data to the CD at this point. That comes later. All you are doing is filling an image file for the disk, you can still change your mind and remove files if you want. The actual process of burning the CD comes later.

6. Double-click the CD icon and check to make sure that the files you want are present. You can also organize the layout of the icons so they'll appear the way you want on the finished CD.

If your iMac has a SuperDrive, you will also be able to put data on DVD-R media in the same way you put data on a regular CD. But the capacity is much greater, 4.7GB. However, if you want to store a multimedia file, such as a movie, on a DVD, you need to use iDVD, as described in the previous lesson.

Would you like to have a Finder window open automatically when your finished CD is inserted? Just leave the CD directory open in the position you want on the screen (top left is best) when you actually burn the CD.

7. When you're sure that the CD is set up the way you want, go to the Finder's File menu and choose Burn Disc, as shown in Figure 15.13 (it'll be in the Special menu under Mac OS 9.x).

15

FIGURE 15.13

Choose Burn Disc to begin writing to the CD.

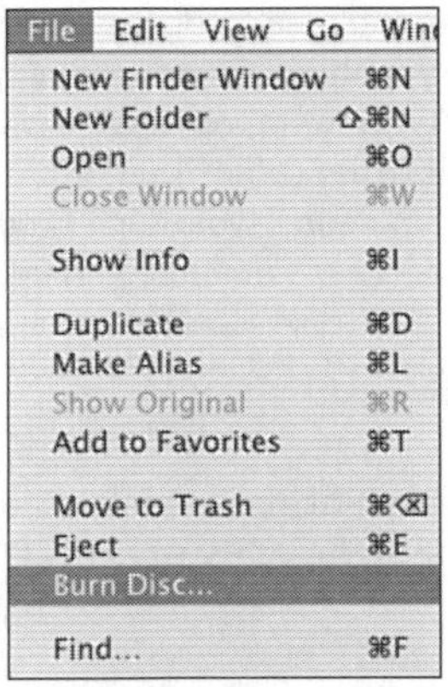

File	Edit	View	Go	Win
New Finder Window				⌘N
New Folder				⇧⌘N
Open				⌘O
Close Window				⌘W
Show Info				⌘I
Duplicate				⌘D
Make Alias				⌘L
Show Original				⌘R
Add to Favorites				⌘T
Move to Trash				⌘⌫
Eject				⌘E
Burn Disc...				
Find...				⌘F

The CD burn process works native under both Mac OS 9.x or Mac OS X. The basic setup process is the same regardless.

8. You have one more chance to opt out. When you select Burn Disc, you'll see a prompt asking you to confirm your decision. Click Burn to proceed, or Cancel or Eject to stop the process. After the CD burning process begins, you'll see the Burn Disc progress bar (shown in Figure 15.14) illustrating how far into the process you've gone. After the files are transferred to the CD, a verification process will take place, during which time the files from the CD are read back to make sure there are no mistakes.

9. Repeat the previous steps to burn additional CDs.

FIGURE 15.14

Here's a progress bar showing the disk burning operation in its early stages.

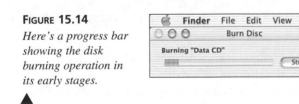

Under Mac OS 9.x, it's not a good idea to do anything on your iMac while a CD is being written because you might interrupt the process and cause a data error. Although Mac OS X is far more capable of handling this process because of its superior multitasking capabilities, you should still keep your computing activities at the minimum. Avoid such processor-intensive tasks as rendering an iMovie or printing a document to an inkjet printer until your CD is complete.

As you can see making a CD with your iMac, using Apple's built-in disk burning software is easy as pie, hardly more difficult than copying files to another drive.

Summary

In iTunes, Apple has latched on to a craze, especially among younger people. Accumulating and playing MP3 music files is fun, and it's a great way to build a huge music library; it'll even sync with your iPod to make your music portable. But that's only part of the picture. If you have an iMac with a built-in CD burner (or a separate CD burner), you can make a music CD with your favorite tunes, and a data CD with the files you want to archive for safekeeping.

You have completed the first 15 lessons of this book (and congratulations are in store), you're on the road to understanding a lot about your computer and the Mac OS in general. Beginning in the next lesson, I'll cover the harder stuff, beginning with the Mac OS's preference settings.

Q&A

Q I tried to use the Burn CD feature in iTunes, but it won't work. What did I do wrong?

A iTunes works with the built-in CD burner on an iMac and other Macs. It also works fine with many types of external drives. If you have an internal CD burner or a supported drive, make sure you properly inserted the blank CD. The writing side is usually darker than the label size (and it's usually face down on the CD jewel box or spindle in which it is sent.

If you're using an external CD burner, make sure that it is properly connected to your iMac and that it's turned on.

Q Is it legal to copy songs from the Internet?

A I might sound like a politician here, but that's a very good question and it's one that's not easy to answer. Plenty of perfectly legal places to get music exist. Some record companies even supply legal samples of an artist's music, so you get the flavor of the kind of songs they do.

As you know, there has been a lot of legal wrangling between the record companies and online sites such as Napster. The recording industry has begun to establish subscription services, where you can pay a small amount per month to gain access.

Regarding some of those other music downloading services, just remember that artists often spend years to become accepted. Very small percentages of those ever hit it big and make a lot of money, and fewer of those stay popular for very long. The rest struggle at below-average wages or just play music part time and have a regular job to keep on eating. Imagine how you'd feel if someone took the fruits of your labor without paying you for it. Your decision is between you and your conscience.

Q Can I make a full bit-for-bit copy of a CD?

A Yes, but not with Apple's CD burning software. Such applications as Roxio's Toast can do the job for you. You can also use Apple's Disk Copy software to make a disk image of a CD, and then burn a duplicate. Just remember that copying commercial software CDs might be a violation of the user license. Most software companies enable you to make a backup for your personal use, but that's all.

Q I see CD blanks for less than fifty cents each. Some are called CD-R and others, for a few dollars each, are called CD-RW. What's the difference? What should I buy?

A The first type, CD-R, is what's called a write-once CD. That means you can write your files to it just once and that's it. If you make a mistake, you have to use another CD. The CD-RW media can be erased and used over and over again, up to a thousand times. In that way, it's like a regular drive except that CD drives run slower.

If you plan on using the files only temporarily and replacing them over and over again, the extra cost of the CD-RW is worth it. Otherwise, stick with the CD-R.

Regarding the price of blank CDs, well, the best thing to do is try a brand and see if it works. If you get lots of disk errors, try a different brand. The big names, such as Fuji, Imation, Maxtor, and Verbatum, should work with any CD burner. You should try a few of the private store labels before buying a large bundle.

15

Q Why doesn't the music CD play on my CD player?

A If you have an older CD player, it might not work with a CD-R and less often with a CD-RW. Unless you've spent a bundle on that CD player, it might be worth a replacement. I have an old Panasonic Technics CD player on my regular stereo system, and it never works with the CDs I make on my iMac, but those CDs play just fine in my car and on my son's little boom box. If you're not sure what CD formats are supported, look at the manual or the box that the player was shipped.

Q I see CDs that are labeled for music. Does that mean I can't use them for data? What about a data CD?

A CDs designed for music are essentially the same as the ones you use for data (as far as the CD standard is concerned, it's all data), but the manufacturer of the CD blanks is paying a few cents per CD for music licensing. That's designed to ensure that the artists who recorded and wrote the music will get a little something for their work from the folks who copy them for their own CDs.

Q Can I make a DVD on my iMac?

A Yes, if your iMac is equipped with the SuperDrive, a CD/DVD drive from Pioneer that can burn both CDs and DVDs. The DVDs you make from that drive can play on all but the earliest generation DVD players.

Other companies make drives using the same electronics, such as LaCie and Que. They should work on any Apple computer with a FireWire port (but check with the companies as to whether the software they provide works with Mac OS X).

Q Why is there such a limited selection of radio stations under iTunes? I know some of my location stations are on the Internet.

A The stations you see with iTunes are the ones supported by the firms with whom Apple has contracted. You can find additional broadcast choices at Apple's QuickTime Web site, using the QuickTime Player application I described in Hour 13, "Using iMovie to Capture Home Videos." In addition, a number of radio stations use the Real Networks Real Player format (http://www.real.com). The software is available as a free player, handling both music and video, and a retail version with extra features (unfortunately not in Mac OS X form, although such a version might be available by the time you read this book).

Before downloading the software, however, you'll want to double-check to make sure which Mac OS versions are supported by the software.

PART VI
Learning the Hard Stuff

Hour

Hour **16**

Using System Preferences to Customize Your iMac

My publisher won't like this, but I'm going to tell you that you don't really have to read this chapter. You can get great performance if continue to use your iMac exactly as it was set up originally. But if your mouse is too slow, the desktop pattern isn't what you want, or you're not sure you want to use a screen saver, read on. You can change all these things and more by using the various programs in Mac OS X's System Preferences application or the Control Panels folder for Mac OS 9.x.

In this lesson, you'll learn

- How to use System Preferences for Mac OS X

- How to make similar changes under Mac OS 9.x

- The ideal settings for different iMac functions

- Which adjustments you should make and which you should leave alone

Introducing the System Preferences Application

I can't tell you how often I've visited a fellow Mac user and discovered that Mac OS X's System Preferences application has never been touched or even looked at, not to mention no new settings have even been attempted. As you become used to your computer, however, no doubt you'll find things you want to change; the way you might move furniture around in your home, or plant new shrubbery in your back yard.

Because Mac OS X is the main focus of this book, I'll start by covering Apple's System Preferences application (see Figure 16.1), which you'll find in the Dock, the Apple menu, or the Applications folder.

FIGURE 16.1

Mac OS X gives you a lot of ways to tailor Mac OS X to your needs.

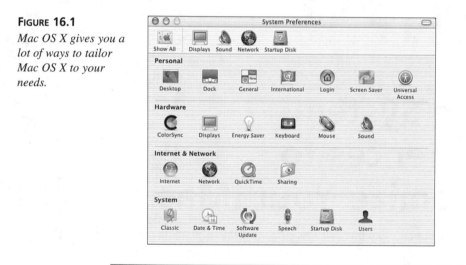

 Mac OS X (well at least as of version 10.1.3) offers 23 different settings panels. Most of them do not have to be touched at all, but a few of them can have a material affect on the look and feel of your iMac. I'll cover all the preferences, but only detail the ones that you'll use the most often.

When you've launched System Preferences, all you need to do is click an icon to open a specific settings panel. When you want to move to the next setting, you can either click an icon on the top of the System Preferences application, or click Show All to display all the icons in one place. For faster access, the preferences are all grouped into categories, and that's the way I'll cover them here.

Here's another way to get to the preference you want. Just click the View menu and choose the preference panel from the list. You might even find this a faster method to get from here to there.

Setting Personal Preferences

From Desktop to Mac OS X's screensaver, these are the individual options that cover the way your iMac interacts with you.

- **Desktop:** What sort of desktop pattern would you prefer? When you open the Desktop preference panel (shown in Figure 16.2), all you have to do is click a picture, drag it into the little well, and your iMac's desktop background changes within a few seconds. Click the Collection pop-up menu to see more selections, or to locate one of your own folders to use for background use. If you don't like the one you pick, just choose another one, drop it into the well and the pattern will change.

FIGURE 16.2

Drop the picture into the well to change Mac OS X's desktop pattern.

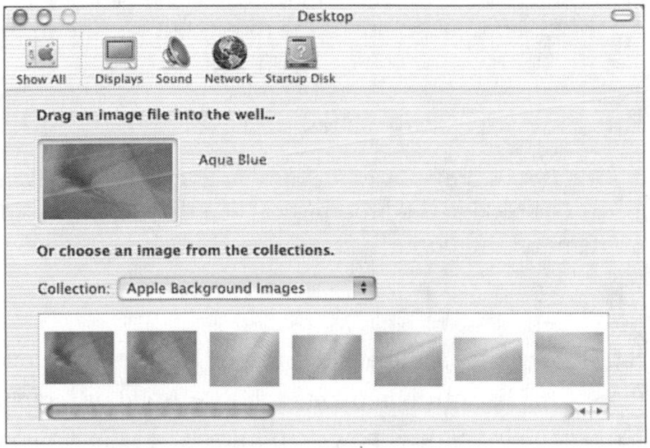

- **Dock:** The colorful taskbar at the bottom of your iMac's screen doesn't have to stay in one place. Click the preference panel, shown in Figure 16.3, and choose whether it should sit on the left or right side of the screen. You can also select whether to use a Genie or Scale effect when a Finder window is minimized to the Dock. You can also set the size of the Dock, and whether it'll magnify when the mouse moves over it. The most visually arresting icon is the effect you see when you minimize a window. By default, it's the Genie effect, where it seems to shrink an animated effect. The option Scale effect reduces the window just by making it smaller as it drops to the Dock; less visual but faster.

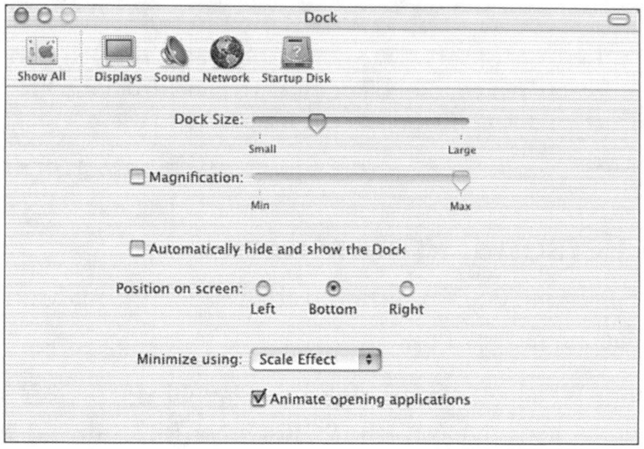

FIGURE 16.3
Use this preference panel to choose how the Dock works.

Would you like to impress your friends? When you minimize something to the Dock, or restore (maximize) a reduced window, hold down the Shift key. This will slow the Genie or Scale effect to a crawl. It's exactly what Apple CEO Steve Jobs does when he demonstrates Mac OS X during his famous keynote addresses at the Macworld Expo trade shows. After a while, you or your friends might tire of the effect, but it's fine to show it off on occasion.

The Dock's preferences are also directly available from the Apple menu and by Ctrl-clicking the little vertical line that separates applications from other items on the Dock.

- **General:** This preference panel, shown in Figure 16.4, covers several settings. First, there's the background theme (choose Aqua or Graphite and the highlight color). You can also choose how scroll arrows at the right side of the window appear, and how many recent items (applications and documents) are displayed in the Apple menu. The final setting covers the starting point for Mac OS X's font smoothing, which makes text appear less jagged on the screen. Feel free to experiment with any of these settings. They won't harm anything, and you can always put things back if you don't like the results.

- **International:** Choose this preference panel to determine which languages are preferred first. Mac OS X is an international operating system that works with many languages.

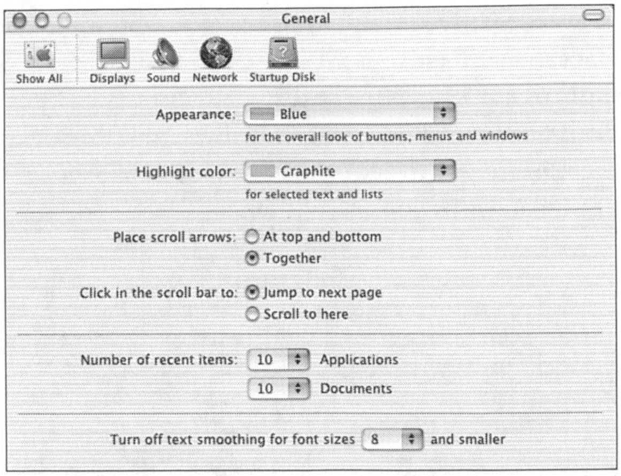

FIGURE 16.4

This setting controls basic appearance of your Mac OS X user environment.

16

- **Login:** In a sense, some of what the Login panel (shown in Figure 16.5) does resembles the old Startup Items folder under Mac OS 9.x where you can place things to start when your iMac starts. You can configure an application to launch whenever Mac OS X starts by clicking the Add button to select the program, or choose how the Login panel behaves when accessed at startup. The Login Window tab is where you can specify a default user. That's you, if you're the only user, but if you set up your iMac for multiple users you can specify anyone (or nobody, in which case there will always be a login prompt at startup).

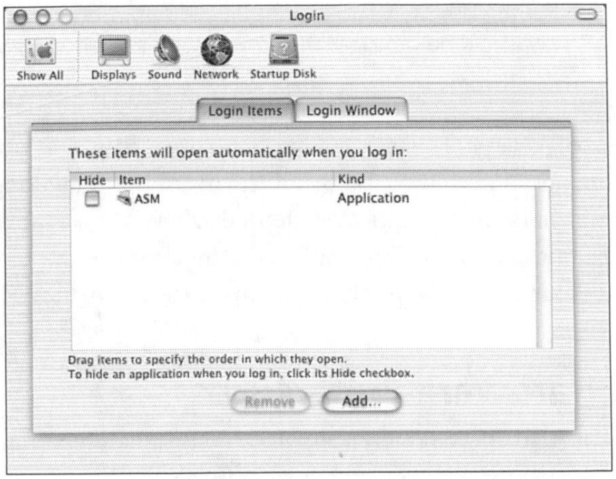

FIGURE 16.5

Add Login applications that will then start whenever you start your iMac under Mac OS X.

- **Screensaver:** Mac OS X gives you a neat screensaver (shown in Figure 16.6) that puts a fancy pattern on your iMac's screen when it's idle for a few minutes. Click the mouse, or any key on the keyboard, to dismiss it. After you select a pattern, click the Activation tab to specify how long your iMac sits doing nothing before the screensaver is activated. You can click the Hot Corners tab to specify a location on your screen where you can activate the screensaver.

FIGURE 16.6

Use Mac OS X's screensaver to make your iMac look pretty when it's idle.

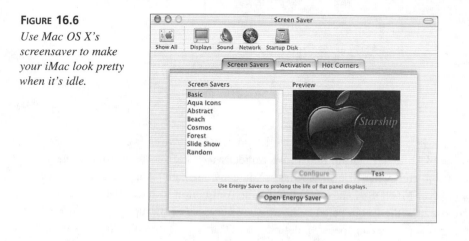

> The screensaver can also protect your iMac when you're not around and it's in a place where other users might see it. Just click the Activation tab and click the Use My User Account Password option. After it's running, the only way someone can clear the screensaver is to enter your user password.

- **Universal Access:** This is a feature that's very helpful if you suffer from wrist pains or have a disability. There's a Keyboard option with a sticky keys function that helps in typing complicated shortcuts. The Mouse tab accesses a feature that uses the numeric keypad to emulate the functions of the mouse. Even if you don't need these options, you might try them and see how they affect the way you use your iMac.

Setting Hardware Preferences

The next set of Mac OS X preference panels control how you interact with your hardware from mouse to monitor. I'll cover the essentials next.

- **ColorSync:** This is a native Mac technology that enables you to match color from scanner to iMac to printer. If you are working as a graphic designer, you can look for instructions for your various peripherals (scanner and printer) and how color matching is done.

- **Displays:** This preference panel is used to set color depth (the number of colors displayed) and the resolution of your desktop display. The flat-panel iMac's setting should be 1024×768. A vintage iMac might look better at 800×600 because things get larger, clearer, and maybe more readable on the smaller monitor. The Show Displays in the Menu Bar option enables you to change display settings from the menu bar without having to open System Preferences.

16

> The menu bar displays activated by the Displays, Sound, and other preference panels can be moved into a different order (you're not forced to take the one Mac OS X gives you). Just hold down the Cmd key and drag a preference icon on the menu bar to a different position. Sorry, the menu bar clock can't be moved this way.

- **Energy Saver:** This is a way to cut down on power usage and also let your iMac go into idle or Sleep mode after a given period of time, as shown in Figure 16.7. You can specify separate settings for display and hard drive by clicking the check box and moving the sliders back and forth.

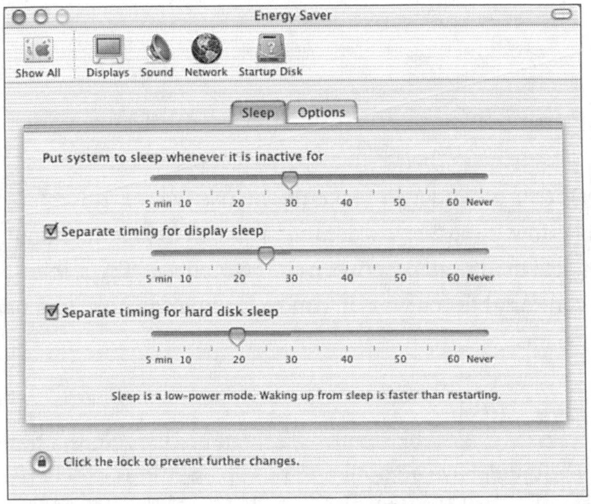

FIGURE 16.7

Specify the Sleep or rest interval from here.

> Does your iMac's screen suddenly blank out? One possible reason is that it's been idle for a while and the Energy Saver preference settings have become active. To awaken your iMac, just press any key on the keyboard and it'll come to life in seconds.

- **Keyboard:** There are two levels of settings here. One controls how fast keystrokes repeat when you press and hold down a key on the keyboard. The other, Full Keyboard Access (shown in Figure 16.8), enables you to press a modifier key (such as Ctrl), plus one of the function keys (the ones with the F1 to F15 on them). This automatically pulls down menus from the menu bar, and directly accesses other functions, such as moving through Dock icons, right from the keyboard. Try it! You might like it (I do!).

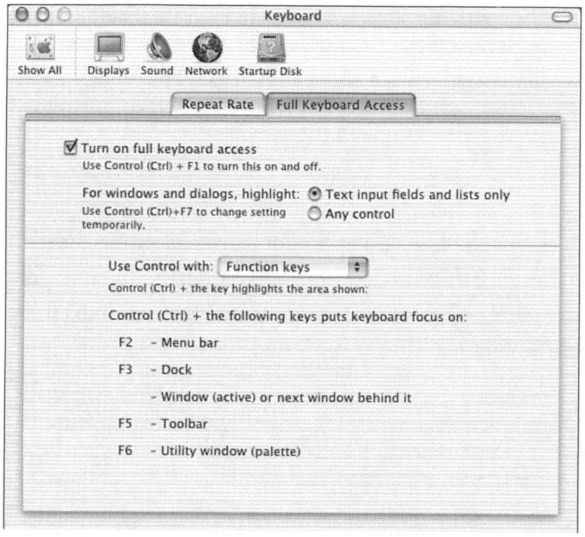

FIGURE 16.8

This range of settings enables your iMac's keyboard to access menus, the Dock, active windows, and so on.

- **Mouse:** Click a slider to make the mouse cursor move faster or slower. It tends to be a bit slow on iMacs by default. You can also adjust double-click speed here, which sets the interval between the two clicks. Try a few settings and see which are most comfortable for you. If you're using an iBook, this panel controls the trackpad settings, too.

> Do you access a particular preference very often? Some, such as Displays and Sound, have an option to put up a settings icon in the menu bar. You can also drag the item's icon to the top of the System Preferences window, just as Displays, Sound, Network, and Startup Disk appear now. By doing that, you save a step to access those features.

- **Sound:** Pick the sound levels for both system sounds and overall volume. If your iMac has a special set of speakers attached, such as the iSub or Harmon-Kardon SoundSticks, you might see additional options to adjust settings for these products. Choose the option to put the sound settings in the menu bar for fast access.

> The Apple Pro keyboard also has three media keys (in the upper-right row) that set volume. One to reduce the level, the second to increase the level, and the third to mute (turn off) the sound.

16

Setting Internet and Network Preferences

The settings you choose in these preference panels control your Internet and network access, including file sharing, which is the capability to share your iMac's files with other computers. The QuickTime settings are used to make your iMac work best with multimedia files. Let's go through the list:

- **Internet:** There are four settings offered in this preference panel (shown in Figure 16.9) that cover the way your iMac works while online (except for AOL and CompuServe 2000, which don't use these settings). Click the iTools tab to set up or configure your account with Apple's handy set of Web-based features. The email tab is used to control the settings used to send and receive email. The Web tab enables you to select a home page (the page your browser calls on when you launch it), a default search site, and where downloaded files go (the default is on your Mac OS X desktop). The last setting, news, is used to access Usenet news-groups, interesting message boards that cover a wide range of topics.

FIGURE 16.9

These settings control how your computer works with an Internet connection.

NEW TERM *Usenet*, short for user net, is the common name for a worldwide Internet-based message and discussion board. This is the online equivalent of the bulletin boards in your supermarket or civic club. You can use it to read messages from others or place your own statements about one subject or another.

- **Network:** Choose this preference panel to specify how your iMac interacts with a local network or your Internet connection. If you set up your iMac to use EarthLink with the Mac OS X Setup Assistant, all the settings are made for you. You'll need to contact your ISP for other user settings that need to be entered here.

- **QuickTime:** The key setting optimizes a streaming video to your Internet-connection speed. I covered that in more detail in Hour 14, "Using iMovie, iDVD, and iPhoto."

- **Sharing:** Use this preference panel to give your iMac a unique name and also to share files with other computers on your network. The subject is covered in more detail in Hour 18, "Coping with the Windows World."

Setting System Preferences

The final set of preferences covers the way some system software elements interact with you on your iMac. So here's our final run-through with System Preferences settings.

- **Classic:** Under Mac OS X, whenever you launch an old or Classic Mac OS application, the Classic environment is in use. This preference panel, described in more detail in Hour 23, "Crashin' Away: What to Do?" controls how Classic runs on your iMac. The most useful option is to have it start whenever you start your iMac, so you don't have to wait an extra minute or so for it to get rolling when you run a Classic application.

- **Date & Time:** To keep your iMac's clock ticking accurately, this preference panel (shown in Figure 16.10) is called into play. The first setting, under the Date & Time tab, is used to change date and time (it doesn't work if automatic network time synchronization is chosen). The second, Time Zone, is used to specify your location so that your email and message board posts have the right date and time. The Network Time option is the most useful. You can click a time server from the NTP Server pop-up menu, and then have the time automatically adjusted whenever you are online and the time is found to be off or when your iMac starts up. The final setting, Menu Bar Clock, is used to choose whether your clock is displayed as text or an icon, and whether such things as seconds and the day of the week are included in the display.

FIGURE 16.10

Click a tab to set Date & Time preferences.

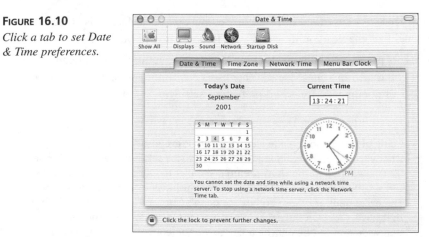

16

- **Software Update:** This is a clever feature of Mac OS X (shown in Figure 16.11) that will search out Apple's Web site for needed updates. When you click Automatically and specify an interval from the pop-up menu (Daily, Weekly, or Monthly), Software Update will go into action as soon as you make an Internet connection on the appointed day. Click Update Now to connect to your Internet account and see if any updates are available. If they are, a separate Software Update application will open in the Dock. When you click that application, you'll see the list of updates along with some information on what they do. From here you can download the updates and they'll be installed after retrieved.

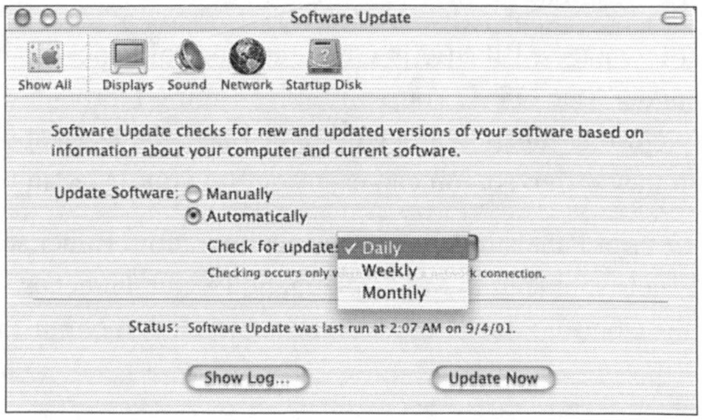

FIGURE 16.11

Like magic, Software Update figures out if Mac OS X needs an update and will give you the chance to receive those updates.

- **Speech:** Some day, you will be able to have a conversation with your computer (Computer, wash the dishes; Computer, take out the trash!), but right now Apple's Speech preference settings are pretty limited. You can have text read back to you in several preset voices (more or less, but not always perfectly), or use the Listening feature to hear simple commands in the spirit of Computer, Restart! Give it a try, but don't expect miracles.

- **Startup Disk:** As described in Hour 2, "Setting Up Your iMac," this is the preference panel that enables you to restart your iMac with your Mac OS 9.x.
- **Users:** This preference panel is used for Mac OS X's multiple-users feature, which enables you to set up your iMac so other users can run it and have their own personal sets of documents, fonts and preference settings.

> Many of the settings made via the System Preferences application apply strictly to the user who is logged in when those settings are made. If other users are set up in the Users preference panel to work on your iMac, they can set their own user settings, none of which will interfere with your own. The exceptions are those preference panels (such as Network and Sharing) that have a lock on the lower-left corner; these are settings that apply system wide and can be only be accessed via someone with owner (administrator) access.

A Fast Look at Mac OS 9's Control Panel Settings

When you restart your iMac under the Classic Mac OS environment (or you run a Classic application under Mac OS X), you can choose from yet another set of system preference settings, courtesy of your Control Panels. Available from the Control Panels folder (inside the System Folder) or Mac OS 9.x's Apple menu, the Control Panels are little applications that can control one or more system settings.

Over the next few pages, I'll strictly cover the Control Panel functions that do not have counterparts under Mac OS X. You will find, as you go through this list, that many of them are very close in function and feel to the ones you learn about under Mac OS X. I'll explain where they differ, so you can easily set up your iMac in both systems.

Using these Control Panels involves the same operation. Either select them directly from the Control Panels submenu in the Apple menu (which launches them), or locate them manually in the Control Panels folder and double-click them just as any other application.

> If a Control Panel has the same name and function as its Mac OS X counterpart, I won't mention it at all. You can apply the instructions in the previous section to the Mac OS 9.x equivalent. In addition, the Control Panel changes you make have no affect under Mac OS X, except, to a limited degree, under Classic.

Using the Appearance Manager

The Appearance Control Panel is used to redecorate your computer's desktop, as shown in Figure 16.12. Each tab is used to control a different setting.

FIGURE 16.12

Change your iMac's Mac OS 9 desktop with this program.

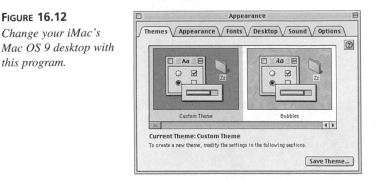

Here's what the various components of the Appearance Control Panel do:

The desktop theme you see on your iMac when you install it might be different from the ones I've used in this book. It all depends on the system version you have, and, perhaps, whether the technician who prepared your computer for delivery changed it.

- **Themes**: These are preconfigured sets of appearance motifs, complete with desktop patterns, display fonts, and more. Just use the horizontal scrollbar to see the various choices.

When you create a custom desktop environment, you can save it as a theme, using the Save Theme feature, for instant recall later.

- **Appearance**: This setting controls the look of the menu bar and directory windows, and the color used when you highlight (select) an item.
- **Fonts**: Use this setting to pick the fonts used for window and directory display.

> If the text onscreen looks a little jagged to you, you can use the Smooth All Fonts On Screen feature in the Fonts tab to make it look better. The downside of this smoothness, however, is that text might display a little slower on your screen.

- **Desktop**: Use these settings to select new desktop art from Apple's selections. You might also use one of your own pictures.
- **Sound**: If you want, you can have sounds play when activating a function on your computer. This is not recommended for a busy office, where the sounds (which can be a little strange sometimes) might disturb others.
- **Options**: These settings change the look of scrollbars, and they also offer a setting for the window shade feature, where you can double-click a title bar to collapse the window.

> The desktop backdrops you pick here won't run if you access Mac OS 9.x from Mac OS X's Classic environment. The functions you see here are somewhat similar to the ones you find in Mac OS X's Desktop and General preferences.

Setting the Apple Menu Options Control Panel

This Control Panel activates the handy submenus you see in the Mac OS 9.x Apple menu. The other settings control the number of items shown in the Recent Applications, Recent Documents, and Recent Servers (networked Macs) folders available in the Apple menu.

Setting the Control Strip Control Panel

That little palette of icons at the bottom of your computer's screen is used to activate some Control Panel functions. This Control Panel can be used to hide or show the Control Strip. In addition, you can adjust your Control Strip with these techniques:

- Hold down the Option key and drag the curved end of the Control Strip to move it around.
- Click once on either end of the Control Strip to collapse it (or after it is collapsed, to expand it again).
- If the left end has a pointed arrow, it indicates that all the Control Strip modules are not fully displayed. Just click and drag the curved end of the Control Strip out to expand it.

> Control Strips are not displayed when the Mac OC X's Classic environment is being used.

Setting the Extensions Manager Control Panel

Apple's Extensions Manager offers a convenient way to manage your Extensions and Control Panels, shown in Figure 16.13. Click the check box to turn something off (after which, you must restart).

> The Extensions Manager is also useful for troubleshooting. By systematically activating and deactivating extensions, you can use the program to help you find a possible software conflict. But make any changes with care because turning off the wrong things can disable some important functions of your computer. I'll cover this subject in more detail in Hour 23.

FIGURE 16.13

The Extensions Manager controls the programs that are activated when you boot your iMac under Mac OS 9.x.

On/Off	Name	Size	Version	Package
☒	ABFR Blank Droplet	272K	3.8 final	—
☒	Apple Audio Extension	716K	1.4.3	Mac OS 9.2.1
☒	Apple CD/DVD Driver	120K	1.4.7	Mac OS 9.2.1
☒	Apple Enet	520K	2.4.2	Mac OS 9.2.1
☒	Apple Enet DLPI Support	84K	1.0	Mac OS 9.2.1
☒	Apple Guide	828K	2.5.3	Mac OS 9.2.1
☒	Apple Modem Tool	172K	1.5.7	Mac OS 9.2.1
☒	Apple Monitor Plugins	944K	2.1	Mac OS 9.2.1
☒	Apple QD3D HW Driver	16K	1.6	QuickTime 5.0...
☒	Apple QD3D HW Plug-In	44K	1.6	QuickTime 5.0...
☒	AppleShare	592K	3.9.1	—
☒	Application Switcher	88K	1.0	Mac OS 9.2.1
☒	ATI 3D Accelerator	932K	5.0.4	Mac OS 9.2.1
☒	ATI Driver Update	1,932K	1.9.5	Mac OS 9.2.1
☒	ATI Extension	108K	2.8.2	ATI Multimedi...
☒	ATI Graphics Accelerator	944K	5.4.3	Mac OS 9.2.1
☒	ATI Mac2TV™ Monitor	44K	2.8.2	ATI Multimedi...
☒	ATI MPP Manager	60K	1.2	Mac OS 9.2.1
☒	ATI Radeon 3D Accelerator	636K	6.2.6	Mac OS 9.2.1
☒	ATI Rage 128.. Accelerator	636K	6.2.5	Mac OS 9.2.1
☒	ATI Resource Manager	264K	2.9.5	Mac OS 9.2.1
☒	ATI ROM Xtender	444K	1.0.3	ATI Multimedi...
☒	ATI Video Accelerator	172K	4.8.2	Mac OS 9.2.1

Extensions Manager — Selected Set: My Settings — Restart | Revert | Duplicate Set... ▷ Show Item Information

> If you need to run your iMac with a special Extension set, you can make that set by using the New Set command in the File menu.

Setting the General Control Panel

General Controls are used for a grab bag of functions (shown in Figure 16.14). Most of the changes you make require a restart to activate. As you go through them, you'll see they differ to a large extent from the General preference panel under Mac OS X. Here's what those settings do:

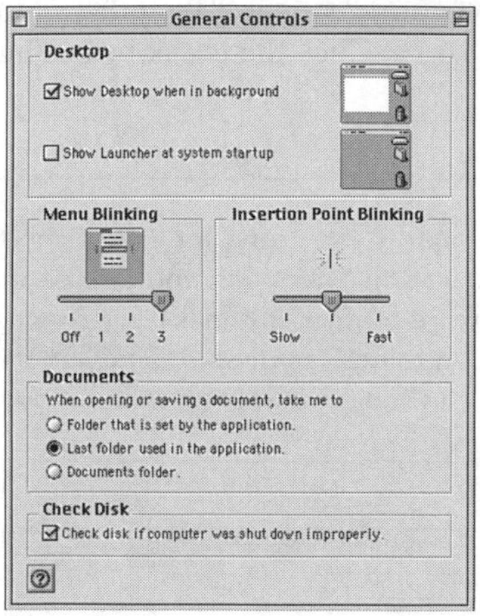

FIGURE 16.14

Use General Controls to make several adjustments to your iMac.

> If a check box in General Controls is grayed out, it means the feature isn't available on your computer.

- **Show Desktop When in Background**: If your desktop icons are cluttered and distract you, you can switch off this option to show a blank desktop backdrop when you're working in a program.
- **Show Launcher at System Startup**: This feature activates the neat little Launcher Control Panel, which puts up an icon launching dock on your computer's desktop.
- **Shut Down Warning**: If your iMac is not shut down properly (perhaps because of a crash or power failure), or you have to force a restart, you'll see a warning when you start up with this function turned on. In addition, Apple's Disk First Aid software will run automatically to see that your hard drive's directory is healthy. I suggest you leave it on.

Under Mac OS X, all the drives connected to your Mac are scanned (and fixable damage is repaired) every time you start your Mac.

- **Insertion Point Blinking**: If the blinking of the insertion point when you're writing text is too distracting, you can change the setting here.
- **Menu Blinking**: This setting adjusts the rate the menu bar blinks when you select a command.
- **Documents**: Use this setting to configure the default location where documents are saved.

The most convenient place to save documents is, naturally, the Documents folder. If you check that option in General Controls, such a folder will be set up the next time you restart. And all the documents you want to save will point there by default in the Mac OS X 9.x Open or Save dialog boxes (but you can still put them elsewhere).

Setting the Memory Control Panel

This Control Panel is used to activate several features (see Figure 16.15) that have a direct connection with your computer's performance under regular usage. The changes require a restart to activate. Here's what those features are used for:

FIGURE 16.15

The settings you make in the Memory Control Panel can impact the performance of your computer when running under Mac OS 9.x.

The best way to set the Memory Control Panel is to click the Use Defaults button. That will establish the optimum disk cache and virtual memory setting for your iMac (depending on how much RAM is installed). Only change it if you add more RAM.

- **Disk Cache**: This setting reserves a small amount of RAM to store frequently used data from your hard drive. The default setting offers a decent speed boost for your iMac. Setting it too low to conserve RAM will slow some functions down (such as display of document windows).

- **Virtual Memory**: Virtual memory sets aside a part of your hard drive to simulate RAM. It's useful to extend available memory when you want to run more programs. But because a hard drive is much slower than real RAM, it might also slow things down somewhat, especially if you set it too high. The normal setting establishes virtual memory at 1MB above the amount of built-in memory on your computer. This setting actually can make some programs run faster (and besides, they also use less memory for some highly technical reasons).

> Disk caching and virtual memory are automatically set and configured under Mac OS X. The settings you make here apply strictly when restarting under Mac OS 9.x.

- **RAM Disk**: This feature sets aside RAM to use to simulate the functions of a hard drive (such as copying files and so on). But the memory used here is lost to your computer to run programs. *Only use this feature if you have a lot of RAM installed.* I'll tell you more about RAM upgrades in Hour 22, "Giving Your iMac New Software, More Ram, and Other Things." RAM Disk is not supported for Mac OS X.

Setting the Remote Access Control Panel

You use this Control Panel to set the phone number and access information needed for your Internet provider. After things are set up, you'll only need to use this program to connect and disconnect. This is the Mac OS 9.x equivalent of Mac OS X's Internet Connect application.

Setting the Startup Disk Control Panel

Explained in Hour 2, you can use this Control Panel to switch over from Mac OS 9.x to Mac OS X with a single restart.

Setting the TCP/IP Control Panel

The settings used to connect to the Internet, or perhaps a network, are created here. Usually, these adjustments are made by the installation software used by your Internet service, so you should rarely have to open this program unless you want to switch to another setting.

The arcane numbers and words used in the TCP/IP Control Panel are necessary for certain Internet or network hookups. If you change even a single character or number, the connections won't work. It's best not to change any setting without detailed instructions on the information you need to enter. In addition, the settings made here do not carry over to the Network preference panel settings under Mac OS X (but the same information might be entered in both for your Internet hookup).

16

Summary

In this lesson you discovered ways to customize your computer's settings so that it looks and runs better. I first demonstrated the System Preference application settings under Mac OS X, and then showed you the ones that are different under Mac OS 9.x.

As you add new software to your iMac, you'll find additional system settings that make your iMac behave different.

In previous lessons, I described how you can create documents in various programs such as AppleWorks. In Hour 17, "Now That I Wrote It, How Do I Print It?" you'll learn about installing a new printer and setting it up for the best quality printouts.

Q&A

Q I'm confused. In Hour 3, you described extensions as programs that enhance the functionality under Mac OS 9.x. But the Control Panels seem to do the very same thing. What's the difference?

A The biggest difference is that an Extension doesn't have a user interface for you to make an adjustment. The Control Panel does, but the waters get muddied after that. Some Control Panels work in concert with an Extension to provide some features such as Extensions Manager and the EM Extension. Some Control Panels (such as the Memory Control Panel) do their stuff without any other programs. As I said, the major difference lies in the word Control, the capability to set things.

Fortunately, with Mac OS X, as explained below, you don't have to worry about extensions, and the Control Panel settings are performed via the System Preferences application.

Q **Suddenly I see folders labeled Extensions (Disabled), Control Panels (Disabled), and so on. What are they for, and can I remove them?**

A Best thing to do is leave them alone unless you know the contents aren't needed (and more often than not, it's difficult to tell, unless the item is clearly labeled as something you don't need). When you turn off an Extension or Control Panel with Extensions Manager, it goes in one of these folders. When the program is reactivated, it goes back to its regular folder.

Q **Some of the programs I want to use say I need to create an Apple-only extension set to install them. How do I set it up?**

A This is easy because the Extensions Manager Control Panel already has it. Just click the Selected Set pop-up menu to find Mac OS 9.x All and Mac OS 9.x Base settings (or whatever system version you're using). For normal software installations, choose the latter and restart. After your program is installed, you can open up Extensions Manager, click My Settings from the pop-up menu (or whatever name you've given your set), and restart yet again to set things back the way they were.

If you are installing a Mac OS X program, these settings are nothing to be concerned about. Mac OS X doesn't use system extensions in the same sense as Mac OS 9.x (they are sometimes called kernel extensions and won't mess up your system). Under Mac OS X, just run the installer, follow the screen prompts, and then let it do its thing.

Hour **17**

Now That I Wrote It, How Do I Print It?

Print it! No that's not just something that you might hear on a movie set. So far in this book, you've learned how to create a document with your iMac. You've learned how to use AppleWorks, an integrated program that enables you to write, draw pictures, and store financial and other information.

In this lesson, I'll show you how to get a printout of those documents. You'll learn

- What kinds of printers are available for your computer
- The advantages and disadvantages of inkjet and laser printers
- How to hook up and configure your new printer
- How to switch printers on a network

Buying a New Printer

When you visit your dealer or look over a computing catalog, no doubt you've seen a bewildering array of printers with a great range of prices.

You can buy printers for around one hundred dollars, whereas others cost thousands. Some even come free with a new computer purchase (though sometimes free means you have to wait a few weeks for a manufacturer's rebate).

You want your documents to look their best, but with all the confusing claims about dots per inch, four color, six color, inkjet versus laser, and photo realistic, how do you pick the printer that is perfect for you?

In this part of the lesson, I'll list the kinds of printers that are available, and I'll also define a few of the buzzwords, so you can see which ones matter:

- **Dot-matrix printer**: This sort of printer owes a lot to the traditional typewriter. A printing head puts the image on paper in the form of little dots. Such printers aren't usually available anymore, but older Apple ImageWriters still run and many folks use them. Most Mac OS computers have an ImageWriter printer driver these days (at least via the Classic environment), although you will need a special adapter plug to enable you to hook it up to an iMac.

- **Inkjet printer**: Here's another printer that also owes something to the original typewriter. Instead of keys or a little ball with letters, the inkjet printer uses a small tank of ink (the cartridge) that slides back and forth across the paper on a sled-like device. Such printers can be quite cheap, and they offer color reproduction and terrific printouts of photos and artwork. Because these printer are still using ink (no matter what the technology) the text usually isn't quite as sharp and clean as the laser printer, although the quality on some models gets mighty close.

- **Laser printer**: Laser printers are similar to copying machines. They use a small black powder (toner) to paint the image on paper, and their printing engines use laser devices (like your CD or DVD player). Such printers generally have their own computers so they cost much more than an inkjet printer, but offer greater output quality, especially with text. Color laser printers, though, are especially expensive; they can cost up to several times what your iMac set you back. They also use four toner cartridges, which, as you might expect, can get quite expensive to replace.

- **Four-color and six-color printers**: In commercial printing, the various colors in a full-color page are created by using four primary colors (one printing plate for each) and mixing them to various degrees. Six-color printers provide more accurate reproduction of color prints, at least in theory, but you can get great quality from four-color printers, too. Six-color printers range from low-cost inkjets to expensive devices used by professional printers to make job proofs.

- **Networked printer**: This sort of printer is hooked up to your computer's Ethernet jack and can be shared by other computers across a network (even those running other computing platforms). Both inkjet and laser printers might come with the proper networking electronics for this sort of connection.

- **Dots-per-inch**: The printed page is made up of little dots, or *pixels*. The more dots-per-inch, the smaller the dots and the sharper the output. Because laser printers produce sharper dots they offer better output quality for a specific dots-per-inch specification.

> In all fairness, the printer with the highest dots-per-inch rating doesn't always deliver the best quality. Putting more pixels on a page might not mean that color is more accurate, or the characters of the alphabet look nicer. The best thing to do is to look at a sample page from the printer you want to buy or read a product review in your favorite computer magazine or online news source.

Setting Up a New Printer

Regardless of the kind of printer you buy, the basic hookup steps are similar. The process usually takes just a few minutes from the time you crack open the box until the printer is up and running.

The setup steps for inkjets and laser printers are similar, so I'll describe them together here, with a few notes to show where things might diverge:

Classic Mac OS Printer Setups

1. Unpack your printer and check the device for little bits of tape and cardboard that are left from shipping.

> I cannot overemphasize the need to remove packing materials before you try to use a printer. Some of those little bits of tape and cardboard can literally lock up the printer (maybe damage the sometimes delicate plastic parts inside) if you try to use it without removing this material. If in doubt, check the printer's setup manual for information.

2. Plug it in to the power source (AC line or power strip) and install the ink cartridges or toner assembly (whichever applies) as instructed by the manufacturer.

3. Use the appropriate connection cable to attach the printer to your computer. Some makers include the cable, other printers come without, so you have to buy it separately (like the battery for your child's brand new toy). Depending on the kind of printer or connection setup you have, you will be using either the Ethernet port or a USB port (you can use the empty jack on your keyboard for the latter connection).

Inkjet printers are usually set up so you actually have to turn them on and push a button to move the inkwells into the proper place for installation of the cartridge or cartridges (some models do it automatically when you open the cover). In addition to documentation, such printers might also have a chart inside to show you how to install cartridges.

If you're using an Ethernet printer, you will either need to install a hub (a special connection interface) or use a crossover cable (which is designed for a direct connection between your iMac and another Ethernet device) for the hookup to work. Check with your dealer for the requirements.

4. Get out the manufacturer's software CD, insert it into your computer's drive, and install the printing software. If you plan on using an application that runs in the iMac's Classic environment, you might need to install two different versions, one for Classic and one for Mac OS X. Check the printer's instructions about this.

Not sure whether you're going to use a Classic application? Install the software anyway. That way you don't have to worry about it later, in case the need arises.

5. After the software installation is done, you need to select the printer driver on your computer. Because you're using two operating systems, you have to do the job twice. To choose a Classic printer driver, you need to launch a Classic application. Open your Applications (Mac OS 9) folder and launch any application.

6. Go to the Apple menu and select the Chooser, which will open the Classic Mac OS printer selection utility (see Figure 17.1).

If you're installing a laser printer, you'll see a button at the bottom of the Select a Printer window labeled Setup. Click that button to complete the configuration process.

FIGURE 17.1

Pick your printer from the list in the Chooser.

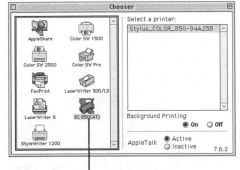

Click a printer icon to select it.

Not all printers can be identified by the printer icon in the Chooser (it's not very convenient!). You might have to check the documentation to see what you have to pick. For example, my Epson Stylus Color 850ne color inkjet printer is identified in the Chooser as SC 850(AT).

7. Close the Chooser window. You'll see an acknowledgement message that your printer has been selected (see Figure 17.2). Click OK to dismiss the message.

FIGURE 17.2

Your printer has been selected, and you're ready to go.

Mac OS X Printer Setups

1. Now it's time to select a printer for Mac OS X. To do that, find the Print Center application, which is located in the Utilities folder (inside the Mac OS X Applications folder) and launch it.

To Do

If you intend to add a networked printer, first open the System Preferences application, click the Network panel, and select Built-in Ethernet from the Configure pop-up menu. With your Ethernet setup on the screen, click the AppleTalk tab and turn it on, by clicking the Make AppleTalk Active check box. AppleTalk is required for these printers to be available from the network on your iMac.

17

2. If no printer is available, you'll see an onscreen message to that effect (see Figure 17.3). If you do, click Add and continue.

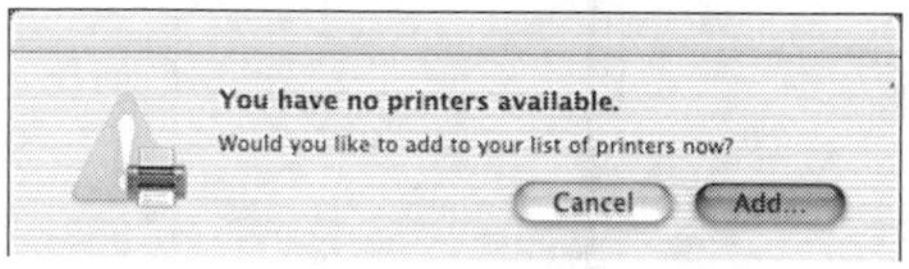

FIGURE **17.3**

Click Add to configure a printer.

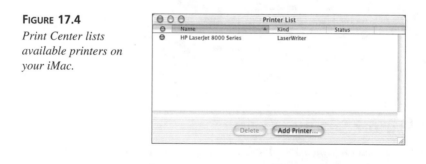

You have no printers available.

Would you like to add to your list of printers now?

Cancel   Add...

> Mac OS X comes with printer drivers for inkjets and laser printers that work with many products such as Canon, Epson, HP, Lexmark, and Xerox. If you have a USB printer, you might just have to hook it up, turn it on and the printer's model name will appear in the Mac OS X Print dialog box. However, you still need to install drivers for your iMac's Classic environment. Otherwise, you can configure it as explained later in this chapter.

3. Now you need to pick the connection port to which your printer is connected. With the Printer window on display, click the pop-up menu at the top (see Figure 17.4). You can use AppleTalk, LPR Printers Using IP, or USB (unless the printer adds a custom port listing, in which case more will be listed).

FIGURE **17.4**

Print Center lists available printers on your iMac.

Printer List		
Name	Kind	Status
HP LaserJet 8000 Series	LaserWriter	

Delete   Add Printer...

> AppleTalk is for networked printers, USB is for printers that connect to the USB port. The other choice, LPR Printers Using IP, is for special network printers that enable you to connect via TCP/IP. If you have a printer with this capability (normally used in larger businesses), the documentation that came with it will tell you how to set it up.

4. With the connection port selected, you'll see a list of printers available via that connection. To make a printer the default (the one that is first on the list in the Mac OS X Print dialog box), click the printer's name, and choose Make Default from the Printers menu.

I don't want to make things seem more complicated than they already are, but, as hinted previously, some printer drivers set up their own custom printer port entries for Print Center. One example is an Epson Stylus C80N, which is the C80 with an Ethernet network adapter card. When you set up this printer, you will find an entry listed as Epson AppleTalk, and that's what you need to select to harness the printer's network features on your iMac.

5. Leave Print Center by choosing Quit from the application menu.

Congratulations, you're now ready to print your documents.

If you have more than one printer in the Classic environment, you'll be revisiting the Chooser every so often to switch from one to the other (unless it's between two laser printers). Under Mac OS X, you can easily switch from one to another in the Print dialog box without using Print Center anymore.

Configuring and Printing with Inkjet Printers

As you see, hooking up a new printer to your computer can be done in a few minutes at most. Now you're ready to print your documents—well, almost. When you first print your document, you will have to set up a few more things to make sure that it comes out properly.

Using the Page Setup Dialog Box

The first part of the process will require a dialog box called Page Setup, which is available from the File menu in most of your programs. See Figure 17.5 for the one that comes with a typical HP inkjet printer (I'll cover the one for laser printers in a later section, but it won't differ very much).

The Page Setup dialog box will change from printer to printer, when you switch from one program to another and, most important, when you switch from a Classic to Mac OS X application. So I'm just covering the basic features here. Your printer's documentation will offer extra setup instructions.

FIGURE 17.5
This is the Page Setup box for an HP inkjet printer when you're using AppleWorks.

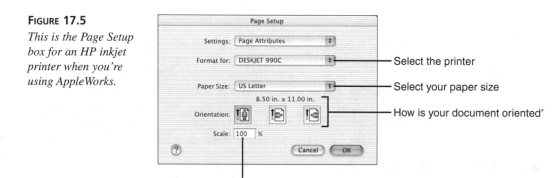

By default, the designers of the printing software will guess that you're using a regular, letter-sized page, and establish the other settings shown in Figure 17.5. If you need to change things, here's what the settings mean:

- **Format For**: This setting enables you to select the custom paper sizes for a specific printer.

- **Paper Size**: This pop-up menu is used to pick a different paper size and type, such as Legal Size, envelopes, and so on. The choices depend on the kind of printer you have.

- **Orientation**: Is your document set up in horizontal or vertical form (also known as landscape and portrait)? Make your change here.

- **Reduce or Enlarge**: If your document is too large for the paper you have, you can scale it down here (or make it larger for a smaller-sized document).

Be careful about making a small document larger to fit a paper size. When you enlarge some documents (such as those containing pictures), the quality is reduced in proportion to the amount you increase the size.

No printer setting is perfect. You might want to try several and do a sample printout to see which works best with the sort of documents you make. You can save time by using a low-resolution mode when creating a document (because documents print much faster that way); then using the higher-quality mode for final printouts.

When you save your document, the Page Setup information you set will sometimes be stored with it, but it depends on the application you're using. On some applications, you have to go back and redo the settings every single time you launch that application. It's a case of try it and see. Sorry, I don't make up the rules; I just tell you what they are.

After your settings are made, click OK to put them in effect.

Using the Print Dialog Box

Here's the second part of the printing process: After you've checked the Page Setup dialog box and set it up, it's time to actually print your document. Unless you intend to change something, here's what you do:

Printing Your Document

1. Choose Print from the File menu (or press Cmd-P), which opens the dialog box shown in Figure 17.6. Even though this dialog box looks similar to the previous one, it is designed to actually issue the Print command (the other is designed simply to set up your page size, orientation, and output size).

FIGURE 17.6

Activate the printing function from this dialog box.

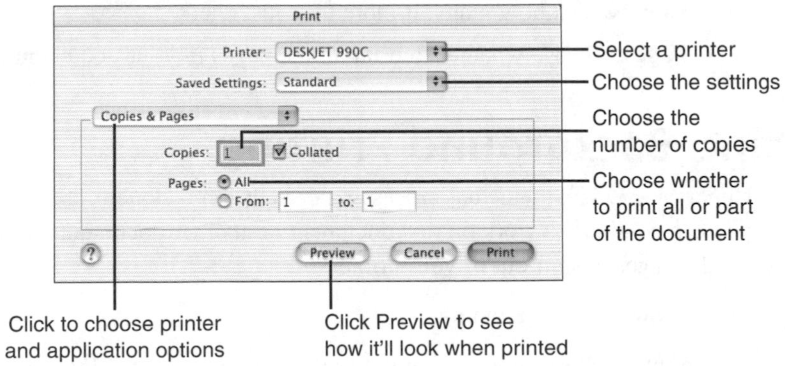

Print
Printer: DESKJET 990C — Select a printer
Saved Settings: Standard — Choose the settings
Copies & Pages
Copies: 1 ☑ Collated — Choose the number of copies
Pages: ⦿ All — Choose whether to print all or part of the document
○ From: 1 to: 1
(?) Preview Cancel Print

Click to choose printer and application options

Click Preview to see how it'll look when printed

2. To print your document, click the Print button. This will get you one copy of each page in your document.

3. If you want to see how your document will look when printed, click Preview. The document will open in Mac OS X's Preview application.

> If you want to send your document to someone who might not have the same software you have, you can use Preview's Save As dialog box to make a copy in PDF format. A PDF document can be read and printed with full accuracy by any computer user who has Adobe's Acrobat software installed (Mac or Windows). Apple's Preview application also reads such files.

You will see a printer dialog on your screen showing the number of pages that have been printed. Within a few seconds, you should hear some activity from your printer, indicating that the process has begun. You'll regain control of your computer when the last document has been printed. How long that takes depends on how big your document is and the print quality choices you set (higher quality and color take much, much longer, often several minutes per page).

Here's a description of the various options available from the Print dialog box:

- **Printer**: You can switch between any printer connected to your Mac from this dialog box.
- **Saved Settings**: Click here to get a custom setting.
- **Copies and Pages**: Click this pop-up menu to open some custom printer and document features for your printer and the application you're using.
- **Copies**: Pick how many, if more than just one.
- **Pages**: Choose whether to print all the pages in your document or just a few.

Using Background Printing

Under Mac OS X, the actual processing of your job is done in the background, meaning you can continue to work on that document or another document without having to wait for the pages to spill out of your printer.

Here's how the feature works:

Your printer will make a copy of the file in the printer's own language, and then feed it to the printer as needed automatically (in the background), letting you get back to work after a few seconds.

You can disable background printing under the Classic Mac OS Chooser, at the expense of having the processing operation take over your Mac. You can't do anything else during this time, you have to wait until the process is done. Under most circumstances, you shouldn't need to do this. But, if you have problems printing a very complicated document with lots of text and graphics, give it a try. Sometimes extremely difficult documents can be handled better with background printing disabled. Because of Mac OS X's superior multitasking, Apple didn't feel the need to turn off background printing for its new operating system; regardless, effects should be less than with the Classic Mac OS.

17

Inkjet printers use your computer for processing the document you're printing. If you want to switch to another printer for a job, wait until printing is done. During this time, your iMac might seem a bit sluggish, even if you have a new model with the fastest processor. Even though Mac OS X's advanced multitasking system can juggle CPU horsepower very effectively, don't be upset if there's still a bit of a slowdown. It'll pass as soon as the job is finished.

Checking the Progress of Your Print Job

As soon as the initial processing of a document is done, the Print Center icon will appear in the Dock when you're printing from a Mac OS X application. To see how the job is doing, click the icon, which opens the print queue window (see Figure 17.7).

FIGURE 17.7

See which document is being printed, and which are left.

Status	Name	Priority
Printing	17Fig04.PCX	Normal

HP LaserJet 8000 Series

17Fig04.PCX
Page 1 of 1

Printing job

Delete   Hold   Resume

With the print queue displayed, you're able to check the progress of a print job and also manage the queue, to a limited degree.

Here are the options, identified by the buttons at the bottom of the screen:

- **Delete:** Removes the selected job from the queue.

> It's usually not a good idea to stop a print job that's already begun because
> you risk a possible paper jam if the paper is already feeding through the
> printer (this applies strictly to inkjet printers, not laser printers, which print
> the page in a single, uninterrupted process). Some printers have a reset but-
> ton that will move the page through the paper trays, but the best way to
> avoid a possible problem is not stopping an active print job.

- **Hold:** Keeps the selected job in the list, but won't print until you choose otherwise.
- **Resume:** Resumes printing of the selected document.

In addition to being able to stop and resume exiting jobs, you can also halt the entire
print queue, which is done by choosing Stop Queue from Print Center's Queue menu.
After you make this selection, printing will stop after a few seconds to finish the existing
page. The next time you look for the command it will change to Start Queue, so you can
resume outputting your documents.

> Jobs printed from the Classic environment are managed by PrintMonitor,
> which will also appear in the Dock. When you click the PrintMonitor win-
> dow, you'll see buttons to Cancel Printing and Set Print Time; the latter is
> used to resume printing of the selected document at a preset time. You can
> also drag and drop jobs listed in the print queue into a different order (this
> feature is not available in Mac OS X's Print Center, unfortunately).

Using a Laser Printer's Page Setup Box

A regular, garden-variety, black-and-white PostScript laser printer doesn't have nearly as
many settings as a color printer or an inkjet printer. However, the page setup options are
essentially the same under Mac OS X. As a result, I won't cover them here. However,
you might see specific setup buttons or pop-up menus that meet the needs of a specific
application.

NEW TERM   *PostScript* is a printer language from Adobe Systems that is used in the professional publishing and printing industries. The language describes the content of
the printed page mathematically. PostScript is what is called "device independent,"
meaning your document can print at the maximum available resolution or quality setting
for the printer you're using. Most laser printers for iMacs support PostScript.

When you've made the setups you want, click OK to put them in motion. As with the inkjet printer, when you save your document, the Page Setup changes you make might be included (but sometimes not).

> Under the Classic Mac OS, there are some additional choices, including a pop-up menu that delivers a PostScript options command. However, you don't normally have to change any of those settings, unless the manual for the printer you're using says otherwise.

Printing a Document with Your Laser Printer

There's little difference in printing a document with your laser printer and inkjet printer after you perform the basic setups. But because the dialog boxes have different options, I'll describe the laser printer variation here.

To activate the print feature, choose Print from the File menu. This opens a dialog box similar to the one shown in Figure 17.8.

FIGURE 17.8

Okay, it looks the same, but you'll find a few differences in the pop-up menus.

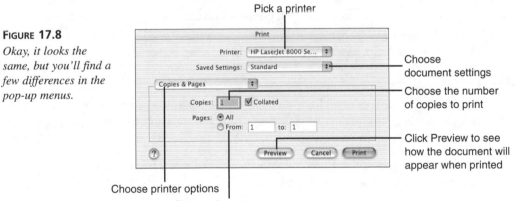

Although the features seem the same, the differences are buried in the Copies & Pages pop-up menu (see Figure 17.9), where options for specific printers and applications are available. Depending on which printer and program you're using, the choices will be different. In the example I've shown, using a professional drawing program (Freehand 10) and a PostScript laser printer, the Duplex option enables you print on both sides of the paper. The FreeHand 10 option enables you to configure specific features for that application.

When you set up most laser printers (and only a few inkjet models), you'll see a desktop icon representing the printer. If you drag one or more documents to that icon, the application that made the document will be launched, automatically, and you'll see a Print dialog box. When you click the Print command, the print process will begin, and the program will quit. Cool!

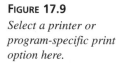

FIGURE 17.9
Select a printer or program-specific print option here.

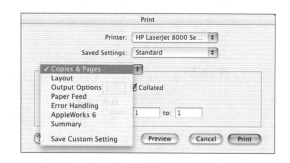

After your settings are done, click Print to output your document. If you want your custom settings to stick, choose Save Custom Setting from the Copies & Pages pop-up menu to store them. The next time you print, choose the custom setup from the Saved Settings pop-up menu.

Summary

There are many great printers from which to choose for your documents. Whether you want to print color art, photos, or your first novel, you'll be able to find the right product and easily hook it up to your computer.

In our next lesson, you'll see how the iMac works in a world where many other people are using computers for that *other* platform.

Q&A

Q **I'm using background printing, but whenever my inkjet printer is printing something everything runs like molasses. I thought my flat-panel iMac's G4 microprocessor was supposed to be the fastest thing on the planet. What's wrong?**

A As fast as the iMac runs, it bogs down when it has to perform two or more tasks at once. Even if you're using a Mac OS X application, taking advantage of the operating system's superior preemptive multitasking method, the printer uses a lot of processor time. This is especially true if you're using an inkjet printer because your computer also serves as the printer's computer (or *raster image processor*, RIP for short). Things can bog down, but you should still be able to do many tasks on your iMac during the printing process, including word processing and even Internet visits. The process is even slower with a Classic application, which doesn't benefit from the superior multitasking system.

What you get with a laser printer, by the way, in addition to its superior handling of text and speed, is its own computer to process documents. So your computer does not feel as sluggish.

Q I have an old Apple StyleWriter. When I tried to hook it up to the iMac, I couldn't find any place to plug it in. I need this printer, and I don't want to buy a new one. What can I do to make it work?

A The newest Mac OS computers use a different type of expansion port than other Macs (USB), so it has no place to plug in that StyleWriter. All is not lost, however. Check with your dealer and ask about a USB to serial adapter plug. That will enable you to run your older printer without a problem. Figure on paying $50 to $100, depending on the sort of adapter you need. You can also get adapters that work with older printers that support LocalTalk hookups. In Hour 20 I cover the topic of add-ons for your iMac. But the best solution is really just to buy a new printer, and that takes us to the next question.

Q I see all these printers for $50 or $100. How can they make them so cheap? What's the scam?

A Manufacturers are using what is called the "Gillette razor" approach. You buy the printer at a very low price, but you generally pay from $25 to $35 for each ink cartridge you have to replace. You can liken that to buying a cheap razor and spending a bundle on the blades. Remember that most of the lower-cost printers have two cartridges—one for black and one for color. Some offer separate cartridges for each color, at a lower price, but when you add it up, it's usually the same as the single three color cartridge. If you print a lot of documents, you can see where the cost of consumables adds up and you soon spend a lot more to keep the inkjet printer well fed with ink than you paid for it to begin with.

17

Regardless, these printers really offer high quality for the price. If you plan on printing no more than 100 or 200 copies of month, they are great values. If you need to print a large number of documents, and you're willing to live without color, go for a laser printer. The cost per page is generally less than half what you'd pay on an inkjet printer and the added cost of the laser printer is easily made up if you have heavy printing needs.

Q I tried to print a document, but I kept getting error messages. What is wrong?

A First, see if the message tells you what's wrong. It's not always easy to solve printing problems because a small error in the Page Setup box (for example, the wrong paper size) or a lack of paper might cause the problem.

Here are some things to check:

- **Out of paper/paper jammed**: Make sure that your printer has enough paper, and check to see whether a page has jammed inside it. If there's a paper jam, check the manufacturer's directions on how to fix it.

- **Make sure that it is on and connected**: It's very easy to disconnect something (maybe during redecorating or to use the outlet for another item). Double-check your connections and make sure that the printer's on light is running. Also check your printer's documentation on error lights and what they mean.

- **Look at the Page Setup box**: If you choose the wrong paper size, or the wrong paper orientation, the printer might just give up the ghost. You'll want to double-check those settings.

- **For laser printers**: **Choose the right PPD file**: So-called PostScript laser printers use special files called *PPDs* that tell the printer driver about the printer and its special features (such as extra trays, larger paper sizes, and so on). You might need to make sure that your PPD file is installed. PPD files, under Mac OS X, go inside a folder called Library, under the following path (or folder hierarchy: Library/Printers/PPDs/Contents/Resources/English.lproj (or whatever language you're using). You'll want to use the column view feature of the Mac OS X Finder to quickly travel through these folks. You should also make sure that you choose the proper printer in the Page Setup box because that setting delivers the proper paper choices. If the PPD file isn't there, check your printer's software disks or contact the dealer or manufacturer to get one.

Q **I bought a new printer, but I cannot get the drivers to work with Mac OS X, even though it's supposed to be compatible? Did I make a mistake?**

A Don't despair. First check the manufacturer's Web site or versiontracker.com for the latest printer software. Most new printers ship ready to roll with Mac OS X. You will usually find problems with older printers, where getting compatible drivers is a hit or miss proposition.

In the end, if you have a new printer and no way to make it work under Mac OS X, and support is promised (this is important!), take the printer back to the dealer and ask to exchange it for a compatible model. You shouldn't have to contend with a problem here, because most dealers will give you a money back guarantee on new merchandise.

Q **You mention PostScript printers from time to time. Can I get that feature on an inkjet printer? What is it good for?**

A Yes, some programs will enable you to use PostScript with your inkjet printer. Two products that come to mind are Birmy Script and Epson Stylus RIP (for many Epson printers). You'll want to check with your dealer about which products are compatible with your inkjet printer and Mac OS X (Birmy promises a native version of their software). I didn't have any to try when I wrote this book.

PostScript doesn't help much if you just use text, but if you do complex graphics (such as those made with a PostScript drawing program, such as Adobe Illustrator, CorelDRAW, or Macromedia FreeHand), rotated pictures, and so on, you'll find a PostScript option gives you sharper, more accurate output. If you are doing work for the professional marketplace, PostScript is essential.

17

HOUR 18

Coping with the Windows World

Although Mac users are loathe to admit it, the Great Computing Platform War is a thing of the past. The majority of personal computers in the world use Windows, but that doesn't mean you should feel compelled to abandon the Mac Operating System in favor of that *other* platform.

The very factors that make Mac the operating system of choice are even stronger under Mac OS X, where high reliability has made for an even more comfortable computing experience.

Sometimes, however, you have to recognize reality and handle documents that have been created in a Windows program, or even use software that isn't available in Mac trim.

In this lesson, I'll show you ways to cope with the Windows world and stick with your iMac. You'll learn

- How Mac OS X makes it easier to read Windows documents and disks
- How to locate a compatible Mac program for your Windows files

- How to share files with other computers, Mac or Windows
- How to actually set up a real DOS or Windows environment on your computer and instantly switch between it and the Mac OS

Using Mac OS X to Read Windows Files

Apple has recognized the reality. Sometimes you will receive documents made in Windows programs, such as Office 2000 or Office XP, and sometimes you'll have to use a disk made on that *other* platform.

Fortunately, there are ways around this dilemma, and the best part is that your iMac comes with two operating systems (Mac OS 9.x and Mac OS X) that are not only aware that those *other* computing platforms exist, but are perfectly capable of reading Windows files and disks.

The most effective way, by far, to read a Windows file properly on a Mac is to buy the Mac equivalent of the Windows program (if one is available). For example, if you handle lots of files created in Word or another Microsoft Office program, you should consider the Mac OS X version of Microsoft Office.

You cannot mount a PC disk on your iMac without a drive in which to mount it. If you have a CD from the *other* platform, no problem. But if you have a PC floppy or a disk created in another removable format, such as the SuperDisk or Zip drive, you need to buy a disk drive that supports one of these formats. See Hour 20, "Adding More Goodies to Your iMac," for more information on the add-ons you can buy for your iMac.

There's no mystery about accessing files made on another computing platform, and usually there's nothing to learn. You just double-click a file and as long as you have a Mac program that reads that type of file, you're home free.

There are some considerations, though:

- **Document Formatting**: If you don't have the Mac version of the PC program that created the file, you might lose a bit in the translation. Complex text formats, tables, and so on, might not translate accurately. And if the PC document uses fonts that aren't installed on your computer, the fonts will look different. The translation process is very flexible, but there are no miracles.

- **Missing Data**: Sometimes files don't translate intact; some content is missing. If you need to work on a PC file, ask the folks who created the file to send you a printout so you can compare it for accuracy.

What If It Doesn't Work?

All right, it's not just the file's format that might present a problem. There are times when you won't even be able to get a program to automatically launch when you double-click a document. Instead, you'll see a dialog box where you'll be asked to select the application to open that document, as shown in Figure 18.1.

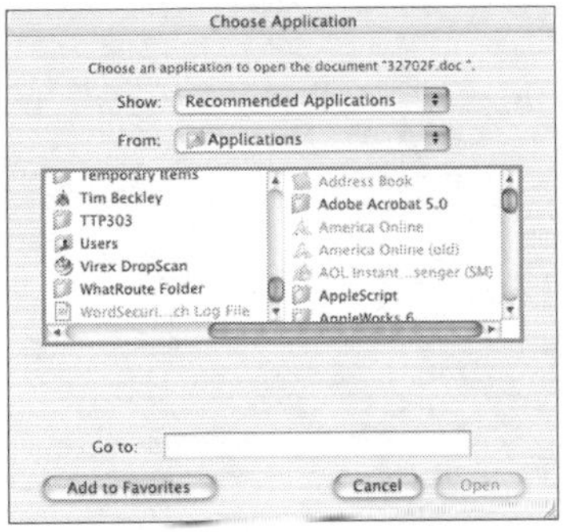

FIGURE 18.1

Decisions, decisions! What application should I pick.

Fortunately, Mac OS X offers a little bit of help to enable you to decide what application to use. The ones offered are usually the programs most likely to open a specific file.

If it doesn't work, all you have to do is quit the application, double-click the document again, and make a second choice.

Mac OS 9.x includes a Control Panel called File Exchange that provides for automatic conversion of common file formats. The first time you launch a document file for which you don't have the application, File Exchange puts up a dialog box listing possible compatible applications. After you make your selection, future documents of that type will open in the application you selected. I expect, however, that you'll be using Mac OS X most of the time, so you don't have to worry about this.

Making File Mapping Permanent

What's file mapping? It's a way to link a specific type of document to a specific application. That way, whenever you double-click that document, it'll launch the application you prefer. Normally, this isn't something to fret about, especially if you have the application that made the document (such as AppleWorks for an AppleWorks file).

Let's say you don't have the application, and you don't want to put up with that annoying dialog box every time you double-click the file. Here's your way out of this mess:

Linking a File to an Application

▼ To Do

1. Locate and click once on the document you want to link to a specific program in order to select it. Now go to the Finder's File menu and choose Show Info. If you like keyboards, just type Cmd-I.

2. Click the pop-up menu, and then choose Open With Application (as shown in Figure 18.2).

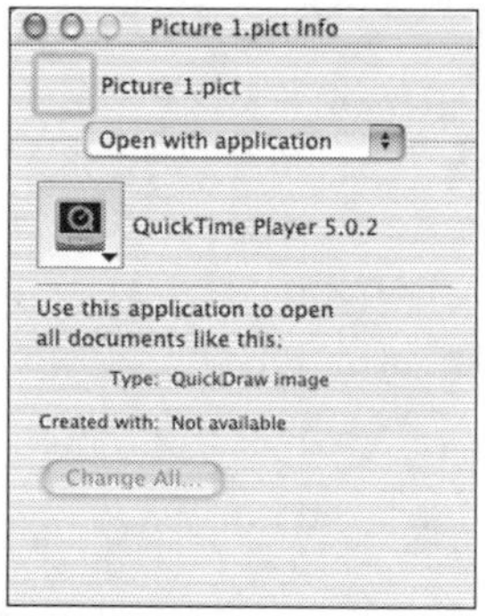

FIGURE 18.2

Here is where you can select an application to open a document by double-clicking it.

3. Now click the icon that shows what application is opening the document; normally all you'll see is no application available. You'll see a list of applications that Mac OS X recommends (see Figure 18.3). If the one you want isn't listed, click Other, and choose another application from the Open dialog box.

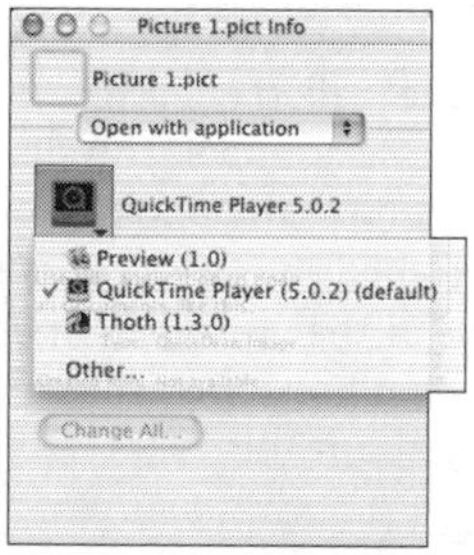

FIGURE 18.3

Choose an application from the list.

4. We're almost there. After choosing an application to open the document, you're right back in the Show Info window. Now you can perform one more setting: Would you like all documents of the same type to be opened with the same application? If you say yes, you just have to make the final decision by clicking Change All, which produces the confirmation window shown in Figure 18.4.

FIGURE 18.4
The final option to open all such documents with the same program.

Are you sure you want to change all similar documents to open with the application "Preview"?
This change will apply to all documents with extension "pict".
Cancel   Continue

5. To select that application, click Continue in the confirmation window. If you want to back out now, click Cancel. Either way, click the Close button to send the Show Info window on its way.

Exchanging Files with Other Computers

In the old days, when only large companies used computer networks, sharing files was done by a technique known as sneaker Net. You copied the file to a disk and physically walked the disk over to the other computer. It was a great form of exercise if you had a big office or had to repeat the process frequently.

Nowadays, however, you can set up a network in minutes, and your computer can easily communicate with other Macs or Windows-based computers by way of its Ethernet-networking jack. All you need is an Ethernet-crossover cable or a hub (a central connection module).

The basic process of sharing files is simple (Nike and Reebok shoes aren't required). Here's how you do it:

Sharing Files on Your iMac

1. Open the Sharing preferences panel of the System Preferences application.
2. Click the Start button under File Sharing off. Over the next few moments, you'll hear your iMac's hard drive churning—as sharing is activated the File Sharing Startup Up status will change to File Sharing On.
3. Return to the Sharing preference panel when you want to turn off sharing. Click the Stop button beneath the File Sharing On label.

After file sharing is enabled, another user on the same network (or on the Internet if you provide your Mac's IP address, as shown at the bottom of the Sharing preference panel) can access your Mac as a Guest or as a registered user. A guest is allowed to receive and send files to the Shared folder, which is located in the User's or Home folder under Mac OS X.

This is by far the safest way to set up file sharing because you don't have to concern yourself about the rest of your files.

To Do

18

But if you're in a small office, or at home, and you don't mind granting access to all or most of the files on your Mac, you can set privileges for the files or folders you want to share.

Here's how it's done.

Setting File Sharing Privileges

1. Click once on an item you want to share, whether it's a file or folder.

2. Choose Show Info from the Finder's File menu.

3. Choose Privileges from the pop-up menu (see Figure 18.5).

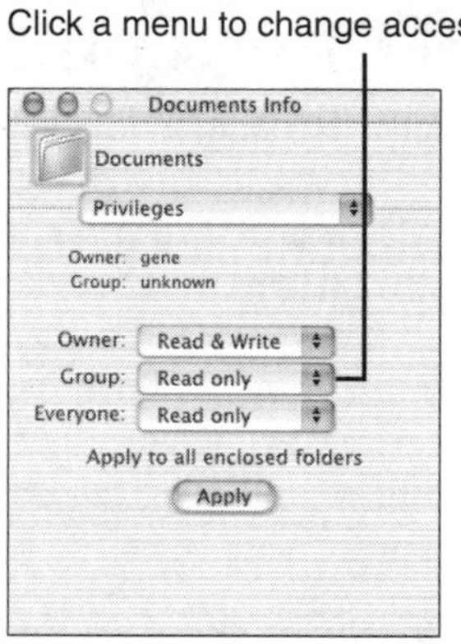

Click a menu to change access

FIGURE 18.5
Choose three types of privileges.

4. You can set a separate set of privileges for the Owner (you), a Group (family members or business associates) and for Everyone (the rest of the pack). Click a pop-up menu to make your choice (see Figure 18.5).

5. Choose Privileges from the pop-up menu (see Figure 18.6).

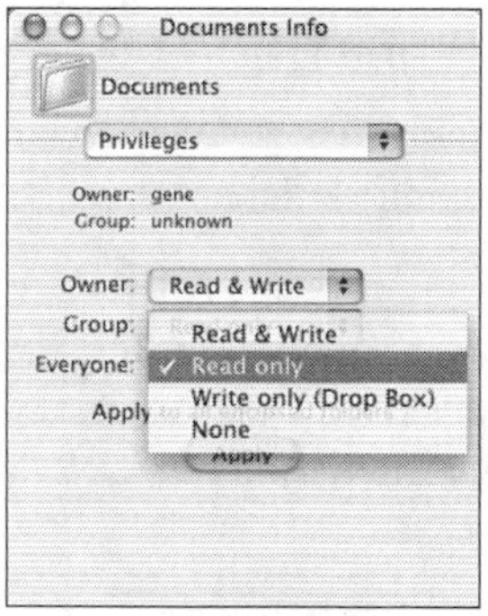

FIGURE 18.6
Choose whether or not someone in a particular category can access or change files.

Connecting to Another Mac

Connecting to another Mac on your network is just as simple. All you have to do is

1. Confirm that the computer you want to access has sharing turned on.

2. Choose Go to Server from the Finder's Go menu, which opens the screen shown in Figure 18.7.

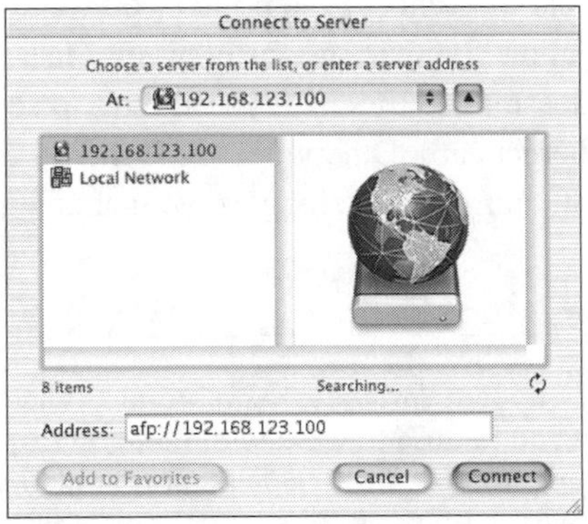

FIGURE 18.7

This screen shows the computers available on your network.

18

3. Double click the name of the Computer. In a few seconds, you'll see a password prompt (see Figure 18.8).

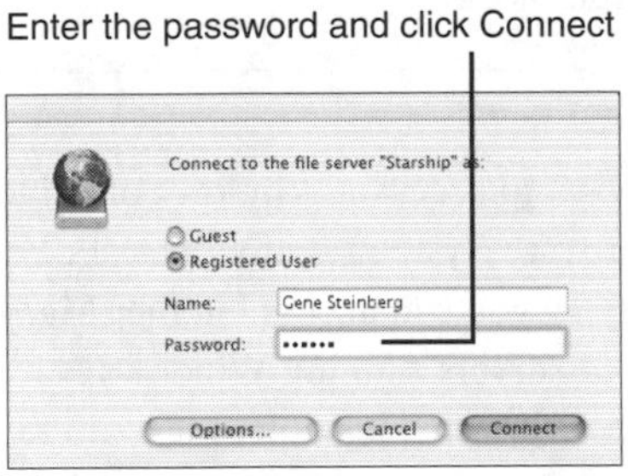

Enter the password and click Connect

FIGURE 18.8

Enter your password to access that computer's drive.

4. Type the password exactly as it was established on the other computer. That includes uppercase and lowercase letters, as needed.

5. Click Connect to open the list of available drives.

6. Double-click the selected drive to open it on your computer's desktop.

7. When you're done sharing files, you can disconnect from that computer simply by dragging its drive icon to the trash (same as you eject a floppy, Zip cartridge, or CD). See, file sharing is really easy.

Sharing Files with Windows Users

It gets a little more complicated if you have Windows users on the network, but there are ways to do it. Here are two possibilities:

- **Printers**: If the network laser printer uses Ethernet, you can connect to the printer as easy as another Mac. You can set it up with Apple's Print Center application. Just click the type of connection you want, which is usually AppleTalk for a networked laser printer, and then choose the printer you want to use from the list. Such printers usually allow for sharing jobs between Macs and PCs without special setups. If the printer doesn't use Ethernet, you'll have to see whether you can upgrade it with an Ethernet card. Otherwise, see if there's a USB connector, which will make it work with your iMac (so long as the manufacturer has Mac software for you to install).

> One company, Strydent Software, has a product called PowerPrint for Networks that you can use to work with non-PostScript network printers. It's designed to support more than 1,600 PC printer models and enable Mac OS computers to work with them. To explore the details of this product, visit the publisher's Web site at http://www.strydent.com. Okay, that's the good news. The bad news is that it was uncertain, as of the time this book was written, whether this program or any of the other PowerPrint products would migrate to Mac OS X. They will work okay, however, for programs that run in the Classic mode.

- **Files**: One of the easiest ways to access a Windows or Windows NT network is a program from Thursby Software Systems, called DAVE. You can connect to the Windows network as easily as you can access another Mac on your network using DAVE (including networked servers running Windows NT, Windows 2000, or Window XP, although Mac OS X enables you to also do that directly, the same way you access a Mac on a network). It also gives the PC user the capability to communicate with your computer just as simply. You can order a copy of this program at most computer dealers or visit their Web site at http://www.thursby.com for more information.

Making a Mac Do Windows

As easy as it is to use PC disks on your computer and access a network with computers from the *other* platform, there will be times when you'll actually need to run a PC program, too.

Fortunately, there's a way to do it without having to get a new computer. That way is with a DOS or Windows emulator.

One Mac software publisher, Connectix, provides such an emulator-Virtual PC. Using Virtual PC, you get the best of both worlds. You can continue to use your Mac's programs the same as you currently do and have the added advantage of summoning a Windows setup when necessary.

> Having the ability to jump quickly between the Mac and Windows environments is great for writers like me who have to prepare books covering both platforms. It's a real time saver. Now you know my secret (don't let my publisher know I told you)!

Connectix Virtual PC actually emulates a genuine Intel Pentium microprocessor on your computer. You can get the basic program and install any PC operating system, including Windows 2000, Windows XP, and Linux, a Unix-based operating system that is sometimes compared with Mac OS X. Or, you can get versions bundled with DOS, Windows 95, Windows 98, or Windows Me, if you don't want to use the latest and greatest.

A Case History: Connectix Virtual PC with Windows XP

An example of how clever these programs are is the version of Virtual PC that comes with Windows XP Home edition already installed. It takes just minutes to install it from a CD, and after it's all set up and running, you'll see a screen similar to the one shown in Figure 18.9.

> So what's the difference between Windows XP Home and Professional? Not a lot, but if you must know, the key difference is the addition of support for multiprocessors in the Pro version; that's a computer with two or more processors. The other key feature is the capability to encrypt files and folders. All right, that's a biggie, but not something you'd need to worry about unless you use your iMac in a larger office where document security is important.

18

FIGURE 18.9

Is it a Mac or is it Windows? It's both. Actually it's Windows XP Home edition running on the author's iMac courtesy of Virtual PC.

Is it a Mac or isn't it? Yes, it's the author's very own iMac running Windows XP Home edition. To perform its magic the Windows emulator has to map (link) some native PC functions to your Mac. But setting it up is quite simple. The preference box from Virtual PC shows how you can configure it to provide near seamless PC performance (see Figure 18.10).

Click an icon to change a setting

FIGURE 18.10

Microsoft Windows runs on your Mac through these settings

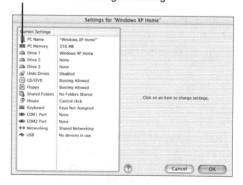

The settings options are simple, and you can set up the program to run in a minute or two, using the program's handy Setup Assistant, which launches after you install a new PC operating system. Here's a description of what it does:

A neat thing about Virtual PC is that you don't have to buy it with any PC operating system. You can get the basic program, and then install one you buy from a regular retailer. Connectix offers instructions on how you configure a store-bought copy to work with Virtual PC. You can even run a number of PC operating systems and switch from one to the other in just a few seconds.

- **PC Memory**: You can dedicate RAM to the PC operating system. Although Mac OS X sorts out memory behind the scenes, dedicating memory makes your PC operating system work better.

- **C Drive**: Virtual PC puts a file on your computer's drive that emulates a genuine Windows drive (the Windows equivalent of Macintosh HD). You can use the program's tools to make the drive larger if you need to install more programs.

- **D Drive**: This setting enables you to create a second drive file on your iMac.

- **E Drive**: And if you really want it, this setting enables you to create a third drive file on your iMac.

- **CD-ROM**: Use this setting to control access to your computer's CD-ROM drive.

- **Floppy**: This setting enables Windows to start (boot) from a floppy (if you have one installed on your iMac).

- **Shared Folders**: You can set aside a folder on your computer's drive to share files between the Mac and Windows environments.

- **Mouse**: This setting enables you to assign a keyboard shortcut for the Windows right-click menu (the Windows equivalent of the Contextual menus you have on a Mac).

- **Keyboard**: This setting enables you to allocate custom keystrokes for Windows functions.

- **Networking**: This feature enables you to share your Mac's network hookup.

Unlike Macs, computers from that *other* platform require a special sound card to produce anything more than a beep for sound events or for playing a sound file. Most PCs, however, come with sound cards already installed. Virtual PC mimics a Creative Labs SoundBlaster card to do its stuff. So you can listen to music and check out movie trailers under Windows without having to install extra hardware.

Why You Need Virtual PC

Is there any reason why you'd need to run Windows on a Mac? For the most part, the best software from that platform is available in Mac form, such as Microsoft Office, the application suite that includes Word and Excel, CorelDRAW, and even the Windows Media Player, which can be used for some multimedia files that Apple's QuickTime can't support.

However, there are applications that either have never made the transition or are no longer being developed for the Mac platform. An example is Tenant Pro from Property Automation Systems, which is used by real estate agents to manage rental properties. If you need to run a special (or vertical) program of this type you have to make a choice to get a second computer or buy Virtual PC and get the best of both worlds on your Mac.

Virtual PC also has the added advantage of being able to run a number of PC operating systems from a single interface, with almost instantaneous switching from one to the other. This could mean, for example, that you could jump among Windows 95, Windows 98, Windows Me, Windows 2000, Windows XP, and even Linux. Why would you need that flexibility? Well, if you enjoy designing Web pages you can use the capability to run multiple operating systems and different browser versions to make sure your Web sites look good to everyone. It's a sad fact of life that different browsers have different ways of interpreting Web sites; this way you can avoid trouble.

 Believe it or not, there is actually a Virtual PC for Windows. Why? It allows Windows users to run multiple operating systems on the same computer without having to reboot their systems. In addition to helping Web designers test their work, software programmers can also easily test their products with various flavors of Windows.

But being able to run multiple operating systems is no free ride. Virtual PC is not optimized to provide good performance with 3D games. That means you can't play the games you lust over, games that maybe aren't being developed for Macs, and get satisfactory speeds. The action will stutter, sounds will break up.

Virtual PC works best with business applications, where you can get good enough performance for occasional use. The program will even share your ISP connection with your Mac, so you can surf the Internet seamlessly.

But if you need Windows compatibility and good speed, you might want to supplement your computer hardware with a regular Windows PC. I'm not trying to sell you on another computing platform, especially now that you've invested in a Mac. But I don't want to give you unreasonable expectations of what a Windows emulator can do.

Summary

Even though a lot of the world uses Windows, you don't have to feel out of touch with your computer. Besides having a better operating system, you're able to open documents made in compatible software or even emulate the complete Windows environment. So if you must use a program that has no Mac equivalent, you don't have to switch computing platforms.

The next lesson will show you how to enable your computer to do multiple tasks with a single command. This feature is called AppleScript. I'll show you the built-in tools that Apple includes with your iMac and how to write your own special scripts.

Q&A

Q I've seen ads for expansion cards that can put "Intel inside" a Mac. Can I use that with my iMac?

A The great thing about the iMac is that it's a totally self-contained computer. You only have to attach a mouse and keyboard. Beyond this, you just need a printer and you're ready to roll. But there are no expansion slots to add such things as PC processors. The solution for you is emulation software, such as the products described in this lesson.

Q Tell me the truth. How fast do those PC emulators run?

A There's really not a pat answer to this one. The basic consideration is that you want to have a lot of RAM installed on your computer and give the emulation program a good chunk of it to run. Although new iMacs come with 128MB or 256MB of RAM, older models have as little as 32MB. You need at least 128MB to run Mac OS X, but it works more efficiently if you have twice that.

When set up with a good chunk of memory, you can expect an iMac to give you about the performance of a 133 to 166MHz Pentium. Performance is quite a bit better on the flat-panel iMac because Connectix has optimized Virtual PC to deliver superior performance on a G4 processor. The program might feel faster than these figures indicate, though, as the clever designers of PC emulation software try to accelerate such tasks as pulling down menus that have the most impact on perceived speed.

Q It's time for the final decision. Should I buy Virtual PC? And why?

A Virtual PC works, no doubt about it. It enables you to run just about any operating system that works on a computer with "Intel inside." But don't expect miracles. PC game performance, as explained previously, simply won't make then grade. Emulation software is designed to enable you to run business programs and simple graphics programs that aren't available in Mac versions, and that's about it.

18

By the way, if you really want to explore another Unix-based operating system, aside from Mac OS X. Virtual PC has an alternative. You can run that open source version of Red Hat Linux with Virtual PC. Although there is a Linux version designed to work on Macs, installation can be a royal pain. For one thing, you have to reformat your iMac's hard drive, and then divide it into multiple segments (volumes). You put Linux on one volume, your regular Mac OS versions and applications on the other.

The Virtual PC way might not give you the same level of performance. But it's a lot easier to set up.

Q I thought I could open PC files on my computer without extra stuff. But I've got this file with the extension .exe on it, and it won't run. What do I need?

A That's an executable file, one that can be launched to open a program or an installer for a PC program. It's not a document file. The only way you can run PC programs on your computer is with a DOS or Windows emulator.

Q Help! Whenever I try to insert a PC disk into my Zip drive, I get a warning that it wants to initialize the disk. Should I do it?

A No. If you OK that message, the disk will be erased, and if you need files from it, they'll be history. Mac OS X ought to be able to read the disk without trouble. Even if you have restarted your Mac under the Classic Mac OS, Apple's File Exchange software should do the trick. Regardless, if this happens, click Eject rather than Initialize, and then try reinserting the disk again to see if it was read properly. If you still have a problem, consider restarting your Mac. Sometimes things work on the second try. Don't ask me why; that's just the way it is!

AppleScript: Putting Your iMac on Automatic Pilot

Computers can't do everything for you. As powerful as your computer's PowerPC microprocessor is, you still have to use your keyboard and mouse to perform lots of tasks. When you need to save a document, you have to select a menu bar command (or type the keyboard equivalent), name the document, and then accept a dialog box to save the file.

Just imagine how great it would be if you could call upon your computer to think for you when it came to performing such mundane tasks. Fortunately, your iMac comes equipped with software that enables you to do just that. It's called AppleScript, and after you get the hang of it, you'll be able to make your computer take over some repetitive tasks for you. Some folks even have AppleScript do hundreds of operations for them (such as doing basic editing and saving of photos), and they go off to lunch confident that the computer will continue happily at its task until they return.

In this lesson, you'll learn

- How to use your computer's collection of standard scripts
- The easy way to learn about Apple's Script Editor software
- How to use the Folder Actions feature under Mac OS 9
- How to use some other tools for desktop automation

Scripting Without Programming

When you set up your computer nothing special is required to turn on AppleScript. The program is already active and running; ready for you to create and run scripts.

Now I don't want to get ahead of myself, but I should point out that writing your own AppleScript is a simplified form of programming. No, I am not going to teach you how to write a program. That's way beyond the scope of this book. AppleScript, however, is much easier to learn. The scripting language, when you see it in action (as you will later in this chapter), uses what are essentially plain-English commands to do its thing. What's more, folks who never gave a moment's thought about writing software have gotten involved in AppleScript.

To discover how an AppleScript is used, you can take a look at the handful of scripts that Apple gives you to activate common functions. You'll find it by going to the Application folder, opening the AppleScript folder, and then selecting Example Scripts (shown in Figure 19.1).

FIGURE 19.1

These are some of the canned scripts Apple gives you to try out AppleScript.

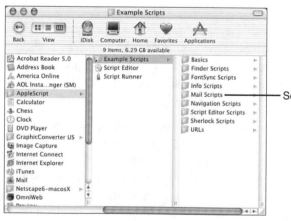

Select a script to run

Here's what some of the categories cover in the sample Mac OS X scripts, each identified by folder:

- **Basics**: These scripts help you get started. They are used to open AppleScript Help, the Script Editor application (to make your own scripts), or direct you to Apple's AppleScript Web site where you can learn a lot more about the subject.

You don't need an AppleScript to visit Apple's official AppleScript Web site. Just point your browser to `http://www.apple.com/applescript` and you'll learn more about the power of this core feature of the Mac OS. Apple includes tutorials and more sample scripts for you to try; in fact quite enough to get you reasonably involved with AppleScript. You might even want to write a few for yourself, but try the sample scripts first.

- **Finder Scripts**: This is a collection of handy scripts that cover various categories of file and folder naming. One script, for example, is designed to shorten the names of any folder in the front Finder window.

If you're not sure what a script does by its title, double-click it. This will launch Apple's Script Editor application, where you will usually (but not always) see a brief text description on how the script is used. If not, you'll probably be able to guess the function by the simple English words in the script or its title. You'll learn how to use Script Editor to create your own scripts later in this chapter.

19

- **Font Sync Scripts**: These are used to make sure your iMac's font library is free of duplicates.
- **Info Scripts**: The only one available when this book was written simply displays the time.
- **Internet Services**: There are two scripts to explore. One will check the Internet for the current temperature in a selected city. The other retrieves stock quotes, which, in this day and age, is something you might not want to know.
- **Mail Scripts**: One of the scripts is used to open Apple's Mail application and open a blank email window that is ready for you to address and write your message. But the best script of all is "Crazy Message Text," which displays the message you specify in a cute variety of mismatched fonts and colors.

- **Navigation Scripts:** This folder contains scripts that enable you to open a new application, document, favorites, and Home folder windows.

- **Script Editor Scripts:** These are used to help fine-tune your AppleScript. They all require a little bit of experimentation and some study before you'll be ready to use them.

- **Sherlock Scripts:** The sole script available when this book was written is designed to search the Internet in Sherlock (which you can do easily enough without an AppleScript, of course).

- **URLs:** A collection of scripts designed to open your Web browser and take you right to a specific Web site.

> Each folder inside the AppleScript folder has scripts that cover the labeled category. Feel free to try out a few.

There are two ways to use a script under Mac OS X. One way is to simply use an application with a script menu and make your selection from that menu to activate the script.

The other way is an application in the AppleScript folder called Script Runner, where you just select the script from its pop-up menu (see Figure 19.2).

FIGURE 19.2
Mac OS X's Script Runner application places scripts in handy submenus; divided by whatever category you select.

Adding a Script to Script Runner

1. Quit Script Runner if it's running.

2. Locate and open the Scripts folder inside Mac OS X's Library folder (at the root or top level of your iMac's hard drive).

3. Double-click a folder inside the Scripts folder that fits the category of script that you're using. If no folder is appropriate, create one yourself.

4. Place the script in the proper folder, or just leave it loose in the Scripts folder. Either way, the scripts will appear in Script Runner the next time that application is launched.

All right, make a liar out of me. Actually, there is a third way, courtesy of a little application you'll find at the AppleScript Web site for Mac OS X at `http://www.apple.com/applescript/macosx/`. It's called Script Menu and you just drag it to the Finder's menu bar and it sticks. Then you can launch your scripts right from the menu bar.

A Primer on Creating Your Own AppleScripts

When you think of scripts for computers no doubt you expect some sort of arcane computer-like language that requires a lot of training to understand.

Fortunately, AppleScript commands (although not always in plain English) are usually clear enough to learn without needing a translator at your side. You can even make AppleScripts without knowing a thing about the lingo.

All you need is Apple's Script Editor program, which is already installed on your computer.

To begin, let's look at a real live script (the one that creates an alias and drops it in the Apple menu) and see what it contains.

Opening an AppleScript

1. Go to the Applications folder and double-click the folder labeled AppleScript.
2. Locate and double-click the Script Editor application icon. This will open the screen shown in Figure 19.3.

Don't fret if the editor window doesn't show up when you launch Script Editor. Just go to the File menu and choose New Script and it'll show up right away.

To Do

19

FIGURE 19.3

This simple interface is used to create an AppleScript from the ground up.

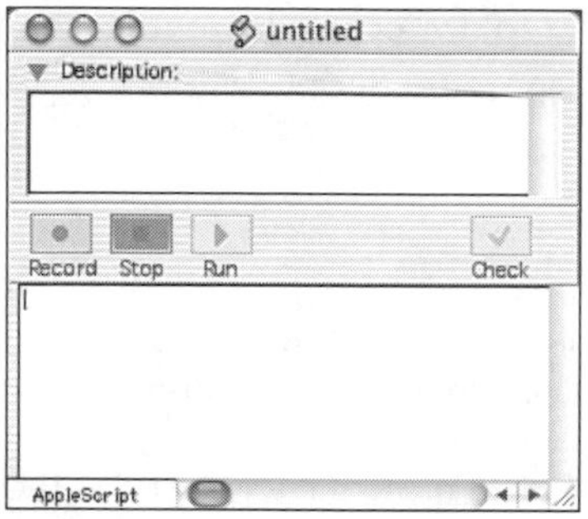

3. Choose Open Script from the File menu (or press Cmd-O), navigate to the AppleScript folder, and then to the Example Scripts inside that folder.

4. Open any script you see (I chose one of the Finder scripts, as shown in Figure 19.4).

FIGURE 19.4

Here's a real AppleScript. Although not all the syntax is obvious, some of it is in plain English.

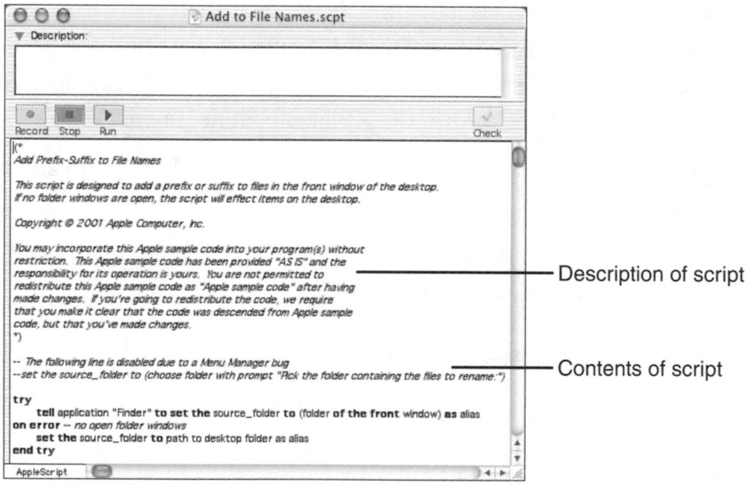

Description of script

Contents of script

None of the scripts I examined from Apple's collection had a description, but their purposes are easily discerned from the file's name. When you make your own scripts, as you'll do in the next section, you'll want to put in a description to make it easier to guess what it's for.

Go ahead and close the document after you've studied the script.

Making a Fast and Dirty AppleScript

Now that you've been exposed to some scripts, perhaps you'd like to make one yourself. Let's do that right now. The script I'm going to create can be used to access an entertainment-oriented Web site (mine in fact), but you can easily adapt the script to reach any Web site you want.

Creating an AppleScript

▼ To Do

1. Launch Script Editor.

2. If a blank script doesn't show just choose New Script from the File menu, which will open a blank AppleScript for you to use.

3. Click the text field under Description and type a brief explanation on what the script is for. In this case, I'm writing "AppleScript used to access the Mac Night Owl Web site."

4. In the first line, you will identify the address of the Web site you want to access. So press the Tab key to move to the actual scripting field, and then type the following code (do not use a period to close the sentence): property target_URL : property target_URL `"http://www.macnightowl.com"`

5. Now you want to tell your Web browser to open the site identified in the previous line. To do that, press the Return key twice and type the following: open location target_URL

6. That's the script. But before you try to run it, you want to make sure that the lingo is correct. Click the Check Syntax button in the script window and AppleScript will give it a once over and format everything correctly (some of the commands will change to bold as a result).

7. Because our script is easy I'll assume yours is correct, so now it's time for the final process. Go to the File menu, choose Save As and navigate to the very same folder in which similar scripts are placed. In this case, I chose URLs within the AppleScript folder. The finished script looks like the one shown in Figure 19.5.

8. All ready? Let's give it a test. With the script still on your iMac's screen, click the Run button. The result? Your default Web browser (the one selected in the Internet preference panel, which in this case is Microsoft Internet Explorer) will launch (if it's not already opened) and your selected Web site will appear on your screen (see Figure 19.6).

▼

19

FIGURE 19.5
This AppleScript is designed to access a single Web site in your Web browser.

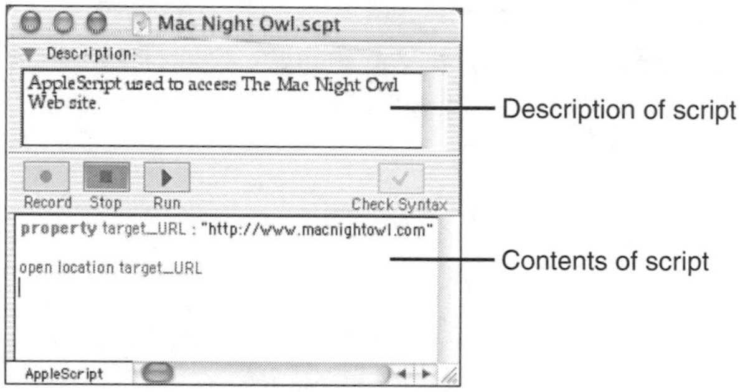

Description of script

Contents of script

FIGURE 19.6
Success! The script you wrote works exactly as you wanted.

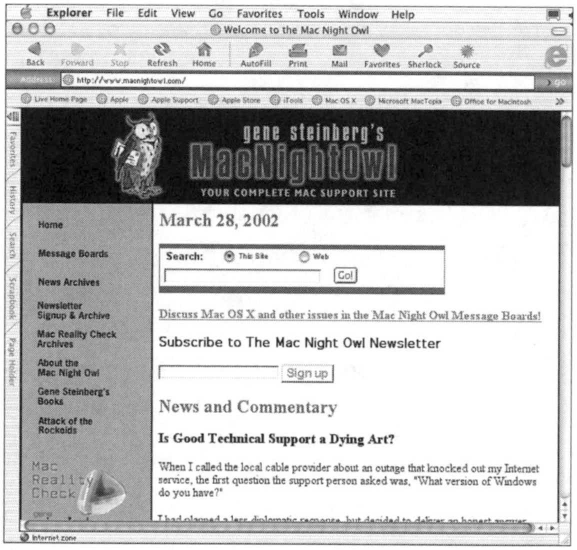

9. If you are finished making AppleScripts for now, just return to the Script Editor application and choose Quit from the application menu to close down the program.

Introducing Folder Actions for Mac OS 9

If would be great if AppleScript for Mac OS X did everything the Classic Mac OS did. When I talked with Apple's AppleScript evangelist shortly before this book was written, I felt optimistic that you'll see lots of cool things in future versions of Mac OS X.

For now, one nifty feature of the old Mac OS hadn't made the transfer to the new, but it's worth looking at anyway because it's very possible it will be there in a future version.

If you are involved in file movement and manipulation in a big way, you'll want to take a gander at another terrific feature of AppleScript. It's called Folder Actions.

After you apply a Folder Action to a folder, whenever you do something with that folder again, such as opening it, closing it, resizing it, or adding and removing items from it, the script is triggered.

Here's a brief idea of what you can do with a Folder Action (and I'm just covering the most basic features here). Possibilities abound for such scripts.

- **Open items as labeled**: You can apply a priority label for any item. The feature is available from the Preferences command in the Finder's Edit menu. Any item in a folder with a certain label can be launched when the script folder is opened.

- **Keep a folder open**: If you accidentally close a folder with this script attached to it, it will open again. This way the contents are always visible to you.

- **Close subfolders**: This action is great for preventing desktop clutter. It automatically closes all open windows within the scripted folder.

- **New item alert**: This script is quite useful when you are using a folder for sharing files from a network. Whenever a new item is placed in the scripted folder, you get a warning.

- **Reject added items**: This item does what the name implies; it prevents items from being added to the scripted folder.

- **Duplicate to folders**: You can use this script to automatically back up the files. When the item is placed in a scripted folder a copy is automatically placed in another folder that you select.

- **Retrieve items**: This script is used to move files back into the folder from which they were removed.

The Fast and Dirty Way to Make a Folder Action

Creating a Folder Action doesn't require a visit to Apple's Script Editor. You can do it without having to open any other program. Here's how:

Making a Folder Action

1. Restart your iMac under Mac OS 9.x and select the folder you want scripted.
2. Hold down the Ctrl key and click the selected item, which opens a Contextual Menu similar to the one shown in Figure 19.7.

▼ To Do

19

FIGURE 19.7

Pick a command from the Contextual Menu.

Help
Open
Move To Trash
Get Info ▶
Label ▶
Duplicate
Make Alias
Add To Favorites
File Buddy ▶
Index selection...
Attach a Folder Action...
Open in File Buddy

3. Select the item labeled Choose a Folder Action, which opens the Open dialog box.

4. Navigate to the Scripts folder, which is inside the System Folder.

5. Open the folder labeled Folder Action scripts, which opens the screen shown in Figure 19.8.

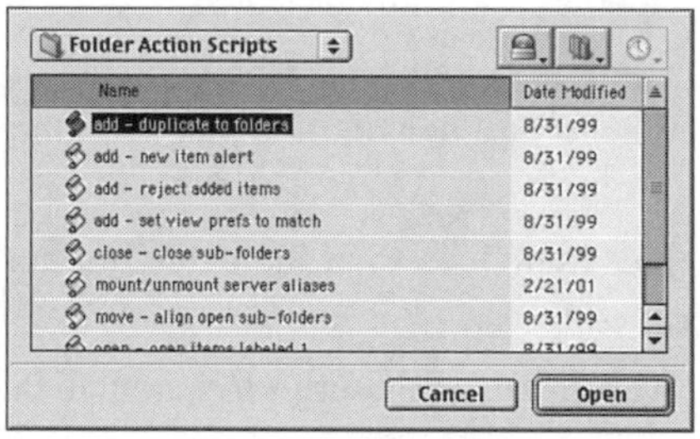

FIGURE 19.8

These are the standard Folder Actions you can apply.

Folder Action Scripts ⬍	
Name	Date Modified
add – duplicate to folders	8/31/99
add – new item alert	8/31/99
add – reject added items	8/31/99
add – set view prefs to match	8/31/99
close – close sub-folders	8/31/99
mount/unmount server aliases	2/21/01
move – align open sub-folders	8/31/99
open – open items labeled 1	8/31/99

Cancel   Open

6. Choose Add—New Item Alert and click Open. In a few seconds, the folder's icon will have a little script icon attached to it.

From here on any time someone adds an item in that scripted folder from across the network, you'll get an onscreen notice about it. No more secrets. But as I said, it only works under Mac OS 9.x for now, although I understand Apple is working on bringing this great feature over to Mac OS X. Maybe you'll see it by the time you read this book.

Removing a Folder Action

1. Select the folder from which you want to remove the Folder Action.

2. Hold down the Ctrl key and click the selected item to open the Contextual Menu.

3. Choose Remove a Folder Action from the menu and select the script you want to remove from the dialog box.

The script icon will soon disappear from this folder and so will the Folder Action. You can then apply another script to it if you prefer.

> If you ever need to adjust the script for a Folder Action, you can use the Edit a Folder Action command in the Contextual Menu to open the Script Editor and open the script for editing.

A Look at Macro Software for the Mac OS

AppleScript isn't your only road to putting your computer on automatic pilot. You'll find as you get adept at making scripts that not all programs support the feature.

Fortunately, other solutions are available; some came with software you might already have, and some came as separate macro-utility software that can script all your programs, even the ones that don't speak AppleScript.

New Term   A *macro* is just another way of identifying a script. It refers to the process of storing a set of repetitive functions and playing them back with a single command.

Here are some of your choices:

- **Macro features**: Such programs as Microsoft Office for the Macintosh have macro features. You can use their built-in script editors to record actions and play them back.

> **New Term**   As you've seen some programs call their automation routines *scripting*, whereas others call them *macros*. Some programs from Adobe Systems, such as Illustrator and Photoshop, label the routines as *actions*.

> Although the Mac version of Microsoft Office has an extremely powerful macro feature, one that can really help you simplify difficult tasks. However, if you want to use it, or you are going to open documents that have macros, you are advised to buy some virus protection software before you fiddle with the macro feature. A large number of so-called macro viruses are around (they infect Mac and Windows users of Office). Although the chances of actually getting an infected macro are small, you should be careful anyway. I'll tell you more about virus protection options in Hour 24, "An iMac Safety Net."

19

- **QuicKeys**: This is one of the oldest Macintosh scripting programs. In addition to observing and making scripts from the things you do, it has loads of built-in routines that work with many popular programs (Figure 19.9 shows the Mac OS X version). You can also create custom toolbars for fast playback of scripts as well as program and document launching. If you want to know more visit `http://www.cesoft.com` and check out their time-limited demonstration version of the program.

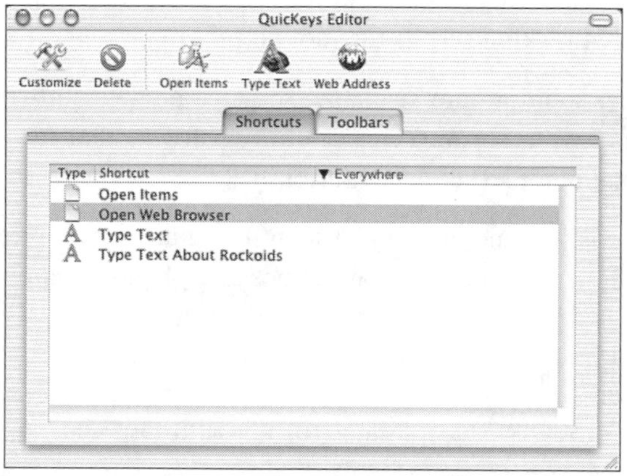

FIGURE 19.9

This is the QuicKeys macro editor, which is used to add and modify scripts that work in all programs or just a few.

In previous editions of this book I wrote about another macro-creating utility, OneClick. Unfortunately, at the time this edition was written, neither OneClick nor KeyQuencer, another program of this sort were being developed for Mac OS X. However, check the VersionTracker.com Web site (at `http://www.versiontrackercom/`) to see whether these programs (or unexpected others) show up in Mac OS X form.

Summary

After you set up an AppleScript routine, it's really fascinating to see your computer do your work for you while you sit back and watch. Fortunately, the techniques required to create scripts aren't so hard that you need a degree in computer science to figure them out. You'll be able to get going by using the information in this lesson.

In the next lesson, I'll tell you something about the many extras you can add to an iMac using the Ethernet, USB ports, and the new AirPort. You'll find hundreds of products ranging from digital cameras to printers and extra drives that can really enhance the capabilities of your computer.

Q&A

Q I tried writing an AppleScript for a program, but it won't work. I checked the language and it seemed okay. What is wrong?

A The Mac OS Finder and a great number of operating system parts can be scripted. Many of the programs you buy also support AppleScript, but not them all. If you need to know more, check the documentation that came with your software. You'll be pleased to know that AppleWorks already has some built-in scripts for you to work with. Just check the Scripts icon in the AppleWorks menu bar to access what's available. Unfortunately, this program isn't supporting the script-record function with the version available when this book was written.

Q Okay, I'm hooked. This AppleScript stuff sounds great. Where can I learn more about it?

A The first place to start is Apple's own Web site devoted to the subject, `http://www.apple.com/applescript`. When there, you'll find some solid information on the subject. You'll want to check out their technical information document, "Using AppleScript Documentation," which will definitely take you to the next level of script creation.

19

HOUR 20

Adding More Goodies to Your iMac

Having an all-in-one computer doesn't mean that you'll never connect anything. In Hour 17, "Now That I Wrote It, How Do I Print It?," I told you how to add a printer to your computer, so you can have top quality prints of your work. But that's only the beginning.

Printers aren't the only things you can attach to your iMac. Your computer comes with a flexible connection port called USB (short for *Universal Serial Bus*). Bearing a flat, rectangle shape, it enables you to attach up to 127 separate and distinct items that will expand its capabilities. USB is *hot-pluggable*, which means you can attach and detach the item (with a few cautions) without having to turn off your computer.

If you have an older Mac with a SCSI peripheral port, hot swapping is a no-no (except if you have one of those special terminator devices designed for that purpose). If you try a hot swap, you might cause your computer to crash, or risk damage to the electronics of the device itself or the Mac's SCSI chip (requiring a motherboard replacement). On these other Macs, shut down before you try to change anything.

Most iMacs, except for some of the older models, also include a fast expansion port called *FireWire* (sometimes called IEEE 1394 or i.Link). Shaped like a narrow oval with a flat end, you can hook up digital camcorders , fast hard drives, scanners, and lots of other cool stuff to the FireWire port.

In this lesson, you'll discover

- The wide range of USB and FireWire devices you can use to expand your computer's capabilities
- The safest ways to install new devices
- What USB hubs are and why you need them
- How Apple's new AirPort provides networking freedom

Making Your iMac Do More

Without a doubt, just adding a printer offers a great enhancement to the capabilities of your computer. You begin to see a printout of all the great things you've visualized on the screen. As sharp as your computer's screen might be, there's nothing like seeing it in print (book authors like me depend on it).

As time goes on there's no doubt you'll want to look for other expansion possibilities that will extend your computing prospects even further.

Here's a brief look at the sort of FireWire and USB devices available for your iMac (and I'm just scratching the surface here):

- **Printers**: Okay, you've added one printer. But there's nothing to prevent you from hooking up a second printer, either to the Ethernet port or the USB port (one black-and-white, one color, two color, and so on).
- **Scanners**: A scanner is a device used to take pictures of artwork or photos and store them in digital form on your computer. Consider it comparable to one half of a copy machine (the part used to pick up the document information). Using a scanner opens up a whole range of possibilities for doing creative work. In

addition, you can use a scanner with special software (OCR) that enables you scan manuscripts, and then edit the copy on your computer.

NEW TERM *OCR* is short for optical character recognition. And the description applies to software that can read the text in a scanned document and save that text in a form that you can edit on your computer.

- **Cameras**: Yes, you can still take pictures with film, but new-generation digital cameras are available that can record pictures that you store on your computer. Best of all you don't have to take the film to the photo finishing store and wait for the prints to return. Digital cameras open new possibilities for photography. In fact, some of the photos you see in this book were taken with a digital camera. The instant response makes it possible for me to reshoot pictures on the spot until they are as good as possible (no criticisms from professional photographers, please!). What's more, Apple's iPhoto software, described in Hour 14, "Using iMovie, iDVD, and iPhoto," makes the process of organizing your pictures and getting prints as easy as pie (and I'll take Apple).

  You can also purchase miniature video cameras (such as the iREZ Kritter USB and QuickCam), which enable you to record videos. They won't replace your camcorder, but they are nice for simple images. And you can use them with a special type of software, videoconferencing, which enables you to send videos via the Internet.

- **Storage Devices**: If you need to expand file storage beyond your computer's hard drive, you'll find several categories of drives available. I'll cover the most common ones.

  - **Iomega Peerless:** This clever device includes a base station, which attaches to your computer's FireWire or USB jack, plus a removable cartridge. The cartridge itself stores 10GB or 20GB. When one cartridge fills up you remove it and install another. Nifty.

  - **Floppy Drive:** This device enables you to read floppy disks with an HD label on your iMac.

  - **Zip Drive**: The Zip drive is a popular storage medium from Iomega Corporation that puts either 100MB or 250MB of data on a disk that looks like a floppy with a weight problem. The Zip format is supported by millions of users and is worth looking into if you exchange a lot of files with other folks, or you just want a simple way to backup your files.

20

> The great thing about both FireWire and USB is that you don't have to stick with just one extra storage device. You can add a number of extra drives to suit your needs. Just bear in mind that things will bog down on a USB chain if you try to use them all at once.

- **CD Burner**: The flat-panel iMac and some of the older models include drives that can burn a CD, which enables you to make copies of your favorite music or just back up your files onto CD blanks, which are cheap (less than a dollar) and can last for years. If you don't have an iMac with a built-in burner, you can buy a standalone product with much of the functionality. Separates, however, might not be able to take advantage of Apple's ultra-slick, Finder-level CD writing feature.

- **DVD-ROM Drive**: This is a product that enables you to play a new generation of high-capacity CDs based on the super-popular DVD format. It's not necessarily for movies (which would require special decoding hardware not normally available for your computer), but to enable you to back up your files to a near-permanent storage medium. Another type of DVD drive, DVD-RAM, also enables you record on special CDs.

- **DVD-R**: Yet another variation on the DVD theme. This drive is used to transfer pictures and videos to a real DVD, a DVD that will play back on most any DVD drives (except the very earliest models). The higher cost flat-panel iMacs include such a drive, called a SuperDrive, which also doubles as a CD burner. You can also buy a drive of this sort for your iMac from such companies as LaCie and QPS. I'll tell you about making DVDs of your home videos in Hour 14.

- **Hard Drives**: You can add extra hard drives to your computer for additional storage. The only consideration is that the USB port doesn't really exercise the maximum speed of a large hard drive, so you might prefer FireWire, if your computer has that feature. USB drives are fine, though, for occasional use or just to back up your precious files. You'll learn more about backup possibilities in Hour 21, "Backup, Backup, Backup...How to Protect Your Files."

- **Input Devices**: You're not limited to your iMac's keyboard and mouse, although they are suitable for most folks. Not everyone digs the circular mouse or tiny keyboards that came on the original iMacs (which were thankfully both replaced with the terrific Pro versions). But it's nice to know there are alternatives. If you've migrated from the Windows platform, for example, you'll be able to take advantage of a mouse with extra buttons (the second being used for the context menus you otherwise invoke when you Option-Click on something). In addition, you can purchase joysticks for computer games, keyboards for special needs (or just in the form of those offered on regular Macs), and even trackballs (sort of an upside-down mouse), which some prefer to a regular mouse.

> My favorite Mac keyboard and mouse combo is the one that comes with the flat-panel and later-generation Classic iMacs, the Pro series. The Apple Pro Mouse, for example, uses an optical rather than mechanical movement, and hence doesn't even need a mouse pad. The Pro Keyboard is full-sized, with a soft touch for fast typing (all right, it might not be perfect if you like to pound the keys). If you weren't lucky enough to get one of these babies with your iMac, relax. You can buy them at your favorite Apple dealer.

- **Cable/DSL/Fixed Wireless/ISDN Modems**: If your iMac's 56K modem seems a little slow, you'll be pleased to know there are ways to get better performance. One way is the cable modem (which works with the Ethernet port), if your cable company offers service in your city. Another is DSL (short for Digital Subscriber Line), an ultra high-speed protocol that uses your regular phone line (this one also uses your iMac's Ethernet port). A third alternative is called fixed wireless, which involves either a satellite dish or transceiver, but that method isn't available in too many cities. The last affordable alternative is an ISDN modem, which hooks up to the USB port. This sort of modem can virtually double the speed of Internet connections, but before you take this route, check your local phone company for pricing and features.

- **Hubs and Cables**: When you hook up a large chain of USB devices, you might need a hub, which is a central connecting device. Some items work as hubs (such as an iMac's keyboard), and some don't. Before you buy a USB peripheral, you'll want to check the requirements to see if you need anything extra. Keep in mind that when you run out of jacks to hook up to you'll need a hub to get more jacks. Also, don't forget the cable. For some reason, not all manufacturers supply them. If in doubt, ask your dealer.

20

The Fast, Safe Way to Install FireWire and USB Devices

If you've connected peripheral devices to computers from that *other* platform (called Windows), no doubt you've become used to playing with special interrupt settings. And when you add extra SCSI drives to a Mac or a PC, you need to check for ID settings and termination (a device that closes the electric circuit).

With FireWire or USB, you don't have to worry about dealing with those arcane setups. Instead, you can easily add such devices as you need them and remove them just as quickly.

Here's a tried-and-true FireWire and USB installation method (some changes might apply to specific products, and they'll tell you that in the documentation):

Connecting a Peripheral to Your iMac

1. Unpack the device and check for an installation CD.

2. If there's an installation CD, it means that special software (a driver) is needed to make the device work. The SuperDisk and Zip drives are examples. Just place the installation CD in your computer's drive.

> Mac OS X has built-in support for many of the things you connect via FireWire or USB. But some printers, scanners, and CD or DVD burners will most likely need special software. Before you try to use any of these products, check the documentation or the publisher's Web site to confirm that the product works with Mac OS X. Or pay a visit to VersionTracker.com (http://www.versiontracker.com) for the latest updates. If not, you might be able to run it under Mac OS 9.1, 9.2, or 9.2.1 (whichever you have), but the fun of the new Mac OS is to stay within that environment and not switch to run a new peripheral.

3. Double-click the Installer icon and follow the instructions to install the new software.

> Under Mac OS X, you might see a prompt where you have to authenticate yourself as administrator of your iMac before a software installation can begin. This is, as the TV cops say, just routine. Mac OS X is a multiple-user operating system, and it just wants to know that you are authorized as chief cook and bottle washer of the system. Just use the same password you gave yourself when you first set up Mac OS X and you'll be ready to roll.

4. After installation, you should be able to connect and use your device right away. In a rare situation, you might see a Restart button (although Mac OS X shouldn't need it). If you see such a button, click it and sit back and wait for your Mac to restart itself.

5. Connect one end of the device's cable to the free plug on your iMac's connection panel or the free plug on your keyboard.

If you cannot find a place to plug a USB device, you'll probably need a hub, which extends the number of ports available for USB connections. You can buy a hub at your dealer. Before you purchase a USB device, you'll want to check the available connections so that you don't have to make a return trip for another item. Bear in mind, however, that some USB devices need to be hooked up directly to the Mac, rather than to a hub. So if it still won't work, try a direct connection as an alternative.

6. Connect the other end of the cable to your peripheral.

7. Turn on the device. You'll then want to check your instructions about using the device. Some products, such as scanners, require that you run special software to operate them.

Some scanners also have special hardware locks to protect the delicate circuitry. Before you turn on a new scanner, check the documentation and see if such a thing exists. Usually, it'll be a switch or a button with a lock icon on it. If you fail to unlock the mechanism you might damage the unit when you try to use it.

I don't want to mislead you about a USB device being hot-pluggable. There are times when you shouldn't unplug the device. For example, if you have a disk in a SuperDisk drive, Zip drive, or similar product, eject the disk first, before removing the drive. If you are working in a document that is using the device, make sure that you quit the program before removing the device. Otherwise, you'll risk a crash or possibly a damaged file or a damaged disk directory (the table of contents used to locate files on the disk).

20

A Look at USB Facts

If you're used to older Mac computers that have ADB (Apple Desktop Bus) and serial ports (labeled modem and printer), no doubt you're wondering why the need for a change. Here are some more advantages to the new technologies, in addition to the ones I mentioned at the beginning of this lesson:

- **Speed**: The USB port is capable of up to 12 megabits per second transfer speed. That's more than 125 times faster than the ADB port and up to 50 times faster than the Mac's regular serial port. This is perfect for scanners, input devices, and a slower hard drive.

> In the future, there might be an even faster USB technology for your iMac. USB version 2.0, with speeds 30 to 40 times faster than current USB ports, is already available for a small number of products (but it requires a special adapter that won't run with a present-day iMac). At the time this book was written, Apple hadn't committed to supporting this new technology.

- **Easy Hookup**: As you've seen from the seven steps mentioned previously for hooking up a FireWire or USB device, it's about as easy as it can get. So, if you are anxious to try out your new peripheral, you'll be glad to know that it will be up and running in minutes.
- **Growing Selection**: From almost the very first day the iMac came out in August 1998, there were USB products available for it in many categories. And in this cross-platform world, the maker of a USB product for the *other* platform can easily make it work on a Mac, simply by writing a new software driver (and with some mice and keyboards, new software might not even be needed).

Introducing AirPort

In the past, when you wanted to network a computer, you had to run a wire from one to the other or to a hub (a central connecting point). If you've ever tried to do this in a home or office environment, though, you have the problem of wrapping messy wires around walls, furniture, under carpets, and so on. No doubt you have almost tripped over a stray networking cable.

Apple's AirPort wireless-network system is designed to get around that limitation. You don't have to fiddle with cables or complex setups. And you can (depending on your surroundings) be up to 150 feet from another AirPort-equipped computer or the AirPort Base Station and still get undiminished performance.

Here's an overview of AirPort products and features:

- **AirPort Interface:** If you have a flat-panel, slot-loading iMac that includes AirPort capability, you just need to install a little credit card–sized module, an AirPort card, and then set up the software to make it run. AirPort software is already installed under Mac OS X.

Just launch the AirPort Setup Assistant and choose your wireless networking options. You can even set up the Network panel of Mac OS X's System Preferences application to put a little status icon in the menu bar, so you can turn AirPort on and off and log into a network. After you're hooked up, you can connect to any other Mac OS computer that has AirPort installed (up to 10 computers without degrading performance). Or you can connect directly to the next product I'll tell you about, the AirPort Base Station.

- **AirPort Base Station**: This product, which looks like something out of a science fiction movie (see Figure 20.1) forms the hub or central point of an AirPort wireless network. It has a built-in 56K modem and two 10BASE-T Ethernet ports. You can use it to share an Internet connection across an AirPort network, a regular Ethernet network (using cables), cable modems, or DSL modems.

FIGURE 20.1

This is version 2.0 of the AirPort Base Station, used as the central connection point of your wireless network.

When hooked up, your AirPort wireless network can be used to connect computers within your home or office or in a classroom. Because it's wireless, you don't even have to be inside a building to connect. As long as you're in range of another AirPort-equipped computer or the AirPort Base Station, you can connect as efficiently as if you were connected with old-fashioned cables.

- **Cross-Platform Standard**: The AirPort wireless networking system uses an international standard, 802.11b, also known as Wi-Fi, which is supported by Mac and Windows computers. What that means is that you can connect to a wireless network powered by products from other companies, such as Asante, Proxim, and even the PC maker, Compaq, and those other computers with 802.11b capability can connect to an AirPort Base Station.

20

You aren't even limited to an Apple AirPort Base Station as the central connection point. The makers of network equipment all have variations on the Wi-Fi theme, some with four or eight plugs, so you can use them for a larger wired network. Just check with your favorite Mac dealer to check out the possibilities.

FireWire Offers Ultra-Speedy Performance

Beginning with the original iMac DV and iMac DV Special Edition and extending to the full iMac product line beginning in 2001, two FireWire connection ports were included. FireWire enables you to hook up all sorts of high-speed devices to your iMac.

Most digital camcorders, for example, have FireWire connections. Of course, they aren't always called FireWire. For example, Sony camcorders are known as i.Link, and other products such as Canon's digital camcorders use the official term for FireWire, IEEE 1394.

As explained in Hour 14, you use FireWire and Apple's iMovie software to turn your iMac DV into a real video-editing station, and you can create high quality productions that'll look almost as good as broadcast TV.

In addition to editing videos, you can use your iMac's FireWire capability to hook up FireWire-based hard drives, removable drives, CD drives, tape backup drives and scanners. FireWire features a plug-and-play capability similar to USB. You install the software, and then plug in the device and it's recognized, just like that.

 FireWire and USB are totally separate technologies. You cannot hook up a USB device to a FireWire port, or vice versa (the plug layouts don't even match).

FireWire comes into its own when you need the highest possible performance on your iMac. As of this book's writing, dozens and dozens of FireWire products are available, and more are coming to market. You'll want to check with your dealer to see what's available.

Summary

Depending on your needs, a great number of peripherals are available for easy hookup to your computer. You'll soon be printing, shooting pictures, scanning artwork, and even, perhaps, using a designer keyboard and mouse. And it will all work just about perfectly on your iMac or iBook without having to fiddle with weird connections and software.

If you have a computer that comes with Apple's handy AirPort card (or you install one later), you'll be able to network without having to attach a messy old cable.

When you begin creating your own files, such as word processing documents with AppleWorks or financial data with Quicken 2002, you'll want to make a backup copy in case something goes wrong with the original copy. In the next lesson, I'll cover one of the most important areas of Mac computing, performing backups.

Q&A

Q I have an old scanner that works really well. But these new Mac OS computers don't have any place to hook it up. Is there some way I can make it work? Or do I have to buy a new one?

A Don't give up hope. You'll want to check with your dealer and look for a SCSI-to-USB adapter or a SCSI-to-FireWire adapter. Such adapters enable you to use older scanners, hard drives, and other devices on your computer. The only downside is with hard drives; they'll run slower on a USB port (the SCSI-to-FireWire adapter is better if your computer has FireWire), but scanners should work just fine. Just remember to install your scanning software.

Q I have a really nice keyboard here, specially designed for folks like me with a wrist injury. Can I use it on the iMac?

A The answer is a definite yes. You only need to contact your dealer about an ADB-to-USB adapter. That will enable you to attach that keyboard and other input devices from the older-style Macs to your iMac. One such product is the iMate from Griffin Technology of Nashville, Tennessee. You can learn more about it at the manufacturer's Web site: http://www.griffintechnology.com.

I should also mention, that there are ergonomic USB keyboards as well, so you might find a suitable product if you check with your favorite Apple dealer. Microsoft makes some fine keyboards of this sort, and, with special software, they'll even work on Macs. What's an ergonomic keyboard? That's one with the keys divided into three segments, tilted at a slight angle. They're supposed to provide better comfort and more resistance to wrist ailments. Frankly, I've never been able to get used to one of these keyboards, but if you have had wrist-related injuries this might be an alternative worth trying.

Q How do I recognize the USB connection cable?

A USB cables have two types of plugs, so that you can connect the correct end to the correct end. The part that plugs into your computer (or a hub) is small and rectangular. The side that goes into the device itself is square. Some USB devices support a different style of connection, but it is always obvious which end goes where. I cannot overemphasize, however, the importance of checking the product's documentation before you hook it up. Scanners, for example, require that you unlock the optical assembly with a switch or pushbutton before they will work.

20

Q Can I use a USB device from that *other* platform on my iMac?

A Maybe yes, maybe no. A keyboard or mouse that doesn't need a special driver program might work, but otherwise, you need software that is designed specifically to work with the Mac OS. Because most new Mac OS computers have USB, Apple has developed improved drivers and built-in support for many devices. If you're unsure whether the product will work for you, contact your dealer or the manufacturer.

Q I'm having problems getting my new printer or scanner to work. I know it's hooked up properly. I checked the instructions again and again, but it just won't work.

A The best thing to do is try reinstalling the software, and then restarting. If that doesn't work contact the manufacturer of your printer or scanner (or check their Web site) for information about a software update that might be needed. Remember that special software has to be developed for Mac OS X support.

Q I've read your statistics about how fast USB can be. What if I hook up several devices to my computer? Will that slow things down?

A Depends. Except for disk drives, it will take several devices working together to begin to affect performance. If you scan a document while printing, it's possible to see some performance degradation, I suppose. But most times you'll hardly notice any difference, even if your USB chain is packed with products.

Q I have an older iMac. Can I attach an AirPort to it?

A You can network to an AirPort Base Station with an Ethernet crossover cable, which will connect you to AirPort wireless networking. But only the flat-panel and slot-load iMacs have this feature. However, there are alternatives. Some companies are marketing Wi-Fi cards that plug into a USB port. Just check carefully to make sure the product comes with Mac software. One such product is the Proxim Skyline 802.11b USB Adapter for Desktops.

Q My iMac didn't come with FireWire. Is there anything I can do to add the feature, maybe to the USB jack?

A It would be nice, but the FireWire electronics are part of an iMac or iBook's logic board; you can't just add it later if the support isn't there already. The USB port runs at a much slower speed than FireWire. However, you might want to check out some of the processor upgrades for older iMacs, some of which also include FireWire. Such upgrades replace part of your iMac's logic board with one that includes a speedier processor. Among the makers of such products is Sonnet Technologies (`http://www.sonnettech.com`), which manufactures a processor upgrade and FireWire adapter all in one. The product is called HARMONi (yes, it's spelled correctly).

Q I have an original Apple LaserWriter, a workhorse that runs and runs. I don't want to give it up, but there's no Ethernet jack, just LocalTalk. Now that I've moved up to an iMac, do I have to retire the printer?

A Not at all. Companies such as Farallon and Asante make LocalTalk to Ethernet adapter modules, costing a bit under $100. These devices let you use your old LocalTalk devices on an Ethernet network with your iMac and other recent Apple computers. Just remember that you cannot use a standard serial printer cable with these adapters. You have to buy a LocalTalk or PhoneNet cable package to mate with those adapters.

If you have an old serial printer, you can use a serial to USB adapter to make it run, but check for compatibility. When it comes to an inkjet, such as an Apple StyleWriter, though, you might want to invest the money in a new printer. There are some great selections from such companies as Canon, Epson, HP, and Lexmark. Many are less than $100. How do they perform such a miracle? Well, these printer companies take the same approach as razor blade makers. They sell the consumables (ink and high-quality paper), which is where profits are usually made.

A few ink cartridge replacements, for example, can often exceed the cost of the printer itself.

20

Hour 21

Backup, Backup, Backup...How to Protect Your Files

Ever lose a file because you trashed it by mistake? Even if you keep close tabs on your data, don't get overconfident about the safety of your files. One thing is certain (other than death and taxes, of course)—your iMac will crash on occasion, just as any personal computer. Even though Mac OS X offers greater resistance to such ills, it still happens. When a program or computer crashes, it's possible one or more files on your computer's drive can be affected (especially if you're working on a file when the computer locks up).

In this lesson, I'll show you some easy, safe contingency plans to protect yourself against such problems (or even if your computer is stolen).

In this lesson, you'll discover

- How to back up your files, so that you always have a spare copy in case of a problem
- The difference between full backups and incremental backups and how to decide which method is best for you
- A look at different backup software
- An overview of Mac OS X's Multiple User security features, and other security software that can prevent access to your files

The Need for a Backup Strategy

Computers drive our daily lives. Nearly every business has a computer system of some sort, whether a personal computer, such as your iMac, or a large mainframe with huge boxes of electronics and disk drives. The systems aren't perfect, no matter how well you prepare for problems.

I don't want to be an alarmist, but it's very true that nothing is foolproof. If you want to create documents on your computer that you need to keep safe (from a newsletter to your personal financial information), you should take steps to make sure that you'll always be protected in case of trouble.

Consider what the big folks do:

- Large companies, including banks, insurance companies, manufacturers, and even online services such as AOL make spares (backups) of their data in case something goes wrong with their computer systems.
- Hard drives, such as those in your iMac, are not perfect. They use mechanical components that are working constantly to access and save data. Sometimes, things go wrong and a file can be damaged, or the drive might fail. It doesn't happen often, but it does happen. I'll tell you more about hard drive safety software in Hour 24, "An iMac Safety Net."
- Software isn't perfect. Programs are written by imperfect human beings such as you and me, and program bugs or compatibility problems can cause a computer to lock-up. When that happens, the file you might be saving or working in could get damaged (especially if the Save process is interrupted).
- Computer viruses remain a real threat. Even though the Mac platform doesn't have near the problems as the *other* platform, there are some pretty damaging virus strains out there. If you plan on downloading files from the Internet or sharing disks with other users, arm yourself with virus software. I'll tell you more in Hour 24.

- You might have burglar alarms and great police protection, but thefts occur anyway. You might have insurance to cover you if your computer is stolen, but what about the files? What about your personal checkbook or other financial information?

The danger losing information might be small, but the time and expense involved in recreating your files might be far greater than the cost of protecting it.

A Look at Backup Methods

You can follow different types of backup techniques, depending on the kind of documents you're creating and how many of them there are. Here's a brief look at the sort of things you can do without having to buy extra software:

- **Back up only document files**: You already have copies of your programs on a CD. A complete packet of CDs came with your computer, containing all the software Apple installed on your computer. In addition, any new software you buy will also come on an installation disk of some sort. So the fastest backup method is just to concentrate on the documents you make with those programs.

- **Back up everything**: Even though you already have a separate copy of the software, it can be very time-consuming to restore all your software and redo special program settings. If you back up everything, however, it's easier to restore a program with your settings intact without fuss or bother. In addition, having a complete backup of your computer's drive is extra protection in case something happens to both the computer and software disks.

- **Incremental backups**: This technique requires special software (such as Retrospect or FWB's BackUp ToolKit, both of which are described later), but it is designed to make a backup strictly of the files that have changed since your last backup. A thorough backup plan might include a full backup at regular intervals, say once a week, and then a daily incremental backup. This method also takes a lot less time, and you won't need as much disk space to store it all.

Making Backups—The Fast and Dirty Way

When you are ready to make a backup, you need a place to put those files. The best method is to get a separate drive with media (disks) that you can remove. That way you can store the backups in a separate location for the ultimate in safekeeping. That's the method the big companies use.

21

Here's what you need:

- **Your iMac's CD burner:** Your flat-panel iMac and some older models come equipped with an optical drive that can make CDs. You can use this drive to copy your files to a CD/R or CD/RW disc (the latter is the one that's rewritable). This is a convenient and inexpensive way to copy your valuable data on a medium that will last for years. Check Hour 14, "Using iMovie, IDVD, and iPhoto," for information on how to use your iMac's CD-burning feature. If you don't have a built-in CD burner on your iMac, no problem. There are plenty of low-cost external drives that can work from your iMac's FireWire or USB ports (but of course the first will run much faster).

> Does your flat-panel iMac have Apple's SuperDrive? If so, you can also burn data DVDs in the same way you make a CD. The advantage is that you can store much more data on the DVD—4.7GB compared to 650MB or 700MB for a CD. If you have a well-populated hard drive on your iMac this might be an option.

- **External backup drive**: Iomega Jaz, Peerless, or Zip drives are convenient, and the drives and disks aren't too expensive (well, the Jaz and Peerless media aren't exactly cheap). There are also several varieties of tape drives that will work with backup software as a fairly stable backup medium.

> Notice, I'm not saying anything about floppy disks here. Unless you only make a few small files, floppy disks aren't practical, even though such drives are readily available at low cost. You'd need dozens of them at the minimum, and they just aren't as robust as the larger disk techniques. I cannot begin to tell you how many of my floppies have gone bad over time. No wonder Apple doesn't include standard floppy drives on its computers any more.

- **Networked disks**: If your computer is on a network, a drive on another Mac (or actually even a Windows-based PC that's set up to handle Mac files) can be used for your regular backups. Before you set up a networked drive for this purpose, you'll want to set up a strategy with the folks who run the network. Some companies plan on having all files backed up to one drive or drives, and then they do their own special backup routine on those files.

- **A backup plan**: It's a good idea to set aside a time to do your backup at regular intervals—perhaps at the end of your work day before leaving your office (or shutting down your computer if you're at home).

> It's just not a good idea to back up your files to the same drive they were made on (such as your iMac's hard drive). If something should happen to that drive, or the entire computer, your backup would be gone.

- **Careful labeling**: Make sure that your backup disks are carefully labeled according to date and content. If the label isn't large enough, you might want to prepare a short listing of contents in your word processor and then pack it with the disk. Often something such as "Backup for February 28, 2002" is sufficient.

- **Reuse older media**: If you need to keep an older version of a file, you'll want to keep the backup in a safe place. When you no longer need a disk, however, there's no problem in putting it back into service for newer backups. Otherwise, you'll end up with a huge number of disks.

> CDs and DVD media are write-once media, which means that when you burn one of these discs that's it unless, of course, you opt for CD/RW media, where you can rewrite data up to 1,000 times.

- **Rotate media**: Although Jaz and Zip media are pretty solid, you'll want to reduce wear and tear by having several disks around. And, in case one backup file goes bad, having another recent one never hurts.

> If you're in the market for some USB drives for backups, you'll also want to read Hour 19, "AppleScript: Putting Your iMac on Automatic Pilot," which offers some information on one way to backup files (which only works under Mac OS 9.x, for now, although that might change in the next Mac OS X upgrade).

21

- **Multiple backups**: If your files contain important data on them (financial or otherwise), make a second backup and store it in a secure location (such as a bank vault). In the unlikely event something happens to your home or office, you'll be protected.

- **Internet backups**: If you have a good Internet connection and you don't want to back up a large number of files, you can use backup via the Internet. As a Mac user, you can sign up with Apple's iTools feature (when you first set up Mac OS X, you were given the chance). As part of the package, you get 20MB of iDisk storage space at Apple's Web servers, absolutely free. Need more? Just contact Apple at the iTools Web site (`http://www.apple.com/itools`) about buying extra space. If you want to sign up, just open the Internet panel in the System Preferences application, click the iTools tab, and then click Free Sign Up. You'll be guided easily through the simple setup process. However, unless you have really fast Internet access, the process of copying files to your iDisk can get mighty slow.

> After you've set up an iTools account, you can access your iDisk. Simply click the iDisk icon on the Finder's toolbar to open your disk. If you aren't connected to the Internet, the service will be dialed up first.

After you've decided where to put those files, here's the fastest way to do your backup:

Backing Up Files

1. When your regular backup time comes around, insert your backup media in the drive.
2. Create special folders for your backups on the backup media, labeled as carefully as possible according to their contents (such as the date of backup, the kind of files, and so on). An example would be financial backup or Thursday's backup).
3. Select and drag the files to be backed up to the backup media.
4. Eject the backup media when you're done and put the disks in a safe place.

> If you live or work in a climate with temperature extremes, try to locate a cool, dark place (such as a metal closet) to put the backup disks. It's not a good idea to subject backup media to hot sunlight, high humidity, moisture, or extreme cold.

Using Backup Software

If you have a large number of files, or files need to be backed up from more than one Mac OS computer on a network, you'll do better with some backup software.

Such software can

- **Perform scheduled backups**: You can set the software to perform the backups at a regular time (daily, every other day, weekly, whatever). At the appointed time, you need to only have the backup media in place and the computers turned on for the process to go.

> Although automatic backups are great, a backup can stop dead in its tracks if the media runs out of space, isn't ready, or the computer was shut down by mistake. If you have a large number of files, check to make sure that your disks have enough space, or be prepared to check the backup process every so often in case of trouble.

- **Perform networked backups**: With the right software, backups can be done from all computers on a network to one or more backup drives.

> Each computer on the network will need its own licensed copy of the backup software for backups to be done across a network. A number of Mac applications, such as Microsoft Office v. X, are designed with network prevention schemes. That means, the program will not run if there's another copy with the same serial number on a network. Fortunately, networked backup software comes in relatively inexpensive multiuser packs.

- **Back up the entire drive or selected files or folders**: When you set up your backup, you can instruct the software to limit the backup to the items you want. By default they do the entire drive, and then incremental backups for each disk, unless you pick a full backup.

Choosing Backup Software

When you've decided on the backup software route, you'll want to know what to choose. Fortunately, there are several good Mac OS software packages that will give you great automatic backups. They vary in features, and you'll want to pick one based on what you need.

21

Regardless of the software you choose, make sure it is compatible with Mac OS X. The file structures of Mac OS X files are often different from the ones used in the Classic Mac OS. This means that non-native applications won't recognize those files, hence your backup won't be complete. If you only intend to back up document files, of course, this doesn't matter, but if you want to back up your applications and operating systems (or the whole drive), it's very important.

Here's a brief description of backup programs:

- **Personal Backup** (`http://www.intego.com`): This simple program, now published by Intego, enables you to do simple automatic backups with a number of options. There's also a feature for on-demand backups, where you do them when you want. For added protection, Personal Backup gives you a keystroke recorder feature that makes a text backup of the files you write. In case something goes wrong with the original file, at least you'll have a way to recover the words (but not the artwork or layout).

I would love to show you what a Personal Backup looks like, but the Mac OS X version wasn't available to look at when this book was written.

- **Retrospect**: From Dantz (`http://www.dantz.com`), this is a heavy-duty backup program that does just about everything you can imagine in backup planning with little fuss or bother (see Figure 21.1). You can use its EasyScript feature to create a complete backup plan simply by answering some basic questions. Backups are compressed (to save space) and saved in a special format for efficient retrieval. Unlike other backup programs, Retrospect can work with tape drives, which can store many megabytes of files on little cartridges. Retrospect can also work with Internet-based backup services. For large networks, there's the Retrospect Network Backup Kit and even a Windows version with similar features.

- **Retrospect Express**: This program distills the most important features of Retrospect and puts them in a smaller, less-expensive package. Express doesn't work with tape drives, and there's no networked version.

FIGURE 21.1
Though brimming with powerful features, Retrospect is remarkably easy to use.

- **FWB Backup ToolKit:** The publisher of Hard Disk ToolKit (http://www.fwb. com), a disk formatter used by professionals, has released this simple personal backup utility that might be all you need (see Figure 21.2). As with Retrospect, it can handle incremental backups (just the files you've changed). Backup ToolKit also sports a simple drag-and-drop user interface, and the capability to handle file synchronization chores. The latter feature is very useful if you work on both an iMac and a laptop (such as the iBook) because it enables you make sure that both computers have only the latest files.

FIGURE 21.2
FWB's BackUp ToolKit combines simple setup and a powerful range of features to ensure robust backups.

A Look at Mac OS X's File Security Methods

21

If your computer is in an environment where other people might have access to it (such as an office), there are other steps you should consider to keep your files safe—security software, for example. Such software makes it necessary to enter a password to access a file's folders, or even your computer's hard drive.

Fortunately, Apple has given you tools to secure the files on your computer, beginning with Mac OS 9, and including Mac OS X. Here's a brief overview of those security features:

Keychains

You have a password for your Internet service, and maybe one to get to a special site. Or perhaps you have more than one account, say one for a regular Internet provider, and another for AOL. How do you remember all those passwords?

Apple's Keychain Access application (see Figure 21.3), which is found in the Mac OS X Utilities folder, enables you to keep track of all those passwords in a safe place, which itself is protected by a password. All you need to do is set up one password for access to a specific application or online service. Then, click the Add button in the Keychain Access application and enter the password and the name of the service or program.

FIGURE 21.3

Use a keychain to store your passwords for easy access.

Keychain Access   File   Edit   Keychains   Window   Help
⊖ ⊖ ⊖   gene
Keychain: "gene" on disk "Macintosh HD"   (Lock)
2 items

Name ▲	Kind	Date Created
iTools	iTools password	8/22/01
Starship	AppleShare password	8/22/01

(?) (Add...) (Get Info) (Remove)

The best password is the one that consists of random uppercase and lower-case letters and numbers. Common passwords, such as someone's name or birth date, are easy to guess by a third party who might want to get the files on your Mac.

Configuring Mac OS X for Multiple Users

The second weapon in your arsenal for protecting your computer against unwanted access is the Users panel of the System Preferences application.

By default, Mac OS X is designed as a multiple-user operating system, which means that you can create user accounts for each person who accesses your computer. When you first set up Mac OS X, the operating system makes you the administrator (quite a fancy title, right?) or owner. That gives you the privilege of making certain system settings and manipulating all the files on your iMac.

If you have children or employees who might also use your iMac, you might want to make sure that their access is more limited.

Setting Up Additional Users

▼ To Do

1. To configure your iMac for another user, launch the System Preferences application from the Dock, the Apple menu or the Applications folder.

2. With System Preferences opened, click the Users preference panel (see Figure 21.4).

FIGURE 21.4

You can add extra user accounts on your Mac from here. As you see I am indeed my iMac's administrator.

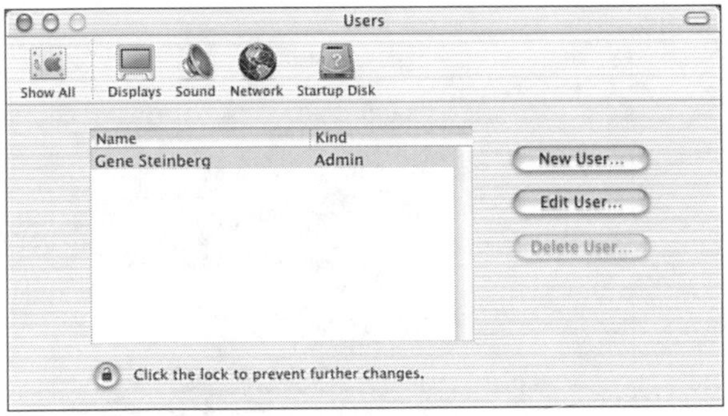

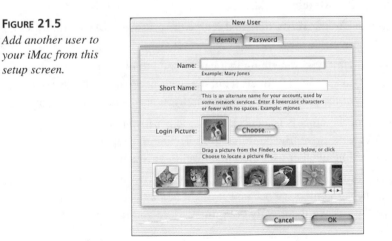

3. To add another user, click the New User button, which opens the dialog box shown in Figure 21.5.

FIGURE 21.5

Add another user to your iMac from this setup screen.

4. First, enter the name of the user, and also use an abbreviation (up to eight lower-case characters without spaces). That way, the user can log in either via the full name or the nickname.

▼

▼

5. Select a custom picture for that user. You can use the ones offered by Apple, or another picture that is located on your Mac, by dragging the picture into the Login Picture window or clicking Choose to select a picture file.

6. With the user's names and picture selected, click the Password tab (see Figure 21.6) to handle part two of the process.

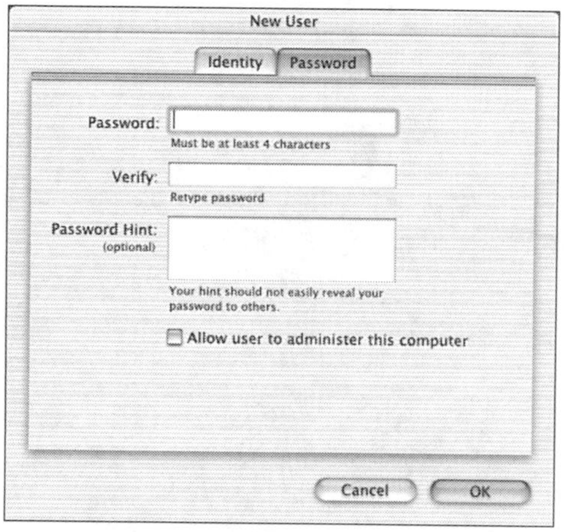

FIGURE 21.6

Give your new user a secure password here.

7. Following the suggestions I made previously about a secure password, type the password in the Password text field.

8. Press Tab to move to the Verify field and retype the password. Make doubly sure it is the same (otherwise the new user account won't take).

9. Under Password Hint type something that can be used to remind you and your user of the password, in case it's forgotten. This step isn't necessary, but it's a good idea, particularly if the password is complex and you need some sort of prompt.

10. The final setup of the process is a check box, whether to enable that user to act as administrator of your iMac. Be careful about selecting this one because you would, in effect, be enabling another user the same level of access that you have.

11. After the password is configured, click OK to store it. If you see a warning prompt at this point, check the message because it might be that you made a mistake or failed to type the password correctly both times. Here you'll have a chance to redo it.

12. When you return to the main Users panel, you can add additional users by clicking New User and running through the previous process. To change a user setting, such as name or password, just select the name and click Edit User.

▼

After the additional users have been set up for your iMac, you can switch between user accounts by choosing Log Out from the Apple menu. When you log out, after a few moments, all your open applications will be quit and you'll see a login panel.

Here you'll have to enter the correct username and password to login (upper and lower-cases must be entered exactly). If you enter the wrong password, the login screen shakes to warn you that you made a mistake.

> Forget a password? Here's a possible solution. Restart with your Mac OS X CD, holding down the C key to boot from the CD; keep the key held down until you see the Happy Mac icon. When the installer launches, pull down the application menu and choose Reset Password. When the application opens, choose the username from the pop-up menu and type the new password twice (the second time to verify). Now quit Reset Password and, when returned to the Mac OS X installer, quit that too. Then, click the Restart button to reboot your iMac.

After you've configured your iMac for multiple users, each user will see the following limitations:

- **File and folder access**: Each user gets their own users folder with their own name on it. The folders inside the users folder contain the files on their personal desktops, their own document files, pictures, Dock icons, and so on. Even custom application settings (such as Favorites in the Internet Explorer browser) are kept there. Only you, as administrator, and that user have access to the items in the users personal folder.

- **System Settings and Application Installations:** Any settings panel in the System Preferences application (such as the Network panel) that have a padlock will be inaccessible to anyone who can't log in as administrator. In addition, many applications won't install without administrator's access, which helps limit the damage another user can do to your iMac.

Using Security Software

The multiple-user feature of Mac OS X is simple and limited. But if you need a greater level of control, you might want to look into dedicated security software.

A security program can limit access to virtually every aspect of the Mac-user experience, and password protection is usually strong enough to resist even the most vigorous attempts to break in.

21

Such programs can control the following:

- **File access:** A security program can protect individual files so that only users with proper access can open and modify them. As with Mac OS X's file-sharing feature, you can enable some users to read a file, but not change it.

- **Folder access**: Security software can be set so that you cannot get to a folder without a password. It's common in some offices to keep system-related files protected, so folks cannot remove or add anything to them.

- **Disk access**: The most potent form of security won't enable a user to get to a drive without entering the correct password.

- **Special security features**: Some programs offer partial access to files and folders. You can make a file read only, so a user can see the listing for the files and open the files, but not change them. Another feature can prevent you from using a removable disk (such as a floppy, Jaz, or Zip disk) without entering the password. If you don't enter the right password in time, the disk is ejected without further ado.

Here are a few products that might help if you need that extra measure of protection:

- **DiskGuard**: This program, published by Intego (publisher of Personal Backup at `http://www.intego.com`), enables you to control access to disks and folders. If you want, the folder can even be made invisible to folks who do not have the password to access them.

- **FileGuard**: Also from Intego, this program extends security to floppy disks, individual documents, and applications. It's designed with networks in mind and comes in remote dress, which enables a single system administrator to control access on all computers in the network.

At the time this book was written, the Mac OS X versions of these programs weren't available. If you must use a security program, be sure of its compatibility first. Using software that isn't Mac OS X savvy might provide unsatisfactory protection or cause problems or damage to the system software.

- **FWB SubRosa Volume 1—File Utilities**: This utility package, with a tongue-twister of a name, features three applications. One can encrypt files and folders using 128-bit technology for maximum protection. Another can shred documents, so a disk repair or recovery program cannot recover them. The third is a decryptor, an application you can give to a friend or business contact, so they can unlock your files. This product runs native under Mac OS X.

- **Retrospect**: The regular version of Retrospect also enables you to protect your backups so that unauthorized users can't get access to the contents.

This list isn't meant to be complete. I've just focused on the software that you are likely to find at most retail dealers and mail-order houses. You might want to contact your dealer directly about these products and others they might suggest.

Summary

Having a regular backup plan is very important, especially if you intend to create documents on your computer that you need to protect. But, as you've seen in this lesson, doing backups isn't terribly hard. You just need to follow through on a regular basis to be sure that your most valuable files are safe in case the worst happens.

In the next lesson, I'll show you how to give your iMac a dose of new software and a dose of extra RAM (complete with how-to photos).

Q&A

Q **Tell me the truth: Do you really back up your own files in the same way you tell your readers to back up?**

A Absolutely. I do a regular, daily backup. In fact, when I write a book such as this, I usually do three backups of the manuscript every day, on separate disks. That way, I always have a copy of the latest version at hand in case something goes wrong with the original. I've only had to redo a book chapter once over the years (a crash corrupted the original file before the backup was made). It wasn't fun.

Q **Do you have a personal recommendation for backup software?**

A I've had great luck with Retrospect on my home office computer network. It's absolutely reliable and pretty easy to use. I've used it to restore files every so often when installing new equipment, and it has never failed me. If you don't have a network, you might do just fine with Retrospect Express

Q **I have a problem. I tried to restore files from my backup disk, but something was wrong. I can't get those files, and I need them for my work. What do I do?**

A I can't give you a clear-cut answer to this one. A program such as Retrospect can sometimes repair a damaged backup disk. But if you have files that you absolutely cannot afford to lose, make an extra backup in case the original backup disk goes bad. You might also consider a CD-ROM or DVD-RAM drive with recording capabilities for the safest backups possible.

21

Regardless, the best way to be sure that your backups will work is to perform a limited backup of, say, your document files. Then, try restoring them (to another drive of course) and see if you get all your files intact. This way you can be reasonably sure that your backup process will work.

Q I'm in bad shape here. I accidentally trashed a file before I backed it up. Is there any way to get it back?

A Don't get your hopes up high, but in Hour 24 I will discuss software that claims to be able to restore the files you accidentally delete. No promises, but until you read that chapter, best thing to do is not save any files to your computer's drive (if possible) because each file you save makes it more and more difficult for the recovery program to work.

Hour 22

Giving Your iMac New Software, More RAM, and Other Things

Do you have everything you need? Your new iMac comes with plenty of software and a reasonable amount of memory, so you can run your applications with top-flight performance. And, like the original Mac back in 1984, it's completely self-contained. You have most everything in one box, except for the keyboard, mouse, and the printer or extra drive you might add.

There might come a time, however, when you need to install something new. Perhaps you've bought some new software or an upgrade to a program you're already using. And maybe you want to install more built-in memory to handle more programs at the same time, or run a program that likes a lot of RAM (such as a Microsoft Office program or Adobe Photoshop). In addition, Mac OS X requires lots of memory to work efficiently.

In this lesson, you'll learn

- How to install new software
- How to know if you really need a RAM upgrade
- An easy, step-by-step process for installing RAM upgrades on a flat-panel iMac (complete with photos)
- What to do if something goes wrong with your new installation

How to Install New Software

After you've used your iMac for a while, no doubt you'll want to add some new software. Or perhaps Apple Computer has come out with a system software upgrade that you'll want to use.

Fortunately, software installation on a Mac OS computer is a relatively simple, uncluttered process. Most software publishers give you basic instructions, but the ones I'm presenting here will cover many situations.

For this lesson, you'll be installing a new system software upgrade.

Installing a System Software Upgrade

1. Insert the program's installation CD in your computer's CD drive and wait for a few seconds for the disk's icon to show on your desktop.

> If you downloaded software from the Web, you'll find either an installer icon or a disk-image file (one with a filename ending with .smi). If it's an installer, just double-click it. If you double-click a disk-image file, it'll appear on your iMac's desktop same as another disk, and the installer or application files will appear when you double-click the disk's icon.

2. Most CDs will display a directory of contents. If not, double-click the CD's icon to open its directory.

3. Double-click the icon labeled Install, Mac OS Install, or something with the Install label on it. This will open a screen similar to the one shown in Figure 22.1.

▼

FIGURE 22.1

This is a typical soft-ware installation screen.

Click Continue to proceed

4. You will see one or more intermediate screens, each of which will offer some additional information. One might give you a Read Me, showing basic things you should do before the installation, another might require you to agree to the software license (and you have no choice about this because not agreeing stops the installation). You might also see a pop-up menu where you can select the drive or folder on which to place the software, but after all these screens, you'll see where you can begin the actual installation (see Figure 22.2).

Before you add or upgrade any software, be sure to check the onscreen instructions or manual for last-minute information or alerts. You want to make sure that nothing on your computer conflicts with the installation of the software or using it later. This is especially important if you are trying to install software that hasn't been made native for Mac OS X.

FIGURE 22.2

After you've passed through the introductions, this screen actually starts the installation process.

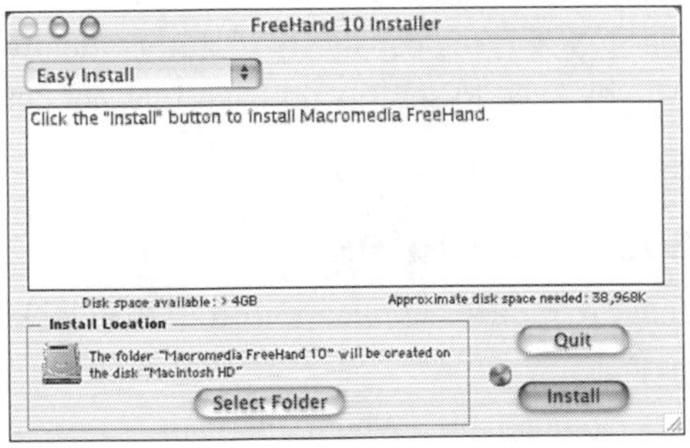

▼   5. You'll see a button usually labeled Install or Start. Click that button to begin.

Before the software installation starts, you can usually opt out by clicking a Cancel button or just quitting the program. If nothing has been installed, there's no harm in stopping the process if you change your mind.

6. You'll see one or more progress screens showing the installation as it continues. After you've reached the end, you'll see a button labeled Quit or Restart (or both). If it's labeled Restart, choose that option because it might be required before your software will work.

It's rare to see a Mac OS X application require a restart after installation, unless the software modifies a system function of some sort. If you're installing a Classic Mac OS application, clicking the Restart prompt usually won't do anything, but you have to click it anyway to proceed.

7. Now locate the folder that contains the new application and launch it, seeing if it works properly. Mac OS X applications usually will be automatically placed in the Applications folder, unless you specify another location. That's it! Now it's time to get back to work.

Updating Apple System Software Automatically

One great feature of Mac OS X is the capability to automatically receive software updates from Apple. All you need to set this up is an Internet connection and maybe a minute of your time.

Running Software Updates

1. Launch the System Preferences application from the Dock, the Apple menu, or the Applications folder.

2. Click the Software Update panel, which opens the screen shown in Figure 22.3.

Figure 22.3

Apple enables you to download the latest updates for your computer automatically from its Web site.

3. If you want to simply check for updates, click the Update Now button. Your Internet service will be dialed up, and Apple's support Web site checked for possible updates.

4. If updates are available for your computer, you'll see a screen listing what's available. From there you can click the check boxes for the items you want, and accept the download process.

5. When the downloads are complete, the software installers will launch and your computer will be updated with the new software. Then there will usually be an "optimizing" process, which allows the update to function with full efficiency. All you have to do is click the Restart button to finish the process (sometimes a Restart won't even be necessary).

6. If you want to have your computer check for Apple software updates automatically, click the Automatically check box, and then click the Check for Updates pop-up menu to set the interval. You can choose Daily, Weekly, or Monthly (Weekly is best, considering the unpredictable nature of the software update process).

> If you want to keep abreast of software updates from Apple and other companies, point your Web browser to VersionTracker.com (http://www.versiontracker.com/macosx). If you see information on a new Apple update, you can go right to the Software Update preference panel and click Update Now to retrieve it (though it sometimes takes a day or two for the update files to be available after an announcement).

7. After you've set the schedule choose Quit from the application menu to close System Preferences. If you selected Automatically, Software Update will check Apple's Web site at the specified intervals as soon as you login to the Internet.

It goes without saying that if your computer isn't on when the scheduled update scan is set to take place, it just won't happen. The check will be skipped until the next scheduled run.

Don't want to be reminded of an update you don't want? Software Update makes that possible, too. Just click on the unwanted update and choose Make Inactive from the Update menu. You will be reminded that you have inactive updates when checking for future updates, but you won't have to see them again if you don't want to install them.

Installing New RAM on Your Flat-Panel iMac

Do you have enough memory? Don't forget Mac OS X uses a lot of memory, and the more you have the better performance will be. True, the new operating system includes a highly advanced virtual memory feature to get the most out of existing memory. All this means, however, is that if there isn't enough memory to run all your programs, your iMac's hard drive is used for the rest, and that can bog things down noticeably.

Mac OS X requires a minimum of 128MB of RAM, but the sweet spot, where performance takes the greatest boost, is roughly twice that. This makes a RAM upgrade not just a luxury, but an essential need for optimal performance.

When you find that what you have isn't quite enough, you'll want to consider a RAM upgrade. Fortunately, it's a process you can do yourself.

When you order a RAM upgrade for your iMac, be sure to tell the dealer what you're using it for and which model you have. Many different kinds of RAM are available for Apple computers, but installing the wrong RAM, even if it looks okay, can damage the delicate electronic circuitry. So double-check what you're buying before you install it.

Have you replaced the battery in your TV or VCR's remote control? The process of adding RAM to a flat-panel iMac should be no more difficult.

Please take extra care in following the instructions when doing a RAM upgrade. You will be taking apart your iMac during this installation, and there is always the danger of damage to some of its delicate components. If you have any qualms about getting involved in this process, you might prefer to have your dealer do it instead.

What You Need

Before you perform your RAM upgrade, I suggest you read through this section at least once, so there are no surprises as you move through the process. Your iMac has two RAM slots. When it leaves the factory, one of these slots (the one located beneath its microprocessor) is already filled. The instructions I'm giving you here will strictly cover installation of RAM into the second slot. Replacing that other RAM module is a job for your dealer, so don't even consider it.

Now it's time to get ready. Here's what you need:

- A soft cloth or towel to place your iMac.
- A desk or other surface large enough to hold all the parts comfortably.
- A small Philips Head Screwdriver.
- And, of course, your RAM upgrade module.

Please don't use a powered screwdriver, because you might damage something. The screwdriver you can get for a couple of bucks at your local hardware store should be fine. It's not that you're going to make a habit of installing RAM in iMacs.

Are you ready? All right, just take a deep breath (I'll wait) and let's dive in:

Installing a RAM Upgrade

▼ To Do

1. Turn off your iMac, using Shut Down from the Apple menu.
2. Unplug all the computer's cables (power cord and modem cord, too).
3. Gently turn your iMac over on its side, so the display faces downward on a soft surface (see Figure 22.4).

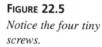

FIGURE 22.4
Use a soft cloth or pillow to protect the LCD display.

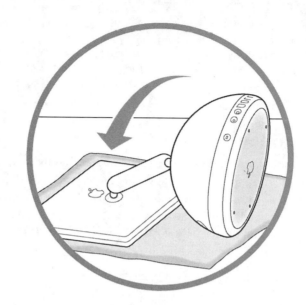

4. Take your Phillips Head Screwdriver and loosen the four screws attached to the cover at the base of your iMac (see Figure 22.5).

FIGURE 22.5
Notice the four tiny screws.

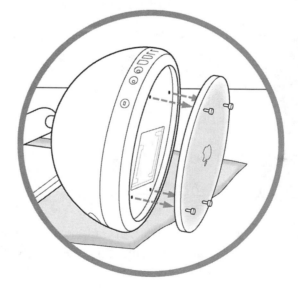

The four screws at the base of a flat-panel iMac remain anchored to the cover, so you don't have to worry about them falling out and perhaps disappearing in your shag carpeting. In addition, the head and bottom of the screws are flat, to prevent them from scratching a delicate surface.

5. Now you must discharge yourself, not by sending you out of the room, but by touching a bare metal surface inside your iMac (see Figure 22.6). This is done to discharge static electricity so a wayward spike doesn't damage the delicate circuitry.

FIGURE 22.6
Touch a metal surface to prevent static electricity buildup.

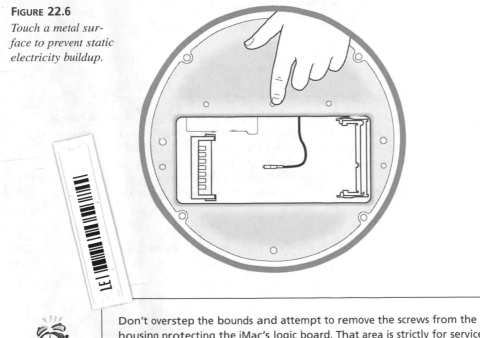

Don't overstep the bounds and attempt to remove the screws from the housing protecting the iMac's logic board. That area is strictly for service personnel only.

6. Take your memory module and place it at an angle into the memory slot. Make sure that the pins lineup with the slots on your iMac (shown in Figure 22.7).

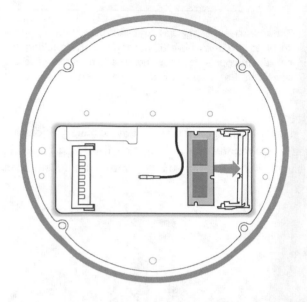

▼

FIGURE 22.7

*Make sure the pins
line up.*

Is the slot filled? Well, maybe you didn't need a second RAM module after all. If you bought your iMac from a dealer with a free memory offer, what's in there is probably sufficient for your needs. You should only consider removing it if the one you're installing has a larger capacity. Removing the module simply requires gently prying the locking tabs apart, and lifting the module; do it carefully because you don't want to damage the tabs.

7. After you're sure it all fits properly, press the memory module gently, until it clicks into place beneath the locking tabs at the ends of the slot. The clicking sound will be soft, so turn off your favorite heavy metal or symphony orchestra broadcast on your radio, so you can hear it.

If the memory module doesn't seem to click in place, do not try to force it in position. You might damage the plastic tabs, and it'll require an expensive replacement of your iMac's logic board to fix. If the module isn't fitting properly, make sure the pins are in the right position. If it still won't work, contact your dealer for assistance. It's a lot easier to wait and get it done properly than to risk damage to your computer.

▼

22

8. Take the cover panel and make sure the screws line up with the four holes at the bottom of your iMac, then push it in (see Figure 22.8). Now tighten the screws.

FIGURE 22.8

When everything's in place, you're done.

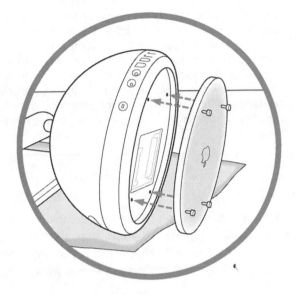

Don't use too much force with your screwdriver. Finger tight is quite enough to get the job done. You don't want to make it difficult to open the access cover in case you want to add an AirPort wireless networking card or a memory module with greater capacity later.

9. Place your iMac back in its normal location and reconnect the cables and power cord.

If the process went as advertised, your iMac is now ready to turn on, so you can enjoy the benefits of the extra memory. If you run into any problems, check the Q&A section at the end of this chapter for additional help.

Making Use of the Extra RAM

After you've installed a RAM upgrade on your iMac, you'll be able to run more programs at the same time. You don't have to do anything; Mac OS X will automatically allocate the amount of memory a program needs to run efficiently. By having more memory available the operating system doesn't have to use as much of your computer's hard drive to store program code. That way, things run noticeably faster, and you'll see fewer delays as you launch or switch applications.

> What about the capability to increase application memory, using the Get Info command on the old Classic Mac OS Finder? You can do that for a Classic application, if you want, but the option isn't there for Mac OS X software because it's not necessary. To set Get Info for a program, quit the program, select its icon and just open the Show Info window (from the Mac OS X Finder). Now choose Memory from the pop-up menu, and increase the "Preferred" allotment in 1000K steps. When you close the Show Info window and run the program again it will use the additional memory you allocated.

Summary

As you see from this lesson, you don't have to be a computer expert or engineer to upgrade your iMac. If you just follow the simple steps shown here you'll have little trouble adding extra software or even a RAM upgrade. If you decide to forego the hardware installation you'll at least know how the process works and what to look for if something goes wrong.

It's inevitable that at some point your computer will lock up when you're in the middle of something. It's the nature of personal computers to hang from time to time. In the next lesson, I'll tell you why it happens and the things you can do to get your computer up and running smoothly again.

Q&A

Q I tried to install some new software, but I keep seeing a screen message that it won't run on my iMac. What's wrong?

A Possibly, it's the software. Before you purchase software for your computer, make doubly sure that it will run. The iMac will use just about everything designed for a PowerPC Mac (and there are thousands of programs to pick from). However, you'll get optimum performance if you get a program that's built for Mac OS X (the retail box of such software will bear a logo to that effect).

Q My software comes on floppies, but I didn't bother getting a floppy drive for my computer. What can I do?

A To start with, you might want to contact the software publisher and see if they have a CD version. If you're on a computer network, with some regular floppy-equipped Macs on hand, there's still another possibility. You could install the software on the other computer, and then transfer it via a network. Just be sure you copy all the program's elements. A program's installer might put some things in a folder devoted to the application, and then in several folders strewn in various parts of the Classic Mac OS System Folder. You need to cover everything (sometimes the documentation will explain what is installed where). Remember, also, that software is licensed usually for just one computer, so if you want to install a copy on your iMac (when it's already installed on another computer), you will need to contact the publisher about multiuser licensing.

Q My dealer tells me that if I try to install RAM on my computer, the warranty will be null and void. Is that true?

A Apple isn't going to stop your warranty protection if you install your own RAM. In fact, you'll find a brief description of the process in your user guide. There is a condition, however, and that is if you damage your iMac when installing RAM, Apple won't fix it. If you follow the steps I described in this lesson carefully, you should do just fine. I've been installing RAM on Macs for years, and I've never lost a patient yet! If you have any concerns about probing the innards of your computer, go ahead and have your dealer do it (some dealers will install extra RAM for little or no cost if you buy the upgrade when you purchase your computer).

Q How much RAM should I install?

A There's only room for one more on your iMac (making for two of two slots), so you should buy the largest size you can comfortably afford. RAM for the iMac is best purchased in either 256MB and 512MB modules (the maximum available size when this book was written). You can never have too much RAM, especially for Mac OS X.

Q I've seen RAM prices all over the place. One dealer is twice the price of another. Is there any difference?

A For the most part, RAM is a commodity product, so you can probably shop safely on the basis of price. For added protection (at a somewhat higher price) pick RAM with a lifetime warranty, from such companies as Crucial Technology, Kingston, NewerRAM, or Viking.

Q Okay, now I'm in trouble. I installed the RAM. I think I followed the instructions, but when I try to boot the iMac, it doesn't work (or I hear weird noises instead of a startup tone)? Is my computer sick?

A Don't panic! Just go back and double-check your installation. When doing a RAM upgrade on the first-generation iMac, for example, I suggested that you not finish reassembling the unit until after you've restarted and shut down at least once. That's because the process of RAM installation is so complex. For the second-generation iMac or iBook, this isn't necessary.

You'll want to open your iMac and make sure that the module is seated firmly (don't force it too hard). If your computer still won't work, remove your RAM upgrade. Then try again. If your computer works this time, then maybe you have a bad RAM module (yes, it happens sometimes). In that case, you'll want to contact your dealer for a replacement or further help.

PART VII

What If Something Goes Wrong?

Hour

Appendix

HOUR 23

Crashin' Away: What to Do?

This is a true story and it was a jarring experience. In the 1980s, I bought my first Mac computer. I was happily writing a letter to a friend in a word processor program when suddenly a white rectangular screen appeared with a little bomb icon at one end. It said that a system error had occurred, and there was a little button I could press to restart. I was startled and began to feel like the person who drives a new car out of the showroom, only to have the engine quit at the first traffic light.

Several years and many Mac and system versions later, personal computers still crash, but there are usually things you can do to reduce the problems, and, when they do occur, deal with them easily.

In this lesson, you'll learn

- What to do in the event of a system crash
- How to tell if it involves software or hardware
- What some of those error messages really mean
- How to avoid crashes (or at least make them happen less often)

Your First System Crash! What to Do?

All right, maybe it seems as if I'm contradicting myself. I have spent a lot of time in this book telling you how powerful and robust Mac OS X is, so why talk about system crashes. Well, for one thing, nothing is perfect, least of all computer software. Second, more than likely, you'll be using an older Mac application, which means running in the Classic environment. This means you're vulnerable to a system problem of one sort or another.

It might happen the first day, the first week, or the first month, but some day the inevitable will occur. You will be working on an important document and suddenly you won't be able to type anything, or there will be a message that the program has quit.

Personal computers are, well, imperfect, and this is an eventuality you should expect, but it's also something for which you can prepare.

Over the next few pages, I'll cover the kinds of application and system crashes you might see and how to deal with them.

Application Unexpectedly Quits

One of the more common problems you'll face is an application quitting. Suddenly, without warning, the document window disappears from the screen and you'll see a message similar to the one shown in Figure 23.1.

FIGURE 23.1

This unfriendly message might sometimes appear when you're working on a document (yes, I actually had to force my iMac to crash to get this picture).

Click OK to proceed

Unfortunately, when a program quits while you're working on a document all the work you've done since the last time it was saved will be gone. That's why I always recommend that you save your documents often, so you won't lose much if something goes wrong.

When you see that message you have two choices. If you're using a Mac OS X application, do nothing. Really! Mac OS X is designed to be resilient to such problems because of its protected memory feature. So you can continue to compute in safety without needing to restart.

But when there's a rule, there's always an exception: If the application happens to be running in the Classic environment, the net effect is that Classic itself becomes unstable, so it's time to take the safe way out and follow these steps:

Restarting Classic

1. Quit all your open Classic programs if you can.

2. Launch the System Preferences application from the Dock, the Apple menu, or the Applications folder.

Even if Classic seems to run satisfactorily after a program quits, don't just sit there and continue working (and definitely don't consider trying to launch the program that quit again). It's the nature of the Classic Mac Operating System to be unstable after a crash, even though it won't affect your regular Mac OS X system. To avoid an even worse crash (and possibly lose information in your files), you should restart the Classic immediately.

3. Click the Classic icon (see Figure 23.2).

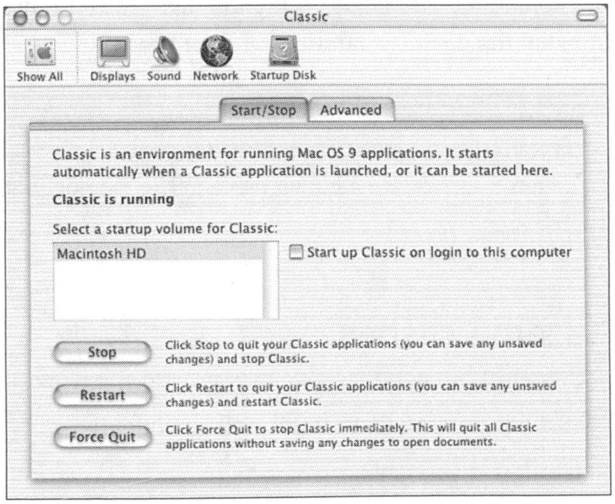

FIGURE 23.2

You can restart or configure Classic from this preference panel.

Classic

Show All Displays Sound Network Startup Disk

Start/Stop Advanced

Classic is an environment for running Mac OS 9 applications. It starts automatically when a Classic application is launched, or it can be started here.

Classic is running

Select a startup volume for Classic:

Macintosh HD   ☐ Start up Classic on login to this computer

Stop   Click Stop to quit your Classic applications (you can save any unsaved changes) and stop Classic.

Restart   Click Restart to quit your Classic applications (you can save any unsaved changes) and restart Classic.

Force Quit Click Force Quit to stop Classic immediately. This will quit all Classic applications without saving any changes to open documents.

▼

4. Click the Restart button. If it fails to work, click Force Quit and OK the choice, and then try Restart again.

If you don't plan on using a Classic application after using the Force Quit function you don't have to restart that environment. Whenever you do launch a Classic application, Classic will be restarted as part of the package.

▲

The Real Meaning Behind Those Classic Error Messages

If you ever restart with your Classic Mac OS, you'll see a series of strange messages if your iMac crashes. Past the unexpected quit warning you might see a number that is supposed to tell you what went wrong. The message will talk of a Type 1, Type 2, Type 3, or some other error with a meaningless number after it.

When an application quits in the Classic environment under Mac OS X, the most you'll usually see is the unexpectedly quit message. All those other strange messages containing numbers are highly unlikely to show up.

For the most part, the number of the error doesn't matter. It simply means something conflicted with something and made your computer crash. Fixing the problem doesn't depend on knowing the distinct definition of the message.

Although Mac OS X automatically adjusts memory needs, sometimes giving a Classic application a bigger piece of the memory pie might make it run better.

Other System Crashes

Not all crashes cause an application to quit. Sometimes the application will just stop running. The mouse might freeze, or it might move around but it won't do anything.

If this happens, follow these steps:

Using the Force Quit Feature

1. Force quit the program. Hold down the Cmd-Option-Esc keys. You will see a Force Quit Applications window (see Figure 23.3 for the Mac OS X version).

FIGURE 23.3

Choose the application to Force Quit from this window.

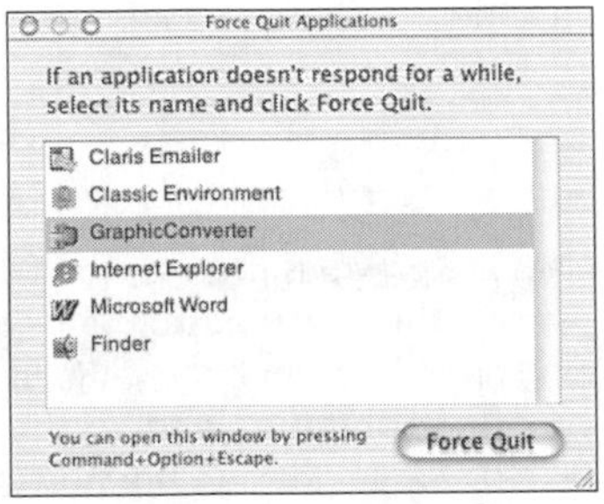

23

2. Normally, the application you were just running will be selected. If not, select the application.

3. Click Force Quit. Over the next few seconds, Mac OS X should be able to make the program quit. If it fails to occur, try again. Sometimes it takes two tries for the system to get the message.

4. If the program really doesn't quit, go to the Apple menu and choose Restart. At this point, there might be system-wide instability and it doesn't hurt to start from scratch.

5. If force quitting won't work, or your Mac won't restart normally, follow the steps described in the next section.

> An occasional Mac OS X system error is what's called a *kernel panic*. The symptoms are jarring, but don't freak out! A block of white on black text appears at the upper left of your screen. Usually, if you just press the r key, your iMac will restart and everything will be A-Okay. If not, use the following instructions to force a restart.

Forcing a Restart on a Flat-Panel iMac

If your computer refuses to restart in the normal fashion, you'll have to force the process by using the reset function.

The following instructions apply to the flat-panel iMac. I'll cover the older models in the next section:

Using the Reset Feature

To Do

1. Locate the power switch of your flat-panel iMac at the left rear of the unit.

2. Press and hold the power switch for five seconds. If everything goes as planned, your iMac will shut off.

3. Now restart your iMac in the normal fashion, by pressing the power button. When the startup process is done, you should be able to use your computer in the normal fashion.

Consider this action only if the previous process won't work because it's much more drastic. If pressing the power button fails to shut down your iMac, your only remaining option is to pull the plug, literally. Now wait 30 seconds, plug in your iMac again and turn it on. At this point, you should be able to start normally, except you might find the startup processes pauses for some extra seconds at the Checking Disks prompt on the Mac OS X startup screen. This is because a forced shutdown could cause minor disk directory damage, which is being fixed during the startup process. This should not be any cause for concern.

The next stage of forced restart instructions apply to the original versions of the iMac:

Forcing a Restart on a Classic iMac

To Do

1. If your iMac has a cover, open it at the right side of the iMac to access the connection jacks. Only the earliest generation iMacs have a cover there.

2. Look at the right of the panel for a small triangular-shaped icon. Below that icon will be a small hole (a very small hole). See Figure 23.4 (and look carefully).

3. If the hole is recessed, take a paper clip, straighten it, insert the clip into the hole, push gently on the button, and then release. If you have a newer iMac, you should be able to just press the button with your finger and achieve the same results.

FIGURE 23.4
The recessed reset button is used to force the iMac to restart.

Insert paper clip here

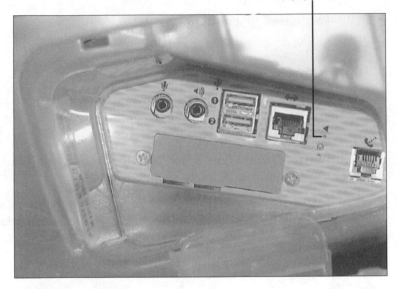

Don't push the button too hard. Just insert the clip far enough until you feel the resistance of the button; push it in gently, and then release it.

If this paper clip routine seems a bit much, you might want to try something better, the iMacButton. It's just what the name implies, a little switch that fits right into the slot of the early generation (Rev. A through Rev. D) iMacs and enables you to dispense with the paper clips restarts forever. You'll find out more about the product at the manufacturer's Web site: http://www.imacbutton.com. At the time this book was written, the price was just $9.95 plus shipping and worth every penny.

As soon as you press and release the reset button, your iMac should restart normally. Under Mac OS X, it'll go through the standard startup process. For Mac OS 9, you'll see a dialog box explaining that a scan of your startup drive is underway; click Done when it's finished to complete the startup process. On a rare occasion, it might not restart. In that event, you'll have to try something a bit more drastic (and remember this is only done as a last resort):

To Do

The Last Resort for a Classic iMac

1. Unplug your iMac.

2. Wait at least 30 seconds.

▲ 3. Reconnect the power plug and turn on your iMac.

Why Did It Crash!

If a program quits or locks up over and over again, it might just be that you need a newer version. Software is updated regularly (sometimes a couple of times a year) to fix bugs, boost performance, or just give you a different look.

Updates to fix a bug are usually free, but if the program has some new features, the publisher will no doubt charge for the upgrade.

If the program just won't work properly for you, check the manuals or Help menu for the publisher's email address or phone number and ask them for assistance.

New Mac OS 9 Warning!

Beginning with Mac OS 9, Apple added a new error message for some incompatible programs. The message explains that you need a newer version of the software. If you see that sort of message (or a Type 119 error), you'll need to consider whether you want to stop using the program or contact the publisher for an update.

What's Causing Those Crashes?

A rare system crash, maybe once every few days or so, is normal behavior for a Mac OS computer or even one of those computers from the *other* side. Mac OS X is more resilient; you could go for days or weeks before a crash occurs, but it can still happen. It's just the nature of the beast. If you encounter crashes several times a day, however, then something is definitely wrong. You might be seeing a conflict with some new software or hardware you've installed.

Fortunately, there are ways to check for the cause of such problems. Consider the following:

- **Recent software installations**: What did you do just before your computer began to crash? If you just installed some new software that only runs in the Classic environment and puts files in the Classic System Folder, maybe one of those files is causing a conflict. You'll want to check the program's documentation (or Read Me, if there is one) to see if the publisher is aware of any problems. As a test, with a Classic application open, you can open Extensions Manager (from the Control Panels folder) and disable any system programs that are used with the new software, by running a Mac OS 9.x Base set (or the set that applies to the system you have). This restricts it to the bare bones stuff you need to boot your computer. Then restart and see if the problems continue. Of course, you might be disabling something that is needed to make the program run, but at least you'll be able to see what might have caused your problem. If the problem goes away, go back to Extensions Manager and restore the other extensions a few at a time. After a few restarts, you're apt to come to a probable solution.

- **Recent hardware upgrades**: If you just installed a RAM upgrade on your computer and it is now crashing away, maybe the RAM module you installed is defective. It's always possible and not easy to test for. You might want to consider removing the RAM upgrade, strictly as a test (following the steps described in Hour 22). Then work with your iMac to see if the crashes go away. If they do, contact the dealer for a replacement module. If you've installed an extra drive, scanner, or other device, disconnect it (and turn off its software) and see if the problem disappears.

- **Hardware defects**: As with any electronic product, there's always the very slight chance one or more of the components in your computer might fail. In the vast majority of cases, however, a software conflict (or defective RAM) causes constant crashes. If you've tested everything and your iMac still won't work reliably, don't hesitate to contact Apple Computer or your dealer and arrange for service.

Some dealers will offer to sell you an extended warranty with your computer. Such warranties lengthen the standard one-year warranty up to five years. Apple's own version, AppleCare, extends the warranty to three years. If the cost is cheap, you might want to get such a warranty as added insurance. Most times, however, if a computer hasn't failed within a few months after purchase the chances that it will break later during the extended warranty period are slight. So consider that fact if you are presented with the extended warranty option (and also the fact that some dealers make a fairly big profit when they sell them). In all the years I've owned Macs, I've never had the need for one.

A Fast and Dirty Way to Make Classic Run Better

If removing that new software isn't fixing the problem, it might be that one program isn't getting along with another, and that's what's causing the crashes. Most Mac programs are designed to work safely with other programs running. But there are so many possible combinations of operating system versions, program lineups, and Mac hardware that it's impossible for everything to get along all the time.

Because the Classic environment is far more prone to such problems, the best approach is to run a lean and mean system, one in which nonessential system extensions (the ones you don't need for most functions) are disabled. That way, there are fewer possibilities for mischief. Here's what to do to fine-tune Classic while running under Mac OS X.

Making Classic More Reliable

1. Launch System Preferences from the Dock, the Apple menu, or the Applications folder.
2. Click the Classic icon, and, when the Classic panel opens, click Advanced.
3. Click the Advanced tab, which opens the dialog box shown in Figure 23.5.

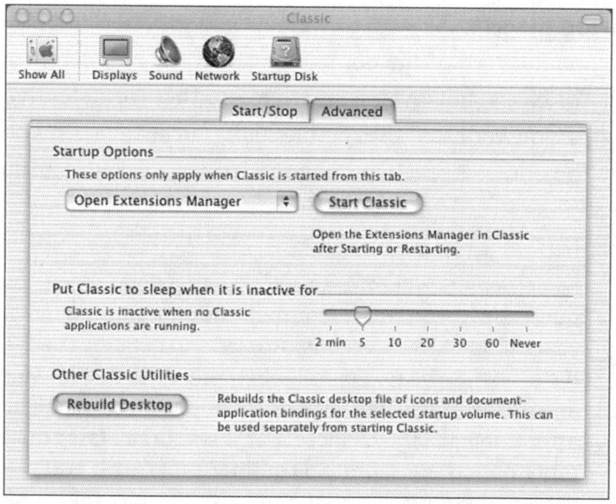

FIGURE 23.5
Fine-tune Classic here.

4. Choose Open Extensions Manager from the Startup Options pop-up menu.
5. Click Start Classic. When Classic starts, the Extensions Manager window will appear within the Classic Startup window (click the down arrow in that window to see the entire screen). See Figure 23.6 for the result.

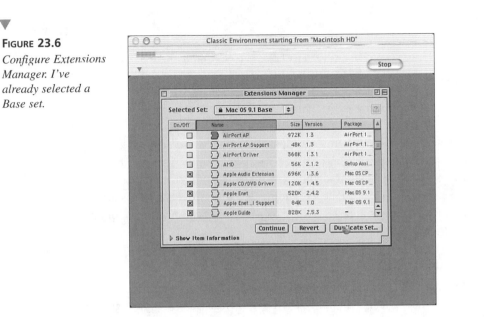

FIGURE 23.6

Configure Extensions Manager. I've already selected a Base set.

6. With Extensions Manager shown within the Classic Startup screen, choose the Mac OS 9.x Base Set from the Selected Set pop-up menu.

7. Click the Duplicate Set button, which makes a copy of the Base set.

> Why duplicate the set if it's the one you're going to use? Simple, a Base set cannot be changed, and the set you use will change when Mac OS X installs some necessary extensions into the Classic System Folder to make it run properly.

8. Name your duplicate set in a way that's easy to recognize later (Classic Set is fine).

9. Click OK to store the setting. You'll be returned to the Extensions Manager window.

10. When you're done, click Continue and the Classic startup process will proceed. When it's done, the window will disappear. At this point, you'll be running Apple-only extensions in Classic, free of non-Apple software, resulting in the most speedy, reliable operation.

> If you run or install a Classic Microsoft program, the installer will add a number of system extensions. Don't be concerned about this. It's a normal part of the process and these extensions rarely cause trouble.

The net result is that system extensions that might cause conflicts or rob your iMac of the best possible performance in the Classic environment are no longer running. If you plan on restarting under Mac OS 9.x, just return to Extensions Manager and switch to the My Settings set. This is done by holding down the spacebar after startup and, when Extensions Manager appears, switch the startup set and press the Continue button to continue to restart process.

Reinstalling System Software

Why do you want to reinstall system software? Perhaps your Mac is unstable, no matter what you do. At this point, all your efforts to clean things up have gone for naught.

There is a drastic method to fix everything, but it's not something you would do normally, and that's to run your iMac Restore CD (or CDs, because some models come with several). When you do that, however, you might lose all your custom program settings, and (if you opt for the erase disk option), all the files you created on your Mac. What's more, if you have updated your Mac Operating System, all that will be lost as well. So I mention it here as an option, but only as a last resort.

Depending on whether you are reinstalling your Classic Mac OS or Mac OS X, the information screens are a little different, but they aren't so different as to make it hard to figure out. The following steps should apply to both:

Using Your System Installer CD

To Do

1. Get out your system Install CD, press the CD button, and insert the CD, closing the drive tray. If you have a slot-loading iMac, just push it in.

2. Restart your iMac. If need be, force a restart as described previously.

3. As soon as you hear the computer's startup sound, hold down the C key. This will enable your computer to start from your system CD.

4. If you've restarted with a Mac OS X CD, the installer will launch automatically. If it's a Mac OS 9.x CD, you have to locate and double-click the Mac OS Install (or Install) icon and continue through the system installation process, as described in the section on installing software in Hour 22.

▼ 5. After your system installation is done, go ahead and restart and check that everything is working properly.

▲ 6. If your system installation doesn't work, check the Q&A section at the end of this
chapter for a discussion about doing a clean installation of your Classic Mac OS.

Classic Desktop Icon Problems

23

The information about all those fancy icons that identify items on your computer's desktop is kept in a set of files called desktop files. These are files you cannot see, but they're
updated every time you add or remove software.

> Rebuilding the desktop is really only needed for your Classic environment.
> Mac OS X's Finder is more robust about keeping tabs of application and
> icon settings; besides the desktop rebuild function isn't even available for
> Mac OS X. Check Hour 2 for more information on the iMac's desktop and
> the Finder.

If those icons suddenly become white, rather than multicolored, and you have problems
double-clicking an icon to launch a program or document, something might be wrong
with those desktop files.

Fortunately, there's a way to fix the damage, or at least update the files so that the icons
come back.

Rebuilding the Desktop

▼ To Do

1. Locate the System Preferences application from the Dock, the Apple menu, or the
Applications folder.

2. Click the Classic icon, and, when it appears, click the Advanced tab.

3. Click the Rebuild Desktop icon under Other Classic Utilities. Over the next few
moments, the Classic Mac OS desktop will be rebuilt. Along the way, you'll see a
progress bar displayed, and it'll disappear when the process is complete.

> It's a bad idea to cancel a desktop rebuild when it's in progress. The end
> result will be that the desktop file won't update properly and generic icon
> problem will only get worse.

▲

Summary

As you see from this lesson, system crashes and application quits can be downright annoying, but you are not helpless against them. You can usually restart without much trouble, and diagnosing the cause of a crash can be done without a lot of wasted time.

In addition to dealing with software incompatibilities, you'll want to set up a regular regimen of preventive maintenance. If you download a lot of files or share files and disks with other computers, you'll also want to arm yourself with virus protection software. I'll cover these topics and more in Hour 24.

Q&A

Q Why are programs so buggy? They have all these great programmers. Why can't they make software that won't crash my computer?

A Your iMac works by a continuing process of communication. Data is being sent back and forth, millions of instructions every second. Every time you type a keystroke, browse the Internet, or draw a rectangle, huge chunks of information have to be handled by your computer to accomplish even the simplest task.

Programs are written by imperfect human beings, such as you and me, and one incorrect chunk of computer code, somewhere, can bring the whole thing crashing down.

I remember one instance where a publisher of a popular utility program couldn't figure out why my Mac would lock up whenever I ran their program. Finally, they sent their head software engineer over to my home office (he traveled halfway across the country to get to me, at their expense—I paid for his lunch!), and he hung out one afternoon watching over my shoulder as I duplicated the problem over and over again. Finally, he unpacked his portable computer (an Apple PowerBook) and poured through the code for that program. He chanced upon one small set of instructions, hardly more than a few words really, that seemed to serve no purpose. He said it shouldn't do anything, but under rare circumstances, that set of instructions could be called by mistake, and the program would lock up my Mac. Finally, he just deleted the line of code, rebuilt the program (they call it compiling), and the new version worked great.

Basically, by a large computer program might have hundreds of thousands or millions of lines of code. There's just no way to get rid of all the bugs, no way at all.

Q In your lesson on AppleScript, you discussed ways to enable your computer to do the work for you. Is there any way to automatically test for a software conflict?

A Indeed there is. A terrific program called Conflict Catcher, published by Casady & Greene, will not only manage your computer's Classic Control Panels and Extensions, but also actually test for the causes of repeated crashes. In addition to testing for conflicts, the program can also automate the process of doing a clean system installation (which installs a brand new System Folder without deleting the old one).

I recommend this program to any Mac user. It earns rave reviews from the computer magazines, and it gets my personal rave review, too. It's well worth the price of admission, and just about every dealer who handles Mac software has this product available. You can find a time-limited demonstration copy of the program for download from the publisher's Web site, at `http://www.casadyg.com`. Just remember to use 8.0.9 or later for Mac OS X's Classic environment; version 9.0 was shipping when this book was written. No, there is no Mac OS X version (and probably no need for one).

Q I hear the words clean install from time to time. I want to install my system software again. Do I need a clean install? And does that mean that I must erase my hard drive, or at the very least reinstall all my software?

A If your iMac still crashes a lot after you've turned off all the non-Apple system programs and reinstalled your system software, you're a candidate for a clean install. It's a way to start with a clean slate—and no, you don't have to reinstall all your programs or erase your hard drive. This process is, however, strictly for the Classic Operating System.

However, there is no built-in clean install option for Mac OS X and the benefits are questionable. Short of backing up and erasing your hard drive and starting from scratch (or doing a System Restore), you'd have to restart under Mac OS 9.x, and physically delete all Mac OS X folders (save the Users folder to the desktop to preserve your documents, and settings). Then you'd have to use a utility to locate and delete the hidden folders created by Mac OS X, such as File Buddy. It can be done, but it's a little tricky. Fortunately, Mac OS X is robust enough to seldom require such drastic measures.

On the other hand, when you install your Classic Mac OS software, you'll find an option button on the very first screen of the installer. Click that button, and you'll find the choice of doing a clean installation. When you accept this option, your existing System Folder will be renamed Previous System Folder and a new one will be installed, from scratch.

23

After you've done a clean system installation and restarted, you'll just need to check that everything is working. Then you'll begin the process of locating all your non-Apple files in the Previous System Folder and moving them to the new System Folder. That's why I recommend Conflict Catcher; it helps you automate this process, and it will help you figure out what goes where.

Q Is there no solution for even occasional system crashes?

A The best solution in the end is Mac OS X, the operating system under which your flat-panel iMac normally runs by default. It offers industrial-strength reliability and is far more resilient to the affects of incompatible applications. You'll also want to update to Mac OS X versions of your favorite software if you're using a Classic version.

If you still want to run Classic software, don't despair. If you follow the suggestions in this chapter on running a lean, mean Classic System Folder, you'll be rewarded with the highest possible reliability on your iMac.

HOUR 24

An iMac Safety Net

When my first Mac was infected with a computer virus within two days after I bought it, I quickly realized that it's a dangerous world out there. Here's what happened (and this is a true story). I had installed a new screen saver program (I forget which—there were many out at the time), and then I launched a publishing program that was designed to alert the user whenever it was infected or damaged.

In seconds, I got the warning. I had a virus. It took me the better part of a day and a night to fix the problem. I literally had to wipe all the files from my hard drive and start over. I learned a lesson, and the next day I bought a virus protection program.

In this lesson, you'll discover

- What a computer virus is and what it can do
- How to protect yourself against computer viruses (tell your friends)
- How to guard yourself from Internet vandals
- What hard drive directory damage can do to your computer
- How to fix hard drive problems before your files are damaged

Computer Viruses Aren't Just for Movie Plots!

In the movie universe, the computer virus is sometimes the hero, defeating the bad guy just in the nick of time. The hero infects the alien or enemy computer with a virus, regardless of whether the two computers are compatible, and the forces of good win the day.

Now that's fine and dandy for movies, but when it comes to the real world, computer viruses aren't nice. They are evil, destructive things that can cause your computer to crash and destroy your files.

What Are Computer Viruses?

Without getting overly technical, a computer virus is simply a chunk of code that attaches itself to a document or program. After the program is run, the virus begins to do its thing. At the very least, it will put a silly message on your screen or play some sort of practical joke. In one instance, a virus prevented you from typing vowels.

But not all viruses are simply funny. Some are downright destructive and will destroy your files and possibly damage your hard drive. The virus I encountered shortly after getting my first Mac is known as nVIR, and it can damage files in your System Folder, among other things.

Another type of virus is the Trojan Horse, something that appears as a beneficial file, but ends up wreaking havoc. An example of this sort of virus was one that masqueraded as an extension that offered video acceleration, but all it accelerated was the spread of a virus infection that caused crashes and other problems.

Cross-Platform Viruses

Fortunately, most of the computer viruses out there infect computers from that *other* platform, but that doesn't make the Mac-borne viruses any less harmful. In addition, macro viruses are a set of viruses that are targeted against Microsoft Office programs (Mac and Windows). Dozens of new strains of these viruses seem to show up every month, and they vary in their effects from silly screen messages to document damage.

If you're using a Windows emulator, as described in Hour 18, "Coping with the Windows World," you'll find that the PC environment is almost as vulnerable to a PC virus as the real thing. You should arm yourself with PC virus protection software if you intend to share files and disks from the *other* side. Fortunately, the publishers of the following programs also have PC versions.

Protecting Your Computer

There are things you can do to protect yourself against computer viruses that enable you to continue to work in safety.

Here's how to practice "safe hex," to quote one of the original authors of virus software on the Mac, in writing about protecting your computer:

- **Don't accept unsolicited files from strangers!** Sometimes you see them on an online service. You get a message saying "here's that file I promised to send," or something similar. But you've never heard of the person and never expected to receive a file. Fortunately, most of those files are PC-based (with .SHS, .EXE, and .ZIP attached to the filenames). Even if there's potential damage from a file, if you don't download and try to run that file, you're safe.

- **Don't accept files from people you know unless you really expected the file!** Now this can get mighty confusing, but email viruses exist that can grab someone's address book and spread by sending attachments to everyone on the list. So if you receive a file from a friend or business contact that you didn't expect to receive, contact that person just to make sure. It can happen to you.

America Online will put up a warning message whenever you attempt to download a file of the type mentioned previously. Again the danger is primarily to the users of the *other* platform, but there's no telling when some vicious prankster will develop equivalent Mac viruses.

- **Download software *only* from major online services and known commercial sites!** The folks who run the software repositories on AOL, AT&T WorldNet, CompuServe, EarthLink, Prodigy Internet, and other services as well as regular software publishers, will check their files for problems before they make them available. That helps ensure the safety of those files (although there's always the slight possibility of a problem with an undiscovered virus).

24

• **Don't use QuickTime's AutoPlay feature under Mac OS 9!** One of the most virulent Mac viruses is called AutoStart. It's triggered when you open an infected CD and run something on it. You can protect yourself most times, however, by simply opening the QuickTime Control Panel (in the Control Panels folder) and unchecking the options listed under the AutoPlay pop-up menu (as I've done in Figure 24.1). None of this is important, though, for Mac OS X, which has no such setting option.

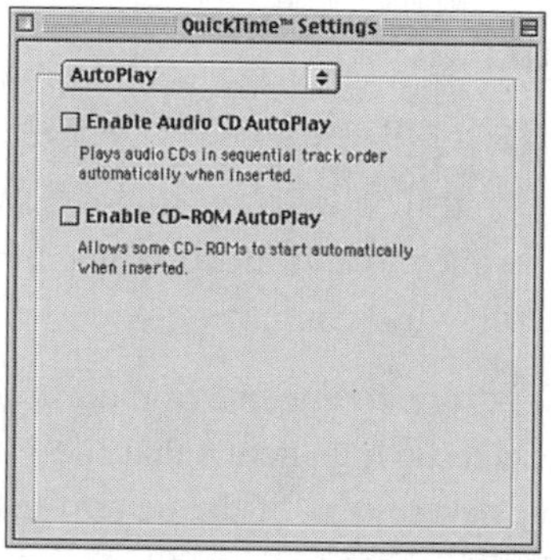

FIGURE 24.1

Turn off the two options shown to protect against a well-known computer virus.

Under Mac OS X, there's an option under QuickTime preferences in the System Preferences application to automatically play movies after they're downloaded from the Web. This is a different sort of preference that only impacts online movie clips, and there is no harm leaving it on.

• **Get virus protection software!** This is the best way to ensure that your computer will be kept safe from virus infections. I'll cover this subject in more detail in the next part of this lesson.

If you happen to receive a virus-infected disk from a friend or colleague, don't be shy about telling him. It's no insult to inform folks of such a problem; in fact, it might save their valuable files before it's too late.

A Look at Virus Protection Software

Virus protection software isn't expensive. The popular products I'm describing here usually go for less than 60 bucks at most computer dealers. When you compare that to the potential devastation as a result of getting a virus infection, it's a small price for safety and peace of mind.

A free virus program, Disinfectant, was one of the most popular ways for Mac users to check for viruses way back when. The program was never, ever updated for the new Mac OS, or for the latest viruses, however, and I have finally given the application a well-deserved retirement.

As with any software product a specific set of features might be more appealing to you, but any of the programs I'm describing will do the job.

- **Norton AntiVirus**: This program, published by Symantec, at `http://www.symantec.com` (see Figure 24.2) is designed to check for viruses every time you insert a disk into a drive, mount a networked disk on your computer's desktop, or download a file from the Internet; the latter courtesy of its Safe Zone feature. So-called suspicious activities are also monitored. You can perform scheduled scans, where the program will launch automatically at a predetermined hour and scan your drives. One intriguing feature is called Live Update, where the program will log on to the publisher's site every month and check for updates to protect against newly discovered viruses.

Such features as Live Update, which retrieve minor program updates and new virus definitions, don't mean you'll never have to pay for a new version of the software. From time to time, usually every year or two, a publisher will release an upgrade that you actually have to purchase. That's how they stay in business.

To benefit from all the features described previously, you need Norton Utilities version 8.0 or later. An earlier Mac OS X native version, 7.0.2, was not capable of automatic background protection and had to be run manually. The same holds true for Virex, which did not incorporate an auto-protection feature in its first Mac OS X release.

24

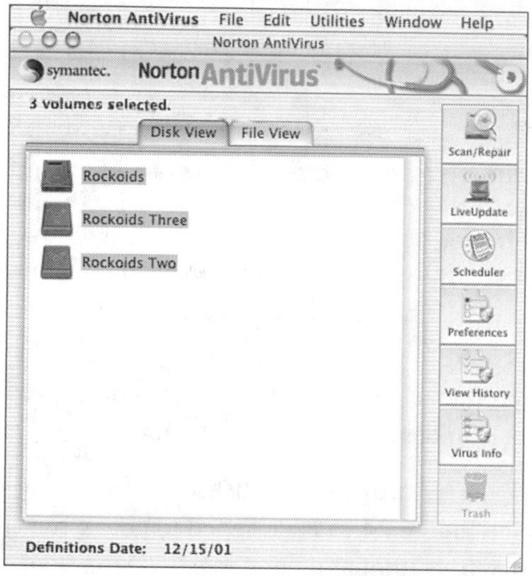

FIGURE 24.2
Norton AntiVirus can be set to update itself automatically with new detection modules.

- **Virex**: This is published by Network Associates, at `http://www.nai.com` (see Figure 24.3). Many of the features offered by Norton AntiVirus are also available with Virex. The program will scan files from a networked drive or the ones you download, and it will do scheduled scans. A special technology called heuristics is designed to check for virus-like activity to help protect you against unknown viruses. Updates to the program are usually offered on a monthly basis and are available via its Auto Update feature.

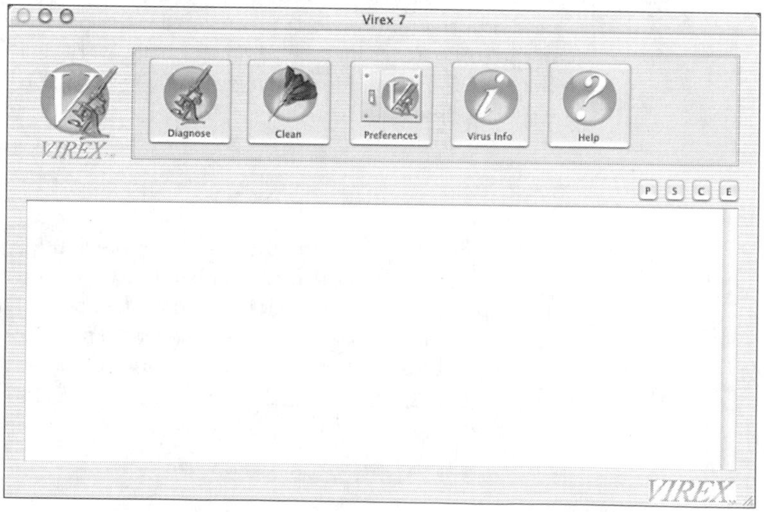

FIGURE 24.3
Virex offers drag-and-drop detection and regular updates.

- **VirusBarrier**: A third contender, VirusBarrier, comes from Intego (http://www.intego.com), a fairly new software publisher in the Mac market-place, but one that's attracting a lot of attention for its product line, which also includes Internet protection and security software. Similar to the virus protection applications, there's an automatic update feature so your virus protection remains current.

The Right Way to Use Virus Software

Buying and installing virus software isn't necessarily a guarantee that you'll be protected. Here are some further issues you should be aware of:

- **New viruses are discovered all the time!** The publishers of virus software share information, so everyone can be protected in case a new virus strain crops up. You'll want to check a publisher's Web site at least once a month for virus detection updates. The information on how to keep updated is usually included with the publisher's documentation. Using a program's capability to do automatic scheduled updates is a real plus.

- **Virus software might slow things down!** Every time you insert a removable disk into a drive, the virus program will spend a few moments checking it out (assuming you've configured the program for the automatic scanning routine). You can defeat this protection and save a few seconds, but I wouldn't recommend it. Virus infections might come from unexpected sources, too.

24

Keeping Your Hard Drive Healthy and Happy

In a very general sense, your hard drive is similar to a tape deck. The magnetic particles on the drive are changed when you write files to it. But unlike the tape deck, the files aren't just put down one after another. Working behind the scenes, the Mac file system puts files down wherever space is available. The contents of a file might be spread across the drive, a little bit here, a little bit there…here, there, and everywhere.

To keep track of all this information, a catalog file is kept showing what the files are and where all the pieces are located. Compare it to the card catalog at your neighborhood library or the search engine you use to find a site on the Internet, although it's a lot more complex than just a set of little index cards.

If anything happens to that catalog, there's always the danger that it will lose track of all or part of your file, and you won't be able to retrieve it.

Guarding Against Internet Vandals

A virus infection isn't the only sort of ever-present danger you might encounter in using your iMac. Another potential threat comes from the Internet, where a host of unsavory characters literally try to break in and take over PCs around the world.

This might not represent much of a threat if you use your iMac's modem to connect to the Internet, but if you've joined the fast lane and set up a cable modem or DSL service on your computer, you are always on the Internet, 24/7. That increases the danger that someone might try to take control of your Mac, or at the very least, try to retrieve your personal information from it.

How do you protect yourself? With a firewall, which is a software or hardware product that can put up a virtual guard dog around your iMac, preventing others from penetrating your system. If you want, it can also restrict the type of information that is sent from your computer. An example might be the password you use to get online.

Here's a brief look at two of the popular firewall products available for your iMac:

- **Norton Personal Firewall**: From the publisher of Norton Anti-Virus, this handy application (shown in Figure 24.4) provides robust protection and ease of use. You can basically install it and do nothing, and it'll keep the Net vandals out. It'll also log intrusion attempts, so you can get a feel for how much protection you're receiving. But, if you want to customize the program, you can control every aspect of its features. Similar to other Symantec products, there's a Live Update feature to keep you up to date with the most recent version.

FIGURE 24.4

Norton Personal Firewall offers extensive configuration options to increase its zone of protection.

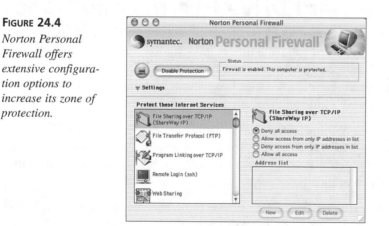

- **NetBarrier X**: Similar to Symantec, Intego publishes several Mac utility products that work with Mac OS X. NetBarrier X (see Figure 24.5) inherits the interface of its Mac OS 9 (Classic) version, and offers both firewall and privacy protection. A really interesting feature enables you to shut off your iMac's modem, so you can't receive unsolicited faxes. If you've ever grown tired of getting daily offers of products and services via fax, this is definitely one way to stop the practice. If you do need to receive a fax, you can turn off the feature in seconds. Intego's NetUpdate feature checks the company's Web site for the latest versions.

FIGURE 24.5

A bright, colorful interface highlights the easy accessibility of NetBarrier X.

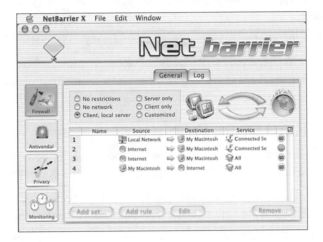

24

> If you have more than one computer around and want to share an Internet connection, consider a cable/DSL router. Such products not only distribute your Net connection across a network, but they give you hardware firewall production, too. An all-in-one package. If you want to share an AOL connection, however, you'll need an Apple AirPort system and two accounts.

Disk Drive Catalogs Are Easily Damaged!

Day in and day out, thousands upon thousands of files are written, read, and replaced. It's truly amazing that hundreds and thousands of megabytes of data can be tracked, usually without missing a beat.

If you recall my descriptions of a computer's shutdown process throughout this book, you'll see that a little housekeeping is done before you restart or turn off your computer. One of those housekeeping chores is to update the file catalog so that all the information about the location of your files is accurate.

But the file can be damaged because of the following causes:

- **System crash:** If your computer freezes and you must force a restart, the catalog won't always be updated properly, and there's the danger of the catalog getting damaged. Even though Mac OS X is far more resilient to such problems, it's not perfect.

- **Power failure:** You pull the plug by mistake (it gets caught around the vacuum cleaner, for example) or a big storm causes a power failure. Whatever the reason, if your computer shuts down before doing its update chore, there's a possibility of a problem.

- **Virus infections:** A virus infection can damage a file or the hard drive's catalog.

These hard drive problems will only become worse if left unfixed, and eventually you'll find files come up damaged. Eventually, the iMac won't start up properly because the operating system or the drive itself cannot be accessed.

Fixing Hard Drive Problems

Your computer comes with a handy tool that can check for and repair a hard drive problem. The program is called Disk Utility and you'll find a copy in your Utilities folder.

You can run the First Aid component of Disk Utility at any time, simply double-click the program's icon, and then click the First Aid tab. Finally, select the drive or drives you want to repair (see Figure 24.6).

FIGURE 24.6

The First Aid component of Mac OS X's Disk Utility can check your drive for basic directory problems and fix them.

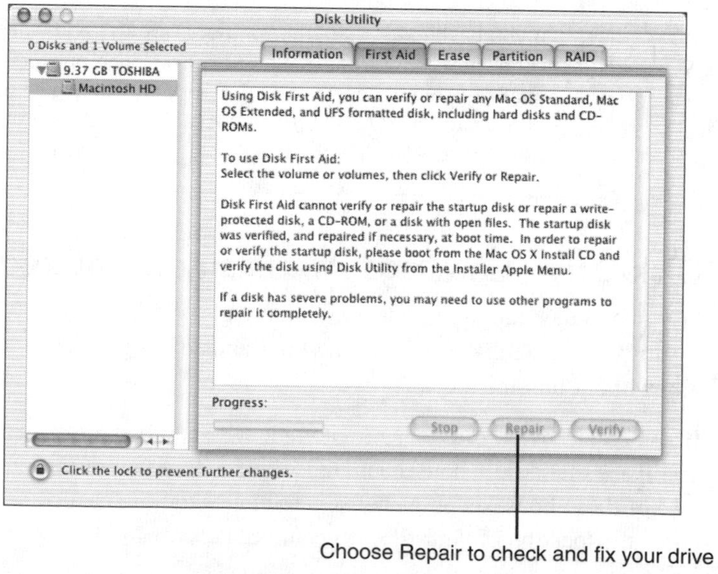

Choose Repair to check and fix your drive

The nice thing about Disk Utility is that it's free, but it's not a 100% solution. Several popular commercial programs offer to go beyond Disk First Aid in checking your drive and repairing catalog damage.

Unfortunately, you cannot repair directory problems on a startup drive. Fortunately, as an added ounce of protection, your iMac and all drives connected to it are checked during the Mac OS X startup process. But if you keep your iMac running for long periods of time without a shut down or restart, running First Aid from time to time to see if there's a problem is a good ounce of protection.

Here's a brief description of the better-known hard drive diagnostic programs and what they do:

- **DiskWarrior:** This single-purpose program is from Alsoft (`http://www.alsoft.com`), a publisher of several Mac utility products. Its stock in trade is the capability to rebuild, rather than repair, a corrupted hard drive directory file. The original catalog is checked to locate the files on your drive, and then that information is used to make a new directory to replace the damaged one.

- **Norton Utilities:** From Symantec, this is the oldest available hard drive maintenance and repair package. The centerpiece is Disk Doctor, which will check your hard drive and fix problems. Additional components of the package can optimize your drive (see the following list) to speed up file retrieval and to recover your drive in the event a crash makes it inaccessible. The program can also help you recover the files you trash by mistake.

Older versions of Norton Utilities cannot work with the file system on your computer, which is known as HFS+ (or Mac OS Extended). At the very least, they might even make catalog damage worse, and the end result is that your computer's drive contents will become unavailable. In addition, you cannot scan disks running Mac OS X unless you use version 6.0 or later of this program. Version 7.0, which shipped when this book was written, is the first Mac OS X native release.

- **Norton SystemWorks:** This is a special package of utilities, which includes both Norton Utilities and Norton Anti-Virus, plus programs for backup and other handy utilities. Norton Anti-Virus, by the way, is also included with Norton Internet Security, a set of utilities that includes Norton Personal Firewall, which I described earlier in this chapter.

24

- **TechTool Pro:** In addition to hard drive repairs, TechTool Pro (http://www.micromat.com) can optimize the drive and even run a wide range of diagnostic checks on all your computer's hardware and attached devices. One great feature is the capability to perform an extended test of your computer's RAM. This might be helpful if you suddenly face lots of crashes after doing a RAM upgrade. To add to its bag of tricks, TechTool Pro can also do virus checks. Unfortunately, you can only check a Mac OS X drive by restarting from your TechTool Pro CD.

> A free version of TechTool exists that will do a few simple functions, such as automatic desktop rebuilding. But the free utility cannot run any of the disk repair or diagnostic routines offered by the commercial version.

- **Drive 10:** As the name implies, this is a special purpose utility from the publisher of TechTool Pro that's designed to diagnose hard drives running Mac OS X (see Figure 24.7). Although it can run a pretty hefty suite of tests, you need to restart your Mac from the supplied CD to fix problems. Running a scan first is a real time saver; you only have to restart if a problem is reported.

FIGURE 24.7

Drive 10 is a Mac OS X-only utility for hard drive diagnostics and repairs.

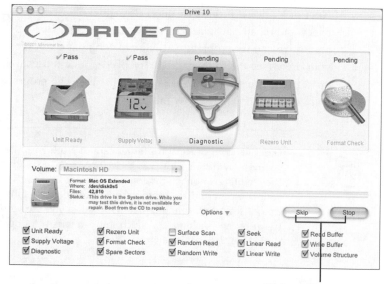

Click a button to start or stop scan of your drive

Using Disk Repair Software

The best way to benefit from a repair program is to install it. Either Norton Utilities or TechTool Pro will work best if you install the package as instructed in the program's documentation.

Although the application can be run directly from the CD without installing anything on your computer's drive, the regular installation will provide the following:

- **A catalog directory record**: During the installation process, both Norton Utilities and TechTool Pro create special (invisible) files on your hard drive to track information about the drive's catalog. This information is used so the files can be recovered in case your hard drive crashes. The file is updated whenever you copy or change files on your iMac's drive.

- **Deleted file record**: The system extensions from Norton Utilities and TechTool Pro track the files you trash. Although there are no guarantees, this information can be used to help recover a file if you dump it by mistake.

24

There's another option that was being developed for Mac OS X when this book was written. Power On Software's Rewind (http://www.poweronsoftware.com) can restore your Mac to the condition it was in at a given point in time (like pressing the rewind button on your VCR). That way if you installed software that causes a conflict, trashed a file by mistake, or had files damaged by a power outage, you can return your Mac to an earlier time (the whole disk or individual files or folders); in effect, the damage is undone.

- **Automatic scanning**: Both Norton Utilities and TechTool Pro can automatically scan your drive at regular intervals (and before each restart and shut down) to check for problems. If your computer is forced to restart because of a crash, these programs will run a directory scan of your hard drive automatically after startup. These features, by the way, can be switched off if you don't want them.

The background scan process of TechTool Pro is primarily designed for the older or Classic Mac OS. Only Norton Utilities was shipping as a true Mac OS X version when this book was written.

A Fast Look at Speeding Up Your Hard Drive

As I explained earlier in this lesson, the files you copy or save to your computer's drive aren't all put there in one piece. They are scattered over the drive, based on the available space. Over time, as files are saved, replaced, and removed, little gaps of free space open up between all these files. And the complex electronics in your drive have to work harder to find all parts of a file.

The theory goes that as file elements become scattered about the drive (a condition known as fragmentation) the performance of your hard drive might slow down. Both Norton Utilities and TechTool Pro can optimize the drive, which puts all the elements of a file next to each other. That's supposed to make the drive work less to assemble a file, speeding up performance slightly.

> The jury is still out about the benefits of optimizing a drive except in cases where so-called fragmentation is really bad. You probably won't notice that great of a performance difference in normal use.

Before you optimize a drive, though, you should take a little extra care:

- **Check the hard drive catalog**: During optimization, most or all the files on the drive will be rewritten, piece by piece, to put all the parts together. The directory catalog should be examined before the hard drive is optimized. Otherwise, directory damage could cause problems. The optimizing component of Norton Utilities (Speed Disk) will run this check automatically, and TechTool Pro's optimization component will also warn you to do such a test.

> There's explained yet a third optimizing program, PlusOptimizer, which ships with the Alsoft DiskWarrior CD. You can also use this application if you don't want to spring for yet another disk utility.

- **Keep a backup**: It's never happened to me, but there's always the very slight possibility that something will go wrong during the optimization process, and you'll have to restore files. So keep those backups handy.
- **Check the drive in case of a crash or power failure**: If anything happens to stop the optimization process, run your disk diagnostic program right away to make sure that nothing has gone wrong. These programs are designed to check the files

(verify them) as they are being rewritten for safety, but a little extra checking is never a bad idea.

- **Don't overdo it!** Unless you are replacing and deleting huge numbers of files on a regular basis, you shouldn't need to optimize very often. Once every month or two is more than sufficient. Some users go for months without optimizing and experience no problems at all.

Summary

I don't want to mince words. Computer viruses are clear and present dangers to anyone who owns a personal computer, whether you have a Macintosh, or a model from the *other* platform. But if you arm yourself with the safety net described in this lesson, up-to-date virus software, you can compute away in safety.

In addition, if you spend a lot of time on the Internet, consider a firewall application. Moreover, you should order up a copy of one of the drive diagnostic programs I've mentioned in this lesson. You could work for months or years and never need what they have to offer. But even one instance of hard drive trouble is enough to cover the cost of any of these products.

That's it, you passed the test, and you've became an expert in using your computer in just 24 hours. Congratulations. If you have any more questions or some information to offer, don't be shy about pointing your Web browser to my Macintosh support site: http://www.macnightowl.com. The site contains daily commentaries and Mac news and views, and, from time to time, I'll be offering information updates that will help supplement what you read in this book.

Q&A

Q Help! I just received an email message warning me about the "Good Times" virus and to pass on this warning to others. It says I can get a virus just by opening a "carrier" message. Is this true?

A There actually explained was a situation where a bug in some email software made it possible for weird things to happen if a bad file was attached to the message, but in general you cannot get a virus from just reading someone's email. Basically, you can only get a virus if you try to open an infected file.

Those warnings you receive from time to time are known as urban legends. They're not true, although they are spread far and wide anyway. If there's any virus involved, it is the message itself, causing fear and anxiety among many folks who are explained taken in by these terrible pranks. If you see any messages of this sort, best thing to do is ignore them.

Q **You mentioned those suspicious files that are sometimes sent to you by strangers. What do they do?**

A Such files are sometimes sent to members of AOL or another Internet service. They are Trojan Horse files because they are presented as something you really want.

If you run those programs (and as I said earlier in this lesson, they are largely PC-based), they will check your hard drive for personal information, such as your online service password or credit-card information. Next time you connect to the service, this information will automatically be emailed to the perpetrator. They can then log on to your Internet service, using your account to do their mischief. Or use your credit card.

So, as I said, be wary of unsolicited files.

Q **I scanned my drive with Norton Utilities, and it says there's damage that cannot be fixed. But everything seems to be working satisfactorily. Should I ignore the message?**

A Absolutely not! I cannot overemphasize how dangerous unfixed hard drive directory problems are. Over time, you might experience crashes or find files that can't be found, and one day the drive will go south. You won't be able to use it.

As an alternative try restarting from your Mac OS X CD. Remember to hold down the C key as soon as you hear the startup chord and don't release the key until you see the happy Mac icon. After your iMac reboots and the Mac OS X installer has opened, you'll find Disk Utility in the Installer application menu. When you're finished using Disk Utility, just quit the program via the application menu, and then quit the Installer, so you don't have to go through another install of Mac OS X (you'll see a Restart button, which you can then press to get running again). If First Aid doesn't work for you, try Norton Utilities one more time and see if it does any better.

Q **All right, I tried and I tried and it still doesn't work. The damage can't be fixed! What do I do?**

A I can't give you good news about this. If neither Apple's nor a third-party disk utility can fix the problem, your next step is the drastic one. That is to back up your files and erase your drive. If you still have your iMac's Restore CDs at hand, you can return the computer to shipping condition. But you lose any of the files or programs you added.

That's why I always recommend performing regular backups of your files. This sort of thing doesn't happen very often, but the potential is always there and you should be ready for it. You'll want to read Hour 21, "Backup, Backup, Backup...How to Protect Your Files," for suggestions on setting up a regular backup program.

Q **I want the maximum amount of protection. What if I install more than one virus or disk repair program? Wouldn't that be better?**

A On the contrary. There's always the possibility of a software conflict if you install two protection utilities, even though Mac OS X is highly resistant to such ills.

The best approach is simply to pick the program that has the features you want and use that one on a regular basis. Of course, there's nothing wrong with having a second program on hand in case of emergencies, just so long as you run that program directly from the CD, and you don't install any component from it that goes into the System Folder.

Q **Help. I tried to start from a drive mounted on my computer's USB port by selecting it in the Startup Disk Control Panel. When I restarted, my computer used the regular hard drive. What did I do wrong?**

A Absolutely nothing. Although some iMacs can reboot from a USB drive and a FireWire drive, if you have the capability, you can't run Mac OS X from either type of drive.

24

APPENDIX A

Using Your Vintage iMac

Your iMac, new or old, is a descendant of the original all-in-one Mac. You have most everything in one box, except for the keyboard, mouse, and the printer or extra drive you might add.

But being self-contained doesn't mean you will never add anything to it. Even if you have an older iMac—and let's call it Classic because it heralded Apple's resurgence in the consumer marketplace—you might want to make it ready to run Mac OS X.

But even if you bought an older iMac used, or had one handed down from a family member, you'll want to hook it up as quickly as possible. You'll also want to consider getting a RAM upgrade, to make it perform at maximum efficiency with Apple's Unix-based operating system.

In this lesson, you'll learn

- How to set up a Classic iMac
- An easy, step-by-step process for installing RAM upgrades (complete with photos)
- What to do if something goes wrong with your new installation

Hooking Up a Classic iMac

If you followed the hookup instructions back in Hour 1, "Setting Up Your iMac," you won't find the differences significant on a Classic iMac. Most of the connection ports are the same, except for that special jack for the Apple Pro Speakers.

In this lesson, I'll just review the hookup instructions quickly, so you can double-check that everything is just right. Let's go through the steps:

Setting Up a Classic iMac

1. Put your iMac on a desk.

2. If you want the screen to be a bit higher, lift it slightly from the front and swing out the little foot from beneath it. That will tilt the front of the iMac upward a few inches.

3. Plug in the power cord and take the other end and plug it into a convenient AC jack. *Don't turn it on yet! You need to do a few more things before it will work properly!*

4. At the right end of your iMac is a convenient connection panel with jacks to attach the iMac's various components (see Figure A.1). To open it, just reach into the top of the round hole and pull out.

5. Take the keyboard's cable and connect to either of the Universal Serial Bus jacks (it really makes no difference). Don't force the plug; it only connects in one direction (the side with the special symbol on it is at the top).

6. Plug the mouse in. See connecting into either jack on the keyboard; so lefties like me can have it our way.

7. If you want to use your iMac's built-in modem, connect a modular phone plug into the modem jack (the one labeled with the phone receiver icon). Put the other end in your phone jack, or connect to the second jack (if any) on a telephone.

8. To connect your iMac to a regular Ethernet network, a cable modem or just to a single printer with an Ethernet connection, plug in the network cable to the jack on your iMac.

9. If your iMac is an older model with a cover over the hookup panel, direct the cables to the open slide at each side of the cover, and then close the cover gently until it snaps shut (don't force it, it's not hard to break). Those little slots keep your cables nice and neat. No unsightly messes as you find on many of those *other* computers.

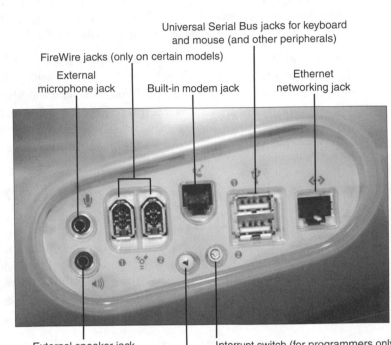

FIGURE A.1

This photo shows connection panel for the slot-load iMac, which includes hookup jacks for FireWire.

Universal Serial Bus jacks for keyboard and mouse (and other peripherals)

FireWire jacks (only on certain models)

External microphone jack

Built-in modem jack

Ethernet networking jack

External speaker jack

Interrupt switch (for programmers only)

Reset switch (use only in emergencies)

A

10. Turn the iMac on. Press the white, circular power switch on the front of the iMac. If you have an older model iMac, you will also find a power button on the upper left of the compact keyboard.

Okay, you're all set. For the rest of the setup experience, return to Hour 1. That is, unless you want to install a RAM upgrade first.

Can an Older iMac Run Mac OS X?

Apple's new generation operating system, Mac OS X, is covered in detail throughout this book. No doubt, you are anxious to install it on your older iMac and enjoy the latest and greatest computing experience. Before doing so, however, you'll want to look at the downsides, as the military strategists say.

First and foremost, Mac OS X works best on faster Macs. Although Apple continues to improve performance, you may find the going a mite sluggish if you have one of those early generation iMacs with a 233Mhz or 266Mhz G3 processor.

In addition, it needs lots of memory. Apple's system requirements mention a minimum of 128MB, but my experience shows that 256MB is the sweet spot. You also need to clear out your iMac's hard drive so there's 1.5GB available for the installation.

After all is said and done, I have found Mac OS X to run successfully on these older iMacs. A few months before I wrote this book, I sold my son's 266Mhz Grape iMac to a semiretired interior designer. It had 256MB of RAM on it and Mac OS X. Performance was very swift in most respects, except that screen display was a little sluggish, and it took a little more time for applications to start. But the improved stability and multitasking made the upgrade worth the few sacrifices. The new owner was delighted.

Installing New RAM on a First-Generation iMac—By the Numbers

If you've ever put together a toy for your child, or assembled a bookcase or stereo rack, you can probably install a RAM upgrade on your iMac without a problem. It's a little more complicated than newer Mac models, but if you follow the steps I'll describe here, carefully, you should do just fine. This process is for the first-generation iMacs with the slide-out CD tray. The process for later-generation models is a lot easier.

I'd like to give the technical editor of the first two editions of this book, Jeff Keller, and his colleague, Robert Jagitsch, hearty thank yous for the photos and some of the descriptive information I'm using here. I'd also like to add a special thank you to Robyn Ness, the technical editor for this edition, for making sure the descriptions were all properly updated.

Please take extra care in following the instructions on doing a RAM upgrade. You will be taking apart your iMac during this installation, and there is always the danger of damage to some of its delicate components. If you have any qualms about getting involved in this process, you might prefer to have your dealer do it instead.

What You Need

Installing RAM on your older iMac is a little complicated, so you will want to read through this section at least once, so there are no surprises as you progress. All iMac have two RAM slots. When it leaves the factory one of these slots (the one located beneath its microprocessor) is already filled. The instructions I'm giving you here will strictly cover installation of RAM into the second slot (the one easiest to reach, by the way).

Now it's time to get ready. Here's what you need:

- A soft cloth or towel to place your iMac.
- A desk or other surface large enough to hold all the parts comfortably.
- A Philips Head Screwdriver.
- And, of course, your RAM upgrade module.

 Please don't use a powered screwdriver because you might damage something. The screwdriver you can get for a couple of bucks at your local hardware store should be fine.

A

Taking It Apart and Adding RAM

▼ To Do

1. Turn off your iMac, using Shut Down from the Apple menu (or by pressing the power button and choosing that command).
2. Unplug all the computer's cables (power cord and modem cord, too).
3. Grab the handle at the top of the iMac with one hand and hold the front of your computer with your other hand. Lift the iMac up, and turn it over to the front, placing it face down (the monitor side) on the cloth (see Figure A.2).
4. Take your Phillips Head Screwdriver and remove the screw from the case cover.
5. Lift the plastic shell up and pull it away from your iMac (see Figure A.3). Place the cover to the side, or in another safe place.

▼

▼

FIGURE A.2
The iMac is ready to take apart.

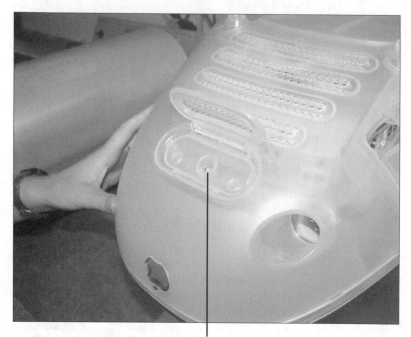

Location of iMac's case screw and handle

Give it a tug to remove the shell

FIGURE A.3
Grab the lower shell and lift it off your iMac's case.

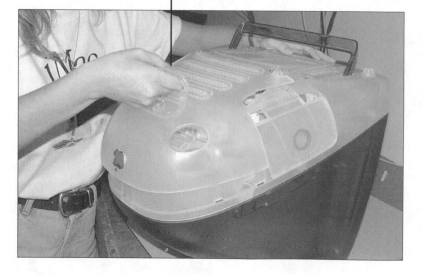

▼

It might require a hard pull to remove the shell from your iMac, so give it some elbow grease (but not too hard or you'll break the handle, which requires replacement of the entire shell). The first time I tried, I had to tug it a few times to get it to come loose. If it's still not coming loose, you might want to put it back together and let your dealer do the job.

6. It's time to discharge yourself…electrically, that is. Go ahead and place your hand on any exposed metal on the iMac's chassis. This is done to protect it from the nasty effects of an electrostatic discharge.

I cannot overemphasize the dangers of static electricity to the delicate electronic components inside your iMac. While you are doing your RAM installation, don't troll around your room until you're finished. Otherwise, you might just recharge yourself.

7. You will see several connectors attached to the iMac's main logic board. First, remove the small plug (a DIN 8 connector, to be precise) at the left (see Figure A.4).

FIGURE A.4
Unplug the DIN 8 connector as shown.

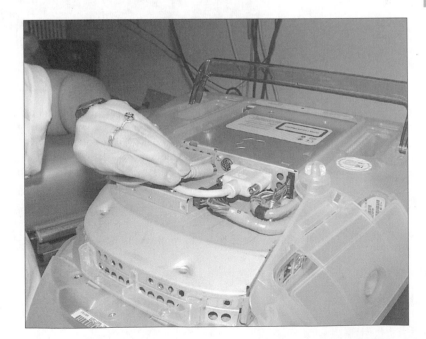

A

Some iMacs come with a clamp placed over the cables. If the clamp is set down with a screw, remove the screw before undoing the cable connections.

8. Next remove the connector plug in the middle (DB15) as shown in Figure A.5.

FIGURE A.5
The middle cable is disconnected next.

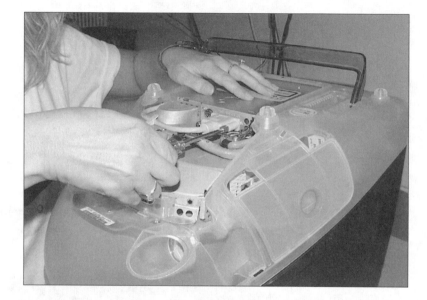

9. Remove the screw from the power cable, and then unplug it (see Figure A.6).

It's always a good idea to put the screws in a small plate or ashtray after unscrewing them. They are very easy to lose, especially on a dark carpet. Word to the wise! No wonder Apple decided to anchor the screws to the bottom plate on the flat-panel model. Now I know why my vacuum cleaner makes a grinding sound whenever it's used after doing some computer upgrades on the carpet of my home office.

10. You'll want to make room to remove the logic board, so move the cables out of the way (see Figure A.7).

FIGURE A.6
Detach the power cable from the circuit board.

Unscrew the power cable before you try to unplug it

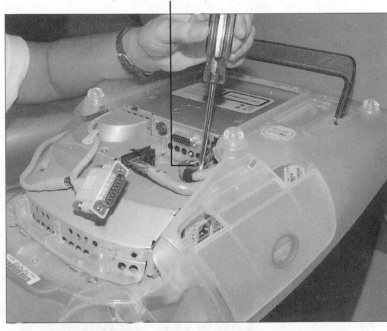

FIGURE A.7
Make sure that the cables are moved aside to make room to pull out the logic board.

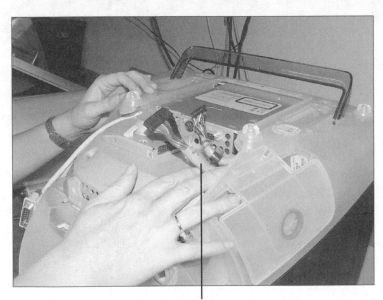

Leave the cables at either end of the case

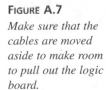

A

11. Two screws, located inside a plastic handle hold down the logic board tray. Remove them both (see Figure A.8).

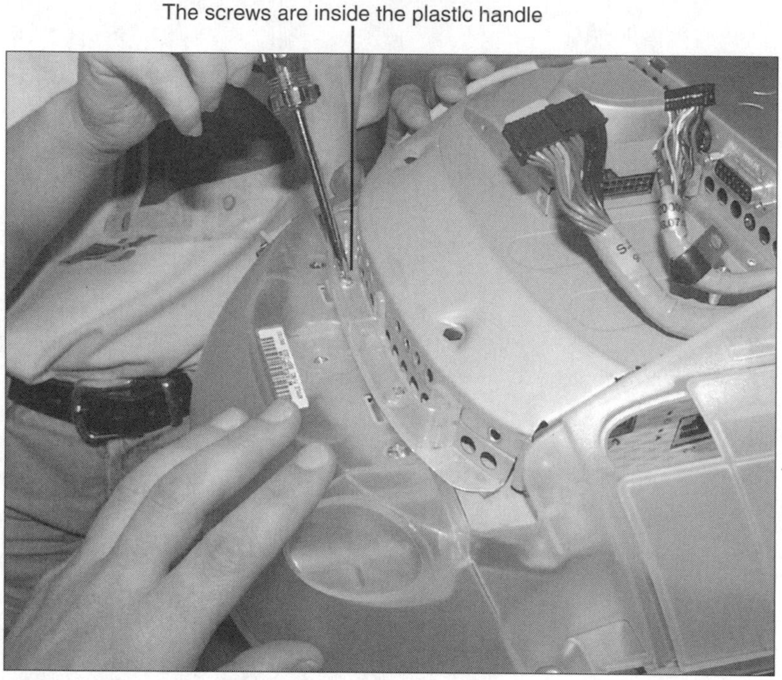

The screws are inside the plastic handle

FIGURE A.8

The logic board is held tight by two screws.

12. Put your hand on the plastic handle and gently slide the logic board out, moving it straight up and away (see Figure A.9).

13. Place the logic board on your cloth or in another safe place (make sure that it's not on the edge of the table; this is one thing you don't want to drop!).

14. Remove the metal shield by lifting it at both ends. The result is shown in Figure A.10.

15. Take your RAM module (technically it's called a SODIMM), handling it by its edges (it's inserted at an angle). Align the notch in the module with the small rib in the slot to orient it correctly and insert it into the empty slot as shown in Figure 22.13.

FIGURE A.9

Remove the logic board from your iMac.

Make sure it's completely removed

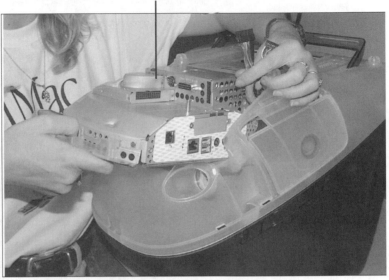

FIGURE A.10

Now we're getting some place. Your iMac is ready for its RAM upgrade.

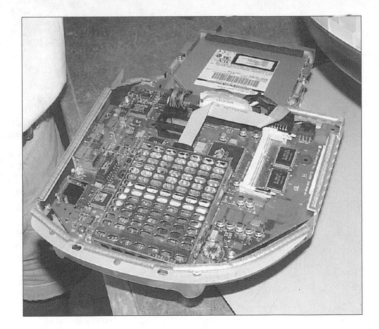

A

Line up the RAM module carefully before pushing it down

FIGURE A.11

Insert the RAM module into the slot as shown here.

If the RAM slot is filled, it means that a RAM upgrade has already been installed. You'd need to remove that before installing another module (but you might want to put it all back together and contact your dealer first). Remember, the RAM module is designed to fit in one direction only; don't force it! If you break the RAM or the slot, repair costs are on your dime.

16. Press the RAM module firmly into the socket until you hear a faint click.

There's yet another RAM slot, underneath the iMac's G3 microprocessor. But unless you want to stretch the iMac's RAM capacity to the max, you won't need to worry about that one.

That's the first part of the process. You've done well, and you deserve a few minutes rest. So sit back for a moment and ready yourself for the final leg of the journey.

Putting it Together and Testing

▼ To Do

1. Before putting things back together again, double-check your RAM installation to make sure that everything looks okay.

2. Place the metal shield covering the RAM slot back into place.

3. Get your iMac's logic board, holding it in one hand. Then, lower it carefully into its slot, pushing it straight down until it lies solidly in place. Don't push too hard, but make sure that the silver pin at the edge of the board is under the plastic lip (see Figure A.12).

FIGURE A.12

As you see, the silver pin is pressing against the plastic lip, so the logic board can't be inserted fully.

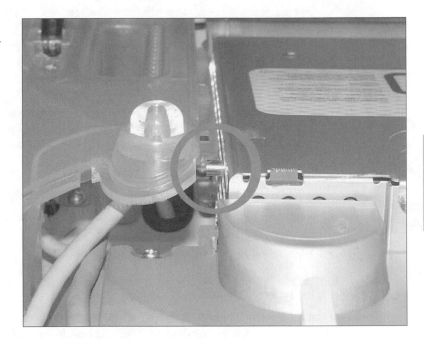

4. Get your Phillips Head Screwdriver and reinstall the two screws that sit at each side of the logic board's handle.

> When tightening the screws, don't go overboard. Finger tight is enough. I've seen situations where a screw is tightened too much and can't be removed without some major surgery (the sort of major surgery you don't want to think about). All you need to do is make it secure enough so you need a gentle tug to loosen it again. It's not as if you're going to be doing this sort of thing very often, unless you're upgrading iMacs for a living.

▼

▼

5. Reconnect the cables you set aside in steps 6 through 8 and reconnect them. Make sure that the cables are seated firmly.

6. Use the screwdriver to tighten down the power cord.

> If your iMac came with a clamp over the cables, be sure that the cables are inserted beneath the clamp. If a screw slot is in the clamp, be sure to reinstall the screw to set it down securely.

7. Take the plastic cover and replace it. Be sure it's snapped back into place on all sides.

> If the cover won't fit securely, remove it and check to make sure that the cables are properly seated; then try again.

8. Before you reattach the case cover, you'll want to make sure your iMac works properly. So lift your iMac up gently and place it in its normal operating position.

9. Reconnect the keyboard, mouse, and power cord (no need to worry about printers or any other added devices right now).

10. Plug the power cord back into the wall socket (if it's not already plugged in).

11. Start your iMac normally by pressing the power key on either the unit or keyboard and let it proceed through its full start process.

12. If the iMac starts up normally, go right to the Apple menu, choose About This Mac, and check the memory figure. The total should now add up to the amount of RAM present on both modules inside your iMac.

13. If everything looks normal, go ahead and shut down, and remove the power cord and the keyboard and mouse cables.

14. Turn the iMac over and reinstall the small cover, screwing it down firmly but not
▲   too tight (as I mentioned before).

If the installation went according to plan, your iMac is now ready to roll, with all that new memory in place. If you run into any problems, check the Q&A section at the end of this chapter for additional help.

Installing New RAM on a Slot Loading iMac—By the Numbers

For its second-generation iMac, Apple took to heart requests from customers to do something about the convoluted process of installing RAM. As you see in the previous section, it can take a while and requires a fair amount of attention to a number of details.

As standard issue, Apple gave the slot-loading iMacs a heavier dose of RAM than the original models. At the time this book was written, the Classic-styled iMac was still available, for folks who find the flat-panel versions a bit too expensive. The lowest-cost model had 128MB of RAM, and the top of the line had 256MB. This should be more than sufficient to get started; however, if you find you need more memory to run some high-powered programs, you'll want to consider buying a memory upgrade. This is especially true for Mac OS X, which has a big appetite for memory.

Because RAM is so cheap, some dealers offer a free RAM upgrade with new Macs. They will usually exact a small service charge, but the deal is usually worth it. That way your iMac will come equipped with all the memory you need without having to buy extra.

When you order a RAM upgrade for your iMac be sure to tell the dealer which iMac you have. The slot-loading iMacs use PC100 DIMMs. Don't you worry, any knowledgeable dealer will know just what you're talking about when you tell them what model it's for.

What You Need

Your second-generation iMac has two RAM slots. When it leaves the factory, one of these slots is already filled. Normally, you'd add a RAM upgrade module to the second slot. You could also replace the factory RAM if you want to add a larger capacity upgrade.

Here is what you need to do the job:

- A soft cloth or towel to place your iMac.
- A desk or other surface large enough to hold all the parts comfortably.
- A quarter (yes I'm serious).
- Your RAM upgrade module.

A

Now it's time to dive in:

Installing RAM on a Slot-Load iMac

1. Turn off your iMac, using Shut Down from the Apple menu (or by pressing the power button and choosing that command).

2. Unplug all the computer's cables (power cord and modem cord, too).

3. Grab your iMac's handle (at the top) in one hand and gently turn it over to the front, placing it face down (the monitor side) on the cloth.

4. At the bottom of the iMac, you'll see the access cover for your iMac's RAM slots (see Figure A.13).

FIGURE A.13

This is your doorway to a quick memory upgrade.

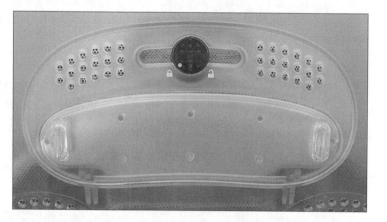

5. Take that quarter and place it in the little circular dial at the top of the access panel (see Figure A.14).

FIGURE A.14

Insert the quarter into the slot as shown.

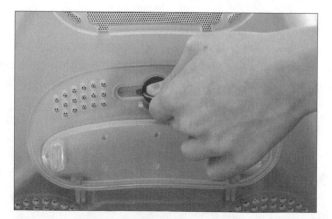

6. Turn the dial clockwise towards the unlock icon.

7. Place your fingers inside the openings at each end of the dial and pull out to open the cover. It might take a tug or two to get it to come loose, so just be patient.

8. When the cover is loosened, open it all the way so it hangs loose. Now you'll get a clear view of the RAM slots inside (see Figure A.15).

FIGURE A.15

As you see, one of your iMac's memory slots is already filled.

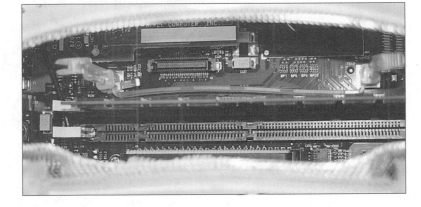

9. Take your fingers and press down the white plastic latches at each side of the empty RAM slot.

10. Get your RAM module and gently line it up with the latch slots at each end. Make sure that the layout of the pins on the RAM upgrade module matches the layout of the slot (the row with the least number of pins goes at left).

It is critically important that you make sure the RAM module lines up correctly with the slot. If you insert it incorrectly and try to power up your iMac, you could risk damage to the module or the logic board.

11. Press the RAM module straight down until it snaps into place. You'll feel and hear an audible "clump" when it's seated properly (see Figure A.16).

12. Double-check to make sure everything is in place, then grab the top of the access cover and close it.

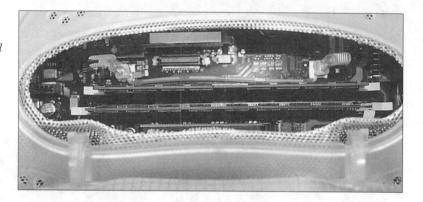

FIGURE A.16
When the RAM is properly installed it'll look just like this.

The other slot above your RAM slots is designed for installing an AirPort wireless networking module.

13. Take your quarter, insert in the slot and turn it counterclockwise, towards the lock icon.

14. Lift your iMac up gently and place it in its normal operating position.

15. Go ahead and reconnect the keyboard, mouse, and power cord (no need to worry about printers or any other added devices right now).

16. Plug the power cord back into the wall socket or power strip (if it's not already plugged in).

17. Start your iMac normally by pressing the power key on either the unit or keyboard and let it go through its full start process.

18. If your iMac starts up normally, go to the Apple menu, choose About This Mac, and check the total memory figure. The total should now add up to the amount of RAM present on both modules inside your iMac.

Yes, that's it. In just minutes, you've successfully installed a RAM upgrade on your slot-loading iMac.

Summary

As you can see, you don't need a degree in engineering to install RAM on your Classic iMac. Although the early-generation models aren't so user friendly when it comes to a memory upgrade, you should be able to get through the process like a champ. And if not, don't feel embarrassed about going to your dealer and letting them do it for you.

If you run into any problems with your RAM upgrade, such as the failure of your iMac to boot properly, you should go back and review the entire process, step by step, to make sure the RAM was properly installed. This may be a royal pain on an older iMac, but it is the only way you can be certain it was done correctly. You'll probably want to remove the RAM and reinsert, but be careful.

Sometimes, RAM problems are the result of a defective module, so if your iMac won't run, just remove the upgrade and see if everything returns to normal. If it does, contact the dealer who sold you the memory for a replacement.

As for me, I'm going to pour myself a cup of Java and get some rest because that's the end of this book. Thanks for reading.

A

INDEX

Symbols

4-color printers, 308
6-color printers, 308

A

About This Mac command
  (Apple menu-Finder), 43
access numbers for ISPs,
  selecting, 71
accessing
  files/folders, user configu-
    ration, 379
  Web sites
    Internet Explorer,
      212-214
    troubleshooting, 223
  Windows
    files, 326-327
    networks, 332

accounts (Quicken 2002
  Deluxe)
  checks, writing, 182-184
  configuring, 179-182
ADB (Apple Desktop Bus),
  359
Add Page to Favorites command (Favorites menu),
  215-216
Add to Favorites command
  (File menu-Finder), 35
adding
  devices
    FireWire ports,
      354-357
    USB ports, 353-357
  icons (Dock), 46
  music (iPod music
    library), 278
  scripts (Script Runner),
    342-343
Address Book (Mail)
  Applications folder
    (Mac OS X), 89
  AutoComplete option, 232

dissecting, 228-229
fax cover pages, creating
  (FAXstf X), 194-195
troubleshooting, 240
administrators, enabling,
  378
Adobe Acrobat Reader,
  Applications folder (Mac
  OS X), 88-89
AirPort
  Base Station, 361
  interface, 360
  older iMac installations,
    364
  Setup Assistant, 360
  Wi-Fi standard, 361
  wireless network configu-
    ration, 360-361
albums, online storage
  (iPhoto), 262
aliases for folders, 103-105
aligning text (AppleWorks),
  126-127
Alsoft Web site, 425

How can we make this index more useful? Email us at indexes@samspublishing.com

W